ST. DOMINGO PRODUCTS.

SANTO DOMINGO,

PAST AND PRESENT;

WITH A GLANCE AT HAYTI.

By SAMUEL HAZARD,
AUTHOR OF "CUBA, WITH PEN AND PENCIL."

MAPS AND NUMEROUS ILLUSTRATIONS.

NEW YORK:
HARPER & BROTHERS, PUBLISHERS,
FRANKLIN SQUARE.
1873.

TO THE

ORIGINAL OF THIS

THE

DISTINGUISHED PRESIDENT OF CORNELL COLLEGE, N.Y.,

IN PLEASANT MEMORY OF

DAYS OF AGREEABLE COMPANIONSHIP,

AS WELL AS OF SOME ROUGH EXPERIENCES AMID NOVEL AND

BEAUTIFUL SCENES IN SANTO DOMINGO,

These Pages are Dedicated

BY HIS SINCERE FRIEND,

THE AUTHOR.

THE author of these pages makes no pretension to be the "historian" of St Domingo; his only endeavour in making this volume is to bring together in a continuous and condensed form, for the benefit of the general reader, the facts connected with the history of the

Island of St Domingo from its discovery by Columbus to the present time, illustrating, as much as possible, its scenes and people by his own sketches, and photographs and engravings gathered from various sources.

At a time when the masses of the people of the United States were watching with interest the action of their representatives in Congress on the question of the admission of St Domingo into the Union, the author was surprised to find how little was really known, either of the present or the past of that historic isle; and in endeavouring to obtain this information for himself, he was astonished to find the great lack of books (at least accessible, and in the English language) giving connected information of an island that had for so long a time, and in so many ways, played such an important part in the history of the world.

Joining afterwards, on the island, the Commission sent out by the United States Government, the author, after almost entirely circumnavigating the island, and traversing its length and breadth, was amazed to find so magnificent a part of the New World so generally uncultivated and even uncivilised, after having been the first chosen spot of settlement of the discoverers from the Old World.

Having seen the comparatively advanced condition of affairs in the sister isle of Cuba (which is not nearly so highly favoured by Nature), and comparing it with the present deplorable state of St Domingo, the curiosity of the author was roused to know, if there were not other reasons than the reputed one of climate why an island so attractive and valuable in every way as St Domingo certainly is, should remain for so long a time unsettled and uncivilised.

Coming to London, and consulting almost every early

writer of note upon the Island of St Domingo found in the treasures of the British Museum, the author is satisfied that the past history, especially of the Spanish part of St Domingo, is little known to the general reader of to-day, and that in that history is found ample reason for the present condition of St Domingo and Hayti—a condition, he thinks, arising only from the fact that this beautiful island has simply been the "victim of misfortunes," brought upon it by its being successively the battle and disputed ground of the Spaniards and Indians, the Buccaneers, the English, the French, the Spaniards, the Haytians, and, finally, the Dominicans themselves.

"The truth is not always to be told," is an old adage, and it is possible that the notes on Hayti may give offence to some; but the author does not see that anything is to be gained by glossing over the present utterly hopeless condition of this part of the island, simply in consideration of the feelings of a few over-sensitive "patriots," because, even in the definition of this word, they and the writer might not agree.

He has been surprised, however, to find, on reading over the accounts of the different writers who have visited Hayti since the expulsion of the French, how perfectly justified are their remarks and experiences by the condition to-day of affairs in that Republic (?). The author is sure no one more ardently hopes to see a change for the better, as well in the government as in the people of Hayti, than he, feeling as he does, that not only will the people of Hayti be benefited, but so will be the great causes of humanity and civilisation.

As there may be readers who would like to follow out

more in detail the subject treated of in this book, the author has given a list of the most valuable authorities which he has consulted at the British Museum, and to which he shall make little or no further reference in his work, though he confesses he has used them freely, even at times quoting their very language. Notwithstanding the number of these writers, they all go over pretty much the same ground in detached accounts, except some few who give greater details, but only in matters peculiarly local, and that would not be interesting to the general reader, who, the author hopes, will find in the present volume all that can interest him.

The map accompanying the work is compiled from the one ordered by the Dominican Government in 1858, from the surveys and data of Baron Schomburgh and the French engineer Mendez, the latest and most reliable chart of the entire island yet published.

PARIS, *October* 1872.

CHAPTER I.

ST DOMINGO.

CHAPTER II.

THE CONQUEST.

CHAPTER III.

THE EARLY SPANIARDS.

CHAPTER IV.

THE DECLINE OF ST DOMINGO.

CHAPTER V.

THE BUCCANEERS AND EARLY FRENCH.

CHAPTER VI.

THE JOINT OCCUPATION OF THE FRENCH AND SPANIARDS.

CHAPTER VII.

THE REVOLUTIONS OF FRENCH ST DOMINGO.

CHAPTER VIII.

TOUSSAINT'S RULE.

CHAPTER IX.

THE WHOLE ISLAND UNITED UNDER ONE GOVERNMENT.

CHAPTER X.

LAND HO.

CHAPTER XI.

SAMANA AND THE SOUTH COAST.

CHAPTER XII.

ST DOMINGO CITY.

CHAPTER XIII.

VICINITY OF ST DOMINGO CITY.

CHAPTER XIV.

CHAPTER XV.

JOURNEY OVERLAND.

CHAPTER XVI.

COTUY.

CHAPTER XVII.

FROM MOCHA TO SANTIAGO.

CHAPTER XVIII.

FROM SANTIAGO TO MONTE CRISTO.

CHAPTER XIX.

THE NORTH COAST LINE FROM MONTE CRISTO TO PUERTO PLATA.

CHAPTER XX.

JOURNEY TO HAYTI.

CHAPTER XXI.

CAPE HAYTIAN.

CHAPTER XXII.

CHAPTER XXIII.

COASTING THE ISLAND.

CHAPTER XXIV.

APPENDATORY.

ILLUSTRATIONS.

2

LIST OF SMALL ENGRAVINGS.

THE BIBLIOGRAPHY OF SANTO DOMINGO AND HAYTI.

ACOSTA (Joseph de)—Historia Natural y Moral de las Indias, 4to, Seville, 1590.

Alcedos (Antonio de)—Geographical and Historical Dictionary of the West Indies, with large additions from Modern Voyages and Travels, by G. A. Thompson, Lond. 1812.

America—The History of the Buccaneers of, gathered from several languages into one vol., with copperplates, Lond. 1699.

—— Voyagien de Spanjaarden na West Indien, Johan Lodewyk Gottfried, Leyden, 1727.

—— Encyclopedia des Voyages, par J. Grausset S. Sauveur, Paris, 1796.

—— An Account of the Spanish Settlements in, 1 vol. 8vo, Edin. 1762.

—— L'Univers Pittoresque, Paris, 1849.

—— or an Exact Account of the West Indies, especially the Spanish Provinces, by N. N. Gent, 12mo, 1655.

Annales des Voyages (Malte Brun), Paris, 1808.

Anonymous—Les Principes de Revòlutions en Haiti, privately printed (by General Cinna le Conte, a grandson of Dessalines).

Antonio del Monte y Tejada—Historia de Santo Domingo, desde su Descubrimiento hasta Nuestras Dias, Madrid, 1860.

Archenholtz (J. M. Von)—History of the Pirates, Freebooters, &c., of America, translated by G. Mason, 1807.

Ardouin (B.)—Etudes sur l'Histoire d'Haiti, &c., 11 vols. Paris, 1853–61.

Atkins (John)—Voyage to Guinea, Brazil, and West Indies, 8vo, calf, 1735.

Barbe de Marbois—Etat des Finances de Saint Domingue, Paris, 1790.

—— Observations Personelles à l'Intendant de Saint Domingue, Paris, 1790.

Barcia (And. Gonzalez)—Historiadores Primitivos de las Indias Occidentales, fol. Madrid, 1749.

Beard (J. R.)—The Life of Toussaint L'Ouverture, 1 vol. 12mo, illustrated, Lond. 1853.

Beckford—Descriptive Account of the Island of Jamaica, with Remarks upon Sugar-cane Culture, Lond. 1790.

Bellin (N.)—Description Geographique des Debouquemens qui sont au Nord de l'Isle de Saint Domingue, Versailles, 1773.

Benzoni (Girolamo)—La Historia del Mondo Novo, Venetia, 1565.

Bergeaud-Stella—Roman Historique d'Haiti, Paris, 1859.

Berlioz d'Auriac (J.)—La Guerre Noire, Souvenirs de Saint Domingue, Paris, 1862.

Biggs (Wm.)—Military History of Europe from the commencement of the War with Spain, Lond. 1755.

Bloncourt—Des Richesses Naturelles d'Haiti, Paris, 1861.

Bonneau—Les Interéts Européens à Santo Domingo, Paris, 1861.

Bonnycastle (Sir R. H.)—Spanish America, 2 vols. 8vo, Lond. 1818.

Bossi (Luigi)—Vita di Cristoforo Colombo, Milan, 1818.

Bouvet de Cresse (A. J. B.)—Histoire de la Marine de tous les Peuples Paris, 1824.

Brasseur de Bourbourg—Bibliotheque Mexico, Guatémalienne, 8vo, Paris, 1871.

Breton (J. B. J. de la Martiniere)—Histoire de l'Isle de Saint Domingue, 8vo, Paris, 1802.

Browne (Dr Patrick)—Civil and Natural History of Jamaica, plates Lond. 1756.

Carderera—Informe Sobre los Retratos de Cristobal Colon, Madrid, 1851.

Casas (Barth. de las)—Obras del Obispo dela Ciudad Real de Chiapa en las Indias, &c., Seville, 1552.

Chanca (Dr Alvarez Diego)—Letter addressed to the Chapter of Seville, 8vo, 1859.

Charlevoix (Pierre Francois Zavier de)—Histoire de l'Ile Espagnol ou St Domingue, Paris, 1730.

Charolais—Les Interets Français et Européens, à Santo Domingo, Paris, 1861.

Charton (M. Edouard)—Voyagers Anciens et Modernes, Paris, 1854. (This is one of the best collections of Voyages and Travels extant, and to which the author of this volume is much indebted. To readers of French it is invaluable.)

Churchill (John)—Collection of Voyages and Travels, 6 vols. Lond. 1744.

Coke (Rev. Dr Thomas)—History of the West Indies, 3 vols. Lond. 1811.

Collection (A New) of Voyages, 7 vols. 8vo, Lond. 1765.

Colombo (Cristofori)—Discorso de Cesare Correnti, Milan, 1862.

—— Paesi Nuovamente Retrovati, Vicenza, 1507.

—— Memorials of Columbus, a Collection of Authentic Documents from original MS. at Genoa, Lond. 1823.

—— Zee en Land Reysen, 1707.

—— Select Letters of C. C., by R. H. Major, Hakluyt, Lond. 1847.

Columbus, Lettre de, publiée d'apres la rarissime version Latine conservée à la Bibliotheque Imperiale, Paris, 1865.

D'Alaux—Sonlouque et Son Empire, Paris, 1856.

Dalmas (M. Antoine)—Histoire de la Revolution de Saint Domingue, &c., Paris, 1814.

De Bry (Theodore)—Works of, principally the Edition of 1595, Frankfort.

De la Gerontocratie en Haiti, Paris, 1860.

D'Hormoys—Une Visite chez Soulouque, Paris, 1859.

Descourtilz—Guide Sanitaire des Voyaguers aux Colonies, ou Conseils Hygieniques des Européens destinée à passer aux Isles, 8vo, Paris, 1816.

—— (M. E.)—Voyages d'un Naturaliste et ses Observations, 3 vols. Paris, 1809.

—— Flore Pittoresque et Medicale des Antilles, 8 vols. Paris, 1829–33.

Dessalles (M. Adrien)—Histoire Générale des Antilles, 5 vols. in 3, 8vo, Paris, 1847–8.

Diez (Juan de la Calle)—Memorial y Noticias Sacras y Reales de las Indias Occidentales, 4to, Madrid, 1646.

Domingans "Alerta," a political pamphlet, Santiago (St Domingo), 1852.

Dorvo Soulastre—Voyage par Terre de St Domingo au Cap Francais. Paris, 1809.

Drake (Sir Francis) Revived, or a Summary of Foure Severeal Voyages to the West Indies, 4to, Lond. 1653.

Drake, Life and Voyages of, by John Barrow, Esq., Lond. 1843.

Du Coeur Joly (S. G. ancien habitant de St Domingo)—Manuel des Habitans de Saint Domingue, 2 vols. Paris, 1802.

Dutertre (J. B.)—Histoire Générale des Antilles habitées par les Francais, 4 vols. Paris, 1667–71.

Edwards (Bryan)—Civil and Commercial History of the West Indies, 3 vols. fol. Lond. 1793, 1801.

France—Colonies, Bibliotheque Historique de la Revolution, Paris, 1810–20.

Francisci (Erasmi)—Ost und West Indischen Lust und Staats Garten, Nuremburg, 1668.

Franklin—Present State of Hayti, Lond. 1828.

Frezier (M.)—Relation du Voyage de la Mer du Sud, &c., Amsterdam, 1717.

Froger (Le Sieur)—Relation d'un Voyage fait en 1695–6–7 aux Indes, Antilles, &c., Paris, 1598.

Gage (Thomas)—Survey of Spanish West Indies, Voyages, &c., Lond. 1711.

Garan Coulon (J. Ph.)—Rapport sur les Troubles de Saint Domingue, Paris.

—— An Inquiry into the Causes of the Insurrection of St Domingo, Lond. 1792.

Garcia (Jose Gabriel)—Compendio de la Historia de Santo Domingo, St Domingo, 1867.

Gardyner (George)—Description of the New World, &c., as in the Year 1649, Lond. 1651.

Gonzalez Carranza (Domingo)—A Geographical Description of the Spanish West Indies, Lond. 1740.

Gomara (Fr. Lopez de)—La Historia General de las Indias, Anvers, 1554.

Granier de Cassagnac (A.)—Voyage aux Antilles, Paris, 1843.

Gryneus—Navigatio Novus Orbis, Basle, 1532.

Guillermin (M. Gilbert E.)—Prècis Historique des derniers Evenéments de la Partie de l' est de St Domingue depuis 1808, &c., Paris, 1811.

Guridi (Zavier Angulo)—Elementos, &c., de la Isla de Santo Domingo, St Domingo, 1866.

Gurney (Joseph John)—A Winter in the West Indies, plates, Lond. 1840.

Hakewell (James)—Picturesque Tour of the Island of Jamaica, 4to, coloured plates, Lond. 1825.

Hakluyt's (Richard) Voyages, History of the West Indies, &c., Lond. 1812.
Hanna (Rev. W. S.)—Notes of a Visit to some Parts of Hayti, Lond. 1836.
Harris—Navigantum Itinerantium Bibliotheca (Indies), fol. 1744.
Harvey (W. W.)—Sketches of Hayti from the Expulsion of the French to the Death of Cristophe, 1827.
Haytian Constitution, Tariff, &c., Pub. Doc.
Haytian Papers published by authority, to which is a Preface by Pierce Sanders, Agent of the Haytian Government, Lond. 1816.
Hazard (Samuel)—Cuba with Pen and Pencil, with over 300 illustrations, Hartford and Lond. 1871.
Helps (A.)—The Conquerors of the New World, Lond. 1848.
Herrera (Antonio de)—Descripcion de las Indias Occidentales, 4 fol. vols. Madrid, 1730.
Histoire Générale des Voyages par Dumont D'Urville, and others, Paris, 1859.
Histoire Naturelle du Cacao et du Sucre, Amsterdam, 1720.
Historie der Boecaniers op Vreybuyters van America, Amsterdam Nicolaas Ten Hoorn, plates, 1700.
Holmes (Abel)—American Annals, a Chronological History of America, 2 vols.
Humboldt et Bonpland—Voyage aux Regions Equinoxiales du Nouveau Continent, Paris, 1825.

INGINAC—Secretaire Haïtien (under Boyer), Memoires, Kingston, Jamaica, 1843.
Irving (Washington)—History of the Life and Voyages of Columbus, 4 vols. Lond. 1828.

JACKSON (Dr Robt.)—Treatise on the Fevers of Jamaica, with Observations on the Intermittent Fever of America, 1791.
—— —— Febrile Diseases, 1820.
Jefferys (Thomas)—Natural and Civil History of the French Dominions in North and South America, fol. Lond. 1760.
—— A Description of the Spanish Islands, &c., Lond. 1762.
Juan (Don George, Capt. in Spanish Navy)—A Voyage to South America, translated, Lond. 1807.
—— de y Ulloa—Noticias Secretas de America, 4to, Lond. 1826.

LA AMERICA—Cronica Hispano Americana, Madrid, 1854.
Labat (R. P.)—Nouveau Voyage aux Iles de l'Amerique, 8 vols. Paris, 1742.

La Croix (Pamphile, Lieut.-General Barno)—Memoirs pour Servir à l'Histoire de la Revolution de St Domingue, 2 vols. Paris, 1819.

Laet (Joan de)—Novis Orbis, Leyden, 1630.

La Harpe—Histoire Générale des Voyages, Paris.

Las Casas—Relation des Voyages et des Decouvretes que les Espagnols ont fait dans les Indes Occidentales, avec le Relation Curieuse des Voyages de Sieur Monteauban, Capitain des Flibustiers, Amsterdam, 1698.

La Vega (Pedro de la)—Cronica de los Frayles, &c., de Sant Hieronymo, Alcalá, 1539.

—— (Manuel de)—Historia del Descubrimiento de la America, Mexico, 1826.

L'Espinasse de Langeac (N. de)—Colomb dans les Fers, a poem, Lond. and Paris, 1782.

Llorente (Juan Ant.)—Annales de la Inquisicion, &c., plates, Madrid, 1841.

Lyonnet (Le C.)—Statistique de la Partie Espagnol de Saint Domingue, Paris, 1800.

MACGREGOR (John)—The Progress of America, 2 vols. Lond. 1847.

Mackenzie (C., British Consul)—Notes on Haiti during a Residence in that Republic, 2 vols. Lond. 1830.

Madiou (Thomas, fils)—Histoire d'Haiti, 3 vols. 8vo, Port-au-Prince, 1847.

Malenfant (Colonel)—Des Colonies, et particulièrement de St Domingue, Paris, 1814.

Marles (M. la Croix de J.)—Histoire Descriptive et Pittoresque de St Domingue, Tours, 1852.

Métral (Ant.)—Histoire de l'Expedition des Francais à Saint Domingue, Paris, 1844.

Métral (Antoine)—Histoire de l'Expedition Militaire des Francais à Saint Domingue, with Notes by Isaac, the son of Pierre Toussaint. portrait, 1841.

Monardes—Historia Medicinal de las Cosas que se Traen de Nuestras Indias Occidentales que sirven en Medecina, woodcuts, Seville, 1574.

Montgomery (James)—The West Indies, a poem, Lond. 1814.

Moore (J. H.)—A New and Complete Collection of Voyages, 2 vols. fol. illustrated, Lond. 1785.

Moreau de Saint Mery—Description Topographique, Physique, &c., de la Partie Francais de l'Ile de St Domingue, 2 vols. Phil. 1798.

———— Partie Espagnol, 2 vols. 1796.

Mosely (Dr Benj.)—Treatise on Tropical Diseases and on the Climate of the West Indies, 8vo, Lond. 1803.
Muñoz (J. B.)—Historia del Nuevo Mundo, 4to, Madrid, 1793.

Navarrete (M. Fernandez de)—Colleccion ineditos para servir por la Historia de España, Madrid, 1842.
Navarrete (M. Fernandez de)—Colleccion de los Viages y Descubrimientos, &c., 5 vols. Madrid, 1825.
Nicolai (Eliud)—Navigationes in den West und Ost Indien der Holland. Engellandischen Compagnien, Munchen, 1619.
Nicolaus—Syllacias Letter, translated into English by the Rev. John Mulligan, New York, 1859.
Nuix (El Abate Don Juan)—Reflexiones Imparciales sobre la Humanidad de los Españoles en las Indias, traducida, &c., Madrid, 1732.

Oexmelin (A. O.)—Histoire des Aventuriers des Boucaniers et de la Chambre des Comtes etablie dans les Indes, 2 vols., maps and plates, Paris, 1688.
Ogilby's Accurate Description of the New World, with the Remarkable Voyages thither, &c., plates, 1671.
Osler (Edward)—The Voyage, a poem written in the West Indies, Lond. 1830.
Oviedo (Gonzalo Fernandez de)—Cronicas de las Indias, various editions; La Historia General de las Indias, &c., 1547, 1535, 1851–5.

Philoponi (H.)—Nova Typis, Navigatio in Novum Mundum.
Pinkerton (John)—General Collection of Voyages and Travels, illustrated, Lond. 1809.
Placide Justin—Histoire de l'Ile de Hayti, Ecrite sur les Documents Officiel et des Notes Communiques par Sir Jas. Baskett, Paris, 1826.
Poey (Andres)—Article on Antiquities of St Domingo in *Transactions of the American Ethnological Society*, vol. iii. p. 1, New York, 1845.
Ponce—Recueil des Vues des Lieux Principaux de la Colonie de St Domingue, Paris, 1791, to accompany M. St Mery's work.
Port-au-Prince—Production Historique, Report des Gardes Nationals, 4to, Port-au-Prince, 1792.
Purchas—His Pilgrimes, 5 vols. Lond. 1625.

Rainsford (Marcus)—Historical Account of the Black Empire of Hayti, &c., 4to, maps and plates, 1805.
Raynal (G. T.)—Histoire Philosophique et Politique des Etablissements

et du Commerce des Européens dans les Deux Indes, 10 vols. Paris, 1820.

Relacion Verdadera del Horrible Huracan que Sobrevino à la Isla St Domingo, Aug. 15, 1680, Madrid.

Remy (Saint)—Solution de la Question Haitienne, Paris, 1854.

—— Petion et Haiti, Mémoires pour Servir à l'Histoire de Haiti, 1851.

—— L'Ouverture, Chef des Noirs Insurgées à St Domingue, Paris, 1850.

—— Memoirs, &c., 1853.

Revue des Deux Mondes (Various Articles), Paris.

Robertson (Dr William)—History of America, 4 vols. Lond. 1812.

—— Charles the Fifth, edited by W. H. Prescott, Lond. 1857.

Robin (C. C.)—Voyage dans l'Interieur de la Louisianne, St Domingue, &c., Paris, 1807.

Rochefort (Poincy de Louis)—Histoire Naturelle et Morale des Iles Antilles, &c., Rotterdam, 1658.

Rogers (Samuel)—The Voyage of Columbus, a poem, Lond. 1812.

Roselly de Lorgues—Vie et Voyages de Cristophe Colomb, 1 vol. 8vo illustrated, Paris, 1862.

SAINT DOMINGO CONSTITUTION, St Domingo, 1854.

—— Cuentas Générales, 1848.

—— History of the Island of (attributed to Sir Jas. Baskett), Lond. 1818.

—— Actos Legislativos, &c., de la Republica Dominicana, St Domingo, 1846.

—— Essai sur l'Histoire Naturelle de l'Isle, Paris, 1776.

—— Dios, Patria, y Libertad, a pamphlet, St Domingo, 1855.

Sanchez y Valverde (Don Antonio)—Idea del Valor de la Isla Española, Madrid, 1785.

San Domingo—Annexation of, pamphlet, anonymous, New York, 1870.

Santo Domingo—Report of the U. S. Commission of Inquiry to, Washington, 1871.

Schoelcher (M. V.)—Des Colonies Françaises, Paris, 1842.

Schomburgk—The History of Barbadoes, Lond. 1847.

—— Notes on St Domingo, in *Proceedings of British Association* for 1851.

Spain—Ordenanzas Reales del Consejo de las Indias, Valladolid, 1603, and Madrid, 1585.

—— (Church of)—Historia y Origen de las Rentas de la Yglesia de España, Madrid, 1828.

TOBACCO—Storia Distincta y Curiosa del Tobacco, &c., Ferrara, 1758.

Trollope (Anthony)—The West Indies, Lond. 1860.

VARNHAGEN (Francisco ad de)—La Verdadera Guanahani de Colon, Santiago de Chili, 1864.

Vastey (Baron de) Essai sur les Causes des Revolutiones et des Guerres Civiles de Haiti, Sans Souci, 1819.

—— Le Système Colonial Devoilé, Cape Henry, 1814.

—— Reflexions Politiques sur les Noirs et les Blancs, &c., Sans Souci, 1817.

WALTON (W.)—Present State of the Spanish Colonies, including a particular Account of Hispaniola, 2 vols. Lond. 1819.

West India Sketch-Book, 2 vols. 12mo, Lond. 1834.

—— Directory, Lond. 1869.

Whitehouse (W. F.)—Essays on Sugar-Farming in Jamaica, 1843.

Whittier (John G.)—Poetical Works, Lond. 1869.

Wimpfen (Baron de)—Reisen nach St Doming Erfurt, 1798.

NOTE.—There have been at times also innumerable Pamphlets published on Hayti by refugees and others, of which, though glanced at by the author, he does not deem it necessary to include in the above.

SANTO DOMINGO.

Harper & Brothers, New York.

SANTO DOMINGO.

CHAPTER I.

> " Nymphs of romance,
> Youths graceful as the fawn, with rapturous glance
> Spring from the glades, and down the green steeps run
> To greet their mighty guests, 'the children of the sun.'"

SANTO DOMINGO—*Its Extent, Location, Physical Peculiarities—The Aborigines—Their Habits, Customs, &c.*

FIVE days' good steaming from New York, or about twelve from Land's End, England, lies in the South Atlantic a famous island—famous in ages past, and to be celebrated in the time to come, as the "cradle of the New World"—St Domingo.

Notorious for its misfortunes and those of its inhabitants in many decades of years, it had in the past almost lost its existence in the political world; and the names even of St Domingo and Hayti were held by many intelligent people to be those of two separate countries, until the efforts of the Republic of St Domingo to find a place of safety and protection among the United States of America has attracted attention to this almost forgotten yet historic isle.

Probably no spot on earth, take it all together, and looking at it in its natural aspects, can be found more lovely; and it is safe to say, probably no extent of territory, the world over, contains within itself, under proper auspices, so many elements of prosperity, worldly success, and happiness as the Island of St Domingo.

Many circumstances serve to render the history of this island peculiarly interesting to every intelligent mind, for here we have realised, in almost every part, the actual existence and daily life of Columbus; here we have the place first colonised in the New World by Europeans—the starting point of that civilisation which, spreading itself out in the New World, is now penetrating to those Indies of which the "Grand Admiral" thought this very island was a portion; here we have also the spot where was first inaugurated the beginning of African slavery in the Western World, as well as the real movement that has served to end it. Upon this spot has been wielded the power of almost every European Government, the blood of whose children has been lavishly poured forth upon its soil.

Though fire and sword, cruelty, persecution, and bloodshed have traversed this noble isle in almost every part, and often hand-in-hand, yet to-day it rests upon the bosom of those tropic seas, as beautiful, majestic, and fruitful in all its natural gifts as when Columbus first discovered it, waiting only the assistance of law and sound government, accompanied by intelligence, industry, and enterprise, to take its place in the political arena as one of the most favoured of states. Lying in the Atlantic Ocean at the entrance to the Gulf of Mexico, second of the Great Antilles to Cuba in size only, Santo Domingo yet, by its position and natural advantages, ranks first of all the beautiful islands in these waters; and though to-day impoverished and a beggar, yet she will prove, under proper care, such a precious jewel to the power that may be induced to take her under its protection, as many kings would be glad to place in their crowns.

The territorial extent of the whole island, from its extreme eastern point to its most western cape (Tiburon), is about 400 English miles; and the extreme breadth of its widest part nearly 180 miles—the area within its boundaries, exclusive of the adjacent isles, being of about the same extent as Ireland, or 25,000 square miles.

Of this territory, the negro Republic of Hayti occupies at the western end something less than one-third the whole extent, the remainder being nominally under the control of the Dominican Republic.

Situated in 18° 20′ north latitude, and in longitude 68° 40′ west from Greenwich, St Domingo has for near neighbours Cuba, from which it is distant about 70 miles south-east; from Jamaica, 130 miles north-east; and about 60 miles west-north-west of Puerto Rico; possessing all the advantages and few of the disadvantages of those three islands.

Such is the peculiar formation of this magnificent land, that within its boundaries is found almost every variety of climate; while in the character of its soils and vegetation, it is equally varied. This fact is due to certain peculiarities of its position, and to the singular manner in which its principal mountain ranges are placed.

These consist generally of long chains, of which there are two principal ones, stretching the whole length of the island, their general direction being from east to west. From these principal ranges, which on each side leave a space nearly equal between them and the coast, but which do not always run parallel to one another, go a number of secondary chains, which, running in different directions, divide the land between into valleys as various in depth as extent; and these valleys are again divided by hills and ridges of dimensions as various as are the valleys they divide, so that the secondary chains and ridges appear like so many supporters given by Nature to the principal mountains.

The secondary chains that run from the sides of the principal ones towards the sea, divide the intermediate space into plains of various figures and extent; and these plains are subdivided and sheltered by other ridges, which, going sometimes even to the beach, serve them as a sort of boundaries or ramparts.

The two great chains of mountains rise as they advance from the east; but this progressive elevation does not continue for more than forty leagues, after which the heights remain the same for a considerable distance. They seem to widen as they approach the west, till, coming to the middle of the narrow part of the island, they narrow again, still preserving their height, until, in fact, towards the western part, the mountains are almost piled on top of each other. For this reason, seen at sea, the whole island appears completely mountainous.

But in this mountainous form lies the very secret of its great fertility, for these mountains act as immense reservoirs, whose waters, by means of innumerable rivers, are afterwards borne in every direction. They are the barriers erected by Nature to repel the violence of the winds, to temper the rays of a scorching sun, and to vary the temperature of the air.

With occasional exceptions, all these mountains are covered with vegetation of some sort, but principally of the most valuable kinds of trees, the wood of which is used in commerce; and though the summits of some raise their rocky peaks bald of trees or vegetation, yet the majority are covered with mould, rich in the accumulated vegetable manure of centuries of decay.

For the general reader, it will suffice to make himself familiar with the names of only the two principal ranges of mountains, the longest of which is the most southern; beginning at the extreme eastern end of the island, and running nearly through its centre, it ends near Dondon in the Haytian part, thus dividing the Dominican portion into two districts, the North and South. This range is familiarly known as the Cordillera or Cibao range.

Nearly parallel, and to the north of the Cibao, extends the great range known as the Monte Cristo mountains;

THE NORTH COAST OFF PUERTO PLATA.

beginning at the bay of that name, and running almost parallel with the line of the north coast, it finally ends in the peninsula of Samana.

Between these two ranges lies probably one of the most fertile, beautiful, well-watered plains or valleys in the world, —the famous "Vega Real," or Royal Plain of Columbus.

The valleys of the Dominican part are more numerous and of greater extent than those in the Haytian, while the mountains of the former are notably rich in valuable mines and minerals; the climate and soil being equally varied throughout the two portions.

Having given thus a casual glance at the general physical peculiarities of the island, we shall be better able to enjoy a journey over it, especially after glancing at some of the principal events of its history.

The Dominican Republic having, by a vote of its people, expressed a desire to annex itself to the United States, application to this effect was made by the Dominican authorities in 1869, and after much discussion in the national halls of legislation, a commission was appointed by the United States Government to proceed to St Domingo, and investigate the condition of affairs on that island and report thereon.

This commission, sailing from the United States in the American man-of-war *Tennessee*, January 17, 1871, reached the island at Samana Bay, January 24.

For his own purposes, as well as to act as an independent newspaper correspondent, the author left New York on the 1st day of February 1871 in the steamer *Tybee*, the only steam-vessel that keeps up communication between the Republic of St Domingo and the United States. The voyage, begun in the bitter weather of a Northern winter, was without any event of interest to the general reader, and he cannot do better, therefore, than occupy the time in reading over with me a few chapters of the history of the famous island for which we are bound.

Those of us who had been in the tropics before, looked

forward to the time when we should once again breathe the delicious air of the balmy clime of the Antilles; for there seems to be something particularly fascinating about the tropics, as well to Governments as to individuals: and we find it the same with both; having tasted of the delights of the tropic clime, there remains always a desire to renew either acquaintance or possession once made therein.

Looking back to the period when the New World was first discovered, we see, in the histories of the most prominent nations of the time, the intense desire of their rulers to become the possessors of domains described invariably in such glowing terms by the subjects sent out on voyages of discovery to those new and wondrous lands comprised in the general name of "The Indies;" desires which, being fulfilled, gave to the monarchies of the Old World, in almost every case, colonies and possessions in the Western World, some of which to this day, notwithstanding changes in government, domestic trouble, and long and bloody foreign wars, still remain attached thereto.

Turning over the pages of the ancient chroniclers, we find they all agree in their descriptions of the flowery lands, uniting as they all do in using the most glowing language, as well as the most highly-coloured hyperbole, in their accounts of these new countries.

Even those adventurers who came from the sunny lands of the South of Europe, and who, it might be supposed, were well familiarised to the charms and novelties of the azure skies, gorgeous colouring, and luxuriant vegetation of the tropics, are in nowise behind their more phlegmatic brethren of the North in their glowing eulogies of the new "Paradise."

Reading some of the descriptions of the great Columbus himself, written to his benefactors under the influence of his first impressions of the West Indies, we seem rather to be reading the warm and glowing descriptions of romantic youth, than the staid, cautious relation of a man of mature life, such as he is described to have been at this period; and as we scan the outlines of the picture that seems more likely to be a true likeness than many of the others of him, we look in vain in the features of the calm, dignified man before us for the writer of such lines as these concerning St Domingo:—

"I swear to your majesties there is not in the world a

Columbus. (Charton.)*

better nation nor a better land; they love their neighbours as themselves, and their discourse is ever sweet and gentle,

* From the portrait in the gallery of Paolo Giovo (born at Como in 1483), who had a beautiful collection of portraits of the distinguished men of his time, and who always considered this as representing with fidelity the features of Columbus.

and accompanied with a smile; and though it is true that they are naked, yet their manners are decorous and praiseworthy."

When Columbus, traversing, in his first voyage in December 1492, the narrow channel that separates Cuba from St Domingo, came in sight of the latter island, he found a land even more beautiful in his eyes than that of Cuba, in the description of whose shores he had already almost exhausted the language of panegyric; and of the actual superiority of St Domingo in every respect he gave practical illustration by founding a colony on its north coast, giving to the island the name, it seems, in honour of his adopted country, of Hispañola, or Little Spain, imagining that it resembled the "most favoured provinces of Andalusia."

As to the number of the original inhabitants found on this island at the time of its discovery, the authorities of the time differ in placing the total at from one to three millions; but of the appearance, manners, and customs of the natives they all fortunately pretty nearly agree.

Columbus himself states, that sending a party of men to one of the villages, now thought to be Grosmorne, in Hayti, they found it to consist of nearly a thousand houses, showing that there were at the time towns of some extent.

The original inhabitants were a mild and peaceful race, recommending themselves to Columbus by their "sweetness of temper;" of rather tall and graceful form, but, on the part of the men, of hideous visage, with nostrils wide and open, and teeth badly discoloured. Their skin was of a yellowish brown colour naturally, but from the habit of anointing their bodies with "roucou," and other extracts of vegetable matter, to protect the skin from the attacks of insects, it had a reddish appearance.

The women were considered as rather comely in face as in form, it being related that they took great fancy to the Europeans; and the Spanish chronicles are filled with romantic episodes of the connections formed between the natives and the adventurers.

Both men and women were abundantly supplied with long black hair on their heads. The females of mature age alone wore clothing, consisting of a simple skirt of cotton cloth around the waist, and extending to the knees; while the men, young girls, and children were usually perfectly nude.

The shape of head peculiar to these people was produced by artificial means, that forced almost entirely away the forehead. This was brought about by the mothers, who took care to hold the head of the child strongly pressed between the hands, or two pieces of flat board, while the children were yet newly born; "from which," naïvely says an old writer, "when the children grew up, their skulls became so hard and compressed, that the Spaniards fre-

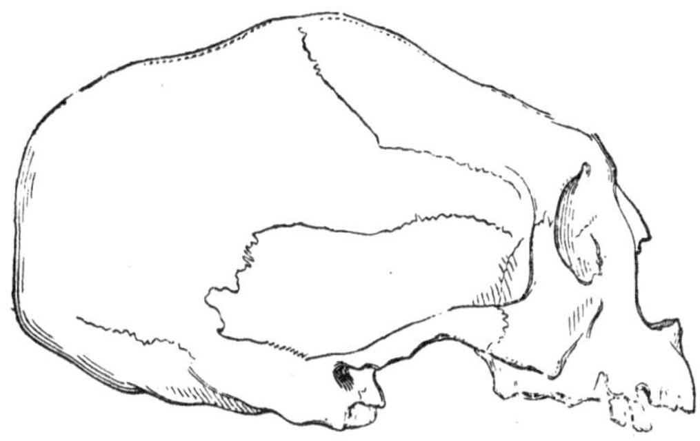

Caribbean skull, after Gall.

quently broke their swords in two when they attempted to cut open their heads."

They all seemed possessed of a phlegmatic temperament, the men especially inclined to melancholy; and it is related they ate very little food, and that of the simplest nature, a peculiarity noticed among their descendants to-day. A crab, a few roots or vegetables, sufficed to nourish them; but they were not endowed with much physical strength, and yet there were many long-lived people among them.

They did no work, passing their lives in the greatest idleness; they danced a greater part of the day, and when they could do that no longer, they slept. They had no hopes, desires, or ambitions, and some writers say they were without passions; but the account others give of their habits of indulgence, of the plurality of wives, and of their fierceness in conflict when roused, show that this was an error.

They had no history, no writings, naught but traditions, upon which have been generally conjectured the theories of the authors of the time; their songs alone gave idea of these traditions, and to these they danced, the accompaniment being the noise made by beating on a tambor or drum of peculiar construction, made of a hollow cylinder of wood, entirely closed except an opening in the side, and this drum was at times beaten by the principal man or chief. The same instrument, somewhat varied in shape, seems to be often used by the Africans to-day in Cuba.

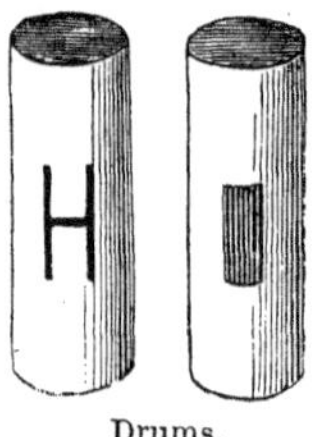
Drums.

These dances were of various kinds; sometimes the men were ranged on one side, the women on the other; sometimes they began one by one, until the whole assembly were on their feet. Reading the account of these people in the early writers, one is not surprised to learn that they were a listless energy-lacking people, for they committed the grossest sensual excesses; they danced until they could dance no more, and falling upon the ground, they intoxicated themselves with the fumes of tobacco, which they produced in a peculiar way. Upon some half-burning branches they spread some leaves of the tobacco-plant not yet quite dry, then they took a tube made in the form of a Y, the foot of which they placed in the smoke, and its two arms in their nostrils, inhaling through it until they were intoxicated by the fumes of the tobacco, when, prostrated upon the ground, they remained in a state of stupefaction, from which they recovered utterly inert and feeble; the Cacique alone being carried from the scene of these orgies by his women to a bed or hammock.

Polygamy seemed to be the custom, and the women had charge of the funeral ceremonies of their husbands, having the privilege (?), if they desired, of putting themselves to death on the bodies of their deceased spouses.

They seem to have had no implements or tools of any kind, if we except a sort of hatchet, made of stone, with which they dressed their canoes or piraguas, which they made exclusively out of trees by burning out the trunks, and to get the tree down, a fire was built round the base of it until

Canoe. (Oviedo.)

it toppled over. These canoes were peculiar in shape, differing from those of the Indians of North America, and yet were very serviceable in the usually placid waters of the islands, being propelled by paddles, and occasionally by a small sail of cotton cloth.

The habitations of these people were in accordance with the mild character of their climate, their houses being simply huts of various dimensions, constructed of the bamboo, roofed with thatch, or roofed and walled with the palm bark or leaf. These huts contained usually but one room, and were always only one story in height, though some of the better cabins had in front a portico, which seems to have been considered amongst them a mark of wealth or distinction.

In the gardens, if they can be called such, of their habitations, the owners grew a few fruits and vegetables, including the maize or Indian-corn, of which latter Benzoni says they harvested two crops a year, and from its grain they made, in the rudest manner, a kind of bread, apparently similar to the "corn dodgers" of the southern United States.

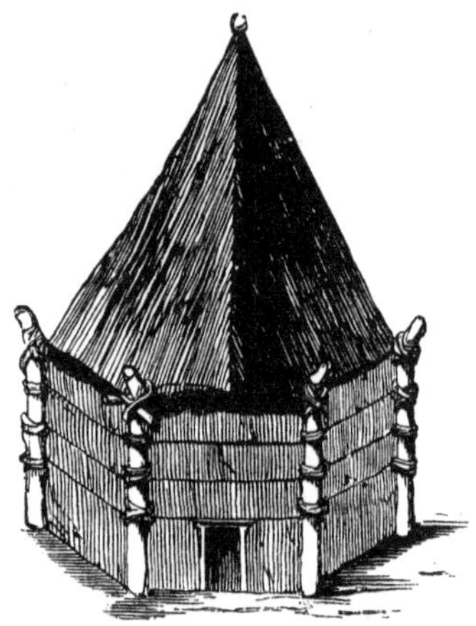

Hut. (Oviedo.)

Benzoni's description of the wine made also from the Indian-corn is not calculated to encourage a taste for that beverage on the part of the novice; for, he says, the grain, at one period of the manufacture, was masticated by the women, who, putting it in their mouths, slowly chewed it, and then, with an effort, coughed the material out upon a platter or leaf, from whence

(Hut. Oviedo)

it was thrown into a jar with the other mixture, and boiled.

Wine-making. (Benzoni.)

Curiously enough, this method of wine-making prevails to-day among some of the islands of the Pacific Ocean.

The natives used also another kind of bread, called cassava, made from the manioc or yuca root; and many of their customs, as described, are similar to those of the people of the interior of the island to-day.

Idol.

The wonderful fertility of the soil, in those early days, may be judged from the fact that the only implement used in its cultivation was a pointed stick, burned hard in the fire, with which holes were made in the ground, into which were placed the seeds of the few plants they needed to cultivate.

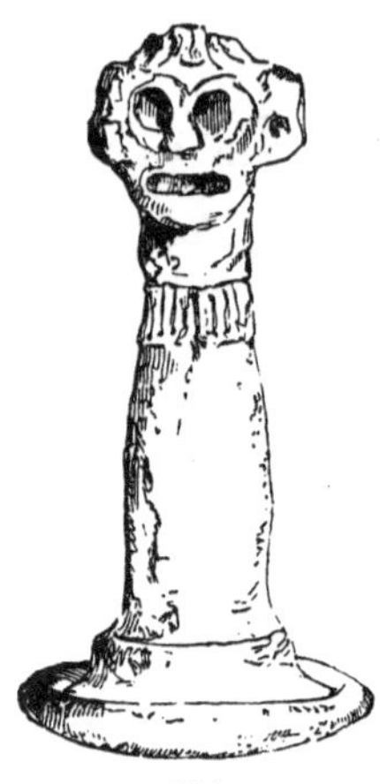
Idol.

The same products brought forth then by the bountiful hand of Nature are still poured out in lavish profusion, almost unaided by the hand of man.

The religion of these islanders was the worship of idols, cut out of stone, in the rudest manner, to represent grotesque animals or human beings, the name of these gods being *zemes*.

One of their traditions was, that the sun and moon came out of a cavern of their isle, and were made to enlighten the world; to this cavern the natives made pilgrimages; one of these had an entrance, it is related, near Dondon, in the northern part of Hayti; and St Mery says, when he visited it, as late as 1789, remnants

Figures cut in the rock.

of rude sculpture on the walls of the grotto, and idols, were yet to be seen there; while traces of the offerings brought for the gods have been found in many of the caverns in the island.

The special ceremony seems to have been one appointed by the Cacique, calling all the people together on a certain day; and they, joining in procession, with the Cacique at their head, resorted to the temple, where were the gods and the priests or "butios," being accompanied in their march

Curing the sick. (Hakluyt after Benzoni.)

by the beating of drums and tambours. Offerings were made of various kinds, often amid the wildest cries and noises; "and others," says Benzoni, "put sticks down their throats when they went before the idols, so that their gods might see that they had nothing bad in their hearts or stomachs when they vomited."

The priests acted as doctors, using plants in lieu of drugs, making particular use of tobacco in most cases, which they administered to the patient until he was stupefied, and upon returning to himself he was considered as cured.

The original name of the island was Haiti, which among the natives signified high ground; and in the eastern part they had another name, Quisqueya, signifying mother of the earth; while, in the western part, it was called Babeque or Bohio, which signified land of many villages or habitations.

At the time of its discovery, it was divided into five large divisions, each under the government of a Cacique (a name equally applicable to a chief or a province), and each of these divisions was subdivided into minor provinces.

The government was despotic, though it seems to have been mild in its execution of authority, except in extreme cases, as in robberies, where the offender was impaled to death. The government of the principalities was hereditary, but if a Cacique died without children, his estates passed to his sisters rather than his brothers, for the reason, as they held, that the children were more likely to be of pure blood.

The following were the five districts, viz.:—

Magua, in the Indian dialect signifying "realm of the plain," its capital being where was afterwards built the old town of Concepcion de la Vega, in the interior of the island; its chief was Guarionex.

Marien had its capital in the vicinity of Cape Haytien or Français, its chief being Guacanarie.

Higuey had its capital in the present village of the same name, so renowned in the annals of superstition of the island, the Cacique Cayacoa having it under his command.

Maguana had its capital where now is San Juan, the Cacique being the famous Caonabo, so celebrated in the sad but romantic history of these people.

Xaragua had its capital in the plain of the *cul de sac* in the Haytian part, where was at one time the old town of the same name. Bebechio was its chief.

Though the island was thus subdivided, there appears to have been but one race upon it, unless the theory that some authors have raised, that those in the western part, from being more warlike and savage in their manners, were of a distinct race: but the same language, with some variations, seems to have prevailed.

This language, says Charlevoix, was not rude or uncouth,

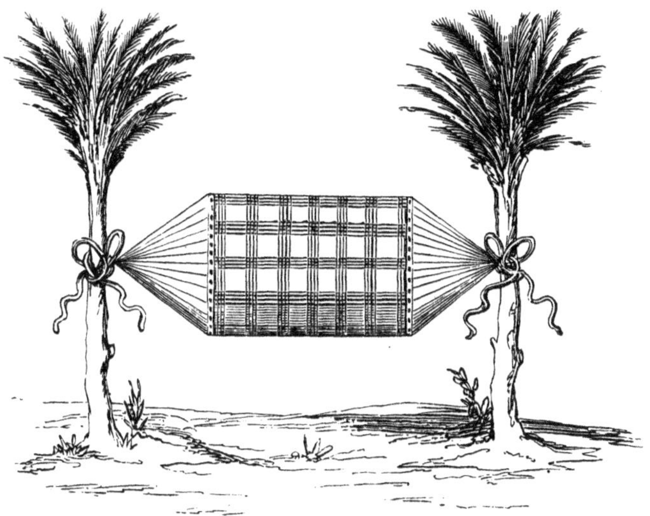

Hammock. (Oviedo.)

but was easy to learn, and some of their words were afterwards incorporated in the dialect of the island. From their word *canoa* came canot (canoe); from *d' uracane* (hurricane), ouragan; while not only was the word *d'amacha* (hammock) adopted, but the article itself found its way into general use by the new-comers.

CHAPTER II.

"When first Columbus dared the Western Main,
Spanned the broad gulf, and gave a world to Spain,
How thrilled his soul with tumults of delight,
When through the silence of the sleepless night
Burst shouts of triumph!"

THE CONQUEST—*Landing of Columbus—First Settlement—Columbus's Return on Second Voyage, and Founding of the First Permanent Colony—Expeditions to the Interior—Settlements there—Rapid Advance of the Island—Columbus's Hard Treatment—Ovando's Rule.*

AT daybreak, on the morning of the 6th of December 1492, Christopher Columbus found himself a short distance from the north-west coast of the island of Hayti; and at vespers of the same day he entered a bay on the same coast, which, in honour of its being the fête day of San Nicolas, he called by that name, and which it has retained up to the present time.

A drawing, said to have been made by Columbus, attempts to give an idea of his first arrival off the island. It suggests, however, but two ideas, that the country was hilly and that the inhabitants went naked; but his written descriptions give a very accurate idea of the country. In fact, the traveller of to-day, with these in his hand, will need no better guide to the general characteristics of this very same coast.

Sailing leisurely along the coast, he entered a port that he called Concepcion; and there erecting a cross upon the shore, he took possession of the island for the King and Queen of Spain, giving it the name, which it bore for a long time among the early writers, of "Hispañola," many of whom spoke of it also as "the Spanish Island."

The first settlement was temporarily made in the Bay of St Thomas, to-day called Aeul (in Haiti), and originated

Sketch by Columbus.

through the wrecking of one of the two remaining caravels; for Martin Pinzon had deserted Columbus off the coast of Cuba with the third. From the materials of the wreck a fort or tower was built, which was called La Navidad.

Here it was that Columbus first heard of the gold regions of the Cibao; but, naturally enough, his great aim was now to return safely to Spain, and make known the news of his great discovery. Having therefore gathered from the Indians many articles rudely worked in gold, as well as other curiosities, he was anxious to set sail, and convey the grand tidings in person to his sovereigns.

The Caravels.

He left, therefore, a small party of men with munitions, provisions, and other supplies, to keep them for a year, giving also abundant instructions as to their conduct during his absence; and on the 4th January 1493 he took his leave of them, not one of whom was he ever to see again.

Sailing eastward along the coast, and stopping occasionally, he was joined at Monte Cristo by the missing vessel that he had parted from in Cuba; and having a favourable wind, he set sail, continuing his voyage. At one of these stoppages, Columbus saw a new sort of creature, which he gravely stated to be sirens or mermaids, but which were the "manati" or sea-cow, which are still found in these waters, and which, from their strange form, their gambols in the water, and the peculiar plaintive cry they emit, might readily, when seen at a distance, be taken by the novice for semi-human beings.

Finally, having reached the Bay of Samana, he determined to set sail for Spain, which place he reached the 15th of March 1493, entering into the port of Palos, from whence he had sailed the 3d of August in the preceding year.

The important results of this great discovery were now to be realised; for, after the reception of Columbus, and the excitement caused thereby, had somewhat subsided, attention was given to the means to profit by this great discovery, and immediate preparations were made to fit out an expedition on a larger scale.

The departure of this second expedition was very different from that of the first, for gathered together in the Bay of Cadiz were seventeen vessels of different sizes, two of them being of the largest class; and upon these were gathered some 1200 men, of every rank and station, from the noble to the humble labourer; there were also skilful pilots, as well as many artisans of various kinds. Stores of all kinds were also put on board, as well for the purposes of existence as for trading, while particular attention was paid to the supplies needed by a new colony in making a permanent settlement. Upon Columbus himself had been bestowed the chief command of the expedition, and to him had been accorded also unlimited power over the new territory.

Among the supplies, one of the most important in the future welfare of the colony was the different animals taken out for breeding purposes; for, strangely enough, the islands of the Antilles do not seem to have been possessed of quadrupeds of any note, and mention is made of only some four kinds, all of which are to-day extinct except the agouti. Of these, the coati, a sort of cat, and the cories or agouti, a species of hare, are only mentioned as furnishing animal food to the natives, if we except the flesh of the iguana, which still exists, and is considered a great delicacy.

On the 25th September 1493, in the presence of a vast concourse of spectators, this second expedition set sail from the Bay of Cadiz, and after a prosperous voyage, touching at various points and islands, the fleet came to anchor in the Bay of Samana, the 22d November 1493.

On coasting the shore of the north coast for the Bay of St Thomas, the Admiral was informed by an Indian of the fate that had befallen the settlers he had left at La Navidad, in that bay, by which every one had perished at the hands of the natives, in revenge for injuries inflicted on them by the Spaniards, and the settlement had been reduced to ashes.

The Agouti.

Columbus then resolved to establish his new city in a different place; and after having sent some parties into the region about Monte Cristo to explore the country, he continued along the coast, until, deeming it a favourable place, he established, on the banks of a small stream, his new settlement, which, in honour of the Queen, he called Isabella.

This settlement, with the intention of making it permanent, he laid out in the form of a regular town, with streets at right angles, and constructed there also a substantial church of stone, as also some of the officers' houses of the same material; the whole being surrounded by a wall and ditch, as a protection against the Indians.

The Coati.

Having thus made a starting-point in the island, he began to send out expeditions to the interior, and so favourable were the reports made by these parties on their return, that he determined himself to penetrate into the interior, to the region described to him at St Thomas, which he called Cipangi, celebrated for its gold; this is the region known then, as now, as the Cibao.

Elated with these descriptions, and anticipating much for the future, the Admiral determined to send advices to Spain, and on the 2d of February 1494, he despatched the fleet, loaded with gold specimens and other products, sending by it also glowing accounts to the King and Queen of the advantages that would accrue to Spain by the rapid colonisation of the island.

Columbus seems to have been unfortunate in the selection of his first site for a settlement, as the spot chosen was a very unhealthy one; and is to-day a noted place for fevers, it being in a low marshy situation, and in some degree sheltered from the healthful breezes of the north; from hence, however, he despatched Ojeda to explore the interior.

Many of his people were taken sick, and he himself, worn out with work and care, fell a prey to the attacks of disease, but happily recovering, he made preparations for a journey to the interior, from which he was delayed by the discovery of an insurrection incited by Bernal Diaz and his friends, that had for its object the breaking up of the colony, and the returning to Spain of the colonists, on the plea that the promises of gold were a delusion, as this mineral was only to be found in the smallest quantity, that which was in the possession of the natives being the accumulation of many years.

Columbus having put an end to this mutiny, and punished some of the mutineers, sallied out the 14th day of March 1494, at the head of 400 men, on his expedition to the interior; and following the route taken by Ojeda in his expedition, he penetrated with much difficulty into the interior of the region known as the Cibao, where, on the banks of the river Janico, he established a fortress, which he called St Thomas, presumed to be in the now impenetrable region known as the Valla de Constanza.

On the completion of this fort, he gave the command of it to Pedro de Margarita, and returned, March 29, 1494, to Isabella, which he had left under the governorship of his brother Don Diego.

Here he found matters in a very unsettled state, for the inhabitants were discontented and sick, many of them utterly disappointed and desponding over the paradise that had been so glowingly described to them. This state of affairs, in addition to the unhealthiness of the locality, was caused from the fact that many of the settlers were utterly useless, inefficient men, who joining the expedition without the slightest knowledge of any vocation or trade, had expected they were simply to pick up gold as they wanted, while leading a life of indulgence and idleness.

Columbus receiving at this time news from the fort that he had established in the interior of a threatened attack of the now united Indians against it, he deemed this a good opportunity to rid the town of these fractious spirits, and under the plea of strengthening that garrison, he selected all such men, to the number of 400, and sent them under Ojeda to the interior.

Columbus now occupied himself in regulating the affairs of Isabella, which being permanently established, became the first Christian settlement in the New World. He created a council, over which presided his brother Diego, composed of the priest Father Boil and four of the most prominent men, and fondly hoped from this small beginning the greatest results would flow.

Columbus, in thus establishing the colony of Isabella, had set up the corner-stone of civilisation in the New World, upon which were to be erected structures that he in his wildest dreams had never pictured; and as little dreamed he that, within 300 years of his great discovery, his own last resting-place, though within the very walls of a city he himself had originated, would be a matter of doubt, uncertainty, and neglect; while the spot which he established in grateful remembrance of the Queen his benefactress, and to which he gave her name, should be a deserted heap of ruins, entirely obscured by the rank vegetation of the land he had described to her in such glowing terms.

But the tide of emigration, once started for these new lands, ceased not to flow; and each year, while he himself was prosecuting further voyages of discovery, saw accessions to the numbers of those who, spreading themselves throughout the island, managed to gain riches which, in most cases, were acquired not only at the expense of the liberty, but of the lives of the native inhabitants.

During Columbus' absence on further voyages of discovery, the Indians had united their forces, and given the Spaniards of the interior much trouble; so that, on the return of the Admiral, on the 4th of September, sick, and worn out with fatigue, he was compelled to take very decided

A Spanish Attack. (De Bry.)

action against them, the more especially as at Isabella the council and authorities had been occupying themselves in quarrels and dissensions rather than with the necessary cares of the colony.

The native chiefs were now, with one exception, united in open arms against the Spaniards, besieging them in their fort of St Thomas; and therefore, taking with him a strong force, Columbus started, March 27, 1495, from Isabella, on a tour of complete conquest, in which he not only rescued the beleaguered garrison, but forced the Indians to make peace, while at the same time he established another fort in the interior, called Concepcion. These trips of the Spaniards into the depths of a savage wilderness infested with large numbers of hostile Indians seem, as we read their accounts in early writers, or the glowing pages of Irving, like fabled romance; and it is only when we discover that these parties of adventurers, small in number as they were, owed great part of their success to the fact that their armour protected them from the rude missiles of the disproportionate numbers of the Indians, while the effect of the fiery Spanish horses, animals entirely unknown to the natives, added to the use of their arquebusses, actually quelled the Indians into submission, as much by their effect morally as by their positive use.

The success of the Spaniards was followed by the capture of two of the principal chiefs, and by the imposition upon the different tribes of a tribute, to be paid in gold and cotton; and from this time forth may be dated the beginning of that servitude of the natives, which, in a very few years, was to sweep them almost entirely from the island, such was the severity of the yoke imposed upon them by the Spaniards.

Before the contemplated return of Columbus to Spain, information was brought him by one Miguel Diaz of the discovery of some gold-mines in the banks of the river Jaina, eight leagues from its mouth, towards the southern side of the island; and such was the enthusiasm created by this news, that Columbus authorised his brother Bartholomew to investigate the fact, and finding the news founded in truth, directed him to establish a fort there, as also to enter into the working of the mines.

Meanwhile, as he himself had determined to return to Spain, he appointed his brother Bartholomew to be chief-in-command during his absence, with the title of Adelantado or Governor, and designating also, in case of accident, his other brother, Diego, to succeed him. The Admiral having sailed for Spain the 10th of March 1496, the Adelantado set himself to work to carry out the plans of Columbus in the working of the mines, and leaving his brother Diego in command at Isabella, he himself went to Jaina, where were established the works known as those of Buenaventura, still in existence in a ruined condition, north of the town of San Christobal. Here he remained some three months, when he deemed it necessary to visit the town of Concepcion, in the interior, to receive the tribute from the natives.

The arrival of reinforcements and supplies at Isabella shortly after brought the news of the safe return of Columbus to Spain, and his honoured reception there, as well as an order from the Admiral for the Adelantado to establish a settlement on the Ozama river, at its mouth, where it emptied into the southern sea. The Adelantado complied with these instructions by going himself to establish on the left bank of the river the town, which was at first called New Isabella, but afterwards received the name of Santo Domingo, the first stone being laid there on the 4th August 1496; and with the foundation of this famous city began the career of glory and discovery in the New World destined to render immortal the names of so many Spaniards.

The Adelantado seems to have been an earnest, energetic man, and every effort was used by him to further the interests of the colony; and we find him at this time making continual journeys throughout the island, now establishing a new town, now developing a mine, and again making war upon the rebellious natives.

Meanwhile, at the first settlement established, the town of Isabella, matters were going from bad to worse, for affairs there were in a most deplorable state, owing to the general sickness of the inhabitants, and the cessation of agricultural labours, caused by the flight of the Indians, who, driven to a labour to which they were entirely unaccustomed, under the harshest kind of treatment, sought relief in the woods and mountain fastnesses.

Following close upon this state of things came the mutiny of Roldan, who had been appointed alcalde-mayor, or chief-justice of the town, and who, in his ambitious projects, desired to have the chief command. Notwithstanding the active efforts of the two Columbuses, this mutiny gained strength and followers among the discontented colonists, and they had even the audacity to sack the public storehouses at Isabella; a state of affairs that continued until Columbus himself returned from Spain, the 30th of August 1498.

Columbus, mortified with the state of affairs in the colony, used every effort to bring about peace and tranquillity among the colonists; but the power of Roldan had increased to such an extent, that, humiliating as it was to the feelings of the great commander to make terms with the rebel, he, for the sake of the welfare of the colony, compromised with Roldan and his followers, by which the former was reinstated in his office of alcalde-mayor, while those of his followers who wished to remain were each allotted a certain amount of land, and a certain number of Indians to work the same; the others were permitted to return to Spain. By this act was established that system known as *repartimientos*, destined to be such a cause, in the future, of quarrels amongst the Spaniards and misery to the aborigines.

Columbus, who had established himself at St Domingo, was not, however, destined to remain without further troubles; for the Indians known as the Ciguayos endeavoured to release their captured chief Mayobanex by a rising against the Spaniards; and this affair was hardly quelled when Ojeda attempted to enslave the Indians for the purpose of carrying a number of them to the newly-acquired lands of Terra Firma. In both these affairs, the former rebel, Roldan, acquitted himself with honour, honesty, and bravery in asserting the rights of Columbus.

Matters being however tranquillised, affairs in the colony began to improve: the mines were in profitable working order, and great advances were made in agriculture, while many towns in the island were permanently established; and we find in 1499 among these the names mentioned of Santo Domingo, Isabella, Concepcion de la Vega, Santiago, Puerto Plata, and Bonao as flourishing places, while others that had been temporarily established were dying out.

The Citadel.

The year 1500 will always be memorable in the annals of the island as that in which the infamous Bobadilla came out from Spain, arriving at St Domingo city at a time when Columbus was in the interior of the island. Although this officer was sent out from Spain clothed with certain powers and authority to investigate matters on the island, he so far exceeded these as to seize upon the persons of Columbus and his brother Bartholomew, and throw them into prison, treating them with every indignity, even to sending them to Spain in chains. The cell in which they were confined is still shown in the old citadel of St Domingo city, and is a moderate-sized square room, with a grated window in the immensely thick wall,—a limited space for a man who had given such immense territories to the world.

Happily for the island, the governorship of this man lasted for a short time only, as no sooner did the news reach Spain of his treatment of Columbus, than Nicholas de Ovando was appointed Governor of the island, as also of all the Indies. Going out in great state, with a large number of followers, Ovando took with him a plentiful supply of arms and artillery; and on the 15th April 1502, he reached the island and relieved Bobadilla of his command.

The superstitious might think, in the events that immediately follow, there was a miraculous intervention of Providence in favour of Columbus, who having been restored to favour, was again in these waters with his fleet on another voyage of discovery; and being desirous of changing one of his vessels, had sought refuge at St Domingo. Ovando, however, declined to allow him to enter the port, and Columbus foreseeing and prophesying a storm, took shelter in the Bay of Ocoa. Meanwhile, some of the property of Columbus had been placed upon the vessels of the fleet in which Bobadilla was intending to return to Spain, and in the same fleet was Roldan, and the chief Guarionex. Though Columbus gave warning of the threatened storm, no attention was paid to it, and the fleet had hardly set sail when the storm broke upon it, and the whole of the vessels, with the exception of two, were lost with all their crews. In these two vessels was the property of Columbus. In the same storm the town of St Domingo was utterly annihilated.

Ovando the Governor, who seems to have been a man of great energy, resolved, however, to rebuild the city, but upon the other side of the Ozama, on the site of the present city; and with its re-erection begins a career of unexampled prosperity for the island, a career which unfortunately lasted but for a limited period of years.

The building of the new city did not, however, prevent Ovando from prosecuting the war for the entire conquest of the island from the aborigines, for he carried on his operations against them with such zeal, that it was not long before the two remaining principalities of Jaragua and Higuey were subdued, but not until deeds of treachery, cruelty, and bloodshed were perpetrated that will for ever cast a blot upon the name of Ovando.

The reader of Irving will readily recall some of the romantic passages in these bloody annals, in which the sad story of the Princess Anacoana and the Cacique Cotubanama are related at length. Suffice it to say here, that with their capture may be said to have ended the period of the conquest of the island.

CHAPTER III.

> "The Spaniard came . . .
> With toil and woes he crushed his wretched slaves,
> Till murdered nations sunk into their graves;
> Then, to replace his victims, fiercely tore
> The helpless negro from his native shore."

THE EARLY SPANIARDS—*Their Treatment of the Natives—Ovando's Rule—Habits of the Spaniards—Negro Slaves—Rapid Decrease of the Aborigines—Sugar-making—Diego Columbus and his Successors—The War of Enrique, and Final Peace.*

WHILE Columbus, on his fourth voyage, after having warred with some furious hurricanes and violent tempests, was obliged to take shelter in Jamaica, the Island of St Domingo was the theatre of several remarkable events.

This colony, the model and the source of all the later establishments that Spain has founded in the New World, acquired by degrees the form of a society regular and flourishing.

The tender care, full of humanity, that the Queen Isabella had evinced for the protection of the Indians, and the special laws passed, by which was enacted their freedom from oppression and enforced labour, delayed for some time the industrial interests of the island; because the natives, seeing happiness only in the indulgence of their indolent habits, could not be tempted to physical labour by the doubtful promises and recompenses of the Spaniards, their conquerors; the result of which was, that the latter lacked the necessary labourers for the working of the mines and the cultivation of the soil.

Accustomed to the service of the Indians, several of the first colonists abandoned the island when they saw themselves deprived of the instruments without which they could do nothing; added to this, some maladies peculiar to it, or, perhaps, created by the imprudence of newcomers, developed themselves; and a great number of those who had arrived with Ovando succumbed to the attacks of disease, and in a short time more than a thousand perished, because, without food and preparation, they had proceeded to the mines, where they died of sickness and starvation.

The demand of half the product of the mines required on the part of the sovereigns, seemed such an onerous condition, that no person was willing to engage in their working at this price, and the ruin of the colony from these causes appeared inevitable. In truth, it would not have been able to have sustained itself from the fate that threatened it, had not Ovando taken upon himself the responsibility of modifying the royal ordinances. It was the new distribution of Indians he made on this occasion that had brought about the uprising of the natives against this enforced labour; and even he, fearing that he would be accused of having forced the Indians again into servitude, ordered that their masters should pay them a regular sum as legitimate recompense for their labour; he also reduced the portion of gold intended for the King from one half to a third, and then to a fifth, a tax at which it remained fixed a long time.

It is curious, in this connection, to read the accounts of the habits of these early adventurers. Many of them were the very dregs of the population of Spain; in fact, in order to get recruits at one time, Columbus had induced the authorities of Spain to pardon all such malefactors as would agree to emigrate to the new colony. Again, though many of the emigrants were of the labouring class, accustomed to work for their living in Spain, yet so strong a hold had the thought of finding gold taken upon them, that they had no idea of labouring themselves in the New World; but constituting themselves masters, they sought to force the natives to labour for them, while they exercised an easy superintendence, swinging in a hammock. Others again, sarcastically observes an old writer, who in Spain had never known

A Spanish Master. (De Bry.)

Spaniard in litter.

even the luxury of riding a mule, were not content, when they had gained some riches in the New World, unless they were conveyed in a luxurious litter, between the poles of which were the native Indians.

The Indians, who had been enjoying the privileges of freedom from labour and oppression, already felt in their first servitude, found this new yoke press so heavily upon them, that they made several new attempts to recover their liberty.

The Spaniards always treated these efforts as rebellion, and took arms against the natives with this idea. It is easy to imagine the result, in a contest between savages, entirely naked, on one side, and, on the other, one of the most warlike nations of Europe, where science, courage, and discipline were pitted against timidity and ignorance. The natives were, from the commencement, treated not as people struggling for their rights and freedom, but as slaves revolted against their masters.

No distinction was made by the Spaniards in their treatment of these poor people; the Cacique was as brutally punished as his most humble follower, and this in spite of the treaty that had been made between the Spaniards and natives; and the unjust war made against the people of the province of Higuey had ended in the unwarranted hanging of the chief for having defended his people with a bravery superior to that of his fellow-patriots.

It was in such a state of affairs that Columbus, returning from his fourth voyage of discovery, in which he had been wrecked on the Isle of Jamaica, had stopped at St Domingo city, where he was well received by the Governor, Ovando; but who offended Columbus' sense of dignity by releasing from arrest one of his men, Porras, whom the Admiral himself had ordered to be confined on board one of his ships, in order that he might be sent to Spain to be tried for mutiny while at Jamaica.

This shameful humiliation was too much for the feelings of Columbus, and caused him such mortification, that he set sail from the island for Spain, never again to return to the New World alive. This event, in 1504, was soon followed by the death of his benefactress, the Queen Isabella, who died the same year, an event that was fraught with such portentous consequences for the Indians.

In memory of her who had been known as the protectress of the Indians, her husband, King Ferdinand, proposed to liberate them all from a state of servitude and threatened destruction, and for this purpose he sent to Ovando new orders, tending to better the condition of the Indians.

As the new plan would destroy entirely the system of the *repartimientos* upon which the colonists now founded their hopes of future riches, it became the object of the most terrible opposition, and the Indians remained subject to their yoke in spite of the royal order, for they were utterly powerless to help themselves. Intimidated and humiliated by the atrocious treatment that they had received, the inhabitants of the whole island submitted without further resistance; and the bloody Ovando, ignoring the royal mandate, and henceforth held by no check, divided the Indians among his friends and creatures.

It is, however, due to him to say, that he governed the Spaniards with a wisdom and justice very dissimilar to the barbarity that he exercised over the vanquished natives.

He established equitable laws, and executed them with impartiality, and accustomed the colonists to respect them; he founded several towns in different parts, and drew to them inhabitants by conceding various privileges. He sought also to bring the attention of the Spaniards to some branch of industry more useful than the mere working of mines, in many cases unprofitable; and the sugar-cane having been brought to the island in 1506 from the Canaries, the richness of the soil and the fertility of the climate appeared so favourable to this culture, that it was soon made an object of speculation.

Though the apparatus for its manufacture was of the rudest kind, large plantations were formed, mills established, and in a few years the manufacture of sugar was the principal occupation of the colonists, and the most abundant source of their riches.

Though the wise measures that Ovando took were principally seconded by the attention that King Ferdinand, gave to the laws and the police of the island, it was menaced by a quick destruction.

Sugar-making. (De Bry.)

The natives, upon whose labours the Spaniards had counted for the success of their enterprises, and even for the supplies for their own existence, died so rapidly, that the extinction of the entire race became probable.

When Columbus discovered St Domingo, it certainly had, at the lowest estimate, a million of inhabitants; fifteen years were now elapsed, and they were reduced to 60,000, a result caused by the combination of certain circumstances.

The natives, possessing a constitution more feeble than that of the Europeans, could not stand the same amount of labour or fatigue; and the indolence and inaction in which they had previously passed their lives, as well as the inroads made upon their constitutions by their habits of excess, rendered them incapable of any sustained effort, especially when suddenly begun and long continued, as was the case when they were driven to their hard daily labour; and though their habits were thus materially changed, it does not seem that their food was improved to a more substantial fare.

The Spaniards, never relenting in their vocation of taskmasters, pushed these poor people to the utmost extremity, until, worn out, without strength or hopes, they put an end in various ways to their unfortunate lives.

Benzoni has made this a subject of one of his illustrations, so well known was this fact among the early chroniclers; and following him, De Bry has represented a perfect saturnalia of suicide, in which every means is resorted to by the natives to end their own lives and that of their families.

Suicides. (Benzoni.)

When we read how these poor people were yoked together like cattle, how men and women were separated, how the men were driven into the mines, while the women slaved in the fields under the burning sun, we can readily put faith in the accounts of the self-destruction of these people, who saw only in this an easy way out of their misery.

Gold-mining. (De Bry.)

The Spaniards, seeing themselves thus deprived by degrees of the arms upon which they were habituated to rely for the culture of their lands, were not able any longer to increase their extent, and, in fact, from this time were not able to continue the work already begun.

Alarmed at this state of things, and wishing to remedy promptly this evil, Ovando proposed to his court to transport to Hispaniola the inhabitants of the Lucayos or Bahamas, a series of numerous small islands lying at the entrance to the Gulf of Mexico, under the pretext that it would be easy to civilise them and instruct them in the

Christian religion, when they should be united to the Spanish colony, where they could be supervised by the missionaries.

Ferdinand, deceived by the specious promises of Ovando, and perhaps willing to resort to any means to keep up a colony, then the "Pride of Spain," consented.

Several vessels were sent to these islands, and with them some persons who spoke the language of the islanders; and these, giving the simple people the most glowing accounts of the Spanish island, and the deliciousness of the life there awaiting them, induced large numbers to accompany them;—the population, it is stated, of Hispaniola being increased to the extent of 40,000 by these deluded people.

Notwithstanding this effort to improve matters, these various causes served to discourage the Spaniards; and their favourite mode of enriching themselves—the digging of gold—being unprofitable, the more adventurous spirits cast about for new regions to explore,—their efforts resulting in a series of most wonderful and brilliant discoveries and explorations, never before or since equalled. The record of these is filled with the names of such bold and brilliant men as Cortes, Balboa, Pizarro, De Soto, and many others.

De Ovando had now been in office from 1501, and although he had undoubtedly benefited the island by his government, many complaints had been made against him, to all of which Ferdinand had turned a deaf ear for a long time; when, with a fickleness said to be a characteristic of this monarch, and sheltering himself under the plea that the Queen Isabella had sworn to chastise Ovando for having put to death Anacaona, the fulfilment of which vow she had confided to Ferdinand at her death, he in 1508 relieved Ovando from his command, and ordered him back to Spain.

Don Diego Columbus succeeded him, but did not enjoy the full rights of his father, the Admiral, who had died in

Spain in 1506; and it was strongly suspected that the son was more indebted to the Duke of Alva, whose daughter he had married, and whose influence at court was great, for this recognition of his rights, than to the justness of his claims as being the heir of his father. He was at first only named Governor of the island, not Viceroy of the Indies, according to the patent given to the Admiral.

The new Governor came to the island accompanied by his uncle, his brother, and his wife, upon the latter of whom in mere courtesy had been bestowed the title of vice-queen. With them came a numerous *cortege* of distinguished persons of both sexes; and the splendour and elegance displayed during Don Diego's residence at the capital astonished the people of the New World, while the presence of so much rank and beauty, it is said, had the effect of softening the manners of the colonists, and gave a higher tone to the state of society at the city of St Domingo, which had then reached its highest state of prosperity.

The unfortunate natives, however, did not profit by these splendours; for, strong in his position, Diego awarded to his friends and followers the Indians, not only in the manner hitherto known as *repartimientos*, but by specifying the exact number to be allowed each person according to his rank.

Although the Spaniards were busy in extending their dominions, Hispañiola seems to have been looked upon as their principal colony; and though Diego Columbus appears to have had the ability to govern it with wisdom, he was not permitted by the changeful Ferdinand to exercise his authority without much interference and many annoyances, the King even curtailing some of his privileges.

Among these was that of assigning the Indians, which privilege he accorded to a courtier named Albuquerque, who was authorised to apportion out the natives independently of the Governor;—the result of which was, that, in anxious haste to profit from the perquisites of the office he held, Albuquerque entered with eagerness into their apportion ment; and the first step he took was to obtain the exact number of the natives, from which we learn that these unfortunates had died out so rapidly, that, from having numbered in 1508, 60,000 souls, in 1514 the total number was reduced to 14,000.

To the credit of the priesthood be it said, they had almost unanimously declared against the system of the *repartimientos*, and especially had the Order of the Dominicans raised their voices against it, availing themselves of every occasion to speak out against the iniquitous practice, not fearing in the presence of the Viceroy and his suite, when present in the grand cathedral of St Domingo city, to appeal to them in eloquent language to remedy this state of things; and carrying out these principles, they refused even to absolve those who shared in this division of the natives.

This proceeding gave great offence, of course, to the authorities; and the Franciscans, who were not so determined in their opposition, uniting with the Government, two parties were in existence, each of whom made complaints to the King.

We can read with astonishment and indignation now the famous edict of Ferdinand, in which he declares it is a divine and humane duty to hold the Indians in servitude, as thus they can become Christianised; but at the time this decree gave great satisfaction, as many even of the higher prelates themselves held numbers of the natives in servitude.

In spite of this, the celebrated Father Las Casas used every effort to bring about the relief of these people; and going over to Spain, he reproached King Ferdinand in person, with such effect, that the King, being then near to death, listened to his appeals, and promised to remedy the state of the Indians, but he died before he could fulfil his promises.

It has been said, at various times, that Las Casas was the author of the introduction of African slaves into the island, but this is not corroborated by facts; for as early as 1511, we find that negroes had been brought there, and previous to this Ferdinand had issued orders for their introduction.

However, Zimenes, Cardinal and Regent of Castile, in the minority of the new Emperor Charles the Fifth, listened to Las Casas; and in order to make a beginning in the new programme he had arranged, he sent out to St Domingo three superintendents of all the colonies, utterly ignoring the rights of the then Governor, Don Diego. These superintendents he selected from the order of Hieronymite monks, hoping thus to get impartial and upright men. Through them he changed entirely the system of the colonies, as, on their arrival, they declared free all the Indians, a proceeding that occasioned general alarm, followed by appeals to the new authorities, who, on the representation that the new conquests of Spain in America would have to be abandoned if these Indian labourers were taken away, found it necessary to tolerate the system of *repartimientos*, but endeavoured to arrange for a more genial execution of its workings.

From the troubles ocasioned by these proceedings originated the introduction permanently of the African; for even Las Casas used his influence to have them brought into the island in larger numbers, in order to lighten the labours of the Indians.

This body of priestly governors, although endeavouring to act with justice and impartiality, did not give entire satisfaction to the colonists; and Cardinal Cisneros de Zimenes dying in 1518, the Emperor Charles the Fifth ascended the throne, and immediately recalled these reverend friars, naming a licentiate, Rodrigo de Figueroa, as Governor, who, manifesting great avarice and rapacity, was carried to Spain in 1521 a prisoner, and Don Diego Columbus was again made Governor.

Reference has already been made to African slaves, and it appears that the Indians died out so fast, that it became absolutely necessary to have some reliable mode of getting labourers to work not only the mines, but the land, now become valuable by the culture of the sugar-cane; and thus, in 1510, a regular form had been given to this traffic in human flesh, by the charging of the Casa de Contracion with its carrying on; and in addition to this, when Charles the Fifth became Emperor, he, by a patent bestowed upon a Flemish favourite, gave an exclusive right of importing slaves to the number of four thousand annually. This patent was sold by the Fleming to some Genoese for twenty-five thousand ducats, and they were thus the first merchants who brought into regular form the commerce for slaves between Africa and America.

So rapidly had these slaves increased in number on the island of St Domingo, that we find, in the records of the second term of the governorship of Diego Columbus, that in 1522 they had strength enough to mutiny on the plantation of the Governor himself, moved thereto by the cruelty with which they were treated.

Punishment of Negroes. (De Bry.)

Some idea may be gained of the cruelties experienced by these poor creatures in the descriptions of many of the old authorities, and of which De Bry has made an illustration. One of these accounts is curious, as showing that the modern theory of "earth cure" in wounds is not new, since it is stated that the slaves were so badly whipped that their backs became raw, and upon their raw wounds brine was poured; a hole was then dug in the ground, the suffering negro placed therein, and the earth piled up around him, in order, says the chronicler, that his wounds might be healed by the salve in mother earth, and he rendered fit to do more labour.

The insurrection, the first of which there is any record, was, however, soon put down by the troops; and hardly was this accomplished, when another, much more important, broke out among the few remaining Indians in the island.

This had been incited by a chief named Enrique, a savage who had been converted to Christianity, and who, notwithstanding the nobility of his birth, had been reduced to slavery in one of the *repartimientos.*

Desiring to avenge an insult that had been offered to his wife by a Spaniard, Enrique called upon his compatriots, and uniting themselves in strong force, they took refuge in the mountains of Bajorucho, where they maintained themselves unconquered.

Meanwhile many complaints had been made against the Governor, Diego Columbus; among these was one that, because he was building a substantial palatial house on the bank of the river, he designed it to be a fortress, and, when finished, he intended to declare himself sovereign of the island, and independent of the authority of Spain.

This house still stands, and though in a sad state of decay, gives a good impression of the solidity and grandeur of such buildings in the St Domingo of those days. The accompanying illustration of it is after Guillermin, who saw it about 1801, when it was in a more perfect state than at present. On account of the above complaints, Diego Columbus returned to Spain, and though he completely disproved the charges brought against him, he was not reinstated in his command, but died in 1526 while petitioning for his rights. His office meanwhile had been given to the

Father Luis de Figueroa, who devoted himself especially to the pacification of the Indians, who, under the chief

House of Don Diego Columbus.

Enrique, had now become formidable from their military organisation. The Emperor, hoping probably to replace their labour, now lost, authorised the Flemings in 1526 to introduce African slaves more freely into the island.

By the death of Figueroa the island came under the rule of one of its best Governors, Don Sebastian Ramirez Fuenleal, who immediately took wise and sensible measures for securing the settlement of the affairs of the island, and improving the condition of the loyal Indians.

Although many overtures were made to the insurrectionary chief, yet such was his want of confidence in the Spaniards, that it was not until Father Las Casas succeeded in inducing Enrique to send an envoy to St Domingo city, that a treaty of peace was signed, in 1533, by which the Indians, 600 in number, under their chief, were permanently established in a village (Boya) by themselves, and land allowed them to cultivate for their own use. With this treaty ended actually the troubles with the aborigines, which in Dominican annals are known as belonging to the time of the conquest. Of this race, not one single pure-blooded descendant exists to-day.

CHAPTER IV.

"Let nobler bards, in loftier numbers, tell
How Cortez conquered, Montezuma fell;
How grim Pizarro's ruffian arm o'erthrew
The sun's resplendent empire in Peru."

THE DECLINE OF ST DOMINGO—*Failure of the Mines—Expeditions fitted out—Depredations on Spanish Vessels—Depopulation of the Island—Neglect of Spain—Its Colonial Policy—Drake's Attack—The Capture and Ransom of the Capital.*

THERE now ensues a long period in the history of St Domingo, in which the island, having gained a position brilliant and striking from its sudden rise and prosperity, as quickly sinks into obscurity, desolation, and misery, the result of manifold causes.

St Domingo city, the capital, had become firmly established; it had been beautified and improved; in fact, had become noted for the splendour of its houses and the regularity of its streets, while its port was the most busy one in the New World.

In addition to this principal city, there had been established in different parts of the island other towns and villages, the most important of which were Azua, Aquin (Yaquimo), Salvatierra de la Savana, Yaguana (Leogane), Puerto Plata, Puerto Real, Monte Cristo, Santiago de los Caballeros, Bonao, Cotuy, Buenaventura, Concepcion de la Vega, Bañica, Hincha, Higuei, and Seybo, to all of which, so important were they considered, had been allowed the use of respective coats of arms.

The number of regularly organised sugar plantations had amounted to nearly fifty, and the products of these, it is related, more than exceeded the products of the gold mines in their best days; in fact, so luxuriant and profitable was the cane-crop, that it was a common remark of the time that some of the handsomest palaces in Spain were built of St Domingo sugar.

Hatero.

The increase of the live-stock originally brought out from Spain had been so wonderful, that the island was literally overrun with the wild cattle, which were left undisturbed, except by occasional visits of the hateros or herdsmen, men who, even at the present day, devote themselves exclusively to the raising of cattle upon the immense plains called "llanos" or savanas.

There was then no reason why affairs should not have vastly improved, and the island itself reached a high state of prosperity, had it not been from a combination of retarding causes.

In the period after the conquest known in its annals as the time of "Old Spain," the island may be said to have reached the very zenith of its prosperity, followed gradually by a series of events which left it almost depopulated, prostrated, and even unrecognised by its parent country; a period in which we see, in strong contrast to the Spaniards, the French, who had gained possessions in the West Indies, show by their energy and talent, as well as by an encouraging policy of the home Government, what could be made of those beautiful isles generally called the Antilles.

In order fully to understand the condition of St Domingo while exclusively under Spanish rule, it may be as well that we take a glance at the policy of Spain in relation to her colonies; for what applied to one as a general rule applied to all. And as she was the first to enter the arena of the New World, so was the system she adopted considered the best by the other powers which followed her, and, with some modifications, pretty generally adopted by them.

The Spanish Indies, the name given by Spain to its colonies in America, having been by law declared an inalienable part of the Spanish monarchy, the King became the sovereign of those newly discovered countries, and exercised all the authority belonging to that title, enjoying to every extent all the rights, powers, and patronage that title gave, and his will became thus the law of the colony, against the exercise of which there was no check or hindrance.

In the exercise of this power, the first agent of the King was the "Royal and Supreme Council of the Indies," a name given to a tribunal created by King Ferdinand in 1511 for the control of the American department.

The powers of this tribunal were much enlarged by the Emperor Charles the Fifth, in 1524, and his successors; so that it became the depositary of all law, the fountain of all nominations, both ecclesiastical and temporal, and the supreme tribunal where all questions, whether of government or trade, in the colonies, were finally adjudicated.

This council, as ancient as the New World itself almost, had always the same limited views, and so far from being moved by great impulses and large ideas fitting to the immense powers bestowed upon it, was, on the contrary, a great drawback to the forward impulses of the youthful colonies, which, like young children, required the most careful nursing and attention from their mother country.

In the earliest period, this council had been organised to benefit the colony of St Domingo, by devising means to advance its interests, to send out supplies of provisions, and to furnish seeds and implements for the agricultural development of the island.

This council prepared all the laws for the Indies; it took cognisance exclusively of all matters by land and sea, and of every kind that in any wise related to the Indies, having full authority over viceroys, presidents, courts, commerce, and even of the army and navy.

It proposed to the King all persons for office, of whatever grade; it presented also the officials of the Church; and, in fact, was endowed with such supreme powers, as, says Valverde, "not even the Roman Senate had so exclusive a jurisdiction."

In the early days of Spanish discovery and conquest, St Domingo was the headquarters of the "Royal Audencia," or court established for all the new provinces; but as the latter grew in extent and number, they also began to have courts of their own.

For hundreds of years the chief commands of the island were bestowed on military officers, the Governor being known as Captain-General, and who in subsequent years, became the President of the Royal Audencia.

The power of the Governor was almost supreme, and with him rested the appointment of the subaltern officers, such as the commandants.

The royal court was surrounded by a great number of formalities, laws, and ceremonies; and at one time, it would appear that St Domingo city was noted for the pomp and display made by the officials in the fulfilment of their duties, which duties were distinctly prescribed in a code made in Spain, known as "The Collection of the Laws of the Kingdoms of the Indies."

The establishment of the royal court was the cause, in later years, of much trouble, for to it were carried all appeals from the decision of the Governor of the island, and there were frequent conflicts of authority therefrom.

An endless cause of bickering and complaint in the island was the constant interference in secular affairs of the priesthood, whose strength and numbers constantly increased; and, under Cardinal Zimenes, we have seen the government intrusted to three of their number.

As the King paid all the expenses of divine worship, the tithes belonged to him in consequence of a concession of the Pope. There was collected on all vegetable products of importance in commerce one measure in ten; on all annual products, even on milk, lard, wool, and on minor products, such as wax, honey, &c., the King took his share of one-tenth. A percentage there was also on sugar and molasses, even the native bread, cassava, paying duty.

The conquerors of the New World, in their desire of making themselves masters of large domains, seized upon immense tracts of land, and held them under what was known as "*encomiendas*," and by degrees they obtained the privilege of converting these into "*mayorasgos*," a species of fief introduced into the Spanish system of feudal jurisprudence, which can neither be divested nor alienated, resulting, as we shall see, to-day, in the system known as "*communeros*."

The Church followed the example set by these adventurers, and became the possessors of large tracts; and, as their revenue was only to be derived by the cultivation of these lands, they were leased out in small lots to those unable to buy or to occupy pieces of their own; and in all the jurisdictions of the Church "first-fruits" were exacted and paid.

The Church had yet another influence in the island, for the Inquisition has played here, as elsewhere, a memorable part in the history of St Domingo; for, as early as 1517 inquisitors were sent to the island, their advent being marked with great pomp and ceremony on the part of the officials and people; and when we read that the inquisitors were paid from the confiscations made by themselves, we can readily understand the motives that prompted their action in many cases. And it is on record that there was only one printing-office, little used, on the entire island; and no books of any kind were allowed to be brought in that had not received the sanction of the Inquisition, a proceeding that is seen in its results to-day, not a single book of any value being found for sale.

The Inquisition, as is well known, was always opposed to the instruction and enlightenment of the people; and in no place was this more forcibly manifested than in St Domingo; and the antipathy of inquisitors against books was only equalled by that against Jews, the results of which are seen to-day in the islands still under the Spanish crown; for, though the Jews may be found in almost every habitable part of the globe, not one hardly is to be met with in Cuba, Porto Rico, or St Domingo.

In fact, the entry of every class of foreigners into the island was discountenanced by the Government, which, with the jealousy peculiar to Spain, looked with suspicion upon the attempts on the part of subjects of any other power to trade with its colonies.

Many other of the Church rules and regulations weighed heavily upon the settlers; and some writers are ill-natured enough to doubt the possibility of the Church, in these times, honestly getting rich, when its servants were so poor. The Jesuits, it is said, managed to carry large sums of gold out of the country in various ways without exciting suspicion, such as sending it as rolls of chocolate, and bones of saints.

In addition to the sources of revenue above mentioned,

there was a tax upon the salaries of the officials, consisting of a levy of half the product of the first year, which is suggestive of the honesty with which these offices must have been filled; while many of the minor positions were publicly farmed out to the highest bidder.

There were municipal governments for the different districts, towns, or villages, presided over by an alderman or alcalde, and he named subordinate officers; and there were besides innumerable fiscal officers, which it would be tedious to mention.

It is, however, from the monopoly created by the organisation of the Casa de Contracion that the colonial interests of Spain have, perhaps, received their greatest injury; for, by an ordinance dated at Alcala, January 20, 1503, a board of trade, with the above name, was constituted, which, though supposed to be subordinate to the Council of the Indies, became in time almost independent of it. The laws and regulations made by this body, although nominally created to encourage and protect the commerce of Spain with her colonies, were ultimately the cause of its decay and ruin.

It consisted of three officers, bearing the separate titles of treasurer, factor, and comptroller, their residence being appointed at Seville, where they were to hold daily meetings in the building known as the Aleazar, for the transaction of business.

This board was instructed to make itself thoroughly familiar with everything pertaining to the colonies, and to furnish the Government with every kind of information concerning their prosperity and welfare.

Laws were passed restricting the entire trade of the colonies with the mother country to the port of Seville; and to the Casa de Contracion was intrusted the supervision of all fleets, their destination, the furnishing them with instructions; and, in the warehouse of the board, at that place, was deposited all the merchandise for shipment, as well as the return cargoes, for the sale of which the contracts were to be supervised by the board.

Seville, therefore, remained the only port for a long time, until the Guadalquiver, which, in the time of the Emperor Charles the Fifth, was navigable up to the town, became, for large vessels, inaccessible, when the port was removed to Cadiz, from whence, at stated times, a fleet sailed for Mexico, and galleons for Porto Bello. This continued in practice until the war of 1732, when register ships were substituted for galleons, which no longer sailed at fixed times, though the "fleet" and these "register" ships continued to sail from Cadiz to Mexico.

Porto Bello was the main rendezvous for this fleet from Spain, known in early times as the "galleons," which consisted usually of about eight men-of-war, of the size known as three or four deckers, each mounting fifty guns, and they were nominally assigned to supply the American ports with military stores; but, in reality, were laden not only with these, but every kind of merchandise, and they also convoyed other ships on private account, to the number of fourteen or fifteen.

In time of peace, this fleet sailed regularly once a year from Cadiz, according as the King ordered it, or the convenience of the merchants permitted; the fleet of galleons being regulated pretty much as was the "flota" or fleet, and designed for the exclusive trade with Terra Firma, as South America was then called, and the South Sea.

The "flota," on the contrary, was destined for New Spain, as Mexico was then called, the port being Vera Cruz, as also the Philippine Islands. It consisted of an annual fleet, that sailed from Cadiz, leaving there about the last of September, being composed of three men-of-war, and sixteen large merchantmen, of from 500 to 600 tons burden.

These were loaded with every sort of goods which

Europe could produce for export, and thus every part of Europe was interested in this fleet, as their manufactures were thus distributed in the New World. Spain itself sent out little more than wine and fruit; this, with the freight and the commission to the merchants, and the duty to the King, was almost the only advantage that the mother country derived from the commerce with the Indies.

This is easily accounted for, from the fact that Spain had, at this time, few or no manufactures, and as she had no goods of her own to send to the colonies, she passed such laws and restrictions as made the whole of Europe one vast storehouse for her, to which she acted as broker, charging commission nominally both ways, to the consumer and the manufacturer; but, in truth, it was the overtaxed consumer, the colonist, who paid the commission; and as the colonist began to realise this fact, so gradually did Spain find her colonies seeking to render themselves independent of her.

In the early days of the New World colonies, all these fleets made the harbour of St Domingo city their haven, in passing to and from Spain, as at that time this was the only strongly and regularly fortified place belonging to that power in the New World.

With the conquest of Cuba, Jamaica, Peru, and Mexico, this arrangement was changed, and the fleets, on their return, almost entirely stopped at the city of Havana, loaded with everything the colonies produced; and here congregated the galleons, the flota, and the register ships, preparatory to their return to Spain.

The register ships originated from the illicit commerce that sprang up by Spain's prohibiting all intercourse with strangers; they were registered, with all the effects embarked in them, in the books of the Chamber of Commerce at Seville.

It was this sort of commerce that induced the English

and the Dutch to step in without waiting for a license; and, with the connivance of the Governors of the different colonies, they all made money.

This practice became finally so flagrant and glaring, that the home authorities sent new Governors with precise orders; and with these came the "guardia costas," or guardships, which, from being established at first for a just and legal purpose, finally made trouble by becoming privateers, and preying upon the commerce of all nations, ending in open war between the powers.

With all these plans to control the trade of the colonies, it would be supposed that every effort would have been made to encourage emigration and increase the value of the colonial lands; but so far from this being the case, certainly, as regards St Domingo, a few years after its discovery and settlement, restrictions were made, and permission had first to be asked of the Board of Trade before emigrants could go out there. Almost every article going into or coming out of the island paid a duty, hindrance even being made to domestic trade; for the principal one of cattle-selling, in the time of the French, had to pay its share of taxes and fees to officials, who occupied their positions, not to further the interests of the island, but to look out for their own profit.

It is very certain that all these restrictions on emigration and commerce had a great deal to do with the decline in the prosperity of St Domingo; for all these laws being enacted at a time when new countries were being opened up, adventurers thought it more easy to seek rapid fortunes in the conquest of those places, than to await them by the slow and restricted processes of agriculture and trade in St Domingo.

In the early period of its history, the population had been increased by the crowds of Spaniards who, insatiable for gold, crowded here from the mother country when expeditions were fitted out for the conquest of

Cuba, Porto Rico, Trinidad, and St Marguerite. Yet the very influence that brought such hosts of these adventurers to this island was the one that assisted more effectually than any other in depopulating it; for the discovery of the gold mines of Mexico and Peru, the glowing accounts of which had come first to St Domingo, tempted the largest part of its inhabitants, particularly the young and adventurous, to seek in those regions for adventures, glory, and riches, the fabulous accounts of which had fired the hearts of a people who seem to have had as second nature that love of adventure which has tended so much to gild with glory the crown of Spain.

Most of the noted expeditions of the time being fitted out from the port of St Domingo, it was not long before the island threatened to become entirely depopulated, such were the numbers who sought a part in these expeditions; and so alarming did this emigration become, that the Emperor Charles the Fifth issued orders against the emigrating of families as well as the recruiting of men on the island. Means were found by those who wished to evade these commands; and it is stated that some of the richest families found it to their interest to seek, with their means and capital, larger fields of enterprise in the new countries now opened.

Up to 1540, the period when this decline began in the affairs of St Domingo, it seems like romance to read the accounts of the comings and the goings of the immense fleets of vessels which were constantly arriving and departing to and from the mother country and the settlements in America, with their products.

Some of the mines, when at first worked, had produced so much silver, that a mint had been established at the capital, where money was struck off the same as in Spain; and in the products of the soil, then mostly new to the Old World, such as cotton, sugar, tobacco, ginger, &c., additional sources of riches were found; add to which the large number of hides produced by the immense herds of cattle then scattered over the island, had produced a commerce at that time which at no period since has reached the same extent.

The traveller to-day, who traverses the streets of the present city of St Domingo, deserted and decayed as they are, as he looks at the immense structures, the solid walls, and the ruins of former greatness, finds himself wondering what has become of those incentives to enterprise which were the origin of the foundation of such a city. From this period to the time when Drake landed, there seems to be little of general importance occurring in the island, other than a series of misfortunes; for the labour of the

An old street in St Domingo city.

mines was reduced to almost nothing, while the agriculture was followed in detached portions only; for the colonists, seduced away by the reports of famous riches on the continent of America, still continued to emigrate.

In 1568 the limited amount of products raised consisted of cotton, sugar, and tobacco, the results of the labours of a few Indians still surviving, as also a few Africans, while the commerce was limited to a few sticks of Brazil wood; when a trade sprang up with the Dutch, which in time would doubtless have helped the colony much, but just at this juncture the English appeared on the coast, to give a new turn to affairs for a time.

Queen Elizabeth of England, being determined to destroy the preponderance of Spanish power in the West Indies, sent out, in 1586, an expedition under Sir Francis

Drake

Drake, to do all the harm he could, as well to the commerce, as to the possessions of Spain in that part of the world. Acting under these instructions, Drake landed on the shores of St Domingo, and succeeded in getting possession of the town. The subjoined account, being that of an eye-witness, affords us some quaint information as to the condition of this famous city and the mode of warfare at that time. I give it in the original text.

"By the way we met a small frigate bound for the same place; in her was found one by whom we were advertised the haven to be a barred haven, and the shore or land thereof to be well fortified, having a castle thereupon, furnished with great store of artillery; without the danger whereof was no convenient landing-place within ten English miles of the city, to which the said pilot took upon himself to conduct us. . . .

"Our general having seen us all landed in safety, returned to his fleet, bequeathing us to God and the good conduct of Mr Carliell, our Lieut.-General, at which time, being about eight of the clock, we began to march, and about noon-time, or towards one of the clock, we approached the town, where the gentlemen and those of the better sort, being some hundred and fifty brave heroes, or rather more, began to present themselves; but our small shot played upon them, which were so sustained by good proportion of pikes in all parts; as they, finding no part of our troop unprepared to receive them (for you must understand they viewed all round about), they were thus driven to give us leave to proceed towards the two gates of the town, which were the next to the seaward.

"They had manned them both, and planted their ordnance for that present and sudden alarm without the gate, and also some troops of small shot in ambuscade upon the by wayside.

"We divided our force, being some thousand or twelve hundred men, into two parts to enterprise both the gates at one instant; the Lieut.-General having openly avowed to Captain Powell (who led the troops that entered the

OLD SANTO DOMINGO CITY.

other gate), that, with God's good favour, he would not rest until our meeting in the market-place.

"Their ordnance had no sooner discharged upon our near approach, and made some execution amongst us, though not much, but the Lieut.-General began forthwith to advance both his voice of encouragement and pace of marching; the first man that was slain with the ordnance being very near unto himself, and thereupon hasted all that he might to keep them from recharging the ordnance.

"And notwithstanding their ambuscadoes, we marched, or rather ran, so roundly into them, as pell-mell we entered the gates, and gave them more care, every man to save himself by flight, than reason to stand any longer to their broken fight. We forthwith repaired to the market-place, but, to be more truly understood, a place of very fair, spacious, square ground before the great church; whither also came, as had been agreed, Captain Powell with the other troop; which place, with some part next unto it, we strengthened with barricades, and there, as the most convenient place, assured ourselves; the city being far too spacious for so small and weary a troop to undertake to guard.

"Somewhat after midnight, they who had the guard of the castle, hearing us busy about the gates of the said castle, abandoned the same; some being taken prisoners, and some flying away by the help of boats to the other side of the haven, and so into the country.

"The next day we quartered a little more at large, but not into the half part of the town; and so making substantial trenches, and planting all the ordnance that each part was correspondent to the other, we held this town the space of one month.

"In which time it chanced that the General sent on his messages to the Spaniards a negro boy with a flag of white, signifying truce, as is the Spaniard's ordinary manner to do there; which boy unhappily was first met with some who furiously struck the poor boy through the body with one of their horsemen's staves, with which wound the boy returned to the General, and after he had declared the manner of this wrongful cruelty, died forthwith in his presence; wherewith the General, being greatly passioned, commanded the provost-marshal to cause a couple of friars, then prisoners, to be carried to the same place where the boy was struck, accompanied with sufficient guard, and there presently to be hanged, despatching at the same time another poor prisoner, with the reason wherefore this execution was done, and with the message, that until the party who had thus murdered the General's messenger were delivered into our hands, there should no day pass wherein there should not two prisoners be hanged, until they were all consumed which were in our hands. . . .

"Upon disagreements with their commissioners, we still spent the early mornings in firing the outmost houses; but they, being built very magnificently of stone, with high lofts, gave us no small travail to ruin them.

"And albeit for eleven days together we ordained each morning by daybreak, until the heat began at nine o'clock, that two hundred mariners did nought else but labour to fire and burn the said houses, without our trenches, while the soldiers stood their guard. Yet did we not, nor could not, in this time, consume so much as one-third part of the town. And so, in the end, what wearied with firing, and what hastened by some other respects, we were contented to accept of five-and-twenty thousand ducats (about 30,000 dollars) for the ransom of the rest of the town."

Five years subsequent to this, the English again committed depredations, doing injury to other towns upon the coast; and the effect of these combined misfortunes was, that the entire population of the island was reduced to less than 14,000 inhabitants, not including some 1200 runaway negroes, who were encamped in the inaccessible parts of the island.

It was thus, from these attacks, that the island rapidly receded in prosperity; for, in addition to the effects on land, the waters of the Spanish Main were filled with vessels bearing roving commissions to prey upon the commerce of nations not at peace with those represented by the banners flying at their masts. From this cause intercourse between Spain and her colonies became very difficult, and particularly so with St Domingo, to which this connection was more desirable and necessary than it was to the mother country, and the trade between the two became almost extinct; for it was only once in two or three years, at most, that a few ships were seen in the port of St Domingo city. Its only external relations were with Mexico; and had it not been for foreigners, the Dutch in particular, the colony would have sunk under the misery which it so long groaned under.

Encouraged by these people, who were anxious to exchange their products and manufactures for the hides, cattle, and produce of the island, the Dominicans entered largely into a contraband trade at the towns on the coast.

The Court of Madrid, entirely unmoved at this condition of affairs, which had arisen in great degree from its own want of administration, and jealous of the interference of any other nation in its trade, shut up, in 1606, all these ports except St Domingo city, and ordered the inhabitants thereof to the interior, where, erecting cabins for themselves, they became only indifferent agriculturists, while their former habitations were demolished. This was another signal for the emigration of numerous families from the island, and such a state of affairs resulted from this, that the authorities of the time state, that the fields were uncultivated, and the farms were depopulated; the houses were going to ruin, with closed doors, their occupants having deserted them; the duties and taxes that could be collected for the Government amounted to absolutely nothing; and to these numberless evils, the island began to be raided on by the buccaneers. But the appearance of these people in the history of St Domingo is of such importance, that I shall devote a chapter to them especially.

While events of this nature were taking place in the western part, there was hardly anything worthy of mention occurring in the other portion of the Spanish part, which was already sunk into decay, when the declaration of war in 1654 against Spain by Oliver Cromwell gives a new interest to the history of St Domingo, in which the English largely figure; and the reader of English history can refer to the details of the disastrous expedition in 1655, sent against St Domingo, for the history of the first attempt of England to make a permanent landing on Dominican soil.

This expedition consisted of a squadron under command of Admiral Penn, having on board 9000 men under the command of General Venables, which, having arrived off the city of St Domingo, April 1655, was divided into two bodies, for the purpose of attacking two different points.

The Spaniards made a united and strong resistance, leading the English into ambuscades, and with such success, that the troops were thrown into disorder, and compelled to retire; and the expedition having signally failed in its object, left the coast of the island for Jamaica.

Penn and Venables, on their return to England, were imprisoned by Cromwell, and their conduct being investigated, they were liberated from prison, but disgraced for their want of skill and success.*

* Walton gives an amusing account of the manner in which the defeat of the English was brought about. He says, "The landcrabs found here are of an immense size, burrow in the sand, and at night issue out in great numbers. On the above occasion, the English landed an ambuscade to surprise the Spanish camp, which being unprepared, and consisting of irregulars, had it been pushed, must have certainly fallen.

"The advanced line from the first boats had already formed, and was proceeding to take post behind a copse, when they heard the loud and quick clatter of horses' feet, and, as they supposed, of the Spanish lancemen, who are dexterous, and whose galling onset they had experienced the day before. Thus believing themselves discovered, and dreading an attack before their comrades had joined, they embarked precipitately, and abandoned their enterprise ; but the alarm proved to be these large landcrabs, which, at the sound of footsteps, receded to their holes, the noise being made by their clattering over the dry leaves, which the English soldiers mistook for the sound of cavalry.

"In honour of this miracle a feast was instituted, and celebrated each year, under the name of Feast of the Crabs, on which occasion a solid gold landcrab was carried about in procession."

CHAPTER V.

> "Dreadful as hurricanes athwart the main
> Rushed the fell legions of invading Spain;
> With fraud and force they swept the isles."

THE BUCCANEERS AND EARLY FRENCH.—*Origin of the Buccaneers—Their Manners and Customs—Settlement of Tortuga, and their Extension from thence under the Auspices of the French—Settlement of St Domingo.*

FILLIBUSTER is a word that has come to be looked upon as almost entirely of American origin, and yet it originated with Europeans, as did also the class of people to whom it properly belonged.

As early as the year 1600 the Spaniards in the New World, particularly that part of it in the vicinity of the Gulf of Mexico, began to stop the ships of other nations found trading in these waters, on the plea that, by right of discovery, all those lands and waters, with their privileges of trade and commerce, belonged exclusively to them.

The result of this was that, though Europe generally was at peace, the English and French, for mutual protection to their commerce, began at first to tolerate the fitting out in their ports of privateers, for the purpose of making reprisals on the commerce of the Spaniards, as well as to resist the arbitrary acts of the legalised vessels, the "Guardia Costas."

As it became necessary to have some depôt for these vessels and their stores in the waters of the Antilles, by a strange coincidence both the English and French selected the same island upon which to establish themselves; but, as it appears, on different sides of the small island of St Christopher, one of the lesser Antilles. This was at first selected as the point most convenient from which to start out on their privateering enterprises.

Here, in this island, the subjects of the two powers of France and England seem to have remained peacefully and quietly in joint occupation, even uniting their forces against the native inhabitants.

The French, it is said, busied themselves in making large boats from a peculiar tree, in which they wandered about among the neighbouring islands, going so far even as to land on the shores of St Domingo, particularly on the north coast, the wild cattle of which offered them tempting inducements. They had thus established themselves in small parties from Samana to Tortuga.

Each nationality being anxious to retain possession of St Christopher for its own Government, representatives returned to France and England to inform their respective Governments of the advantages to be gained in securing and settling this island.

Cardinal Richelieu, in France, immediately took steps to secure these advantages to the French; and a company was formed for the working of this and other islands, in which he himself took stock. This company was known as the "Compagnie des Iles;" and every one embarking under its auspices was required to remain in the islands and labour there three years for the benefit of the company, in consideration of receiving his passage free. This class of persons was known as "engagés," and became of great importance afterwards in the settlement of the New World.

The English, having pursued the same policy, were rapidly growing to be the stronger party in the island, though as yet they both occupied it jointly and peaceably; but the rapid growth of the settlement alarmed the Spanish Government for the safety of its own possessions in those regions, and in 1630 Frederic of Toledo, being on his way with a large fleet to chastise the Dutch in Brazil, was directed by his sovereign to destroy the combined settlement of the French and English at St Christopher.

This he did so effectually, that the inhabitants were all either killed, taken prisoners, or dispersed; and those who effected their escape were forced to take refuge in some of the neighbouring islands, a large number finding their way to the small island of Tortuga on the north-west coast of Hayti.

Here they were joined by some Dutch refugees from Santa Cruz, fleeing also from the wrath of the Spaniards; and being struck with the advantages of the Isle of Tortuga, and finding there only a handful of Spaniards, these "brethren of the sea," as they called themselves, made a permanent location.

They were prompted, also, by a desire to find a more convenient place than St Christopher from whence to attack the Spanish vessels *en route* to and from St Domingo and Cuba; for the currents were so strong, and the winds so contrary, that it was a tedious matter for them to come up from St Christopher, having only their sails and oars upon which to rely.

Thus, then, we have the representatives of three different nationalities in this little island of Tortuga, but which was to be the nucleus of a great settlement. They were all, however, united in one respect, their misfortunes having made them companions in adversity, and in looking upon the Spaniards as their common enemy, whose possessions in Hispañola they made their common hunting-grounds for the immense herds of wild cattle that at the time overran the entire western part.

Thus establishing themselves upon Tortuga, they agreed that, while one portion should remain upon it and cultivate the soil, another portion should occupy themselves in hunting on the mainland, in order to keep the settlers supplied with meat, and a third portion devoted themselves, as they called it, to the commerce of the seas, that is, in seeking out vessels in the narrow channels, which they could attack in their long boats. In this manner these people became divided into three classes, those remaining on the island being known as the "habitans," or planters, and those following the sea, who, in fact, became pirates; for this island was a sort of advanced post by which all vessels going to or from Peru, Cuba, and Mexico, generally passed, thus affording them ample opportunity to indulge their vocation.

This pursuit was followed in a large long boat, most frequently propelled by oars worked by crews consisting of from fifteen to thirty men; who, well armed, did not hesitate to attack most of the vessels that fell in their way. As these boats were made light, and were very fast, they received the various names of *freibote*, *fly-bote*, or *fleibote*, and their crews came thus to acquire the names of *freiboteros* (freebooters), which, in our time, has become corrupted into *fillibuster*.

A Buccaneer.

The third portion were known as *boucaniers* (a name corrupted into *buccaneers*), being those engaged in the hunting of cattle, and getting their peculiar name from the rude manner of cooking their meat, a mode adapted from the Caribs in those islands, who in this manner disposed of the bodies of their victims. This mode was simply to make a frame of green boughs, known as a "boucan," upon which the meat was laid, and under this a slow fire was kept, which partly smoked and partly cooked the meat; which, in that climate, they were thus enabled to keep a short time for use.

A Boucan.

Of these "boucaniers," there were two classes: — one which hunted the cattle exclusively for their hides; and the other, those who hunted only the wild boars and pigs for their meat, which they salted down and sold.

The former had with them a pack of hounds or dogs, usually from fifteen to twenty in number. They carried a long gun, that was made expressly for them in France, the barrel being from four to four and a half feet long, and of uniform calibre, sixteen balls to the pound.

Their clothing consisted usually of a cotton shirt, and a pair of drawers or pants, made loose and baggy like a frock, while for shoes they used the skin of the pigs or cattle they killed. A close-fitting cap, with a small visor, completed this costume. On their expeditions they carried with them into the woods a small linen tent, which they used for purposes of shelter from the sun, and the attacks of the flies, which abounded in the island.

Being thus equipped, these boucaniers joined in pairs, calling each other *matelot*, putting all that they owned into the common stock; and as they increased in wealth and means, they also had servants, who were usually of the class known as engagés, of whom they had paid the passage from France, thus buying them body and soul for the term of three years.

They left Tortuga, and crossing to the main island of St Domingo, were sometimes absent as long as a year in the woods, selecting certain localities which they made known to each other, and where they erected often small huts called *ajoupas*, derived from the Indian word lodge.

They spent their days, attended by their servants and dogs, in hunting the wild cattle, which they slaughtered for their hides only, leaving the meat to spoil. Having found as many hides as they could carry upon their backs, they returned to their place of departure, where they cured the hides in the most primitive manner, partaking also of a repast of meat cooked as described above. Their only amusement seemed to be firing at a mark, and most of them were skilful marksmen.

Having gained hides and meat enough, they returned either to the seaside, where they had opportunities of disposing of their property, or they crossed to Tortuga, where they supplied themselves with the few articles they needed in their rude manner of life, and then delivered themselves up to carousal and dissipation until their means were exhausted.

Their principal vice was drunkenness, which they brought about by imbibing pure brandy, drinking it as freely as the Spaniards did water. Sometimes they bought together a pipe of wine, and staving in the head of it, they never ceased to drink until the wine was exhausted and their money spent.

At first neither the planters nor the buccaneers had other servants than the engagés, and the cruelties practised upon these poor people of the white race quite equal

Merry-making.

anything in the annals of African slavery. They were starved, beaten, maimed, and killed, at the pleasure of their brutal masters, without having any one to look to for redress.

It does not appear that the original settlers of Tortuga engaged in piracy, but settled down to hunting and planting; and it was only after the Spaniards had made their first great attack upon them, murdering those that were on the island, and destroying their plantations, that, in revenge, after having united themselves into a society, they began to make reprisals on the Spaniards and their commerce, which finally extended itself to such a degree, that it was hardly safe for a Spanish vessel to cross the ocean, until, not finding objects for their attacks, the more adventurous of these freebooters led expeditions against the Spanish settlements of Cuba, the Isthmus, and South America.

The first pirate of whom there seems to be any particular mention was one known as Peter the Great, a man who had been born at Dieppe in Normandy, and who, having captured a Spanish ship in a small boat with twenty-eight men, became famous. The news of this rich prize raised such excitement in Tortuga, that many of the hunters and planters determined to follow his example; and leaving their regular occupations, they began their career of piracy, at first in small boats, and as their means increased they invested in large vessels, with which they extended their operations, returning to Tortuga to dispose of their spoils, being sure of finding there ships with merchants ready to purchase them, as in a few years this island became a famous place of business and resort for all people engaged in commerce, whether legal or illegal, in those waters.

Among the most notorious of those leaders who originally started out from Tortuga, was the famous Morgan, afterwards Sir Henry, who, after committing every crime known, ended by stealing the booty of his comrades, with which,

Morgan.

retiring to the Island of Jamaica, he succeeded in making a portion of the world believe he was a high-toned honourable man, becoming actually an officer of the Government, and receiving the honour of knighthood. His portraits represent him as a fine-looking gentleman, and he is said to have sprung from a respectable family in Wales; but the records of some of his comrades show him to be as guilty of hypocrisy as he was of every known iniquity.

There was not much of which to be proud amongst any of these "brethren of the sea," no matter to what nationality they belonged; for though the "Romance of History" has endeavoured to glorify some of them for their deeds, the candid reader can come to no other conclusion than that the whole were a lot of arrant vagabonds, being thieves and murderers on a large scale, the only point in their favour being that they were all men recklessly brave.

The permanent hold of the buccaneers upon Tortuga was not secured, however, until after many reverses; for the Spanish Governor, Acuña, having notified his sovereign of their occupation of Tortuga, caused so much alarm, that a Spanish fleet was sent to St Domingo with orders to destroy this settlement.

The measures to accomplish this were taken with such precaution, that, in 1638, the buccaneers were surprised while many of their comrades were away at sea and others in the mountains, so that it was an easy matter to put those surprised to the sword; and the Spaniards, thinking they had thus extinguished the settlement, retired without taking the precaution to leave a garrison on the island.

The buccaneers who were at sea, on returning to learn the fate of their comrades and find their settlement destroyed, determined, for their own safety, to form a regular organisation, and sacrifice their individual independence for social security; and they, therefore, chose for their leader an Englishman named Willis, who had distinguished himself amongst them by his bravery and judgment, and under whose command, in 1639, they returned and established themselves permanently on the island.

This island, so famous in the history of the New

Plan of Tortuga.

World, was called from its peculiar shape, as seen from the sea, "Tortuga de Mar," or sea-turtle, and is described at this time as a rocky isle, upon whose face grew roots of trees like ivy against a wall; the north of the island, precipitous, rough, and unhealthy, affording no shelter whatever. On the south side there was only one port, indifferently good, but having two entrances, allowing the passage of seventy-gun ships.

The lowlands contained the town of the port, where lived the principal and richest planters. On the island there was abundance of wood for ship-building, fruits, medicinal plants, &c., while wild boars, pigeons, landcrabs, and sea-crabs, abounded.

8

Sometime after Willis had been made captain, a French freebooter arrived on the island, and not being pleased at finding so many of his countrymen under the authority of an English leader, he returned to the Island of St Christopher, where the French were re-established under the command of Chevalier de Poincy, a Knight of the Order of Malta. To him was made known the condition of affairs at Tortuga.

De Poincy immediately took steps to secure the island for the French: and there being at the time at St Christopher an engineer, Captain le Vasseur, an arrangement was made by which he should proceed to Tortuga as Governor. On his arrival at that island he was well received by the French inhabitants; and they being largely in the majority, the English were compelled to leave the island quietly in possession of the French, the former proceeding to Jamaica.

Le Vasseur being thus in command, and fearing the return of the Spaniards, built a fort on the top of a high rock that completely commanded the port and entrance with its battery of two guns.

De Poincy, however, began to mistrust his Governor, Le Vasseur, and therefore organised an expedition to fully establish his authority over Tortuga; but, on its arrival at that island, it was found that Le Vasseur had just died, and the troops of De Poincy being well received by the colonists, order was soon established.

Hardly was this done when the Spaniards in strong force again appeared, and a large number of the male inhabitants being absent, the island was captured, the Governor retiring within the fort, where he was besieged; but making a stout defence, he was finally permitted by the Spaniards to leave the island with his people, with all the honours of war, carrying with them their arms.

The Spaniards then left a garrison of some sixty men, and it remained in their possession until De Rossy, a gentleman of Perigord, and who had previously been a pirate, determined, after the death of De Poincy, the Governor of St Christopher, to recapture Tortuga. Arranging his plans with great skill, he surprised the Spaniards, and took the fort from a side they thought inaccessible; and then sending the Spanish prisoners in a boat to Cuba, he re-established the authority of the French upon the island.

Leaving his nephew, De la Place, as his proxy, De Rossy returned to France, where he died, De la Place governing until 1664, when the West India Company took possession in right of their charter, which gave them exclusive control over the trade of the French Antilles.

This company sent to Tortuga a garrison with a number of military and civic officers, appointing D'Ogeron as Governor; and from that time began a period of prosperity and success for this island and the western part of St Domingo.

D'Ogeron, acting under the company, established storehouses and dwellings for the servants and business of the company; and being a man thoroughly familiar with these islands and their inhabitants, acted with judgment and success.

A guarantee of safety and protection being thus given to this island and its ports, numbers of traders, merchants, and pirates, were attracted there as a place both safe and convenient in which to transact their business, and its port soon became a busy and important place.

The lands began now to be regularly cultivated, and the number of people increasing, soon spread themselves out upon the mainland of St Domingo; and war being declared between the Spaniards and Portuguese, commissions were issued to privateers to make war on Spanish commerce.

With a view to make the settlers on land more contented with their lot, and to attach them permanently to their lands, D'Ogeron had a number of women brought out from France, and either bestowed them upon, or sold them to, the settlers. These women were the very dregs of the Paris courtesans, and were assigned as so much merchandise amongst the rude, uncouth buccaneers; and it is quite amusing to see in what a perfectly matter-of-fact way they took possession of their new helpmates :—

"I take thee without knowing, or caring to know, who thou art. If anybody from whence thou comest would have had thee, thou wouldst not have come in quest of me. But no matter; I do not desire thee to give me an account of thy past conduct, because I have no right to be offended at it at the time when thou wast at liberty to behave either ill or well according to thy own pleasure, and because I shall have no reason to be ashamed of anything thou wast guilty of when thou didst not belong to me. Give me only thy word for the future; I acquit thee of the past." Striking then his hand on the barrel of his gun, he added, "This will revenge me of thy breach of faith; if thou shouldst prove false, this will surely be true to my aim."

Not a very encouraging style of wooing, even for a courtesan.

From this time forward the Island of Tortuga, and the adjoining portion of St Domingo, rapidly advanced in importance, and the history of the French and buccaneers becomes identified.

As Tortuga grew in importance, many of the class of habitans had sought the seaside of the Island of St Domingo, establishing there, on the most convenient places, their plantations of tobacco, corn, &c., until almost the entire coast of the western part of the island was inhabited by these people, and newcomers were forced to go further inland, by which process the main island had gradually became tolerably well settled. The part where these people first located was known as the Cul-de-sac, a large valley in the west, extending to the sea; and the inhabitants increased so fast, that in 1672 there were 2000 planters.

At first they incurred much hardship, as they were not able to leave the island to procure provisions, and the labour of clearing the ground was very great, filled as it was with trees and roots. They first planted beans, but they ripened and died away in six weeks; then the potato was laid, which did well, and following this, the manioc or cassava; and subsequently, when all manner of fruits were raised to sustain life, the culture of tobacco was entered into extensively.

Under D'Ogeron, who seems to have been a man of sound judgment and great energy, the French colony of St Domingo made rapid strides. Although constant disputes were occurring with the Spaniards in reference to boundaries, and although on the frontier the planters were compelled to work in their fields with arms by their sides, yet such was the wisdom of D'Ogeron, who had been confirmed as Governor of the entire French possessions, that, in marked contrast to the Spaniards, the French were rapidly increasing in numbers and wealth.

The year 1666 was a famous year in the annals of the entire island, being known as the year of the "Sixes," and the population suffered severely from the ravages of small-pox, dysentery, and other diseases that prevailed as epidemics.

In endeavouring to extend the influence of French authority over the Island of St Domingo, D'Ogeron met with some opposition from the planters, who, having opened a trade with the Flemings, thought it more profitable to continue that, and refused to recognise the French right to the exclusive trade of the island, on the ground that they were neutrals in neutral territory. But D'Ogeron, with prompt decision, made an attack on the mutineers, and, having defeated them, hung several by way of example. His efforts having alarmed the Flemish traders, they ceased to visit the island, which was thus restored to tranquillity; and as many families came out from Brittany and Anjou, the island from that time began a wonderful career of progress and prosperity.

As the Spaniards, after their various raids on the French settlers, had left no garrisons to prevent their return, the latter quickly returned to their desolated places, and with renewed energy and enterprise rebuilt their plantations.

Still such a guerilla war was kept up, that there was no peace for those hardy settlers who were forced to labour in their fields with their firearms within reach, until D'Ogeron, indignant at these repeated attacks, and the losses his colony had sustained, conceived the idea of conquering the whole of the Spanish part, and with this idea organised a force of 500 men, which he placed under the command of the freebooter Delisle, with instructions to take the city of Santiago, next to the capital the most important town in the island.

Delisle with his troops debarked in 1669 at Puerto Plata on the north coast, and from thence marched upon Santiago, which place he found had been abandoned by its inhabitants, who had taken refuge in the town of Concepcion de la Vega. Finding, however, that Delisle intended to burn their city, they paid him a ransom to leave it intact, with which he retired by the route he had come.

Encouraged by this attempt at retaliation, the French spread themselves out in the beautiful plain of Limonade near Cape Francais, hoping henceforth to be freed from annoyance by the Spaniards; and as immediately opposite the isle of Tortuga there was a fine bay, the shores of which were surrounded by high and fertile hills, a permanent settlement, which afterwards grew into a large town, was located there. This bay was known as Port de Paix or Port of Peace.

D'Ogeron also in 1674 sent reinforcements to Samana,

which had been attacked by the Spaniards, but without success.

So encouraged was the Governor by the rapid increase of the French colony, that he determined to return to France, and endeavour to induce the home Government to send out a strong force, with which he pledged himself he would conquer the whole island for the French—a promise which, without doubt, from the weak state of the

Port de Paix.

Spanish colony, he would have been able easily to have kept. Unfortunately he died the following year in France, and the colony lost in him one of the best governors it ever had. He was, however, succeeded by De Pouancy, his nephew, who, though a most excellent man, does not appear to have been endowed with the same extended and liberal ideas as his uncle; and he, fearing that the settlement at Samana could not be maintained, withdrew the inhabitants of that place to Cape Francais, where a permanent establishment had been already made.

The French, following the example of the Spaniards, had in the past few years gone largely into the slave trade, several fleets loaded with their human freights having from time to time arrived at Tortuga, from whence their cargoes of negroes were distributed among the French planters, by whom they were set to work cultivating their lands upon the main island of St Domingo.

Even at this early period in the island's history, the cruelties practised upon the slaves were so great, that in 1678 a rising among the negroes took place, incited by a negro named Padrejan, who, having killed his Spanish master, had fled to Tortuga for refuge; but fearing to be captured and punished some day by the Spaniards, and seeing the discontent of the negroes on the French plantations, he resolved to make use of this as a means to restore himself to favour with his former masters.

Inciting, therefore, a number of slaves to join him, he began to attack the French settlements, killing the inhabitants and burning their places, finally retiring to the mountain fortress of Tarare, where he intrenched himself. His incursions annoyed the French to such a degree, that there was no peace or safety so long as he remained unconquered, and a number of buccaneers coming into Port de Paix, Governor De Pouancy made a contract with them to attack and capture Padrejan; and they, having carried out their plans with great vigour and resolution, succeeded in killing and dispersing the negro chief and his followers.

Although on this occasion these pirates had rendered such signal service to the island, they were not considered as very desirable colonists, from their restless habits and indisposition to recognise any regularly constituted authority, and though at this time they were much reduced in numbers, there were yet enough scattered throughout the island to make trouble when united with the factious spirits among the planters, who at this time were in a state of discontent from certain restrictions and monopolies of the West India Company, particularly in regard to tobacco.

Up to 1684, neither religion nor justice were administered in the French colony; and in that year two commissioners were sent out from France to concert measures with Governor De Cussy for the better regulation of the colony.

Courts of judicature were established for the several districts, responsible to a supreme council at Petit Goave; and relief was asked from the home Government, without success, for the removal of the restrictions which had been imposed upon commerce, particularly on the article of tobacco.

When De Cussy first arrived on the island, he found the inhabitants there fretting at this monopoly of tobacco by the Government, which farmed it out, and they immediately prayed the Governor to remove it; but this not having been acceded to, they, perhaps fearing a like monopoly, destroyed their plantations of cotton and indigo, and devoted themselves to the culture of cocoa, the first plantation of which had been established by D'Ogeron.

Tortuga having now become almost deserted by the planters who sought the mainland, De Cussy endeavoured to induce settlers to locate on that island, but without success, and the island finally came to be utterly deserted, its inhabitants and trade going to strengthen the new town of Port de Paix, nearly opposite on the main island. And thus this place, once of such great historic interest in the civilisation of the New World, entered a state of decay and oblivion, from which it seems never to have recovered.

In the year 1685, in France was published the celebrated edict by Louis XIV. that became famous under the name of the Code Noir, and that was to have such an effect upon the affairs of the coloured population of the West Indies, as it was made to prescribe the duties of master and slave, and the privileges of the free coloured men.

In 1689, war having been declared between France and Spain, M. de Franquesnay had been sent to the island to organise expeditions of the freebooters against the Spanish possessions in South America and Mexico; the Governor, De Cussy, availed himself of the return of this expedition from Panama to conduct, in 1689, another one against the Spanish town of Santiago de los Caballeros. Although he encountered a force of Spaniards, who made a strong defence, on the banks of the Amina, he succeeded in taking that place, where his men, partaking of the meat left in the houses, were many of them taken suddenly sick, and believing they had been purposely poisoned by the Spaniards, De Cussy in revenge ordered the city to be first sacked and then burned down, having accomplished which he withdrew his forces.

The Spaniards, however, soon took revenge for this attack, for the Spanish part of the island being under the command of the royal admiral, Don Ignacio Caro, he organised a considerable expedition against the French.

This expedition, organised in 1691, consisted of 2600 men that entered the French territory from two points: by land from the frontiers of the Cibao, and by sea at the Port of Bayaja (or Port Dauphin) for the purpose of attacking Cape Francais.

De Cussy, getting news of the movement, organised, with De Franquesnay, a large force, and gave battle to the Spaniards at Sabana Real, January 21, 1691.

The result of this battle was for a long time uncertain, until Antonio Miniel, a native of Santiago, who had held in ambush some 300 lancers, seeing the fight going against the Spaniards, gave the signal to his men to attack, when, falling upon the French, a great slaughter ensued, among those killed being the Governor De Cussy, Franquesnay, and other distinguished officers, the entire French force being defeated.

Following up their victory, the Spaniards entered the French territory, burning and devastating everything in their way, and putting to the sword all the inhabitants they met, until arriving at the town of Guarico (Cape Francais), they sacked that place, giving quarter only to the women and children, after which they retired to their own part of the island, leaving the French in such a prostrated condition, that when the new Governor, Dumas, took command, he was not able to muster a thousand men capable of bearing arms.

It is probable that a long time would have elapsed before the French could have recovered from this severe blow inflicted on them, had it not been that at this juncture the English forces attacked and took the island of St Christopher from the French, owing to which circumstance some 300 persons from that island came to St Domingo, and settled down at Cape Francais and its vicinity, giving thereby a little new life and energy to those people, already harassed to despair.

The Court of France, in 1691, replaced the dead De Cussy by appointing as Governor Du Cosse, who had previously been employed in the French service at Senegal. On his arrival at St Domingo he found the colony almost depopulated, and in a deplorable state, and the fillibusters almost extinct; but with wise administration and skilful management he restored some new life to the colony, and encouraged the culture of indigo.

In 1694, only two years after, he made a descent upon the Island of Jamaica, held by the English, and carrying off 3000 slaves from that island, took also a great quantity of indigo.

In revenge for this disaster caused by Du Cosse, the English Government united its forces with Spain, and together they sent an expedition of twenty-four sail, with 4000 men, which rendezvoused in the Bay of Manzanillo on the north side of the island, where they were joined by a force of 2000 men, that the Spanish Governor, Don Francisco Segura, had sent from the capital of the island.

The expedition proceeded first against Cape Francais, which it took, and afterwards to Port de Paix. Both these places were destroyed, the men being carried off as prisoners by the English, while the Spaniards carried with them to St Domingo the women and children; the allies thinking it better to retire laden with booty than to await an attack threatened by Du Cosse, the Governor, who had endeavoured to collect an army with which to resist the threatened invasion of these combined forces.

The French population was further strengthened by the arrival of some of the inhabitants from the Island of St Croix.

CHAPTER VI.

"How pleasant, in the burning noon of day
Beneath the verdant canopy to stray,
Where ranks of palms their branching honours spread,
That arch in Gothic aisles above the head!"

THE JOINT OCCUPATION OF THE FRENCH AND SPANIARDS—*The Boundary Question—Poverty of the Spaniards—Advance of the French—Successful Agriculture—Tobacco and Indigo Culture—Cocoa Trees—The Introduction of the Coffee Plant—General Improvement of the whole Island—Character of the Inhabitants—French Luxury—Discontent of the Planters.*

ALTHOUGH Spain had at no time, previous to the peace of Ryswick, recognised the right of any other power to locate upon St Domingo, it will be seen how, by that treaty, the French came to acquire a permanent hold upon this island; and while the Spanish inhabitants were rapidly decreasing in numbers, and their settlements decaying, the French had prosecuted their opportunities with such vigour, that they had become masters of the entire western portion of the island.

The allied powers of Europe happily having signed, in 1697, a peace at Ryswick, by which Spain regained all the conquests made from her by France since the treaty of Nimeguen, and the right of France to occupy and hold as her own territory the western part of the Island of St Domingo being conceded, there was, in the next few years, opportunity afforded for the inhabitants of that unfortunate isle to improve their condition, of which the French, with their usual energy, were not slow to avail themselves ; while, on the contrary, the Spanish portion seemed to use it only to sink deeper and deeper into decay. In fact, from the moment the French Government succeeded in getting a permanent hold upon the Island of St Domingo, the Spanish authorities appear to have lost their interest in their share of the colony, and nothing was henceforth done to assist its progress. In truth, the island was almost disowned by the Spanish Government; and such had been the effect of the attack of the pirates on the commerce of Spain, that it was with extreme difficulty that ships to and from Mexico and Peru succeeded in making their voyages.

In yielding, therefore, in 1697, part of the Island of St Domingo to France, Spain made no particular sacrifice. To her the island had been, for many years, only a burden; and it is an undisputed fact, that, so far from this island yielding any revenue to the home Government, the latter had been forced to expend an annual sum of $200,000 for some years in payment of salaries and expenses in keeping this island to herself, this amount being appropriated from the revenues yielded by Mexico and Peru.

In the Spanish territory, such was the lamentable condition of this beautiful island, so rich in every gift of Nature, that the inhabitants, say the chroniclers of the time, had not clothes actually to cover their nakedness, the women being forced to attend a mass specially celebrated at night, in order that their poverty and nudity should not be seen, they not daring to present themselves in the daytime on the streets. Bread was at an exorbitant price ; and we may judge that these reports were undoubtedly true, when we learn that even the clergy had no bread or wine for the sacraments. while the churches were utterly despoiled of their ornaments.

In fact, the poverty of this colony was so extreme, that when the money arrived from Mexico to pay the salaries of the officers at St Domingo city, the day was made one of rejoicing and festivity, the reception of the funds being announced by the ringing of bells and the huzzas of the people.

So far from this condition of things, in the Spanish part, being improved in the following years, matters went even worse, and the island became almost a wilderness; and although an attempt was made to increase the population by bringing some families from the Canary Islands, it did not succeed, for as many inhabitants left St Domingo as had the means; and we learn by the census of 1730, that the entire population of the island was reduced to 6000, St Domingo city itself not having more than 500 inhabitants, its houses being closed, and port and streets deserted, while most of the other towns became extinct, leaving only a few worthy to be called such. These were Cotuy, Santiago, Azua, Banica, Monte Plata, Bayaguana, Higuey, and Seybo.

The first French, as has been before stated, having settled along the coast, followed the chase of the wild cattle as long as there were any to hunt; but as they killed faster than Nature propagated, it was not long before this means failed them, and they soon began to rely upon the supplies of cattle furnished by the Spaniards. The chase was succeeded by the cultivation of tobacco, which seems to have been a favourite labour with them; and although their methods of preparing it were rude in the extreme, it was a source of great wealth to the early planters, until, becoming disgusted with its monopoly by the Government, which farmed out to private individuals this valuable trade, they devoted their attention to other products. It stands now a curious fact in connection with Hayti, that the lands that, under the early white settlers, produced not only enough tobacco for their own consumption, but as an important article of commerce, lie to-day uncultivated and unproductive, not from any fault of the soil, but from the utter worthlessness of the present population.

Preparing Tobacco.

Under such a short-sighted policy of the French Government, although the population increased in numbers, the colony for a few years languished, until revived by the cultivation of the indigo plant. For some time after the discovery of the island, the Spaniards cultivated a little indigo, and at the end of the sixteenth century they sent considerable quantities of it to the mother country; but on the decay of the Spanish part of the island, its culture was soon abandoned, although it continued to grow so luxuriantly in its wild state, as to be looked upon as a mere weed. The French, however, found it greatly to their interest to cultivate it, and prepare it, though in a

Preparing Indigo.

primitive way, for the markets of Europe; and to the culture of this plant the permanent success of the French on the island may be considered justly due.

Every one wished to have negroes and augment his lands, and it was at this time that one planter began to acquire the land of another to augment his own portion.

Now, too, grants were asked for, which formed what was called the second story, or second line of tracts, behind those first established on the coast.

The success of the indigo, the increase of the population, and of the number of negroes produced by those brought by Du Casse from his raid on Jamaica, gave the first idea of establishing sugar plantations. These gave a new value to the lands; and requiring larger tracts than

9

the indigo plantations, several small ones were united, and became the property of one person.

He who had sold his lot on the coast, carried his industry to the second, third, or fourth line, and successively towards the interior of the colony; and thus the whole country gradually came under cultivation with a large population. The only thing not keeping pace with this progress being the cattle, for the French never seem to have paid much attention to cattle-raising, although encouraged to do so by the Government, so that, as this means of subsistence decreased, they became more and more dependent upon their Spanish neighbours, who, seeming to have a natural aptitude for this business, had established "hatos" or grazing farms all over their part of the island; in fact, with one exception, this was their only occupation.

This exception was the cultivation of the cocoa or chocolate plant, which was a native of the Spanish part of the island, and is said, at one time, to have produced in value as much as the mines of the island. In fact, in the sixteenth century, there was no other cocoa known except St Domingo cocoa, and Spain was entirely provided with it from this island alone.

The French, led by the example of their Governor, D'Ogeron, who, in 1665, had planted the first tree on the French part, had created a considerable revenue by the cultivation of this plant, the plantations of which had increased in every direction, particularly in the narrow valleys to the west of the island, where, it is stated, in some of the places there were not less than 20,000 trees.

Up to 1716 this product flourished amazingly, when, in that year, for no known reason, the entire stock of trees failed to produce, and went to decay; and it was not until 1736 they were again cultivated, when they flourished extremely well, many of them reaching a height of thirty feet.

The cocoa of St Domingo has been always considered

as more acidulated than that of the celebrated Caraccas, to which it is not inferior, and experience has proved that a mixture of the two gives a more delicate flavour than that possessed by either alone.

So rapidly had the fortunes of some of the early planters been made, that we find that in 1715–17, many of them, with a view of enjoying their means, gained, in many cases, after long years of toil and absence from their native country, returned to France, carrying with them their means, invested in the securities of the Mississippi Company. Unfortunately they proved worthless, and many of these planters were forced to return to St Domingo, and begin life anew.

Others, however, satisfied to remain on the island and continue their agricultural labour, had created for themselves fine estates, either for the growth of sugar, cocoa, or

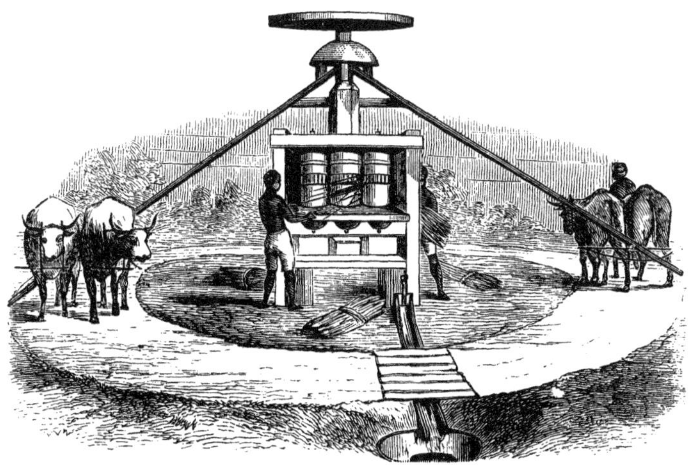

Old French Sugar Mill.

indigo; and although the machinery for the manufacture of the former product would be considered rude in comparison with the superb appliances that steam machinery has called into existence, and which are seen in perfection to-day on the sugar estates of Cuba, yet the buildings on many of these places were erected with not only an eye to comfort and stability, but to beauty also. None of these places are to-day to be seen intact; but from the authorities of the time we get illustrations of what they were.

In 1720, a permission, originally granted to the West India Company, and then revoked, to bring out negroes from Guinea, was renewed, giving them exclusive privilege, in accordance with their offers, to carry to American islands, 3000 negroes per annum.

In its list of members, it is stated, this company had the names of those most distinguished in France, in the army, navy, law, or finance; and the effect at first in the colony was, that every one prepared to increase his extent of land, hoping to secure some of this imported labour to work it.

The colonists, however, becoming dissatisfied with this privilege, which allowed the company to exact such exorbitant prices for the negroes as it chose, and having in remembrance the sad effects of the Mississippi Company, rose up in open hostility to it, insomuch, that when the agents of the company arrived, the colonists burned the warehouses, shouting, "Long live the King, but no company."

While protesting their fidelity to the King, they went so far, however, as to arrest his Governor, Sorel; and a general uprising and discontent was inaugurated, which was not finally allayed until 1728, when the privileges of the company ceased, and quiet was entirely restored.

The whole secret of this trouble appears to have been, that at this time great scarcity of negroes existed in proportion to the number of acres divided among the individual planters; and as their riches would be most assuredly added to by increasing the number of slaves on each plantation, the planters wished to have the privilege of bringing in, on individual account, as many negroes as they desired, as they claimed the company took all the profit of the trade, and none of its risks, since the planter had to bear the loss of the slaves if they died in the process of being acclimated.

Land being so plentiful, it was granted out on certain restrictions for a merely nominal sum, and success then depended upon the number of slaves that could be obtained to clear and cultivate this land.

The slave population at this time amounted to 42,895 negroes, for some of which the West India Company were yet unpaid, the planters having suffered severely from the drought that prevailed in 1726.

Two young coffee-trees had been given to Louis the Fourteenth, by the Hollander Pancras, superintendent of the Garden of Plants at Amsterdam. Some years after they were transported to Martinique by Desclieux; there these trees succeeded admirably, and a short time afterwards they transported numerous shoots to St Domingo, which propagated with an astonishing rapidity, and from St Domingo the coffee-plant spread to all the other West Indies.

In 1732, by an order that seems now very strange, the French Government prohibited, in St Domingo, the cultivation of the coffee-tree, on the plea that its inhabitants, having slave labour, could cultivate other products with profit, while the small planter of some of the other French islands had his existence depending upon this culture alone, as being adapted to white labour. Perhaps had this order not been issued, the planter of St Domingo would not have been so dependent on the slave labour, which was the final cause of the loss of the colony to France; the restriction was, however, taken off in 1735, when cocoa planting was also encouraged.

With all these materials of success, the French colony, notwithstanding the few drawbacks above mentioned, made the most astonishing progress in prosperity up to the period of the French Revolution, and its history in this time presents some curious and interesting facts. One of the native writers, speaking of the period 1737, says, "At this epoch of its greatest splendour, no spectacle more magnificent needs to be seen than the state of cultivation on this queen of the Antilles. Nature appeared to smile upon the laborious efforts of an active population wresting from this most fertile soil the most immense riches."

Old French Plantation.

But the philanthropist trembled at that rapid prosperity which was due to the forgetfulness of the most precious rights of man, in supporting amongst themselves a mere handful of planters. As luxurious as Asiatics, they had became hardened in their hearts; and the poor slave who made their riches was looked upon and treated as no better than a beast of burden.

It was not in the nature of things that the French should make such rapid progress, without a people so near to them as the Spaniards deriving some benefit from the trade that quickly sprung up in the peaceable intervals of the petty quarrels concerning boundaries.

Fortunately, too, for the Spanish part, a Governor had been appointed who displayed great energy and intelligence in improving that hitherto neglected colony. This was Don Pedro Zorrillo, appointed in 1737 to the entire command of that part.

The Spaniards were already addicted to contraband trading, when the war between Spain and England breaking out in 1740, gave a new impetus to this trade, which rapidly assumed the form of privateering upon the English commerce between North America and England.

Following this was the wise and independent policy of the Spanish Governor, in throwing open the ports of St Domingo to the trade of neutral nations, of which advantage the Dutch and Danes particularly availed themselves.

The result was quickly seen in the rapid disappearance of the misery of that part of the island, and the new life given to agriculture, which, with the export of the native products, gave a new circulation to money.

A large increase of population took place with the increase of trade, and with the newcomers came such supplies of merchandise, that necessary articles were no longer beyond the reach of purchase of the inhabitants. New attempts, in 1747, were also made to open up the mines, and this was not confined to the working of the old mines merely, but also to those of copper, iron, &c., though no positive results appear to have been achieved.

In 1751 the Spanish part suffered also from a terrible earthquake, that did an immense amount of damage, destroying entirely the old town of Azua; while in the same year the Ozama, during a heavy freshet, rose to such a height as to wash the very walls of St Domingo city, causing much damage.

The people, however, of the island, seem to have become so habituated to these destructive affairs, that they never entirely despaired of seeing their island in an improved state; and we learn that, in 1756, Monte Cristo, a flourishing town on the north coast, one of those towns which had been destroyed by order of the Government in 1606, was again revived as the port for the embarkation of the products of the great Cibao region, of which La Vega and Santiago were then the principal towns.

A large number of families from the Canary Islands increased its population; while it was declared a neutral port, a step that benefited the whole island; for the French and English being at war, the prizes gained by the privateers of those respective nations were brought in there, and an active commerce was the result. Many strangers flocked to the island; others, gaining riches, settled down to agricultural pursuits, and poor devastated St Domingo again looked up. This progress in the Spanish part was assisted too by the war that broke out in 1762 between England and her ally Portugal against France, Spain, and Naples; for the Dominican Spaniards hastened to resort to a calling with which they were by this time well familiarised, and their privateers soon waged injurious war upon the commerce of the English in the West Indian waters, the prizes they took being carried to St Domingo, where the cargoes were sold to the inhabitants, or to the foreign merchants doing business there. The slave population of the Spanish part by this means was also much increased, as many prisoners were taken from the slavers in those waters.

With the increase of commerce, a large trade sprung up in the cattle of the island, particularly with the French, who were now constantly in need, for food and labouring purposes, of the cattle, horses, and mules with which the Spanish part was immensely stocked.

Many new towns were founded, and, their population increasing, became permanently established; among these were Bani, Caobas, San Miguel, and others, some of which are to-day extinct.

Peace having been declared between the European powers, Charles the Third in 1765 made an immense step forward, benefiting his colonies in opening their ports to a more liberal and general commerce, and removing the restriction which confined the ports of Spain to Cadiz and Seville alone. In this benefit St Domingo shared, as well as her sister isle of Cuba; and prosperous as has been the latter in our day, in the middle of the eighteenth century she was as backward as St Domingo; for in 1730 the entire population of Cuba did not amount to 120,000 souls, while the capital city, Havana, contained not over 500 families.

Up to 1776 innumerable had been the disputes between the two nationalities as to the boundary line that should mark the extent of the frontier between French and Spanish St Domingo; and though no regular agreement seems ever to have been ratified, yet, by tacit consent, a boundary defined by the river Rebouc (now Guayubin), commencing near Isabella, and extending in an indirect line to the south side of the island, in the vicinity of Petit Goave, was observed by both sides, the country west of this being held by the French.

Many quarrels had nevertheless taken place, and much blood was shed, and bad feeling engendered; but, strange to say, the Spaniards, though the weaker party, managed to increase the extent of their boundaries.

At last, however, an act was about to be done that seemed calculated to bring peace and quiet to both parts of the island, and to make amends for some of the misfortunes that had afflicted it. The boundary division of the two powers was to be finally adjusted. On the 29th February a treaty was signed at Atalaya, between the Brigadier Don Jose Solano y Bote, Governor of the Spanish part, and Count Ennery, Governor of the French part, fixing, as plenipotentiaries of the two Governments, the permanent boundary, the which was marked out by an officer appointed by each party by fixing landmarks, some of which are said to be in existence to-day.

This treaty was ratified by the respective home Governments at Aranjuez, June 3, 1777, and distinctly stated the boundary as beginning at the mouth of the river Massacre (Dajabon) on the north coast, and terminating at the mouth of the Pedernales on the south coast, the dividing line being very irregular in its direction, but being marked at different intervals by stone pyramids, numbered from 1 to 221, upon which were cut the words "France," "España." As this treaty has become of considerable importance in Dominican and Haytian affairs, the reader will find it in full in the Appendix. In honour of this treaty, Charles the Third declared free the commerce between the two parts of the island, a first-fruit of peace by which the Spaniards profited much, since they only had cattle to give in exchange for the abundant stores of merchandise of every variety with which the French were well supplied.

Charles the Third also abolished, in 1778, the monopoly of the "Casa de Contracion" of Seville, by which the ports of St Domingo city and Monte Cristo profited very much; and from this period the Spanish part appears to have made considerable progress, though not by any means to compare with the French.

Dajabon, a new town, was established, and rapidly sprung into importance as a trading place on the frontier. St Domingo city, which had been almost in ruins a few years back, was rebuilt. San Juan, Banica, Santiago, and Azua had recovered from the effects of the earthquake of 1751; while Samana, Savana la Mar, and Puerto Plata were all well established and in a flourishing condition.

By the various causes above mentioned, the population had been materially increased; and an immense number of fugitive slaves sought refuge in the Spanish part from the terrors of French slavery, and settling down to agriculture, they soon became an element in the population which had by this time become well mixed.

It is a conceded and curious fact, that while the early Spaniards of St Domingo had been the severest of taskmasters to their negro slaves, as time wore on they seem, for some reason or other, to have lost this habit, and their slaves were infinitely much better treated than those of the French. This may partly be accounted for from the fact that population became so reduced in the island at one time, that master and slave relied upon each other for company and support, and the chains were in this way gradually lightened.

The actual slave laws of the Spaniards were in fact rather mild in their character, and even more lenient in some respects than those of the celebrated Code Noir. All their laws had for their object the facilitating the freedom of the slave who could ransom himself by reimbursing his master for his original outlay; for not only was the master compelled to receive instalments on account of the desired freedom of the slave, but the law fixed a maximum price at which that liberty should be purchased, and which price being offered, the master was compelled to accept. Other articles there were, which, if strictly enforced, would serve to lighten the bonds of the slave very much. This facility of freedom had rendered it easy for the blacks of Spanish St Domingo to secure their liberty, of which they freely availed themselves, to such an extent, that at one time, of a population amounting to 125,000 in that part of the island, 110,000 were freemen. It must however be remembered, that large numbers of slaves escaped from the French and became free Spanish subjects.

It is also a notorious fact that the Spaniards never seem to have had the same stringent laws against their intermarrying with the negroes that the French had. In fact, I find some old authors alluding to this by sarcastically saying, "That the Spaniards appeared to be much more fond of their dusky female slaves, or Indian neighbours, than they were of their lighter-coloured spouses; and though many had left legitimate wives in Spain, they appeared not at all reluctant to take temporary ones from such dusky maidens as were nothing loth."

The effects of this loose system was soon seen in the mixed character of population, which, gradually extending itself as time wore on, has left its imprint on the present population of the island, where it is sometimes hard to tell where the white begins or the black leaves off.

Nearly the same terms came to be applied to this population as in the French part, though, from their Spanish names, they appear to be different. The pure Spaniards coming to the colonies to seek their fortunes were known as "chapetones," just as they are called to-day in Cuba "Peninsulars." The mulattoes were at first known more particularly as the descendants of Europeans and negroes, just as "mestizoes" meant European and Indian; but these distinctions are hardly to-day noted.

If about the only data available is accepted of the increase of this population—that given in the census of the parish priests, taken in 1785—the augmentation in five years is truly remarkable; for by it we learn this amounted in that time to 35,350 souls, 19,350 being free, and 16,000 slaves, making an aggregate population of 152,640; a very rapid increase indeed, if we refer back to the year 1730, when the whole population amounted to but 6000 souls.

It perhaps only shows, however, of what this island is capable under proper government, and protection to settlers, with the right kind of inducements to emigrants.

It is a curious fact to be noted in the history of Spanish St Domingo, that no sooner does its condition promise a speedy advance in wealth, population, and civilisation, than some unforeseen event takes place that throws the island as much further backward as it has advanced; and this proves now to be the case; for the great change that took place in the French part soon drew the Spanish part into that vortex of insurrection, massacre, bloodshed, and horrible civil war, and this too without there being perhaps the slightest similarity in the condition of the affairs of the two parts; for the one was just making a feeble effort to progress from its years of lethargic misery, while the other, perhaps spoiled and demoralised by its rapid increase in wealth and importance, was bringing upon itself, by its pride, luxury, and cruelties, a day of reckoning that will never be forgotten as long as history shall be read.

Some idea of the great state of prosperity at which the French had arrived may be gained from a condensed statement of the condition of the different interests in successful operation in the year 1754, and these were estimated to be, in the commodities of the island, of the value of $6,250,000 (£1,250,000), and the imports to £1,777,500 ($8,887,500). There were 14,000 white inhabitants only, 4000 free mulattoes, and 172,000 negroes.

The sugar plantations numbered 599, while the indigo places amounted to 3379. The cocoa-trees, after being once entirely destroyed, had reached the immense number of 98,946. The cotton, which in the Island of St Domingo assumes more the form of a tree, numbered 6,300,637 plants; while of the banana, cassava, potato, and yam, under cultivation for supplying the means of subsistence, the amount grown was enormous.

Although the French never professed to pay much attention to cattle or stock raising, yet even those had grown to what seems an immense number, for we learn there were on the French part 63,000 horses and mules, and 93,000 head of horned cattle.

From this period up to the time of the Revolution in France, these figures were steadily increased; so that computing the limited number comparatively of the white inhabitants, some idea may be obtained of the unequal manner in which the wealth and the riches of the island were apportioned. This was about the condition of affairs when, in 1776, the boundary was finally fixed between the two parts of the island. It may be well now to give a glance at the character of the population that formed this wonderful French settlement of the New World.

In the early history of the French colonisation, the prejudice of caste was unknown on the Island of St Domingo; for the buccaneer or freebooter made very little distinction between the negro and the European engagé, so long as the latter was in bonds; but gradually the engagés worked out their time, which was usually three years, and became, by economy and labour, equal to other whites; and as the engagés eventually were prohibited being brought out from Europe on account of the introduction of slaves, they ceased to exist as a class.

The blacks, born under a hot sun, supported better the labour of the tropical fields than the whites, and finally, the former were the only class of servants remaining attached to the plantations, the whites confining themselves to the towns, and pursuing trade or commerce.

The whites were composed of those originally settled on the island, having been born in Europe; and to their offspring was given the name "creole," meaning the children of European parents born on the island, a name that has come into general use, as signifying the native white inhabitants of any particular place, though applied for many years to the West Indies exclusively. Also in the towns were a large number of European French, who came out to enter into business as merchants, shopkeepers, and tradesmen, all alike, however, in their desire to accumulate fortunes rapidly, with which to return to Europe.

The Creole soon became an important element in the population, and the effects of climate in those regions are such, that they became as they are to-day—a special type, being usually well made, of good height and regular figure, but not having that rich complexion peculiar to the Saxon race. The temperature of their climate is such, that they acquire a wonderful agility and easy suppleness of frame.

St Mery describes the early French Creoles as a passionate, high-spirited race, with a natural impatience that would not permit of their making even their journeys in an ordinary manner; and as the roads had been put in good order, they either rode or were whirled along at the rate of four leagues an hour.

The Creole women were endowed with lovely figures, beautiful eyes, types yet visible to-day; he relates, however, that these angels, with demoniacal fury, stood by and saw their female attendants punished in such a manner as would move, one would think, a heart of stone to pity.

There can be now no dispute as to the actual demoralisation of a large part of the people of French St Domingo; for the facts are on record by numerous impartial authorities, principally spectators or actors in the state of affairs they describe. In 1760, some idea of the state of things existing may be learned from the report of a commissioner sent out from France by the Government to learn the cause of so many deaths by poison, which had become so frequent as to assume the form of an epidemic,—an extract from which shows in forcible terms some of the habits of the planters:—

"It arises from the too intimate intercourse of the whites and the blacks; the criminal intercourse that the most of the masters have with their women slaves, is the origin of this attack. A legitimate wife, seeing the intercourse of her husband with her servant, in the absence of the husband has her punished severely. If the master is not married, and that is mostly the case (marriage not being popular, and libertinage more tolerated), the inconstancy natural to the men of this climate makes them change or multiply their concubines, from whence arise innumerable jealousies and distinctions; and in the first, as in the second case, are the causes of the taking vengeance now upon the fortunes of the master, in poisoning his negroes, or taking his life, or that of his wife, or even their children."

Up to 1763, it had been permitted that masters might

bring into France with them their black servants; and many of the planters, being enormously rich, had large retinues of servants with them in Paris, where they lived in the most sumptuous manner, making great display of their wealth, insomuch that the expression at Paris became common, "rich as a Creole." Many of those who lived on their estates on the island lived the life of perfect sybarites, indulging in every luxury.

The plains of the north and of the Cul-de-sac were crossed in every direction with spacious roads. The plains and the hills were covered with rich habitations, and with a white population numerous and happy. Fields of cane stretched out in every direction, with their boundaries marked by green and well-trimmed hedges. Many of the houses of the country were surrounded by terraces, upon which thousands of flowers of every tint and colour heightened the view.

In the coffee-places long avenues of graceful palms gave shady approach to entrances of solid stone and iron, while fountains and stone swimming-baths served to cool the air, as well as afford pastime to the planters and their families, many of whom spent half the year in Paris, the other, or winter half, being passed in what it is said were the most beautiful homes in the world.

The planters were only able to increase their labour by importations of negroes from Africa, and therefore were habituated to look upon the blacks and mulattoes as so much human cattle, treating them in many cases with disdain and brutality, while the latter, awed by the superior education and position of the whites, looked upon them with fear. But from the nature of things, in due time there were other relations sprang up between the whites and blacks than those of master and slave.

As early as 1685, when Louis XIV. published the Code Noir, it was seen that great irregularities had sprang up between white masters, who had the power of life and death, and their female slaves, and in order if possible to

ENTRANCE TO COFFEE ESTATE.

prevent these, many articles, now curious in their character, were inserted; such, for instance, as the fining of a white two thousand pounds of sugar who should have children by his slaves. If a white debauched a slave, the woman and her children were to be sold for the benefit of the hospital, without ever having the power to be repurchased.

Notwithstanding these apparently stringent laws, this intercourse became so great, that it was not many years before another race of beings had sprung up. All through the colony, the connection between the white and black resulted in the race of the mulattoes, and eventually from the intercourse of these again with the whites or among themselves, innumerable shades of colour sprang up, giving rise to the distinctions, as we know them, of octoroons, quadroons, &c., and of which St Mery in his work gives a list that is tedious in its numerous details of the ramifications resulting from this intercourse. To all these people, regular or irregular in birth, light or dark in colour, were given the various names of "people of colour," "sang melée," or "mulattoes."

From this class also sprang another, one which, from the force of circumstances, eventually became of the greatest importance in bringing about the freedom of the negroes of St Domingo. This class was known as the "affranchis," or freedmen, being, in fact, the entire people of colour who were their own masters, and not slaves;—a class that had, in a long number of years, been produced by slaves buying their liberty, by planters freeing their illegitimate children, and by irregular marriages of black and white, which, though forbidden by law, were yet sometimes contracted.

The men of colour, though free as far as their personal service to individuals was concerned, were yet considered as the property of the public; and, as public property, they were subject to the caprice and tyranny of all those whom the accident of birth had placed above them.

By the Colonial Government they were treated, however, as slaves, being compelled, on reaching the age of manhood, to serve for three years in a military establishment, called the *Maré Chaussée.* This consisted of a certain number of companies of infantry, which were chiefly employed as rangers in clearing the woods of "marons," as runaway slaves were called; and though this organisation was eventually broken up, from the fear that arose that it afforded the people of colour a means of knowing their own strength, and of holding general communication with each other throughout the island, it was long enough in existence to have that very effect.

Upon the expiration of their terms of service in the *Maré Chaussée*, the mulattoes were also subject to the work of the *corvées*, a species of labour allotted for the repair of the highways, the hardships of which nearly all authorities agree in describing as terrible.

Although they rendered all their military service in the militia of their particular province without pay or allowance, being in fact compelled to provide their own arms and accoutrements, they were nevertheless entirely deprived of any power to hold public office or employment, and were entirely debarred from all manner of liberal professions, and even the taint of blood spread to the latest posterity, so that no white man of any character ever thought of marriage with them. In the courts of justice, also, there was one justice for the white man and another for the coloured.

There were, however, many exceptions; for many of the people of colour had acquired lands and become rich; and these, by secretly buying the metropolitan agents, enjoyed peace and tranquillity, and received favours.

Of the horrible cruelties practised upon the lowest class of the inhabitants—the negroes held in slavery—by their white masters, I shall in these pages give no details. They would fill volumes, and are to be found in the pages of every respectable authority of the time, as well French as Creole. Unfortunately, they are too familiar already to the public.

The blacks proper, or negro slaves, were composed of slaves brought from all parts of Africa, many of them previously having belonged to the fiercest tribes, taken prisoners in battle—many of them even were cannibals—turned loose upon the island among others, to affect them by their presence or example, retaining, as they did, even in a state of servitude, many of their customs of religion, polygamy, and cannibalism; and I need only mention here the religious worship of Vaudoux, which has been known to exist within a few years, and doubtless does secretly to-day, among some of the Haytians.

The Creole language served then, as it does to-day, the colloquial purposes of the whole of the French portion of the island. It is a corrupt French, in which they have mixed some Spanish words Gallicised, and in which sea terms even have found a place. At best it is but a jargon; inflection has a great deal to do with it. It can only be acquired thoroughly when young; no European, it is said, ever fully acquiring it, no matter what the term of his residence may be in the isles.

Many of the servants of the planters had been at Paris a long time, where they had gained new ideas, and where, as there were many freemen of colour, they had profited by their example and instructions; and returning to Hayti, they had carried with them new ideas about their own condition, which made themselves felt in the many plots and insurrections that were constantly being organised among the slaves. But public affairs might have remained in a state of tranquillity as regards the blacks, or their condition being somewhat improved, they might have become more contented with their lot, had it not been that the condition of affairs and the state of feeling existing among the whites towards each other and the home Government also opened a field, and afforded an opportunity, which the mulattoes at first, and afterwards the blacks, seized upon to better their own condition.

Troubles had sprung up between the militia and the regular troops, some of which ended in fatal duels on the part of the officers, and the militia had been forced into special service. Negroes were taken from the plantations, and forced to drill, much to the discontent of their masters the planters, many of whom had besides to pay a certain sum to keep up companies in their localities; and these things caused a feeling of restlessness on the part of many of the prominent inhabitants, and a desire to be independent of a metropolis that asked everything, and gave nothing in return.

The Prince de Rohan came out in 1766 as Governor, with instructions to do all in his power to satisfy the colonists, and regulate affairs in a colony that had been reported at Paris to be in a state of almost open revolt, while its depravity was notorious, according to an account that describes it as "depraved as a country can be, having attained the apogee of demoralisation." Frightful pictures were drawn of the "orgies that these voluptuous colonists had given themselves up to in midnight balls, in the midst of which, the lights extinguished, each man used the woman he had seized at random."

The Superior Council appealed to the King to redress some of the complaints made by the colonists, but De Rohan treated these as seditious.

Then commences a period of internal struggle and bickering between the people, the authorities of the island, and the representative of the King. The prayers of the colonists were unanswered, and their wishes not consulted; bitterness of feeling resulted, ending in the taking of sides, which finally resulted, from various causes, in the rising of the negroes. But this is deserving of a special chapter.

CHAPTER VII.

"Thy chains are broken, Africa, be free!
Oh! ye winds and waves,
Waft the glad tidings to the land of slaves."

THE REVOLUTIONS OF FRENCH ST DOMINGO—*Mode of Government of the French—Discontent of the Planters—Their Desire for Independence—Aspirations of the Mulattoes—Ogé's Attempt at Insurrection—The Revolution in France—Its Effects on St Domingo—Contentions among the Whites—Insurrection of the Slaves—Participation of the English in the Affairs of the Island—Their Defeat, and Success of the Blacks—Cession of the Island to the French.*

THE general and popular idea of the revolution of St Domingo has usually been, that owing to the cruel manner in which the slaves were there treated by their French masters, they rose up and massacred all the whites who did not succeed in escaping from the island; but we shall see that this was only partially the case, and the result of other causes.

The revolution of St Domingo is divided into three distinct epochs;—the first comprises the revolution of the whites; the second, that of the mulattoes; and the third, the revolution of the negroes.

Three times was raised the cry of freedom, each time by different races, followed by frightful mixtures of massacres and conflagrations and of atrocious cruelties; the rich were driven away, and with them riches; the whites were exterminated, but with them also European civilisation. St Domingo conquered her liberty; but it is seated upon ruins, without other companions than disorder and idleness.

The Government of the French part of St Domingo, up to the year 1789, was exercised by a Governor-General and an officer called Intendant, both of whom were nominated by the Crown, on the recommendation of the Minister of Marine, generally for the period of three years. Their powers, in some cases, were administered jointly; in others, they possessed separate and distinct authority, which each of them exercised without the concurrence or participation of the other; and these powers were almost unlimited, against the abuse of which the people had no sure protection.

The Governor, in fact, was an absolute prince, whose will was, generally speaking, the law, the courts of justice even being dependent upon his final decision in many cases.

The Intendant's proper duties were to regulate the public revenues, or administer the finances of the colony. The collectors and receivers of all duties and taxes were subject to his control; he passed or rejected their accounts, and made them such allowances as he alone thought proper; and with him rested entirely the application of all the public moneys.

The taxes and duties were laid on and modified, as occasion required, by a court composed of the Governor-General, the Intendant, the Presidents of the Provincial Councils, the Attorney-General, the Commissioner of the Navy, and the several Commandants of the Militia. This court was dignified by the title of the *Colonial Assembly;* and though the colonists had not a single delegate in it, the reader will see that, in the revolutionary state of affairs in which the colony was shortly to be placed, this Assembly played a very important part.

The colony, for convenience in governing, was divided into three provinces, the northern, the western, and the southern. In each of these resided a Deputy Governor, and in each were established subordinate courts of civil and criminal justice, from whose decisions appeals were allowed to the two superior councils, of which one was at Cape Francois, for the northern province, the other at Port-au-Prince, for the western and southern provinces.

At the breaking out of the Revolution in France, there were at St Domingo several elements of trouble. The colonists, haughty in their pride and riches, absolute lords of vast domains, and arbiters of human lives in the persons of their thousands of slaves, borne down by a hard yoke, were restive under the government of a metropolis so far away, which, as they thought, interfered with the proper development of their interests, commercial as well as agricultural, and controlled by a Governor not chosen from among themselves, but sent from Paris, while they were debarred from sharing in the offices that their own success had created.

The freedom in the United States, too, at this time was a signal of regeneration, and gave rise to new ideas of liberty and government; and, as a result, the colonists wanted to constitute a national sovereignty for themselves, and to demand, in return for the riches they sent to the metropolis, an independence they believed they merited.

These ideas fermented strongly in the colony, and made rapid progress everywhere, when there appeared the first acts of the National Assembly in France.

Every one of all classes and of all colours received with enthusiasm the news of the Revolution; the planters saw therein the sister of the American Revolution, which should bring them also freedom and liberty of commerce.

They hoped to govern themselves, and prescribe their own laws and customs; while the numbers of small traders saw a chance for themselves in the numerous small offices that would be created, and by which, without ever giving a thought to the rights of the mulattoes, they alone expected to benefit.

But the mulattoes thought differently, and they judged that, if the former classes were to have their share in these new rights, they (the mulattoes) also, according to the newly promulgated doctrines of the rights of man, should have a share in the benefits which would accrue.

Thus these very divisions of classes gave ground for divisions of interests and ideas, which were looked upon, especially those of the mulattoes, as monstrous.

Strange to say, the mulattoes, with the negro slaves below them, paid at first no regard to the interests of the latter, having no idea that they should share in this new millennium of liberty; and it was only after being vanquished by the negroes, that the mulattoes consented to receive them as equals.

Many of the mulattoes from St Domingo and other French islands were at this time resident at Paris, where they had gone with their wealth to enjoy the freedom which was debarred them in their native land, as also to bring up and educate their children. Through these a strong prejudice was created against the West India planters on account of the barbarous treatment of their slaves, and this created a sympathy for the black race that took form in the society known as the Amis des Noirs (Friends of the Blacks), and it is probably with them that efforts first began to be made to abolish African slavery.

In that same city, and yet from the same isle, there was another class, very different in position, ideas, and feelings. This was composed of the rich planters, who, accustomed to spend most of their time, as well as most of their means, at Paris, had formed a club known as the "Massiac," being the name of the owner of the house they frequented. They combated *in toto* the ideas of the Amis des Noirs, and demanded an independent government for the Island of St Domingo.

When, in 1789, the National Assembly met, a deputation of mulattoes presented a petition, asking for their civil and political rights; to which the President of the Assembly responded by saying, that "not a single part of the nation should ask in vain its rights from the Assembly of the representatives of the French people."

Meanwhile, at St Domingo, the creoles awaited not even the sanction of the home Government to their independence; for already they had formed primary Assemblies, and afterwards provincial Assemblies, representing the three great divisions of the island, with sittings at the various chief towns of the provinces, Cape Francois, Port-au-Prince, and Aux Cayes.

These Assemblies however, did not, permit the presence of a single coloured man; on the contrary, a petition having been presented by a mulatto named Lacombe to the Assembly of the north, asking that the rights of the mulattoes should be recognised, the Assembly considered it as incendiary, and hung the author.

The three Assemblies (north, south, and west) not being able to agree with each other in the general administration of the colony, resolved to confide these interests to an Assembly, called colonial; and this Assembly, in order to be perfectly free in its deliberations, held its sittings at the town of St Mark, 25th March 1790, taking afterwards the name of the General Assembly of French St Domingo.

This Assembly decided that if, before three months elapsed, the French Government did not send it instructions, it would assume the government of the colony.

A decree, however, came in that time, acceding to the wishes of the colony in making it part of the general government; providing, however, that certain laws incompatible with the interests of the colonists should not be understood as applying to the colony, in these memorable words: "It (the Government) has never meant to comprise the colonies in the constitution (in which all men were declared equal) decreed for the kingdom."

This was a deathblow to the hopes the mulattoes had of securing their share in the "rights of man;" and they asked in vain at the hands of the Assemblies a recognition of their claim. Yet again they did not despair, but appealed to that clause in the decree which says, "that should be considered as active citizens all men, adults, proprietors of real property, or, in default of such property, domiciled in the parish since two years, and paying contributions."

The whites refused to interpret this as making mulattoes active citizens, and refused to receive them as such, placing themselves, on this ground, in open rebellion against the Government of France.

The mulattoes, on the contrary, hoping in time to secure their rights legally, supported the Governor and the agents of the King.

In May 1790, the General Assembly of St Mark published the basis of the colonial constitution, in which it stated very plainly its ideas of independence, and assuming to itself the extreme powers of the government; so that from thence there were two powers,—the legitimate one of the King, and the assumed one of the Colonial Assembly.

The national guard took sides; those who wished the independence of the colony called themselves patriots, and mounted a red cockade; those who wished to maintain the submission to the general Government and the metropolis were called "aristocrats," a term of opprobrium, and these sported the white cockade. The planters took sides according as their interests dictated; while the small inhabitants, knowing well the pride of the rich planters, who composed the patriotic party, sided against them, and with the Government party; while the Provincial Assembly of the north, whose representatives were all more or less legal people, and who had been offended by a decree of the General

Assembly proscribing the laws of usury and legal charges, sided with the Government party.

The General Assembly then declared as traitors to the country the members of the Provincial Assembly of the north, and proclaimed the freedom of trade; licensed two regiments of militia, and ordered their reorganisation. A single detachment of the regiment of Port-au-Prince, induced by extra pay offered by the Assembly, answered its call, and was incorporated in the national guard; and the Assembly, carried away by its desires, called to its bar of trial the colonial chief.

Peynier, the Governor, then deemed it time to interfere, and dissolve an Assembly that was creating civil war in the island. He called upon the captain of the French man-of-war lying in the harbour to give him aid; but the crew hearing orders given to fire upon the "patriots," refused obedience, and sided with the Assembly.

The Governor, not discouraged, after issuing a proclamation declaring the Assembly dissolved, and its members traitors and rebels, ordered Colonel Mauduit to go with some soldiers and disperse the Provincial Assembly of the west, which had made common cause with the Assembly of Saint Mark. They, however, calling to their aid 400 red pompons of the national guard, Mauduit was on his arrival received by a discharge which killed fifteen men; this so exasperated the soldiers that they threw themselves into the room, and dispersed the national guard, whose colours they captured; while the Assembly took to flight, the building being pillaged.

The General Assembly now announced its determination to resist, and the Governor ordered Mauduit against it; while from the province of the north came a body of men commanded by the Baron de Vincent.

Menaced by these forces, the Assembly saw appear at St Mark the same man-of-war (*The Leopard*) whose crew offered to stand by them; but the members of the

Assembly taking a sudden resolution, determined to go to France on board this ship, and appeal to the Assembly there to recognise their illegal acts.

So far from acceding to this, on their arrival the National Assembly of France declared them all traitors, and placed them in arrest.

This news made a great disturbance in St Domingo, and the Governor having called together the primary Assemblies to elect new deputies, the absent members were re-elected.

In the midst of this excitement came the news of the uprising of the mulattoes, inagurated by Ogè.

James Ogè, a young mulatto, son of a coffee-planter, had been sent to Paris to be educated, where, at the age of about thirty years, he had secured the friendship of the Amis des Noirs, who, it is said, procured for him a commission in the army of one of the German Electors. Finding that the claims of his people were not to be allowed by the Assembly at Paris, he made his preparations, and by a circuitous route reached St Domingo, where he immediately addressed the Governor, Peynier, a note demanding a recognition for the mulattoes of their rights as citizens; at the same time preparing, with the assistance of his two brothers, a force among the disaffected to back up his demands.

With him was associated Chavannes; but though encamped at Grand Riviere, near Cape Francois, they were not able to gather together more than two hundred men, and this force was soon defeated; Ogè himself being compelled to flee to the Spanish part, where he took refuge in St Domingo city.

Peynier being succeeded by Blanchelande, the new commander made a peremptory demand upon the Spanish Governor for Ogè, who was most infamously given up to the French, in spite of the noble protest of Doctor Faura, the Spanish Auditor of War. The rendition, however, took place on condition that the French should spare Ogè's life.

How well this condition was kept we can understand when we learn that, in the presence of the whole body of the Provincial Assembly, the unfortunate man was broken on the wheel.

Hardly had the whites quelled the insurrection of the mulattoes, than they re-opened among themselves the rebellion.

Two frigates had been sent to St Domingo carrying troops to support the new Governor; but it appears they had been tampered with, even before sailing from Brest, by the friends of the Council of St Mark; and on their arrival, although they had been directed to land at St Nicholas' mole, they disobeyed these orders by landing at Port-au-Prince.

Their bad example led away the hitherto loyal regiment of Mauduit, and the patriots, mingling with the soldiers, seduced them so effectually, that they gave their assistance to the rebels, and against the authorities they had come to support.

The small whites were also demoralised by the promises and corruptions of the patriot party; and the red cockades marched down to Colonel Mauduit, to ask for the restoration of the colours taken from them by him, the men of his own regiment even appearing against him. Mauduit seeing it would be useless to stem this torrent, came forward to present them the colours, when a voice from the crowd demanded that he should kneel down and beg pardon; but, brave man as he was, he preferred death to dishonour, and baring his breast to the crowd, he fell sabred by a soldier of his own regiment, while the infuriated people fell upon his body, and mutilated and dishonoured it in every way, dragging it through the filth of the streets, foremost among these demons being a woman.

Such were some of the scenes enacted by white men, as an example to the blacks, who were shortly to out-do their teachers in deeds of cruelty and bloodshed; for following rapidly upon this event, the signal of the downfall of the power of the legitimate Governor, came that fearful episode in the annals of St Domingo which made the blood of the civilised world run cold with the horrors there perpetrated.

From France in 1791 came the decree that "the colonial Assemblies actually existing should remain, but that the people of colour born of free parents shall be admitted to the primary and colonial Assemblies of the future, if they have the requisite qualifications."

This was a firebrand thrown into the homes of St Domingo. The mulattoes, on receipt of this news, went crazy with delight, while the whites were enraged with vexation and disappointment.

Open revolt was declared by the latter against the Government, and solemn oaths were taken by members of the Assembly, pledging their lives, their fortunes, and their honour to sustain the cause.

A scene of days of chaos and confusion followed, in the midst of which Jean Francois, a mulatto, with a negro slave, Boukmann, on the plantation Turpin, gathered a force of negro slaves, and marched upon the town of Cape Francois, carrying as their banner of liberty the body of a white infant on a spear-head, and murdering and devastating in their whole march until they reached the environs of the town.

Amidst the confusion that arose in the town on receipt of this news, the mulattoes demanded arms from the whites to assist in repelling the negroes. So far from their request being granted, the whites fell upon them, and massacred them, accusing them of having instigated the rebellion.

The negroes were soon defeated by the assembled forces of the whites, who pursued their advantage by killing and murdering the negroes in every direction; and a saturnalia of blood was inaugurated which makes the heart sick at the accounts of the cruelties practised by those polished whites from that most finished city, "The Paris of the West Indies."

But these deeds brought their own punishment; for the whole black population, finding they had no mercy to expect at the hands of the whites, rose in revolt under the leadership of Jean Francois, and Biassou, his lieutenant.

Everywhere the fires of the incendiaries were lighted, and the once noble habitations were burned to the ground, while the hitherto smiling plains of successful agriculture became vast wastes of desolation.

To add to the strength of this uprising, the minority party of the whites is said to have encouraged the blacks; and the latter assumed, in their first attempts, to be fighting the cause of the King, whom they maintained the whites had in custody at Paris.

The negroes marched to Port Margot, bearing a banner on one side of which was inscribed, "Vive le Roi," and on the other, "Ancien Regime;" and while calling themselves "King's people," their leader marched at their head wearing the decoration of the order of St Louis.

A letter found at one of the plantations after a fight implicated also the Spaniards in this movement of the Royalist party, and subsequent events seem to confirm it.

The crimes committed by one of these negro chiefs (Jeannot) almost pass the bounds of credence, and yet they are verified by many authorities. Young girls ravished in presence of their parents, white men sawed to pieces between planks, others maimed, or their joints dislocated, while the fiend stood by and drank human blood mingled with tafia. His crimes became, however, even too great for the negroes, and he was taken and put to death by Jean Francois.

Meanwhile the patriotic party, so far from being dismayed by the storm they had raised, refused assistance from France, and applied to the English at Jamaica for help; and before sufficient time had elapsed for them to hear from there, the patriot troops mounted the English round hat, with a black cockade for the national colour.

Lord Effingham, the Governor of Jamaica, did not deem it wise at once to accede to the demands of the patriots, but sent supplies of arms and ammunition, and also stationed a man-of-war on the coast.

Meanwhile the negroes were carrying on their attacks and devastations, until the whites were forced to take refuge in the towns, until, at the battle of Limbe, the negroes were defeated.

Yet again the mulattoes, who in all these troubles appear to have been more inclined to the whites than to the negroes, asked for a recognition of their rights, which were refused them.

Claiming then that they had law upon their side, they assembled together and elected their chiefs, among whom were some men of great intelligence, afterwards distinguished in the history of the island (Rigaud, Petion, &c.). They fixed the seat of their operations at the little village of Croix des Bouquets, only a few miles from Port-au-Prince.

A first attack upon the mulattoes by troops from Port-au-Prince was unsuccessful; and the old planters having allied themselves with the mulattoes, as the "Ancien Regime," their power became established in the island, as the nucleus around which gathered increasing power, insomuch that the assembly of Port-au-Prince finally agreed that in future the garrison of that place should consist of equal numbers of whites and coloured men, agreeing at the same time that the Colonial Assembly should be re-composed in accordance with the decree of the 15th May.

When, however, the Colonial Assembly re-united at the Cape, it would not approve of this action, and broke the agreement, again placing itself in communication with the English, without result; and shortly after news arrived from France of the approval by the home Government of its opposition, and civil war was again inaugurated, in which the two parties were arrayed against each other—the mulattoes and negroes each day learning their power better, and the whites of either party committing such atrocious deeds as subsequently were unequalled by the blacks themselves.

The blacks and mulattoes having coalesced, a battle was fought between them and the whites at Croix des Bouquets, March 28, 1792, in which the whites were entirely defeated, and driven back into the city of Port-au-Prince.

It is related by several authorities, that notwithstanding the success of the blacks in this engagement, the negroes, under the command of their black chief Hyacinth, behaved themselves with the utmost propriety. Not a house was burned nor a white man molested subsequent to the battle; on the contrary, the chiefs ordered the negroes to return to work.

In other parts of the island the black and white royalists met with success everywhere, until the agents of the French Government, seeing how hopeless was the state of affairs, returned to France to report the condition of matters in the island.

By the edict of April 4, 1792, the National Assembly of France again declared the right of the free coloured man to a share of the government; and electing three new commissioners, ordered a new election of the colonial Assemblies.

With these three new commissioners came 6000 troops. Slavery was to be legalised, while giving rights to free coloured men. Upon this the mulattoes separated themselves from the negroes in revolt, and joined the troops of the party of the commissioners. These had, on their arrival, declared they recognised but two classes in the island—the freemen, without distinction of colour, and the slaves.

Meanwhile the assembly of Port-au-Prince continued

their resistance, while that of the Cape dissolved. The former place was blockaded by land and sea,—Rigaud, a mulatto general, having command of the troops on land.

The Assembly made a stout resistance; but on the arrival of the French commissioners with troops, the city was, after an attack, surrendered, some of the principal rebels, however, making their escape to Jamaica.

Meanwhile the blacks, ignored by the whites and the mulattoes, were in arms; and various forces, under the command of Rigaud and other mulatto generals, were sent against them; and after various combats, the negroes were subdued, and an amnesty being offered, 14,000 negroes availed themselves of it, and the island was thus almost restored to a state of tranquillity under the commissioners, except in the province of Grand Anse, when war was declared between France and England, May 1793.

Galbaud, a planter of St Domingo, or at all events the owner of a coffee estate, had been appointed Governor of the island by the authorities in France; and his predilections being strongly on the side of the colonists, he rather over-slaughed the commissioners and their acts.

They, on their part, sheltering themselves behind the law that no planter could be appointed to authority in the island, and that at the time he (Galbaud) was given in France his appointment it was not known that he was a planter, refused to recognise his authority.

Nevertheless, they were willing that he should return to France and make known this fact, and be reinvested with his powers as Governor.

Galbaud's brother would not submit to these proceedings, and accordingly collected from among the inhabitants, the Cape militia, and the seamen in the harbour, a strong party to support the Governor's authority.

This dispute led to some terrible scenes and affrays; for in a few days the two brothers, at the head of a large number of followers, marched against the Government House in Cape

Francois, and were proceeding successfully, when a body of seamen, getting possession of a wine-cellar, became intoxicated and ungovernable and their column was obliged to seek shelter in the royal arsenal.

Next day much parleying ensued; but Polverel, the commissioner, rejected the overtures of the Governor; then followed scenes of horror indescribable; for the commissioner, having made overtures to the blacks under Biassou and Francois, which were rejected, they were finally accepted by a negro chief named Macaya, who, with 3000 revolted slaves, entered the town, and murdered indiscriminately men, women, and children. A few white inhabitants attempted to seek shelter on board the ships; but were intercepted by the mulattoes, and a dreadful butchery ensued, which horrified even the commissioners themselves, who were unable to appease the angry passions they had roused, being forced themselves to seek shelter in a neighbouring fort, while Galbaud, with the frightened citizens, seeking refuge in the ships in the harbour, set sail for the United States.

When the revolt among the negroes had begun in the northern province, many emigrations of the whites had taken place to the adjoining islands and to America. Some of the principal planters had even gone to England, and invoked the aid of the British Government, which had been refused until the war was declared between France and England, when, in 1793 the Governor of Jamaica received instructions to receive the submission of those inhabitants of St Domingo who solicited the British protection, and for this purpose he was directed to send a force to hold such places in St Domingo as should be surrendered to him.

The French commissioners, Santhonax and Polverel, although they had succeeded, in addition to the force of 6000 regulars brought with them from France, in raising a large body of men from the national guard, the militia, and even the free blacks and runaway slaves, yet had these troops scattered over a large extent of territory.

On the first information, therefore, of the attack of the English, they desired to strengthen their condition in every way, and for this purpose issued a proclamation abolishing slavery, offering clothes and arms to all slaves who would enrol themselves under their banner.

Many of the negroes availed themselves of this opportunity to secure arms and accoutrements, with which they immediately deserted to the mountain fastnesses, where, with a large number of others, they formed themselves into a sort of mountain republic.

Among the principal leaders of the blacks in the early period of the uprising was Jean Francois, who bore the title of general, and to whom was afterwards joined others of note, as Biassou and Rigaud; but the two former were more closely allied, ravaging together with their followers the same districts on the Spanish frontiers.

As the above declaration of emancipation in the French part jeopardised in a great measure the interests of the inhabitants of the Spanish part, among whom there were a large number of slaves, the frontier towns, with the consent of the local authorities, and in connection with many of the royalist French emigrants, secretly assisted Biassou and Jean Francois with arms and money, in order that these chiefs might increase an insurrection among the people of colour, under the plea that the Liberals were in arms against the King because he had declared the liberty of the slaves.

Notwithstanding this plea, the Spaniards profited by their assistance to the negro chiefs in receiving from them the negro prisoners they took, as well as the slaves they ran off from the plantations, giving in exchange for them cattle and gold; these poor creatures were then shipped, at great profit by the Spaniards, to Porto Rico and Cuba.

The death of Louis the Sixteenth of France made a great change in the state of affairs on the frontier of St Domingo; for Biassou and Francois, on receiving news of this event, renounced the revolutionary Government entirely, and with their companions abandoned the French territory, and seeking shelter among the Spaniards, took the oath of allegiance and service with Charles the Fourth of Spain, and for their services they received commissions of high rank, Francois being made general, Biassou field-marshal, and Toussaint colonel in the Spanish army.

In the contests that followed, Spain not recognising the republic of France, much damage was done by both parties on the frontiers, several Spanish towns being destroyed, and the inhabitants of those districts losing all the advantages they had gained in years of peace. England and Spain having united to divide the island between them, the Spanish troops pushed their black allies under Biassou and Francois with such vigour, that the French rapidly lost possession of a great part of the south, and the whole north of the island.

The English, meanwhile, had landed, though not in very great force, at Jeremie, on the 19th September, being commanded by Colonel Whitelock ; and assisted by several frigates, the town of St Nicholas soon fell into their hands. An attempt on Tiburon was not so successful, failing utterly.

St Mark, Arcahaye, Leogane, and other towns, however, soon fell into their hands; and encouraged by these successes, a second and successful attack was made upon Cape Tiburon, by which means nearly the whole of the western coast was subject to their control, except Port-au-Prince.

Port de Paix, an important town on the north-west coast, was much desired by the English ; but it was stoutly defended by a veteran general of the French service, Levaux; and finding it impossible to take it at once by force, they resorted to corruption, hoping to bribe the old chief to surrender; but he not only declined these overtures, but sent a challenge to the English commander for the insult offered him in making such a proposition.

The English and Spaniards had agreed to divide the

island between them, in consideration of which, the latter were now giving the English their assistance in the attack on Port de Paix, but without success. In this alliance between the English and Spaniards, the famous Toussaint, who, for his valuable services, had been rewarded as stated above by the Spanish Government, was faithfully doing them service. Levaux and Rigaud, meanwhile, had been making war against the English with varied success, assisted in great degree by the delay in the arrival of expected reinforcements; but these having arrived, the city of Port-au-Prince fell into the hands of the English, with a large booty, the 14th of June. The French commissioners, who were at this place, made their escape, with numerous followers, before its surrender, to the neighbouring mountains, taking with them, by means of a number of mules, a large amount of valuable property. Finding, however, that the island was now pretty much in the power of the coloured people, captained by Rigaud and Toussaint, the commissioners sought the first opportunity to return to France, where it appears their proceedings were duly approved of by the French Government. This was followed by the general spread of the English throughout the different portions of the island; but they had come into possession of so many towns, and such an extent of country, that their own troops were not numerous enough to hold them, and they had to rely in many cases on negro slaves, officered by themselves, or those French who were in favour of their cause. In many cases these allies proved faithless, and Rigaud and others were still carrying on their operations, by which the English troops met with disaster, to say nothing of the effects of the climate upon troops that were utterly unaccustomed to its peculiarities.

When Levaux was sorely besieged at Port de Paix by the English, he bethought him of Toussaint, whose influence he knew was very great with the negroes; and by means of a faithful messenger he sent him an offer to induce him to leave the Spaniards and join him (Levaux), with his forces, promising to make him a general of brigade.

Although Toussaint was in the service of the Spaniards, and had been decorated by them, he judged that the interests of the negroes would be safer under a republic than with the Spaniards ; and he therefore persuaded his followers to join him, and accepted the offer of Levaux. Some Spaniards attempting to interfere with his plans, he did not hesitate to put them out of the way, and joined Levaux at Port de Paix.

The peace of Basle in 1795, which ceded the Spanish part of the island to the French, was the means of augmenting the troops of Toussaint, who was now at the head of a large army, by the adhesion of Jean Francois and his troops.

Toussaint, hopeful at this time of the cause of his race, took the name of L'Ouverture, in order, as he said, to announce to the colony, and, above all, to the blacks, that he was going " to open to them the door of a better future."

Although the English were deserted by their allies, the Spaniards, they remained, with varying success, upon the island; until in 1797, the French Government made Toussaint general-in-chief of all the French troops on the island, an authority which in effect he had enjoyed for some time previously.

The war was then pursued with greater vigour against the English, who, although succeeding in making brave resistance against the French, were finally, in 1798, compelled to give up the island, the troops under General Maitland being withdrawn; but not until a treaty of peace and commerce had been formed on the part of the English Government and Toussaint, by which St Domingo was recognised as an independent and neutral power during the war.

It is related that the English, in their attempts to establish their power on the Island of St Domingo, expended the sum of £20,000,000 sterling, losing by disease and death 45,000 men.

In the midst of these operations, the year 1795 brought a peace between France and Spain, the conditions of the treaty of which ceded the entire island to the power of the French; the Spanish troops, it being agreed, should, a month after the promulgation of the treaty, vacate their part of the island, delivering up all the forts, ports, and places occupied by them, as soon as the French troops should arrive to take possession—a sad period in the history of Spanish St Domingo.

In order to consummate the terms of this treaty, the French sent to St Domingo city Commissioner Roume to confer with the Governor Garcia in the arrangements for the details of its fulfilment as to the cession of the Spanish part to the French.

After waiting there a month, and making all preparations, and the French authorities not sending either the means or troops to take possession, the commissioner was obliged to return without having fully accomplished his object, and the condition of this part remained unaccomplished, from the fact that the English invasion and the civil war prevented the commissioners sending the necessary troops, so that the Spaniards remained in possession until December 1795. The Spanish Government having then sent a fleet to take away the troops, and such inhabitants as wished to retire to other Spanish possessions, the opportunity was seized to transport the remains of Columbus, then resting in the grand Cathedral of St Domingo city, to the Cathedral at Havana, where they at present remain.

CHAPTER VIII.

"Sleep calmly in thy dungeon tomb,
Beneath Besancon's alien sky,
Dark Haytien !—for the time shall come,
Yea, even now is nigh,
When everywhere thy name shall be
Redeemed from error's infamy,
And men shall speak of thee
As one of earth's great spirits !"

TOUSSAINT'S RULE—*The Independence of Hayti—Toussaint takes Possession of the Whole Island, giving it a Constitution—Affairs under Toussaint—Napoleon Attempts to Restore the Island to the French—Details of Le Clerc's Expedition—Toussaint's Capture—Rebellion against the French—Cristophe Dessalines—Final Failure of the French, and their Capture by the English Fleet—Dessalines Marches against the Spanish Part—His Discomfiture—His Cruelties in that Part of the Island—Becomes Emperor—His Cruelties and Butcheries of the Whites—Conspiracy against Him—His Death.*

TOUSSAINT L'OUVERTURE,* one of the most remarkable characters in history, was now in almost supreme control of the island, for though commissioners were sent out from France, such was the power he wielded over the people of all classes and colours, that he was able quietly

* Toussaint was originally a slave, but said to be descended from a royal chief in Africa. His early life was exemplary for a person of his condition, being passed upon a plantation of the Count de Noe, where, the overseer taking a fancy to him, he was allowed to learn to read and write, even picking up some Latin and mathematics ; and having been promoted to be coachman, he had increased opportunities to improve his mind, thus laying the foundation of that wisdom he afterwards manifested.

to make the commissioners act subserviently to him (Toussaint).

All authorities seem to agree that under Toussaint a reign of order began in the island that was remarkable. The blacks, proud to see one of their number in chief command in the island, looked up to Toussaint as a god; while he, with a thorough knowledge of his race, prescribed such rules and orders as kept them in a state of tranquillity.

He ordered them all to return to work, as they were before the war; to labour on the plantations, for which they were paid as labourers; and he gave every protection to the whites, even inviting those white planters who had fled the island to return and reoccupy their estates.

Toussaint L'Ouverture.

Under his wise rule St Domingo soon advanced in the most rapid manner in her agricultural and social prosperity; but while Toussaint was wise in peace, he was equally iron-handed in war, and some of the cruelties perpetrated upon the mulattoes, who at first refused to recognise his supreme authority, tarnish somewhat his fame.

The year 1800 saw the island in a somewhat more settled state, the French part, with the exception of a small province in the south, where Rigaud still held out against the authority of Toussaint, was in a comparatively tranquil state, and nominally under the authority of the French Republic, which was represented by the Commissioner Roume. Toussaint was, however, the real authority in the island.

This chief was not satisfied, however, until he was able to claim that the whole island, including the Spanish portion, was under his dominion, and he therefore proposed to the Commissioner Roume that the cession required by the treaty of July 1795 should now be carried out.

Roume seems to have been quite aware of the ultimate intention of Toussaint to make himself independent of the Government of France, but considering it better to hide his suspicions, he so far assented to Toussaint's suggestion as to authorise him to appoint Generals Agè and Chanlette the agents, with necessary powers to accomplish this transfer of authority. While apparently acting thus in good faith, he, with great duplicity, secretly sent word to the Spanish Governor that he should refuse to deliver up the Spanish domain, and should manage to detain the commissioners until a force from France should have time to reach St Domingo city, and hold it for the legitimate authority of France.

Carrying out these secret instructions, the Spanish Governor-General Garcia managed to comply so well, that the envoys, who had with them only a small escort, were made to believe that their lives even were not safe from the Dominicans, who would not listen to the surrender of their city; and they returned to the Commissioner Roume as rapidly as possible, and made their report.

Upon the strength of this, Roume rescinded his order for the surrender of the Spanish part; but Toussaint, comprehending the duplicity of the commissioner, at first imprisoned him, and finally sent him out of the country to France.

The French representative being now out of the way, and Rigaud the rebellious subdued, Toussaint found himself in unmolested supreme control of the island; and deeming it a favourable time to put in operation a plan he had long been maturing, he, on the 9th November 1800, sent a note to General Garcia, demanding satisfaction for the insult offered his officers, and advising him that he should send General Moise at the head of 10,000 troops to take possession of Spanish St Domingo in the name of the Republic of France.

In order to give force to this note, at the same time he despatched it he put in motion the force under General Moise, his nephew, by the northern road through the Cibao country, while he himself, at the head of a column also of 10,000 men, marched by the southern route directly upon St Domingo city.

General Garcia, in command at that place, made every preparation to resist these movements, and while sending word to the authorities of the Cibao to interfere as much as possible with the march of General Moise, he himself took measures to delay the march of Toussaint upon the capital.

These measures were, however, comparatively ineffectual, though much annoyance was caused Toussaint by the activity of the militia against his columns, until he arrived at Ñagá, where a strong force in three columns resisted him so effectually that he was compelled to arrest his progress and resort to diplomacy to carry out his objects.

This he did by writing a note to Garcia, telling him that he, Toussaint, was surprised to find resistance on his journey, which he had not taken as an invader, but as an officer of the French Republic, to carry out the provisions of a treaty made with it by Spain.

General Garcia, fearful that his own conduct in the matter would not be sustained by his Government, and satisfying himself that Toussaint really had documents that empowered him to act for the French, decided to cede his authority, and on the 2d January 1801, opened the gates of St Domingo city to Toussaint, who, at the head of his troops, took possession of this famous city, nominally for the French Republic, the ceremony being solemnly consummated by a *Te Deum* in the Grand Cathedral, at which the principal authorities and the troops assisted.

Toussaint being in possession, there was an immediate embarkation of a large number of the inhabitants; first, the Governor and the Spanish officers and their families; the members of the religious orders; the most prominent of the citizens, all of whom by the treaty were permitted to take with them their property of every kind. Thus for the first time was the island left without the actual descendants of its original discoverers, and the star of Spain, which had blazed with such glory for a time in the New World, now disappeared from St Domingo, to reappear only in later days amid revolution, persecution, and cruelty.

Added to this emigration were all those French and their families who, flying from the revolutions in the western part, had sought shelter from those troubles in the Dominican part, and who now, having no sympathy with the new authorities, took their leave of the island; and, for the same reason, many of the native Dominican families, whose pride would not permit them to remain subject to negro rule, though perhaps many of them counted in their ancestors people of that colour.

These people sought the various islands of Porto Rico, Cuba, and others, which, by this accession of experienced planters of the cane and coffee, reaped immense advantages from this culture, to which they were really the first to give a scientific and systematic form.

Thus the poor impoverished St Domingo of to-day has been the innocent cause of benefiting and enriching her neighbours, while she, with more luxuriant vegetation, richer soil, and better climate, awaits an emigration that will bring peace, order, and riches to her shores.

It is related that after the surrender, Toussaint had the horrible idea of putting the remaining Spanish inhabitants to the sword, and for this purpose he ordered the populace to gather in the public square, where he then directed they should be separated, the women and children together, and the men by themselves, the different groups being surrounded by bodies of troops.

It is even said that Toussaint's sister-in-law, knowing of this intention, had passed the previous night in prayer, asking God to take away from him such thought.

If he ever entertained such idea, he did not proceed to execute it, for though he walked amongst the women asking cruel and rude questions, he finally, on the approach of a terrific storm, allowed them all to disperse without harm; an action that the superstitious thought was the result of a miracle of the Lord in sending the storm at that moment.

Being thus in possession of the whole island, Toussaint seems to have with great wisdom arranged his plans to benefit this part; and in naming Paul L'Ouverture, his brother, as Governor of the south, with headquarters at St Domingo city, and General Clervaux in command of the north, with headquarters at Santiago, he gave to the Spanish part of the island officers who, by their wisdom and judgment, were acceptable to the Dominicans.

Having arranged his authority satisfactorily in this part of the island, Toussaint, by a circuitous route, returned to the western part; it being stated his journey was a perfect ovation from its beginning to its end; and the inhabitants looked forward under his rule to a season of peace and prosperity,—a future they had a right to expect, since, for the first time in its history, the whole island was united under one government. Efforts were made, by systematising the laws, improving the means of communication, and opening the ports of the island to the commerce of the world, to restore it to a peaceful place in the political world.

To better consummate this, Toussaint, who had long meditated his plans, determined to declare the island independent of any European power; and having formed the plan of a constitution for the island, in which he was assisted by several Europeans (Pascal, Abbé Molière, and Maunil), it was submitted to a general assembly of representatives convened from every district, by whom it was approved and adopted. Afterwards it was promulgated in the name of the people ; and in July 1801, the island was declared independent, with Toussaint L'Ouverture as its supreme chief.

Unfortunately for himself and his country, he held this position but a short time.

The autumn of the year 1801 found every part of St Domingo in quiet submission to the authority of Toussaint, rapidly improving in wealth and happiness.

Agriculture had been re-established, and many of the French planters had returned and taken possession of their old estates, though they had no longer any slaves. This name had given way to that of "cultivators," and the law had fixed that they should receive for their labour one-third of the crops. While thus offering liberal rewards to industry, heavy penalties were inflicted for idleness.

The negro population, owing to these wise regulations, which gave them greater ease and more abundant food, was rapidly increasing in numbers.

Among the better classes, following the example set by their former French masters, a great degree of luxury, and even elegance, was maintained, many of their houses being furnished in the most sumptuous manner.

In their social life there was a great degree of ease, cordiality, and even refinement; churches were opened, and religious ceremonies, according to the Romish Church, performed; dramatic exhibitions were given, and some attention paid even to music and painting.

Such was the state of affairs when, the hostilities between Great Britain and France having ceased, Bonaparte, who now held the position of First Consul, was able to turn his attention to St Domingo, and determined to re-occupy that island for France by sending out a large expedition.

In the harbours of Brest, L'Orient, and Rochfort, a squadron of twenty-six vessels was collected in the month of December 1801, and on board this fleet was a force of 25,000 men, completely armed and equipped. In command of this force was Napoleon's brother-in-law, General Le Clerc, and with him were many other distinguished officers, Rochambeau being in command of one of the divisions; Villaret was the admiral-in-chief; while Madame Le Clerc accompanied her husband to participate in his triumphs.

On the 28th January 1802, this fleet arrived in the Bay of Samana. Three divisions were immediately sent to different parts of the island. General Kerverseau was sent with one division to St Domingo city, General Boudet with another to Port-au-Prince, while Le Clerc himself, with the rest of his troops, except a detachment sent to Manzanilla Bay, went to Cape Francois.

St Domingo city, after some resistance, and through the strategy of a native Dominican, Colonel Baron, in getting possession of some instructions from Toussaint to his brother Paul in command of this city, fell into the hands of the French under Kerverseau, the 20th February 1802; while at the same time General Ferrand received the submission of General Clervaux in command of the negro forces of the Cibao.

Thus the Spanish part immediately came under the dominion of the French authorities. Kerverseau, as having been the chief of the expeditionary force, assumed command of the colony, remaining at St Domingo city, where he governed, it is said, with such strictness and severity, that the Dominicans soon grew weary and restless under him.

As this capitulation had been brought about by the Dominicans making an attempt to assist with arms the efforts of the French, Toussaint L'Ouverture, when he received the news of the fall of this capital, which he had directed should be defended to the last extremity, revenged himself in the most cruel manner by murdering in cold blood nearly the whole of a regiment of Dominicans who were at Port-au-Prince with him, having taken the precaution to disarm them, and send them under escort to a place called Verette.

At St Domingo city, General Ferrand, claiming to be the superior officer, had deposed General Kerverseau from his office, and imprisoned him for refusing to recognise his authority, finally sending him (Kerverseau) to France as a prisoner, after which Ferrand appears to have devoted himself with great zeal and energy to the material welfare of that part of the island, improving the capital by seeking to bring to it the waters of the river Higüero, in the vicinity.

Meanwhile a terrible state of affairs was existing in the western part of the island.

General Rochambeau, on the 2d February, landed at Fort Dauphin, on the north coast; and before any demand of any kind was made upon the authorities, the troops were landed on the beach in line of battle; and a number of the negroes having gathered there in mere curiosity, were put to the bayonet, and the fort immediately taken by the French.

The next day, the main body of the fleet and army, under Villaret and Le Clerc, arrived off Cape Francois, and immediate preparations were made to land and take possession of the town. Henry Cristophe, a black man, who subsequently became famous as well as infamous, was then in command of the district of the Cape as general of brigade, and on the approach of the fleet he sent a messenger on board to inform its commander that his superior governor, General Toussaint, was absent at present; and such being the case, he could not permit the French to land a single soldier until orders had been received from Toussaint. In case, he declared also, the French should refuse to await these instructions, and should attempt to force a landing, all the white inhabitants would be considered as hostages for their conduct, and that an attack on the town would be followed by its immediate conflagration.

Le Clerc immediately replied, that if, in the course of the day, the forts Picolet and Belair, with all the batteries on the coast, were not surrendered, he should land his forces the next day at daybreak.

Cristophe replied to this letter, refusing to comply with the demand, and stating that he would make such a defence "as became a general officer."

A deputation of the inhabitants also waited on the French general, and, with the Mayor at their head, begged him to make no attempt on the city, as the blacks would certainly put all the white people to the sword. Le Clerc received this deputation politely, gave them some proclamations to circulate, and refused their request.

On the 6th February he landed his troops some distance below the town, but sailed his fleet up to the mole of the city. Cristophe, however, no sooner received news of this movement, than, knowing the town to be indefensible, he set fire to it, and withdrew with his troops and some 2000 white inhabitants, to whom, though he had threatened to do so, he did no harm.

News had by this time reached Toussaint, who was in the interior of the island, of the state of affairs, and with immediate promptness he issued orders putting the island in a state of defence against the French.

It was at this time that Toussaint was endeavoured, through the medium of his children, to be seduced into giving in his allegiance to the French.

Two of his sons had been sent to France to be educated, and had now reached quite mature years, one being almost of age. These sons the French Government had sent out on the expedition, in hopes that through them Toussaint's sympathies would be worked upon to yield without a conflict the dominion of the island.

Under the escort of their tutor, they were sent out to the home of their father, some ten miles from the Cape, Toussaint having passed his word, which even his enemies say was never broken, that the children and their tutor should be returned in safety, without regard to the result of their interview.

At the same time, Le Clerc sent an epistle, written by Bonaparte, and addressed to Toussaint, in which he was promised all manner of honours if he would give in his allegiance, while the tutor was instructed to make every effort, through the children, to induce Toussaint to accede to these proposals. It is only necessary to say here, that these offers were all unsuccessful; that Toussaint, with a great effort, sent back his children in these words, "Take back my children, since it must be so. I will be faithful to my brethren and my God."

Negotiations failing, Le Clerc issued proclamations addressed to the "cultivators" of the island, endeavouring to enlist them against "their severe tyrant and master," and in many ways directing their attention to the hardships Toussaint had put upon them.

To the black soldiers and officers he made tempting offers; and as many of these were ambitious for themselves and jealous of their chief, numbers were induced to join the French; while the most ignorant cultivators, seeing these things, and probably indifferent so long as they remained unmolested, took no active part.

The campaign was opened by Le Clerc; and then commenced a terrible war, that for months devastated again this beautiful land, in which, with varying success, thousands of lives were lost on both sides. But as Le Clerc was constantly joined by negro troops and officers who became tired of the war, and who doubtless believed they would be as well off under French as negro rule, the island would probably have soon again returned to the dominion of France, had it not been for a fatal mistake of policy.

Le Clerc, carried away by his success, and thinking he had no further obstacles to overcome in the reconquest ot the island, came out boldly with the original programme of the expedition.

This was to declare the negroes restored to their former owners, or their attorneys, a proceeding which, being announced to the inhabitants of the island by a proclamation issued in March, fell amongst them like a bombshell, as every promise had been given all classes that slavery would not be re-established on the island by the French.

Toussaint was far too wise a man not to avail himself of this weapon that the French had placed in his hands; for, knowing full well the spirit of his race, he felt he could now count upon them, even to the humble cultivator, with safety, and he therefore immediately arranged his plans to prosecute the war with renewed energy, and joining his forces with those of Cristophe, he left the shelter of the mountains for the sea-coast, where the cultivators, the class most interested in the French proclamation, were in the largest numbers. Wherever Toussaint went, he called upon the blacks, however, of every class to take arms and join him; and this they did to such an extent that he was soon able to drive the French of the north into the town of Cape Francois, which he would undoubtedly have captured, had it not been that the French hastened to concentrate their forces at that place.

Such was the congregation of their forces at this place, and so closely were they besieged, that large numbers fell a prey to a pestilence which broke out among the troops.

Le Clerc, finding himself thus cornered in the island, and powerless to take active measures, resorted to diplomacy, and issued another proclamation, dated April 25th, which he caused to be distributed among the blacks.

This set forth that when he first arrived in the island he was not familiar with the condition of its affairs, and that therefore some mistakes had been committed, and that in order to remedy these, and provide for the peace and welfare of the island and the liberty of its inhabitants, an assembly should be called of representatives from different parts of the colony, without regard to colour. Negotiations were also opened with Cristophe to bring the prominent officers and their troops to terms.

Although the terms, as proposed by Cristophe, were not very palatable to the French, they were finally accepted; and by the beginning of May a peace was concluded with Toussaint, and the subordinates and troops under him, by which the dominion of France over the whole island was duly acknowledged by all the inhabitants.

One act of treachery on the part of the French remained, however, yet to be performed; for Toussaint, having retired with his family to a small plantation near Gonaives, was, in the middle of the very month in which the treaty of peace had been made, taken prisoner at midnight with all his family, and taken on board a French frigate which had sailed into the harbour in the dead of night. From thence he was transferred to the frigate *Hero*, sent to France, where, being placed in close confinement, first in the dungeons of Joux, and afterwards in those of Besançon, he died, as it is supposed, of starvation, the fact of his death being announced in the French gazettes of April 27, 1803.

This breach of faith on the part of the French opened the eyes of the negroes to their ultimate designs; and Le Clerc having assumed the rank of Governor-General of the island, and issued a decree giving a new form of government, some of the compatriots of Toussaint took alarm, and immediately placed themselves at the head of some bodies of negro troops. Most prominent of these chiefs were Dessalines, Cristophe, and Clervaux.

A rising took place also about this time in the interior

among the mountains, of other chiefs, one of whom was a nephew of Toussaint; and the whole island was soon ablaze with the fires of the insurrectionists, so that the French were soon busily occupied in their new efforts to subjugate the island.

A chapter of horrors might easily be written from the events that followed. French writers themselves speak of the scenes then enacted with loathing and disgust, and it is not perhaps to be wondered at that, when the negroes came into power, they retaliated upon the French some of the revolting cruelties that had been practised upon their own people by the officers and soldiers of that nation.

To this day almost, "Les Noyades" of the French are spoken of with horror; for their usual method of disposing of their prisoners, by making them kneel on the edge of a trench some twenty or thirty feet in depth, and then shooting them until the trench was filled by their dead bodies, was deemed too tedious and troublesome: as an easier means the negroes were placed in vessels, carried out some distance to sea, and, being chained together, were forced overboard and drowned.

Such was the French civilisation that was desired to be introduced into the island; but some of their refinements were truly of a classic kind, for, following the example of the ancient Romans, they had their arenas, in which the performers were naked negroes and ferocious bloodhounds, brought from Cuba expressly to hunt this kind of game.

Retribution followed these deeds, it would appear; for the commander-in-chief, Le Clerc, worn out with troubles of body and mind, died on the island, and his corpse was sent to France, followed by his apparently inconsolable widow.

Rochambeau succeeded to the command, but long months were spent without the French making headway; in fact, they were gradually losing their hold, foot by foot, notwithstanding that new troops had been sent out from France, until, at the beginning of 1803, the French were again cooped up in Cape Francois.

Here the negro chief of the besiegers, Dessalines, gave an idea of the character which he was later to develop into brutal bloodthirstiness. In one of the engagements the French had captured some 500 prisoners, and without taking into consideration that numbers of their own men were in the hands of the enemy, the French general ordered them all to be put to death.

When this news reached Dessalines, he at once ordered 500 gibbets to be erected, and selecting all the French officers he had in his power, and adding a sufficient number of privates to make up the total to 500, he caused them all to be hung up at break of day in sight of the French army.

In the spring of this year, war had been again declared between England and France; and in July an English fleet appeared off the harbour of Cape Francois.

Dessalines immediately opened communication with its commander, asking his co-operation against their common enemy; and although the latter declined positively to accede to this request, yet the efforts of the fleet in blockading the sea front of Cape Francois, materially assisted Dessalines, who, with his troops, cut off communication by land for the French.

Notwithstanding this, the French held out until November, being reduced, however, to the extremity of feeding on the very dogs of the place; and Dessalines at that time making his preparations to storm the town, Rochambeau deemed it best to make terms for its surrender, and the withdrawal of the French from the island.

Articles were signed on the 19th November with Dessalines, by which it was permitted to the French to evacuate Cape Francois and all its forts, with the munitions of war pertaining thereto, while they were to be allowed to retire on board their ships, with all their private property; the sick and wounded were to be left in the hospitals, to be taken care of by the blacks till they were sufficiently recovered to be sent back to France in neutral vessels.

Notwithstanding these terms showed much liberality and great kindness of feeling on the part of Dessalines, the French were not satisfied without attempting to commit another act of treachery with their black enemies ; for on the very day of the meeting with Dessalines, the French endeavoured to treat with the commander of the English fleet for the surrender to him of the city, but in this they were not successful.

This coming to the ears of Dessalines, the surrender of the city was immediately demanded, and the flag of the negroes was, on the 30th November, placed on the walls of the city, the French retiring to their ships, where they were in a state of great alarm ; for the blacks, it is presumed for their meditated treachery, had threatened to sink the ships of the French with hot shot.

The English, who had been watching off the harbour, in expectation of capturing this fleet, had a message sent them by the French commander that he was willing to surrender to them, to escape the threatened attack of the blacks ; and the English commander having accepted the terms proposed, the negro authorities were notified that the French fleet was under the protection of the British flag, and were therefore requested to commit no hostile act.

As soon as the wind permitted, the French fleet sailed out of the harbour with its flags flying, but as soon as they were outside these were hauled down, the broadsides of the vessels fired, and the fleet surrendered.

Shortly after, the small force remaining on the island at St Nicholas' mole took its departure, and thus the power of Napoleon was lost for ever on that part of the island.

Dessalines now devoted himself to placing the island in a condition to benefit by the new state of affairs, and amongst other things, in order to allay the fears of the whites remaining on the island, issued a proclamation promising protection and safety to all, stating that the war that was just ended had been in no wise carried on against the people of the colony. A proclamation having been issued the day before the evacuation of the French, signed by Generals Clervaux, Cristophe, and Dessalines, declaring the island independent, a formal declaration took place to this effect on the 1st day of January 1804, signed by all the chiefs and generals of the army, in the name of the people of Hayti, a name which had been determined on for the new republic. Jean Jacques Dessalines was declared Governor-General for life, with power to enact laws, to make peace and war, and to nominate his successor—powers of which he made most horrible use.

Dessalines has become one of the most prominent characters in the history of Hayti; and his indiscriminate slaughter of the whites in the island, to whom he had promised protection, would cover his name with eternal infamy, were he otherwise a god. On the contrary, he was a rude, uncultivated, illiterate negro, who, by force of circumstances, strong physique, and undoubted bravery, came to have the power of life and death over thousands of human beings, the lowest of whom was perhaps his superior in those feelings which are but the natural adjuncts of man.

His first act was to encourage the emigration from the United States of blacks and mulattoes. He offered $40 per head to the captains of American vessels for each individual of colour they should return to Hayti. He offered to open his ports to the slave ships, and to allow the people of Jamaica the exclusive privilege of selling negroes in Hayti, to be limited to men only. This he did on the plea that he wanted recruits for his army, and that so many slaves would be brought from Africa that his plan would secure them from slavery elsewhere, while making them freemen in Hayti.

Hardly established in his position of Governor for life, this monster in human form issued a proclamation for the purpose of inciting the blacks to murder all the French on the island, stating a long list of the crimes they had committed against the blacks, and appealing to the love of the latter for dead parents, brothers, &c., to rise up and revenge themselves. This, however, not being acted upon by the people or troops, he himself, with his soldiers, proceeded to different towns, and murdered, in cold blood, the French, making no distinction of age or sex.

At Cape Francois, not being satisfied that he had successfully accomplished his object, he issued a proclamation announcing that justice (?) was satisfied, and inviting all who had escaped the massacre to appear on parade. When they did so, they were taken and shot; and it is related that the little stream that runs through the town was actually discoloured by the blood of the slain.

General Ferrand remained in possession of St Domingo city with a small French garrison; and although at first a number of the inhabitants of the Spanish part had quietly accepted the Haytian Government, they had eventually sided with the French, and during the troubles of the blacks in the west, many of the French and their families had sought refuge among the Spaniards, where, it is said, their intelligence and example was having a good effect upon the progress of that part.

No sooner, however, had Dessalines arranged affairs in the west, than he set about compelling the Spanish part of the island to submit to the Haytian rule.

This movement was, besides, quickened by an impolitic order that General Ferrand had issued, that the Dominicans should make slaves of all prisoners of either sex, of more than fourteen years old, that they should take from the Haytians.

In order to accomplish this movement with certain success, Dessalines had endeavoured to keep his preparations secret; but Ferrand, getting information, made every preparation to protect the capital, placing guns in position even on the roofs of the churches and convents.

Dessalines having previously caused to be circulated among the Spaniards proclamations in which he threatened all manner of evils in case of resistance, put himself in march from Cape Francois on the 14th May 1805, and taking a circuitous route through the western and southern provinces of the west, he finally crossed the frontier with a force of 25,000 men.

The Dominicans united with the French; and such a terror had Dessalines' name spread over the island by his cruelties, that the very slaves in the Spanish part took arms against him in favour of their masters, whose kind treatment had strengthened their attachment.

Notwithstanding these resistances, which assumed only the form of guerilla attacks against so large a force, Dessalines' troops succeeded in getting possession of Azua, Santiago, and other places of any importance, and finally sat down before the capital; but he met here with such a vigorous resistance, that he was compelled to arrange his plans for a regular siege, when the arrival of a French fleet off the harbour interfered with their consummation, and he therefore determined to retire suddenly upon the region of the Cibao. This he did by forced marches, laying waste the whole country as he passed along, and murdering the inhabitants wherever he found them. Such was the depredation he committed, that it was years before Spanish St Domingo recovered from the desolation and misery he caused.

On his return from this expedition, Dessalines had himself made Emperor, the empire being made into six military divisions, commanded each by a general, who corresponded directly with the head of the Government. The constitution by which the empire was purported to be formed was signed by twenty-three men professing to have been appointed as representatives of the people ; and in it were some singular declarations, such as the exclusion of white men from acquiring property; the general name of "blacks" for all the subjects of Hayti, of whatever colour; the suspension of citizenship by bankruptcy; every citizen was also required to profess some mechanical art.

The condition and treatment of the cultivators was again prescribed by law as formerly, and they worked the estates, many of which had now become the property of the state, though the illegitimate children of former owners were allowed to make claims.

The sugar plantations had been mostly all destroyed; they have never since been restored in any number. The chief produce then (1805) was, as it is to-day, coffee, of which about fifty ordinary shiploads were produced.

The population numbered at this time about 400,000 souls, the women being in a large majority. In fact, the cultivators were nearly all of this sex, so rapidly had the war carried off the men. After the expulsion of the French, Dessalines was in great fear that they would return, and he therefore used every means to strengthen his army and increase his resources. At this time the regular army amounted to about 15,000 men, 1500 of whom were cavalry. Although well armed and drilled, they were badly uniformed. To this force the militia was endeavoured to be made a strong adjunct, every adult male being compelled to be drilled.

In case of another invasion, Dessalines had so arranged his plans that the troops were to withdraw to the hills and mountains, after having destroyed the towns and laid waste the plain country; and for this purpose a series of forts were erected on the tops of hills within support of each other, and the ground in their vicinity planted with such fruits and vegetables as would serve for food.

Dessalines, however, did not live long to preside over his empire; for his natural disposition to cruelty, increased by the power with which he was possessed, at last passed all bounds, and the horrible deeds he committed, without the sanction of either law or justice, roused the people to rebel against his rule; and his life was ended by some of his own soldiers, who, in arms against him, ambushed him at the "Pont Rouge," a short distance from "Port-au-Prince," the 17th October 1806,—shooting him, it is said, as he charged fearlessly upon them with only a walking-stick for a weapon.

CHAPTER IX.

"And Hayti, from her mountain land,
Shall send the sons of those who hurled
Defiance from her blazing strand
The war-gage from her Petion's hand,
Alone against a hostile world."

The Whole Island United under one Government—Dessalines' Successors—Cristophe and Petion—Civil War—Peace between the two Chiefs—Troubles in the Spanish Part—The Expulsion of the French—Co-operation of the English—Restoration of the Authority of Spain. Rebellion against her Rule—Death of Cristophe and Petion—Boyer's Rule—Allegiance of the Spanish Part to him—Condition of the Island—French Claims—Boyer's Decline—The Republic of Dominica.

ON the death of Dessalines, the power naturally fell into the hands of Henry Cristophe, the second in command of the army, whom we have already seen acting so decidedly against General Le Clerc at Cape Francois.

Petion, a mulatto, however, put forth his claim to be the chief ruler, though Cristophe immediately assumed the title of "Chief of the Government of Hayti;" and civil war was again produced by the contention of these two chiefs.

Horrible and tyrannical as became the after career of Cristophe, there is no question that he began his reign in a wise and most judicious manner, that would have resulted eventually in great benefits to the island; but it seems a peculiarity of the negroes in power in this island, that no sooner do they begin to feel a little assured in their positions, than the negro instinct of display, love of power, or some inherent element of cruelty, induces them to commit acts that bring on their own ruin, while horrifying the world with deeds of bloodshed. Unfortunately the acts of the white man in such periods do not permit us to claim much more for him on the score of humanity.

Hardly had Cristophe assumed the reins of power than the rival candidate, Petion, placed himself in opposition to him; and it is with some little pleasure that the eye, running over the pages of the history of this time, finds in the person of this new chief some solid elements of civilisation, humanity, and education.

Petion, a mulatto general under Dessalines, had been educated at Paris, at the Military Academy, and was said to be a man of letters and of refinement, of gentle disposition and charming manners; and having been educated to the military profession, served with ability as the chief engineer of the blacks.

At Dessalines' death he was in command of Port-au-Prince; and when Cristophe marched against him, Petion endeavoured to check his progress at a place called Cibert, some four miles from that city. But he was then, January 1807, defeated, and forced to fly for his life.

Then began another civil war in the island between the two parties, headed by these respective chiefs, which finally ended in Cristophe's remaining master of the entire northern district, with his headquarters at Cape Francois; and by a sort of tacit agreement, Petion in 1812 remained in possession of the southern province, with his capital at Port-au-Prince.

Thus the western end of the island was in the power of two parties, while in the eastern or Spanish part matters were also in a complicated state.

Notwithstanding the various troubles in the island, and the bad success of the French in their attempts to maintain their control of it, they had still retained some power in the east by their possession of St Domingo city and Samana; and it would seem as though they held on to these places as *points d'appuis*, from which they hoped to renew their efforts to re-establish their power over the western part. To facilitate this plan, many French soldiers, or those favourable to the French cause, had been settled in the Spanish part, and had been armed and organised; and many of the officers even had been encouraged to create families for themselves among the creole women, so that there should be some permanent interest held in the land. This had created quite a strong body; and as the French held all the official positions, they had full power to make themselves obnoxious to the native and Spanish residents.

This they did to such an extent that a revolutionary movement was inaugurated by one Juan Sanchez Ramirez, a citizen of Cotuy, who raised the standard of revolt among the Spaniards, but at first without much success, and he was forced to take refuge in Puerto Rico, where, however, some of the Spanish exiles united with him, and forming a party, they landed in the province of Seybo, and awakened the inhabitants of that part to resistance against the French.

The state of affairs in Spain strengthened this movement; for the Spaniards in the island, taking courage from the example of the mother country in throwing off the rule of the Bonapartes, rose up at the same time as Sanchez Ramirez's landing, and a strong movement was made in the vicinity of Azua, and also in Cotuy.

The movement in Seybo gained such headway, that Ferrand, after making attempts to quell it through his subordinates, was compelled to take the field himself, leaving St Domingo city in charge of a subordinate general, Barquier.

Ferrand, the 8th November 1808, met the Spaniards at "Palo Hincado." At first the French, fighting with great bravery, were successful; but some of the native troops having deserted them, they were quickly defeated by Ramirez and his followers; and the brave veteran Ferrand, after having taken the life of one of their leaders with one pistol, blew out his own brains with the other, on finding himself alone, and his troops all either dead or deserted, not caring to survive his ignominious defeat.*

The whole of the Spanish part was now in arms; and Cristophe deeming it a matter of policy to aid in destroying the last vestige of the power of the French in the island, assisted the Spaniards with supplies of all kinds, the result being that the French were finally cooped up in the two places of St Domingo city and Samana, where they were closely besieged by the revolutionists under Ramirez, who now held the chief command over the Spaniards.

Unprovided, however, with artillery or besieging material, the latter were unable to capture these places, and they sustained a siege of some nine months, the garrisons, particularly that of St Domingo city, suffering immensely, while the Spaniards who were detained in that city had to submit to every cruelty and hardship during this long term.

Ramirez finally sought aid from the English, sending an envoy to the Governor at Jamaica, who fitted out an expedition against Samana, which arriving there in November 1809, the place was captured, the French made prisoners, and their vessels taken by the English, the place being handed over to the authority of the Spaniards.

In July 1809, another British force had been despatched from Jamaica to St Domingo city, under Admiral Cumby, the land forces being under General Carmichael; and after some delay, and just as the English were ready to open

* In later years Santana boasted he had the skull of Ferrand, which had been captured by his (Santana's) father, and that he intended to keep it as an heirloom in his family.

their mortar batteries upon the city from the heights of San Carlos, Barquier agreed to capitulate; and on the 10th July, the French having evacuated the town, the cross of St George was, for a second time in the history of this antique city, flung to the breeze from its walls.

The keys of the city were retained, to be presented by the English Ambassador to the Spanish authorities at Seville, as a token that the ancient domain of St Domingo was once more restored to the authority of its parent country; and on the 11th July, General Carmichael, the English commander, handed over the city to the patriot chief Ramirez, who took possession of it at the head of his troops.

A commissioner was then despatched to Spain to notify that Government of the restoration of St Domingo to its authority; but that country was in a state of war and confusion, and the Government, represented by the Junta of Seville, received this news with indifference, as the question of the home Government then was how to maintain its own safety, without caring to give thought to the reacquisition of territory already parted with by its own volition.

An alliance, however, being formed between Spain and England, which gave a more favourable aspect to the affairs of the former, a commissioner, Francisco Zavier Caro, was appointed and sent out to St Domingo, to give affairs there a regular form. The patriot chief Ramirez was confirmed as brigadier-general, and appointed Captain-General of the island; a decree was also passed entitling St Domingo, as part of the American colonies, to send delegates to the Central Council; and the island was organised into the same form of government in vogue before the cession to the French in 1795, the church organisation being the same.

In fact, the old-time policy of Spain was restored of making the island but a place for official patronage, and the appointments to important offices were made of persons sent out from Spain; the services of those who had been the means of restoring the island overlooked or ignored, and the creoles and other residents of the island found themselves overmatched by newcomers from Spain. This was especially the case with the soldiers, many of whose promotions were revoked, and officers' appointments ignored.

This period is known in Dominican annals as the time of "España boba" (Spanish puppet), for nothing was done to benefit the island; and, as a writer pithily observes, it was a time when there was no distinction between rich and poor, for all the inhabitants alike were in a state of extreme poverty; there was no luxury of any kind—neither theatres, inns, public walks, or any inducements for spending money, for there was no money to spend; in fact, the people vegetated rather than lived, tranquilly devoting themselves simply to their favourite amusements of mass, dancing, and religious festivities—a description that will equally apply to-day.

With the exception of a few trifling incidents, of local importance only, this condition of affairs continued, improved only a little by the accession of some of the exiled families to the population, and by the acts of some of the Governors, until, in 1814, the treaty of Paris gave regularly back to Spain her right upon the colony.

So far from this appearing to have benefited the island, it, on the contrary, seems to have reaped no advantage whatever, and the inhabitants appear to have amused themselves at various times in this period by getting up revolutions, of which, it is said, there were some fourteen, though none of them amounted to anything until Jose Nuñez de Caceres raised a strong party, incorporating in it the principal men of the island, and declared for its independence, which was finally accomplished, with little trouble and loss, in December 1821. Then a new banner was given to the breeze, with the name of "Colombia" as the designation of the new republic. As this lasted, however, only six weeks, it is not worth while to dwell upon it.

Meanwhile we have left the western part of the island in possession of the blacks, under the two rulers Cristophe and Petion, who had agreed to a sort of quasi-peace, and both were devoting themselves to the advancement of their different governments.

Petion's government, however, had been disturbed by the insurrection raised by Jean Baptiste Perrier, who, in 1807, had raised the standard of revolt in the mountains of Jeremie, for the nominal purpose of assisting Cristophe, and he carried on this insurrection for a number of years.

In 1810, General Rigaud had arrived on the island, having made his way from France, and he also raised a revolt, assuming the command of the south, forming a council at Cayes; and thus, in this period, the Island of St Domingo may be seen with five distinctive governments upon it—that of Old Spain, of King Cristophe, of President Petion, of General Rigaud, and of Perrier.

Rigaud dying, however, in 1811, was succeeded by General Borgella, who finally gave in his adherence to Petion.

Cristophe had first made himself king, then emperor, and had set up a court that he endeavoured to make surpass the most gorgeous in Europe.

Petion, meanwhile, as president of the republic, was earnestly devoting himself to the good of the people and the improvement of the country. Though he did not follow the example of Cristophe in bestowing orders of nobility, he yet rewarded his followers with grades of military rank.

During the government of these two chiefs, and after the fall of Napoleon, it was proposed in France to have St Domingo restored to the French Government, and much discussion was thereupon entered into in public as to the feasibility of the plan.

No sooner did an intimation of this reach the blacks in St Domingo, than each chief notified the French authorities that no attempt of any kind would be permitted to be made on the island; each authority proceeding to increase its means of defence.

The French Government, however, having hopes of the accomplishment of this object by diplomacy, if not by force, sent out, in 1814, three commissioners to report upon the state of affairs in St Domingo, and the feeling of its chiefs and people for the project.

These stationed themselves in Jamaica, from whence they attempted to carry on negotiations with Petion and Cristophe individually, and seduce them to their interest.

Further communications from the commissioners were laid, both by Cristophe and Petion, before their councils, and the representatives of France were even invited to the island. The propositions in both cases were utterly refused, and in the case of Petion, with this refusal to recognise the demands of France, a proposition was made that indemnity would be paid for the losses with which the French planters had undoubtedly met in their departure from the island. Bonaparte's return from Elba put an end to all these negotiations.

Petion, although much beloved by his people, seems to have been too mild and gentle a man to rule over such a peculiar population; and the inhabitants, especially the cultivators, had, under him, sunk into such a state of idleness and sloth, that the island suffered much in its commerce and products—so much so, that the revenue was not sufficient to meet the expenses of government. To increase the difficulty, Petion had issued an immense amount of debased silver coin, which eventually only added to the distress.

Petion, who had been appointed President for life, with power to name his successor, was so overcome, it is said, with chagrin and sadness at the fate of his republic, that he gradually pined away, and died in March 1818, naming Boyer as his successor.

Cristophe, Emperor of the north, was still living, and pursuing a very different policy from that of Petion. Understanding full well the nature of his subjects, he had issued the strictest orders compelling every man to work, and punishing with the utmost severity idlers and vagabonds. To see that these rules were complied with, his subordinates not only were compelled to make inspection of the plantations in their districts, but Cristophe himself rode in person at various times in various places to see that his orders were executed. The consequence was, that the whole of that part of the island was in a flourishing state; the revenues were immense, commerce was assured; and doubtless, had the Emperor had a little more judgment and humanity, with a longer life, he would have been just the man to show of what his people and the Island of Hayti were capable.

While there was no end to his pride, ambition, and love of display, he had the good sense to gather around him educated, intelligent men, some of whom were Europeans, by whom he could profit in the rule of his country; he had even the ambitious project of buying up the Spanish end of the island, negotiations for which he had already entered into it is said.

Unfortunately, as he had grown in power, he had more than increased in despotism and cruelty; and if we believe the stories related of him, he eventually became one of the greatest of human monsters.

Finally, to such an extent did he carry his exactions, his punishments, and his tyrannies, that his subjects rose against him, and the troops joining them, his power fast slipped away from him, when, in October 1820, being attacked almost in his very palace by his own guard, he put an end to his own life.

General Boyer, who had succeeded Petion, availing himself of the confusion created by the death of Cristophe, pushed forward to the province of the north, and the people throughout that district receiving him with acclamations and joy, the whole of the western part became united under him into one government called the Republic of Hayti, of which he was made President.

In order to ensure the tranquillity of the island, changes were made in the disposition of the northern troops, they being exchanged for those of the south; all titles were abolished, and those generals who had revolted against Cristophe were rewarded by commands in other parts of the island.

Hardly had this new Government of the west been organised, than overtures were made by some of the inhabitants of the east to recognise the rule of the Haytian republic, and a deputation for this purpose waited on Boyer at Port-au-Prince, and tendered him the allegiance of the Spanish part; for in this part, at this time, there were a great many of the Haytians who were living there, cultivating the ground, and, with the resident coloured people, formed the largest portion of it. Perhaps tired of the disputes between the ambitious leaders of the French and Spaniards, and Spaniards and Dominicans, the mass of the people longed, as they do to-day, for a stable form of government that would secure them in their peaceful labours and its results; and in this feeling the entire population of the country, of whatever colour, shared.

Boyer, therefore, no sooner received intimation of this state of things, than he began to march a force towards the Spanish frontiers, immediately following with his staff, the whole as they advanced being received in the most enthusiastic manner by the populace.

President Boyer made a peaceful entry into the city of St Domingo; and thus the beginning of the year 1822 saw the whole of the island, from Cape Tiburon to Cape Samana, in possession of one Government, the Republic of Hayti, under whose rule it was to remain for upwards of twenty-two years.

As Boyer presided over this republic for many years, it may not be amiss to give a few particulars concerning him.

Boyer.

Jean Pierre Boyer was a dark mulatto, a native of Port-au-Prince, and, at the time of his elevation to the presidency of the republic, was about forty-eight years of age. His father was a tailor; and his mother, a Congo negress, had been a slave. He himself, after taking part in the early troubles on the side of the French, had retired with Rigaud to France, from whence he returned with Le Clerc in his expedition, but joined subsequently Petion, to whom he served as aide-de-camp, finally being appointed his successor, after having served in various grades.

He was below the middle size, with a feeble constitution, and was extremely fond of display and ornament, taking great pride in showing himself on Sundays at the head of his troops in full dress.

In his government of the new republic, Boyer was very far from displaying that judgment and wisdom that had marked the rule of Toussaint; and, so far from profiting by the example set him by Cristophe, the good results of which had been patent to the whole island, in making the culture of the land and general agriculture the basis of a solid wealth and progress for the island, he seems rather to have followed the weak example of Petion in permitting the entire population to sink into a state of idleness, ignorance, and licentiousness.

No effort was made to enforce the cultivation of land; and even the influence that might have been spread around by the working of the public domain, which was considerable, was lost, the President turning his attention more particularly to the working of the mines in the island. This not proving profitable, and the revenues of the island falling short of the expenses, he also had recourse to the issuing of debased coin; and of such a poor nature was this, that it is stated the counterfeit was better than the real, having more silver in it.

But Boyer probably showed his want of wisdom more forcibly by his action towards the French Government.

Although the island was now united under one government, under the flag of the name of the Republic of Hayti, it had not been able to take its place in any way among the body of nations, not one single country having recognised it as having a distinct organisation; even the South American State of Colombia, which almost owed its existence to the aid it had received from St Domingo, had not even recognised its sister republic.

Although, again, this independence of the island from the French had been maintained since January 1804, without any positive denial on the part of France to this assumption, yet now, in 1824, Boyer saw fit to send an embassy to Paris, to ask the recognition from the French of a fact that for years had been tacitly conceded by them —the independence of Hayti.

For this recognition the commissioners were empowered to offer a pecuniary consideration of 100,000,000 francs; but this was promptly refused, the French Cabinet, it is presumed, being wise enough to think, that if Hayti herself recognised the claim of France to her soil, the latter would be unwise to yield it.

Some privileges conceded to an English company for the working of the mines decided the Government of France to send out to Hayti an expedition for the purpose of making demands on account of the above conceded claim.

This expedition consisted of a fleet of vessels of fourteen sail, and is said to have been prepared either for peace or war, in case these demands were not acceded to.

These were placed in the hands of Baron Mackau, an officer of the French navy, who was authorised to carry on the negotiations on the part of the French King.

The arrival of this fleet off the city of Port-au-Prince, it is stated, excited terror and consternation; the object it had in view was unknown, and fears were immediately entertained for the safety of the city, which was in an almost defenceless condition.

The account given of the behaviour of Boyer himself on this occasion is not very flattering, nor does it tend to elevate one's ideas of his courage and decision; but on hearing that the object of the mission was peaceable, he prepared to enter into negotiations with Mackau; and after several interviews and much discussion, an *ordonnance* offered by the French was finally accepted by Ingenac, secretary-general, on the part of the republic. By this document it was prescribed that Hayti, in case the several clauses contained therein were not complied with, should become a colony of France.

As this transaction has lately created some discussion as to its bearing on the Dominican part of the island, it may be as well to give a synopsis of what the treaty was.

This document was dated Paris, 17th April 1825, and signed by the King, Charles the Tenth, setting forth that the ports in the *French part* of *St Domingo* shall be open to the commerce of all nations; that the French ships and merchandise shall be admitted into the *French part* on paying only half duties—exports the same; that the *inhabitants* of the *French part of St Domingo* agree to pay, in five annual instalments, the sum of 150,000,000 francs as an indemnity for the losses of the ancient colonists; and that when the conditions of this *ordonnance* are fulfilled, the *French part* of *St Domingo* is declared independent.

This document, therefore, ceded to France a right which had been strictly forbidden in the original constitution of the government of Hayti, and which says, "Never again shall a colonist or a European set his foot upon this territory with the title of master or proprietor."

To President Boyer, therefore, belongs the odium of this transaction, which saddled the island with an immense debt, that it has found difficult to liquidate, and which has, undoubtedly, had the effect of interfering with its material progress, as to this day the debt remains unpaid.

The joy, however, at the settlement of this negotiation was, it is said, confined solely to the town of Port-au-Prince; in fact, in the other portions of the island, the people were so exasperated that a revolution was threatened, and only prevented by the prompt movement of troops to the disaffected localities. Boyer, however, called upon the legislative body to sanction his action with France, and the measure, under pressure, was approved without debate; the assumption of the debt to France being conceded as an affair of importance to the national honour and credit.

In addition to the money advantage ceded to France by the treaty, there were accorded to her also special privileges of commerce, freedom of duties, &c., that caused great discontent.

Every effort was made by the Government to raise money for immediate payment by a loan from the people; but in this it was frustrated, the people vowing they would never contribute a cent; *the inhabitants of the Spanish part* flatly refused to *be taxed in any way to contribute to this claim, maintaining that they had never belonged to France.*

Many of the most prominent and intelligent of the Haytians protested against the treaty, affirming that it was not binding upon the island, and that even the action of the Legislative Assembly recognising the tribute to the French as a national debt was not binding upon the people; for they had gained their independence by an immense struggle, and supported it at the expense of great bloodshed; in addition to which, the independence of the island from France had now been maintained for the period of twenty-one years, which gave them an undoubted title to it.

In addition to the treaty made public, there was also an additional treaty, kept secret, by which the sum of 30,000,000 of francs was to be paid for the fortifications and public edifices; and of this tribute the sum of 60,000,000 was really paid in coffee and money before the end of the year 1828.

At this time, such was the condition of the finances of the island, that in default of the payments then due to France, it became necessary to declare the Government of the island bankrupt, and all payments were discontinued.

Louis Philippe having succeeded to the throne of France, finding, in 1838, it was impossible to secure the treaty of 1825, entered into fresh negotiations with Boyer, resulting in a treaty which reduced the debt to the sum of 60,000,000 francs, and this has again been reduced by subsequent payments, though the period named (1867) for its entire extinction has since arrived without the Haytians being able to comply.

There were other indebtednesses entered into by Boyer with private firms in France, which have caused great trouble, and involved the country in debt which it has been unable to liquidate.

Nevertheless, on the final settling of the terms of the *ordonnance*, the independence of Hayti was celebrated, 11th July, with much rejoicing and display in the city of Port-au-Prince, the French officers being fêted and dined. This affair remained a source of trouble for a long time after, as in France, before the treaty was formally consummated, there was much discussion and demand on the part of the Government, and the loan with which to pay the first instalment of the treaty had to be raised in France on the most exorbitant terms; in fact, so ridiculous was the nature of these, that at the time, it is said, the "Haytian loan" was a subject of ridicule among the mercantile community.

On Boyer's accession to the government of the entire island, it had been hoped that such rules and regulations would have been made by him as would advance its material interests; these, however, he appears to have neglected, until, finding matters were so rapidly growing worse from the laxity with which the mass of the people were governed, a law was put in force compelling the labourers to remain on the plantations, and to labour at least five days in the week.

It was found necessary even, to carry out this law, to place armed guards to enforce it upon the plantations; but this would seem to apply to the military only, or those in authority: it being stated that on the plantation of the President himself the soldiers were used to drive the negroes to work at the point of the bayonet or the sword.

Such was the result of this laxity in enforcing laws on the part of Boyer, that even the people of the north, who, under Cristophe, had been driven into regular habits of labour, were so demoralised during Boyer's rule, by the example of vice and idleness set by those of the south, that there was no longer any systematic culture on the island, the principal part of the population simply growing enough fruits and vegetables to give them food.

It being seen, however, that the negro would not, in his new state of being, work unless forced both by law and power so to do, resort was had to a series of laws known as the "Code Rural," which was passed by the Chamber of Communes on the 21st April 1826; and on the 1st May, at the agricultural fête annually celebrated in the island, these laws were made known to the populace, by whom they were received with very little satisfaction. In fact, though there can be no question of the good they were intended to do, and would do, the whole code is simply a strong illustration of power used to force unwilling labourers to work.

There were numerous articles in the code prescribing the duties of non-property owners; but their real purport was to declare every man who did not own land, having no ostensible occupation, or not occupied as a cultivator, a vagabond with whom the law dealt severely, placing such at enforced labour on the public lands.

Boyer's rule, however, gave no satisfaction to the more intelligent portion of the Haytians, and many discontents were generated, which finally assumed the form of another revolution; and in 1843 Boyer was deposed from power by a political party, composed principally of the young, active, and ambitious men of the island, some of whom, having been educated abroad, really desired to see the island improved, while others, however, ruined by a course of reckless extravagance and debauchery, hoped to better themselves by a change. But this was effected under the plea that Boyer had made no advance in twenty-five years; that he had not given education to the people; that he had maintained the military system, which retarded the progress of civilisation, and aided him to violate the laws. With the inception of this revolution came a series of others, the results of which are to-day seen in the wretched condition of this once beautiful and cultivated portion of St Domingo.

Boyer's government, although lasting a long time, seems never to have been satisfactorily accepted by the Dominicans proper; and it must be conceded his acts were in many cases arbitrary and despotic, and he is accused of great duplicity in his dealings; as an evidence, the fact that the University of St Domingo, of which the people were justly proud, was entirely closed and discontinued by Boyer, and this too after he had professed himself as being well pleased with it and its students; but no sooner was he fully established in power than he ordered these very students, and many of the young men, immediately into the army—a course which succeeded in driving many of the white families from the island.

As the result of this state of things, when the above revolution in Haytian affairs proper took place, it was quickly followed by the separation and final independence of the entire eastern or Spanish part of the island. But though the subsequent Haytian Governors lost all control of this part, they endeavoured to retain a portion of the territory, an effort that has been fruitful of discords and bloodshed between every succeeding power,—the land thus remaining as a debatable ground still in dispute; and as it is one of the choicest portions of the island, it is evident that it will not be relinquished by either side, unless in the last extremity. In this district are comprised Caobas, Hincha, Banica, San Miguel, and San Rafael.

The Dominicans, in 1844, seeing the state of affairs in the west, raised the banner of revolt, the young revolutionists having at their head a distinguished citizen, Juan Pablo Duarte; and the movement being popular and successful, total separation from Hayti was declared, February 27, 1844. And as henceforth the two Governments remained for ever separated, I shall only refer to them again in my "Present State of Santo Domingo and Hayti."

CHAPTER X.

> "Amidst the heaven-reflecting ocean smiles
> A constellation of Elysian isles.
> . . . .
> The breath of ocean wanders through their vales,
> In morning breezes and in evening gales;
> Earth from her lap perennial verdure pours,
> Ambrosial fruits, and amaranthine flowers."

Land Ho—Arrival in the Tropics—First Sight of Land—Turk's Island—Salt Keys—The Haytian Shore—The Dominican Coast—Arrival off Puerto Plata—Its Harbour—Funny Method of going Ashore—A Night Visit—Historical Notes of the Town—Its Bay—Situation—Trade—People.

ON the morning of the sixth day out from New York, all hands were called on deck, just as day was breaking, to catch the first glimpse of land, which proved to be, on nearer approach, the famed repository of salt, Turk's Island, appearing a barren place enough, though valuable to the English as a salt-mine.

We were now really within the tropics, and enjoying the balminess of air peculiar to these latitudes, an enjoyment the greater when experienced from the deck of a comfortable steamer in the exhilarating atmosphere of a breezy early morning.

Our next sight of land is strange indeed, being the view of some low-lying sandy islands, which at first appear one long strip of hummocked land, but which resolves itself finally into the place known as Salt Keys, also famous for its salt,—the few houses scattered over it being the dwellings of the sparse population who spend their existence, in what is almost a desert island, in procuring this necessity to life for their more favoured brethren in various parts of the world.

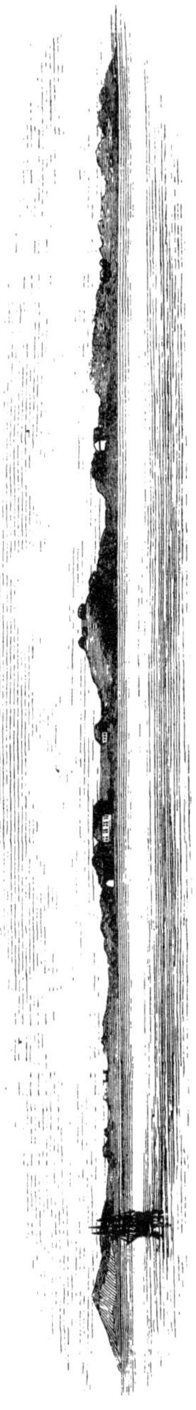

But as the day grows older we come in sight of Hayti itself, running down whose coast we soon have before us its higher mountain peaks; and, as we stand closer in, there comes rapidly into view the bold mountain shore of the Dominican portion, of which it is hard to conceive anything more picturesque and beautiful as one approaches it from the sea. Vast ranges of verdure-clad mountains stretch away diagonally from the sea, the spaces between them forming most lovely valleys and savannas, all, as we see them, teeming with vegetation, for not a sign do we see of abrupt or barren shores, or rocky cliffs. Everything is picture-like, even to the sandy beach upon which breaks the deep blue sea, forming as it falls into foam a belt of almost silver surf.

Salt Keys.

Then came historic headlands, familiar to the readers of Irving's Columbus, and finally the prominent point, Cape Isabella, that marks the spot where Columbus established the first Christian settlement in the New World, the now almost unrecognisable site of Isabella.

Finally we come in sight of the

hills of Puerto Plata (silver port), marked by the most prominent peak on the north coast, known as Pico (peak) Isabella, or, as it is sometimes called, the "saddle," from its peculiar shape. The storm clouds, though, are now rolling their vapoury masses from its peak nearly 3000 feet high, the effect being wonderfully grand and majestic.

Such is the perfect deliciousness of the weather at sea in this climate, that it seems almost a pity to reach the "promised land," were it not that it appears, as we draw near, almost to verify at this distance those lines of the "Emigrant Song," a place—

> "To rear new homes amid trees that glow
> As if gems were the fruitage of every bough:
> Round the white walls to train the vine,
> And sit in its shadow at the day's decline,
> And watch the flocks as they roam at will
> O'er the green savannas so broad and still."

But truly "all is not gold that glitters," as we find on closer acquaintance with this really wonderful domain and its peculiar inhabitants; for here it might truly be said that the aspect of nature is beautiful and grand, and, seen in all its magnificence of luxuriant tropical vegetation, that reaches to the very mountain peaks, is the place where apply those hymn lines so familiar to us all—

> "Where every prospect pleases, and only man is vile."

At five o'clock in the afternoon we are directly off the harbour of the town; and, without waiting to take a pilot, the staunch little steamer goes rapidly in through the narrow and somewhat shallow channel, the surf rolling gently on the sandbars and shoals that are on each side of the harbour, and we quickly come to anchor some distance from the shore.

The bay contained several German vessels, that had lain there for nearly eight months on account of the war between France and Germany. They came out for cargoes of tobacco, of which the Germans have an almost exclusive monopoly in the Island of St Domingo.

The harbour is one of the most picturesque in the island, though not by any means one of the best; for the shore shelves so gradually, that vessels have to anchor at some distance, and even small boats cannot land their passengers, who are compelled to mount upon the backs of the stalwart negro boatmen and be carried ashore—a ludicrous sight indeed.

Going ashore.

Vessels are loaded by large lighters, and these again from small ox-carts, which bring their loads from the shore through the shallow water, such a thing as a dock or wharf when we first arrived being unknown; but a temporary frame wharf was afterwards erected, but only for landing purposes.

Loading Cargo

The change from daylight to dark is very rapid in this climate, as there is no twilight, and darkness found us preparing to make our first visit to Dominican soil. It did not look very promising for a first attempt, as there is no lighting of town streets, and we were told they were filled with mud. Still we had one distinguished gentleman aboard, who, in his desire to taste tropical fruit, could not control his impatience until morning; and so a party of us, with pants tucked in our boots, go, *via* small boat and negro-back, to explore the town.

O shades of Cuba! O poetic dreams of fairy tropic lands! where now are all thy realisations? Or is this, our first introduction to Dominican scenes, a fair sample of what we may expect in all St Domingo? God forbid! for in the gloom of night we find mud and filth, narrow streets shrouded in darkness, swarthy faces, and very, very humble habitations.

The town of Puerto Plata, like the few towns still left in the Island of St Domingo, is a very old town indeed, as far as its location is concerned, for the buildings were utterly destroyed by the Spaniards when they evacuated the island in 1865. The town, however, has been rebuilt after a fashion, with moderate-sized houses of wood, and in the outskirts with small cabins made of strips of the palm and withes, and roofed with thatch. That it had at one time been a place of very great importance and solid structures, is evident from the ruins of many of the warehouses and buildings still standing, which are composed of stone and the material of the country known as "mamposteria," a sort of concrete.

As far back as 1499 the town is spoken of as a flourishing place, and it is even said that Columbus, in one of his later voyages, himself traced the plan of the town, which was afterwards, in 1502, constructed by the orders of Ovando the Governor, who, in order to connect it with the interior, built a fine road, upon which he expended large sums of money, being afterwards reproached therefor, as having committed a useless piece of extravagance. No actual vestige of this road remains.

In those days it was a lively place, being the port at which were embarked the products of the mines and the sugar from Santiago and La Vega—the Spanish merchantmen coming here in great numbers for cargoes. The port was originally discovered by Columbus in his first voyage,

TOWN AND BAY OF PUERTO PLATA.

and being overlooked by the high mountain already alluded to, the top of which appeared at sea so white to the Spaniards, they thought it covered with snow, as it glistened like snow or silver. Being undeceived as to the snow, they called the port, from this circumstance, Silver Port (Puerto de Plata).

In 1543 the place was attacked by privateers, which seemed to be the commencement of its decay; and in 1606 it was one of those ports mentioned in the history of the island as being destroyed by order of the Spanish Government, in order to stop the illicit traffic with other nations. It figures in history as the place where, in 1669, Delisle landed to commence his attack on Santiago; and in 1756 it was one of those towns that shared with Monte Cristo in the free commerce accorded to some of the ports. From that

Street in Puerto Plata.

time to the present it has suffered various successes and reverses. After 1822 it was a flourishing place, possessing handsome houses and stores, ruins of which are yet seen.

The streets were paved, and on the hills surrounding the town were a great many very well conducted coffee estates.

The region in which the town is located has always been noted as having abundance of gold and silver.

Puerto Plata is to-day, however, a very irregularly built town, most of the houses being constructed of wood, usually two stories in height, with balconies on the second floor; and the principal of these, as well as the storehouses, are placed in parallel streets that run directly down from the hills to the waters of the bay. These streets are narrow and badly paved, but the natural location of the town is a very advantageous one, affording ample space for the development of a large city.

The land rises gently up from the shore to some moderate hills beyond the town, and these again are backed by the mountains, the whole spot being fully open to the breezes from the northern sea, while it is also open to the free transmission of the land breezes, which cool the air during the hot hours of the day.

The Old Fort.

The town itself is prettily situated on the side of a high

mountain running gradually to the sea, the shore forming almost a crescent-shaped bay, to the right of which projects a small peninsula almost like an island, forming the most romantic feature in the town and harbour; for on it is the "fortress" (?), a series of dilapidated stone buildings and works built ages and ages ago for protection to the town Now they are dismantled, crumbling ruins, overgrown with moss and vines and grass, and form as pretty a study of ruins as any artist could desire. They still, however, profess to be the protection to the port; and to strengthen this idea, there are about twelve men and one musket, to say nothing of several rusty pieces of ordnance that cannot be fired, all left there as an established Dominican military (?) post.

The actual port of Puerto Plata, though not by any means the best in the island, is capable of being made into a very important harbour. The entrance is not very good, owing to the bars on each side, on which the sea always makes a heavy surf.

It faces exactly north, and a vessel must, in entering, keep very close to the point of the breakers, near the old fort, on the eastern side. The bottom has about three fathoms of water at entering, but shallows very quickly; and large deposits of mud, it is said, are brought down by the two rivers that empty into the bay; but there is anchorage in places seven fathoms deep.

This anchorage is usually good and safe, having once passed the reefs at the entrance, though the squalls from the north and north-west are occasionally felt.

During the rainy season the rivers above mentioned cause a strong outset; and at this period one of them (the St Mark), in the west part of the harbour, is open for boats, and is the best watering-place.

In winter the wind from the E.N.E. comes in about nine A.M., and continues until near sunset, when a moderate land wind comes off from the south-east; but the northers seldom blow strong into this port. The best loading season here begins when it is ended on the other side.

The port of Puerto Plata is the most active one on the Island of St Domingo; in fact, it constitutes, with the capital, the only places worthy of that name; and here is done the principal commerce of the island.

This is almost exclusively confined to the foreign merchants, the majority of whom are Germans, who have the entire monopoly of the tobacco trade of the region of the "Vega Real," which is almost the exclusive seat of its culture, having for the capital of the district the town of Santiago, the first in importance in the island.

This business of tobacco gives rise and life to the entire trade of the town of Puerto Plata. Without it there would be nothing for the storekeepers, as there is in this vicinity no agriculture other than the growing of a few fruits in a shiftless sort of way. There is also the shipping of mahogany and other woods, the loading of which, however, generally takes place at the mouths of various creeks and rivers, or in the bays along the coast.

The population of Puerto Plata is variously estimated at from two to three thousand inhabitants, mostly "people of colour," which may mean jet-black African, mulatto, or not pure white. This name, however, is never bestowed on a Dominican if possible, as they are very "touchy" on this subject, all being equally citizens.

It may be as well here to explain the meaning of the terms applied in the Spanish islands to the different colours of the people.

Creole is a descendant of Europeans settled in America.

Mulattoes, or the offspring of Europeans and negroes.

Mestizos, or the offspring of Europeans and Indians.

Negroes, the pure African.

Of this population, the whites and mulattoes are the storekeepers and tradesmen in the town, and the blacks and mestizos are the labourers about warehouses, ships, &c.

Here in Puerto Plata there are a large number of negroes from the English islands Nassau, St Thomas, Jamaica, &c., most of them speaking English quite well; in fact, a large number of the coloured people speak some little of two or three languages.

I was struck by the free, frank, and manly way in which these men look and speak, evidently showing they feel their importance as freemen—very different from the same class in Cuba.

The women earn their living principally by washing clothes; and, as a smart Nassau negro told me, did better and worked harder than the men. Those who came out from America appear particularly intelligent, retaining all the habits of neatness peculiar to our best coloured people. Some of them, in their towering high bandana head and gay coloured striped dresses, were models in this way. However, in conversation with many of these people, I learned they were all willing to work, and work steadily, if they got pay; many of them were perfectly willing to go upon the farms in the vicinity and perform agricultural labours, provided they were sure of pay; but there is no general agriculture, and those engaged in it are of limited means, and cannot afford to employ labourers.

Dominican American.

Plenty of labour can be had at from $1 to $3 per day,

according to length of time, and by the month all are willing to work for $10 and $12. I found a good many negroes from the United States, who came out in the great emigration scheme some forty years ago. They appear intelligent, industrious, and tolerably well-to-do.

The society of Puerto Plata is very limited indeed, being confined to a very few families, and these mostly foreigners; and their homes, with one or two exceptions, are one-storied frame-houses of three or four rooms.

The prevailing religion of the people is Roman Catholic, but there is a Methodist church established, and freedom of worship is supposed to exist; and, perhaps, does to a certain extent; but my experience in trying to leave the town made me aware that "church holidays" are strictly enforced, the stores being closed and all traffic ceasing, and I could not even hire a negro to carry my luggage until he had obtained permission of the authorities, the reason given being it was "dia de fiesta."

First impressions, it is said, are always best, but this was not my experience of Puerto Plata, for the place improved much on acquaintance, and I spent many days there pleasantly enough, though there was that which, at first sight, astonished and even disgusted me.

Bright and early in the morning, which is always the most charming part of the day in the tropics, our party sallied out sight-seeing. The weather was like a day in early June—crisp and fresh, and everything green and bright; and the town appeared to better advantage than on the previous night; but the streets, mostly unpaved, were filled with mud and filth. We first went to the "Plaza Mercado" or market-square, and a more ridiculous sight cannot be imagined; for here, in a space about one-fourth of an acre, was held the daily market. A few rude booths, made of thatch and poles, composed the butchers' stalls, in which were exposed fearful specimens of various meats. Around the square were seated groups of women and children, with cloths spread upon the ground, upon which were displayed the various fruits in limited quantities, herbs,

Market Square.

salad, eggs, six to eight in a lot, peas by the *cupful*, &c., &c.

This was our first opportunity of seeing the native Dominican chocolate, which is prepared by the country people, and sold in small flat cakes of a quarter or half pound each.

As thus prepared, it has not a very attractive appearance; for so rudely is it manufactured, that the broma or natural oil of the fruit gives the cakes a very greasy appearance and dark colour.

Most of that sold at Puerto Plata comes from the little village to which the fruit gives its name (Cacao), a short distance from the town on the river San Juan, many of these country people coming miles along the coast road with nothing else but this, in small quantities, and a few bananas, to sell.

Thence we strolled to the outskirts of the town, and so on to the small river from which the carriers get the water with which the towns-folk are supplied. A sudden turn in the road displayed to the astonished gaze of most of our party forty or fifty women of various ages, in various

Washing Clothes.

positions in the river, washing clothes. Some were entirely nude, some with only a waist-cloth, but all industriously washing away and chattering like parrots. Our stopping to look was the occasion of much merriment and chaffing, increased by the vigorous screams of a nude old beldame of "Vaya! vaya!" (go away), which we presently did.

Finding ourselves at a small "tienda mista" (notion store), with country garden attached, I engaged the proprietor in conversation, while he kindly took us through his place, knocked the wild, the sweet, and the bitter oranges from the trees for us; showed us the chayote, the mango, the caimito, bread-fruit, yuca, from which cassava bread is made; the banana in its various forms, under the general name of platano; the shaddock; the calabash, from which they make their bowls and cups; the various kinds of palm, including the cocoa, and many other fruits and plants, all growing almost without culture in a little place of an acre or two; and, to use his expression, "It is their nature—they grow themselves."

Amidst mud and mire, in front of this place, stretched the "Camino Real" (royal road, in name only), that runs into the interior to the large town of Santiago in La Vega, one day's journey from Puerto Plata. Upon this road that day, I think, there must have passed at least two hundred mules and horses, each carrying two bales or ceroons of tobacco, of about one hundred and twenty-five pounds each; and as this was the beginning of the tobacco harvest, we were told it was a daily occurrence.

The Dominican tobacco cannot be said to be first-rate, any of it; much of it is very inferior, and all of it is "flojo" (weak), as they say here. But this arises not from any lack of merit in the soil to grow it, but simply from want of attention and knowledge on the part of the cultivators, very different from their Cuban brethren, who spend whole nights watching their plants for the worm, or carefully trimming the plant at the proper time, and by other cares and precautions bringing it to perfection.

The work-horses here are many of them as small as the mule, while none are larger than the ordinary-sized mule with us. Some of those that bring down the tobacco are not larger than a small pony, yet are well proportioned and clean limbed, and withal very wiry and tough, which they need to be from the cruel treatment they receive, many of them being completely used-up in their journeys.

A sad lot they are, as one sees them, sore-backed and covered with mud, resting before the warehouses. The price for a good horse is usually about $40 ; but I was amused, in addressing several horsemen the question, "Horse for sale?" to hear them say invariably, "Yes, señor—$100."

Horse.

The water of the little stream that supplies the town is like that of all the rivers of St Domingo, clear and cold, and very pleasant to the taste; but although it is limestone water, it is considered to be very wholesome.

This is brought into the town by water-carriers, who, each possessed of a small donkey, swing a large cask on each side of the animal, and then, mounting on the back, belabour the poor brute into town, thus carrying the water from door to door.

Water-carrier.

Puerto Plata is considered a very healthy place, as, in fact, the whole island seems to be; the only thing they suffer from being the bilious and intermittent fevers which sometimes prevail, and of which we have so much in the

United States. If it is not healthy the people there should not complain, considering the way they live and the condition in which they keep their roads, streets, and dwellings; but they uniformly pronounce it perfectly healthy, even in the rainy season, which, on this side of the island, occurs in about the months of December, January, and February; though this year, it is said, more rain has fallen than for the past five years.

I find that all the coloured people that came from the United States like this climate, and would not care to go back, except temporarily to see "home." The people are all taking an interest in the United States, and many are trying already to learn English, for which purpose a night-school has been established in Puerto Plata, which is well attended.

Having finished up pretty well sight-seeing in the town and vicinity, we adjourned at twelve o'clock precisely to the French hotel for breakfast, this being the regular hour for that meal, the habits of the people being adapted to the nature of the climate. They rise early, five or six o'clock, have a cup of chocolate or coffee and a roll and some fruit, and then go about their affairs until twelve o'clock, the breakfast hour, followed by the siesta until two; then business again from two till four; after which, at six o'clock, is the dinner. It is the custom for those who have horses, at this hour of the day, to take their "paseo" on horseback, the evening hours being usually delightfully fresh for such exercise on their easy-going horses. I noticed that in many of the habitations the hammock is used in lieu of bed, being made either of grass or canvas. The nearest approach to a bed, except in the better class of houses, is an ordinary cot with pillow and sheet.

The traveller having no acquaintances in the town fares rather badly for hotel accommodations, for there are only two establishments that have the slightest claim to the name. One of these, kept by a German, Emil, has only two or three rooms; and the other, kept by a Frenchman, about the same; the table is, however, very fair.

We had here our first insight into the motives that have induced these people to express a desire for annexation to the United States; for a party of us called to pay our respects to the Government officer of this district, known as the Administrator of Public Property, who has a very charming residence on the borders of the sea, and who received us with the utmost courtesy. Though he spoke no English, he was very ready to converse in Spanish. As Minister of Public Property, he informed me that the principal domain of the Government was in the ports, bays, and sea-coast towns of the island; that in the interior there was no certainty as to the quantity of Government lands, as they were mostly held in private right, but that in each sea-port town there were valuable tracts belonging to the Government; that none of this property would be sold at any price pending the question of annexation, for since it was first broached, two years ago, an order had been issued to that effect; nevertheless, the Government was perfectly willing to lease any of its property for two, three, or five years, or even, in an extreme case, where a *bona fide* purchaser desired to make a home for himself, the "Ayuntamiento" (town council) was authorised to give a deed of such site.

It seemed strange to us, coming from a populous country, where land in any desirable place commands such a high price, to find here that town lots are and can be bought for two or three hundred dollars; that within a mile of the western gate of the principal city 150 acres of desirable land has been sold for $600. Upon this land cocoa-nuts enough can be raised in two years to more than triple pay for the place. But this is the result of the terrible mill in which the island has been ground up, until nothing is left but ruined walls and magnificent earth that is valueless, unless the country can be repopulated with labourers.

The official spoke to me feelingly concerning the motives with which the Dominican authorities were influenced in their desire for annexation, telling me, to use his own words, "I am a Dominican, senor, and I am rich enough to go and live in any part of the world; but then I would have no country. I have no interest at stake except the welfare of my beloved country. Naturally the property that I own here will become more valuable if the island goes to the United States; but why should I be blamed for that? I do not desire office; all I want is to be sure that my property will be handed down to my children with certainty; but under the present state of things there is none. We have no money; we have not enough people in the island to make it prosperous; we are liable to attack from Hayti at any moment they may have a revolution there; and, therefore, for our own safety we want annexation."

We went through the town to examine more closely the stocks of merchandise in the stores, which we found were mostly supplied with goods from St Thomas, which, being a free port, is enabled to undersell all other points in this region. I found, however, that a good many domestic dry goods could be used here to advantage. Straw hats, boots and shoes, hardware, agricultural implements, ice, and many other things, could be shipped here to advantage from English and American markets, if the island should become properly settled and governed.

Leaving Puerto Plata, and going on board the steamer, we found quite a number of passengers, who were taking the opportunity of going to Samana and St Domingo city, some of them quite black, but all equal in cabin or at table. It was a beautiful bright afternoon as we took our departure; and as we ran close along the coast, with the fresh trade winds blowing, it was most enjoyable. The whole coast resolves itself into a constantly changing panorama of noble hills, beautiful savanas, bold headlands, charming curvatures of coast, with its belt of sand and surf separating the rich green verdure from the pure ultramarine of the sea.

Shoals of flying-fish, like myriad bits of pearl, leap and glisten from water into sun, their peaceful sports sadly interrupted by the voracious dolphin, which, with its graceful form in glistening, varied colours, jumps, in its eagerness, high out of water.

No habitations are seen in the entire extent of coast, and only one small harbour, in which lies a vessel loading with mahogany logs from the adjacent hills; and yet this is classic ground, for here were the abodes of over a million of the native Indians; and here too, over these waters, sailed the grand Colon when on his way back to carry to the old world the fresh glad tidings of the new.

Almost all the coast is lined with mangrove-trees, which are usually considered an indication of marshy soil. Some of these trees are so large their trunks would make a good sized rafter; the bark is most useful for tanning purposes, but the branches are the home of myriads of mosquitoes, the roots being inhabited by the crab and the oyster. An eminent physician travelling on board the steamer, a gentleman familiar with every part of the globe, informed me that he found from experience, that wherever this tree grew there was always a certain amount of malaria and its adjunct fever prevailing. This he accounted for from the fact that the mangrove, flourishing in low places at the water side, has, if I may so describe it, its roots growing in the form of an inverted cage, into which the refuse vegetable, dead fish, and other matter is carried by the current and permanently lodged; and this forming a mass of decomposed material, an effluvia is produced creating disease and pestilence. The removal of this tree from localities has always been accompanied by an improved sanitary condition of the vicinity.

There is usually along the whole of this coast a line of surf, but at low water some of the bars are left bare, and on these are found lobsters of extremely large size; basins in the rocks are filled with shell and other fish, while coral and sea-plants are also to be had.

In such places the voracious shark makes its home, and, at more rare intervals, the manati or sea-cow—before

The Manati

alluded to as the siren of Columbus—is found. In "Ogilvy's Voyages" I find a curious account of these animals when they were more plentiful than they are now. He describes it as breeding in the sea, but also as ascending rivers, where, going ashore, it eats grass. One of the caciques kept in a lake one of these strange creatures (Guayando), which was so tame, that when called by its name, Matoom, it would come out of the water and go directly to the cacique's house, where, being fed, it returned to the lake accompanied by men and boys who seemed to charm the manati by their singing, and it often carried two children at a time on its back; being once, however, struck by a pike in the hands of a Spaniard, it would never after come out of the water if there was a *clothed* man near. This particular animal, it is stated, lived twenty-six years in that lake.

Those who nave seen the Frenchman and his pet seals at the London Zoological Gardens, will be prepared to credit this rather fabulous account.

After leaving Puerto Plata the coast line tends in a south-easterly direction to the prominent point Old Cape (Francis), a name given to it by Columbus, just around which is the first settlement of any importance along the coast, the little village of Tres Amaras.

The country for the first twenty miles after leaving Puerto Plata by land, to the little bay of La Goleta, is quite level and singularly adapted to agriculture, there

Cabo Viejo (Old Cape).

being many extremely well ordered and organised plantations, the residences of some American and German settlers, who only await the settlement of the affairs of the country to enter regularly into the production of the fruits and plants for which the island is famous.

Beyond Cabo Viego (Old Cape), almost to the peninsula of Samana, there is hardly a little village of any importance; and though the road, if such it can be called, generally traverses the coast line, with innumerable creeks and lagoons to cross, the country for some distance inwards is quite hilly, and often rocky. At the Bay of Matanzas there is a small village of a few houses, where is stationed a small guard of Dominican soldiers from the interior town of Macoris; but the road to it is so little used, it has become almost obliterated, and the free use of the machete is necessary to open a way. Beyond Matanzas, to the west, the country is almost entirely primeval forest; but the land is low and level, and capable, if cleared, of making a fine agricultural country.

Clearing Old Cape, the steamer makes a direct line almost to Cape Cabron or Lover's Cape, the extreme north-eastern part of the island, the coast line forming between these two points a large bight or bay, on the eastern side of which begins what is called the peninsula of Samana, but which, in fact, may be deemed an island; for though now the channel of the Gran Estero is almost filled up, yet the authorities of the past speak of this passage as being open, though in the time of the early French the peninsula was known as "Presque Isle," while some early maps have it distinctly marked as an island.

Along the whole of this north coast of Samana stretch the coral reefs that form the little groups of islands known as Los Ballaenas, Los Canas, &c., while the shore itself curves to the very edge of the sea in abrupt hills.

Towering above these, at the very extreme point of Cape Cabron, is the landmark of the mariner, the celebrated

"Pilon d'Azuc" (sugar pan), which raises its verdure-clad peak nearly two thousand feet above the sea.

Port Jackson, in this natural bight, is the only bay of any importance, and to which the natives at certain seasons resort for turtle. Its waters are smooth, and protected from the sea by a coral reef that stretches almost entirely across its mouth.

Thus the whole of this coast presents to-day to our eyes undoubtedly the same appearance it did when Columbus, with his heart full of the grandness of his discovery, and looking forward with anxious hope to the moment when he should make it known to his beloved Queen Isabella, directed along this beautiful shore the prow of his little bark in the direction of the coast of Castile.

Sailing over the same waters, amid these same scenes, it requires little stretch of imagination to picture at this vesper hour the tenor and the earnestness of the evening prayers of so devout a man; for—

> "'Twas the hour of day
> When setting suns o'er summer seas display
> A path of glory opening in the west
> To golden climes and islands of the blest,
> And human voices on the silent air
> Went o'er the waves in songs of gladness there."

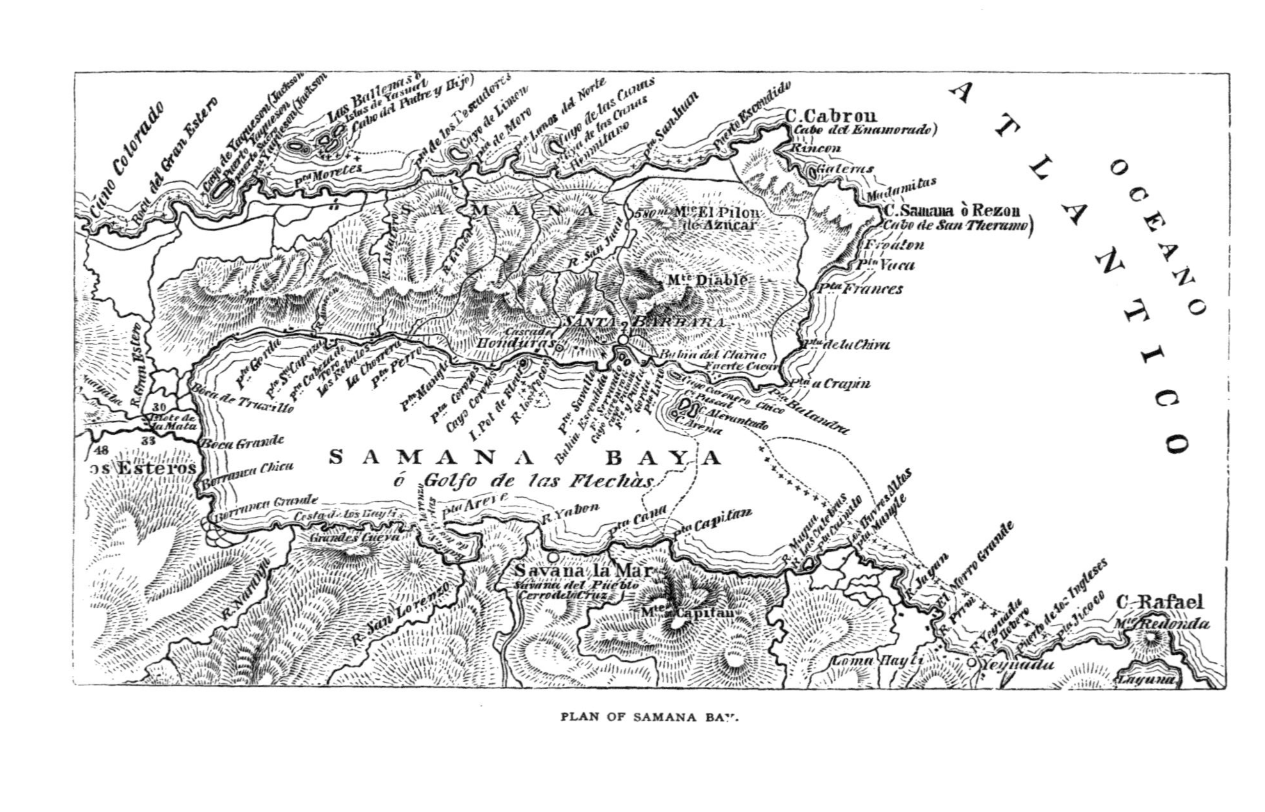

PLAN OF SAMANA BAY.

CHAPTER XI.

"Long on the wave the morning mists reposed,
Then broke, and melting into light, disclosed
Half-circling hills, whose everlasting woods
Sweep with their sable skirts the shadowy floods.'

SAMANA AND THE SOUTH COAST—*Cape Samana—Balandra Head —The Bay of Samana—Santa Barbara—General Account of Samana Bay—The Caves of San Lorenzo—Savanna la Mar —Voyage round the South Coast.*

DAY had hardly broken when, turning out on deck, I found we were just rounding Cape Samana, a bold high headland with apparently a terraced front, an appearance produced by its being a double cliff, the upper of which rises a short distance within the summit of the lower. The face of these cliffs appears steep and gloomy at this early morning hour, but an occasional gleam of light shows their general colour to be red, the levels of the terrace being covered with vegetation.

Although this point is considered as the beginning of the bay shore, with its other or southern point at Cape Rafael, a glance at the map will show that Samana Bay proper begins at the south-eastern point of the peninsula of Samana known as Balandra Head, of which, as day fairly opened, we caught our first sight, as also of this noble bay.

Balandra Head is a remarkable red cliff lying at the foot of Mount Diablo, which, about one and a half miles back, rises 1300 feet high. Between the base of Balandra Head, its continuous line of hills, and the shore, lies a most attractive sloping levee covered with vegetation, and which would be most charming sites for coffee or sugar estates, to say nothing of their beauty and value as places of marine residence for the inhabitants of the future immense city of Samana. But from this point we caught our first sight of the far-famed bay whose name is now so familiar in the United States. Worthy indeed of all that has been said about its size and beauty, it broke upon me as the most superb harbour I had ever seen, and before which even those large and lovely bays of the "Ever Faithful Isle" (Cuba) must pale.

Cape Samana.

Such is the extent of this noble bay, that no picture, however large, could do justice to its appearance; but a glance at the accompanying map will give my readers an idea of the form of this superb sheet of water, the coveted prize of many Governments. In imagination clothe the sides of this bay with bold high hills, varying from 200 to 2000 feet high, from which slope gently to the sea charming valleys covered with trees and vegetation; indent the shore with coves, or here and there small harbours, whose white sandy shores glisten in the tropic sun, and you have some idea of this beautiful bay that Columbus himself has named the "Bay of Arrows," being the place, it is said, where the blood of the children of the New World was first

A TROPICAL MORNING.

drawn by those from the Old. Here resided the subjects of the cacique Cayacoa, whose widow was afterwards baptized in the Catholic faith as Doña Inez Cayacoa.

Balandra Head.

As we enter more fully the bay, we come to a point from which the channel resolves itself into a rather narrow space, with the land close at hand on one side, but shoals on the other that forbid all attempts at entrance there ; and this is the point selected for the site of the old Spanish fort still to be seen.

Having cleared this passage or narrows, the channel widens into a noble bay called the Bay of Clara, and from here, in a north-westerly direction, the steamer heads for the now famous town of Samana, which is situated in a bight or bay indented in the coast, the little island of Careñero lying at its mouth, while other small but most romantic-looking islands are scattered at intervals within it. Looking out into the great bay between two or three of these, with their rich foliage, and the graceful forms of the cocoa and palm reflected in dark shadows in the water,

16

which the glowing glory of a rising sun serves to illuminate, the traveller from the north cannot help being impressed by the richness of the tropical climate, and he begins to appreciate the strong attachment these children of the sun have for their homes amid such scenes.

Samana Bay proper, known also as Port Santa Barbara, may be more properly described as an inlet running one and a third miles east and west, and is one quarter to one half a mile wide. The north shore is formed of irregular hills which rise a short distance from it to a considerable elevation; the head of the bay is low and swampy, the south side being sheltered by a reef and several keys.

The town of Santa Barbara is at the west end of the bay at the base, and on the side of some hills, which are hidden almost from the east by a bold headland, on the summit of which is a small Dominican fort in a rather dilapidated condition. The anchorage off the little town is so good, that it is said a vessel may run its bowsprit ashore anywhere in the harbour; but there is a diversity of

Santa Barbara.

opinion as regards its healthfulness. The town itself is a mere congregation of one-storied houses, some frame, but most of them huts constructed of the palm-leaf, in which the natives swing their hammocks in lieu of beds. There appears no commerce, and really no business, if I except the selling of the few fruits the country produces, the bananas and oranges being particularly fine.

I had here an illustration of the facility with which "a dog is given a bad name," for my companion, having gone ashore to purchase some bananas, selected the very largest he saw. Not speaking Spanish, and the dusky saleswoman not understanding English, a lively time they had together in their trading, much to my amusement while reclining in the boat. On my asking the cause of the extremely demonstrative proceedings, he explained to me in high glee that the woman wished to take advantage of him, by making him take the smaller bananas in place of the large green ones he had selected.

Great was his disgust and chagrin at finding that he had obstinately refused to be honestly dealt with, since the fruit he had bought was only good for *cooking*, while the smaller ones were the choicest kind for eating.

The population is not over 800 or 1000 souls, the majority of whom are blacks, either emigrants themselves, or descendants of those who came from the United States in Boyer's time.

The present site of Samana city is by no means the best for a port, as there are many farther along the coast more desirable, but particularly the place mentioned in old writers as Point Martiniquois or Coroso, about ten miles farther west, where it is said the knowing ones expect to locate the famous city of the future.

Here there is a fine situation, healthy air, plenty of stone and wood, and abundance of pure water; but the whole of the south coast of the peninsula forming the north side of the bay is desirable, having a fine level beach, and gently rolling hills capable of the highest cultivation.

At the bottom of the bay, where the river Yuna enters

by its various mouths through an extensive marsh, there is no desirable shore, and a bar of mud as yet renders navigation up that river impracticable, except to small boats drawing not over two feet of water.

The mouth of this river being cleaned out, will afford a navigable means of access to the great valley of the Vega Real. The right to control this navigation, as well as to build a railroad and telegraph lines from the city of Santiago, has been conceded to a private company on most liberal terms; grants of alternate square leagues of land on each side of the road, not private property, have been given, and permission to use the stone and timber on Government land, without payment, in the construction of the road and its repair, while all material needed on the road imported into the island is exempt from duty.

From the Gran Estero, or salt marshes, at the mouth of the Yuna, along the south side of the bay, the shore is generally rough and irregular, and in many places inaccessible by land and sea, composed as it is of sterile rock; while islets of the same are scattered at intervals along the coast, among which are found innumerable beds of oysters.

At the end of this string of islands is the famous Bay of Pearls, facing to the west, and bounded on the north by a tongue of land; it has good anchorage for vessels of the largest size.

On the shores of this bay are the noted caves of San Lorenzo, which, if time permits, are well worth a visit by the traveller. They are similar in their formation, and are of the same character, as those of Bel la Mar near Matanzas, Cuba.

A narrow aperture opens into a series of large and wonderfully formed chambers, the roofs of which, as well as the walls, are composed of superb stalactites, which reflect every colour of light, while the floors of white sand give a charming air of purity to the scene.

Savanna la Mar, a little farther east, is a small settlement of about a hundred houses, originally peopled by persons from the Canaries, at the same time as its opposite neighbour Samana. It is quite a small place, with a scattered population of about 300 souls. In order to get ashore, the same process is necessary as at Puerto Plata, by boat and negro-back, or wading.

This village is, however, situated at the end of a plain of great extent, being more than thirty miles long from east to west, and extending some twelve miles to the south, where the southern range of hills separates it from the great plains of Seybo. All the land of this plain is capable of extended agriculture, though now devoted principally to grazing purposes, for which it is well adapted, being well supplied with water from some nine streams. This is, in fact, the only extent of land on this side of, and adjacent to, the Bay of Samana capable of culture.

The country round Samana is comparatively unsettled. One sees here and there the huts of the natives, who are engaged principally in "killing time," varied by a slight stroke of manual labour in the small gardens or farms, upon which grows most everything of its own accord that can grow in a tropical country.

The women, with precious little apparel on themselves, occupy their time gaining a livelihood washing for others; but as household expenses are light with them, owing to the fact that the principal sustenance is the plantain, roasted or boiled, and the clothing and schooling of the children costs nothing, since they have neither, they (the people) do not need to earn a great deal, and therefore do not make the effort. One meets them on the borders of the shore with huge baskets on their heads filled with clothes, the only garment worn by them being a loose semi-gown, whilst following are members of the rising generation in a happy state of nature.

The familiar donkey, while in every part of the world a subject of ridicule and amusement, yet seems always to be made a useful servant, no matter how small and odd looking; and here among the Dominicans he is met with, rough, ill-treated, and small, and yet with an immense pack-saddle, constructed in the rudest manner, of straw or palm-leaf, placed upon his back, performing most of the carrying trade that is done.

Donkey.

On the mainland we found the establishment of a New Englander, a young man who had come out from Maine, and established himself in the culture of the banana fruit and growing of cocoa-nuts. With a small capital of some $2500 he has been enabled to establish himself, and feels so much charmed and encouraged by the climate and life there, that under no consideration will he leave unless annexation fails. He plants his bananas just as apples are planted in the North, in regular rows, and the fruit is so much improved by culture, that already his bananas have a reputation in the market. His wife, also from New England, is out here with him, and pronounces the climate the most lovely in the world, and that had she only society, she could desire no pleasanter place in which to live.

Samana Bay, the most superb harbour in the West Indies, in the time of the early Spaniards does not appear to have interested the Spanish authorities as to its great importance, though the early chroniclers refer to it always in terms of high praise as a place where a shipping port for an agricultural people might be established.

They were, however, at that time interested in the smaller ports of St Domingo and Puerto Plata, as places more convenient for the shipment of the ores from the mines, which at that time was the great interest of the island; besides, in those days, when steam was unknown, Samana, from a peculiarity of some of the winds that prevail in the bay, was not a desirable port for the ill-constructed, unwieldy sailing vessels of the time.

The old writers generally agree as to the Bay of Samana being about sixty miles long, but they calculate the bay as beginning at the extreme point of the peninsula at Cape Samana. Modern writers, however, making their calculations based upon various surveys, agree that, starting from Balandra Head to the mouth of the Yuna, the length is about twenty-five to thirty miles; the width between Cape Samana and the southern point, Cape Rafael, being about twenty-one miles; the average width of the bay proper, however, is only about thirteen miles.

The actual entrance to this superb bay is, however, quite narrow, for there extends from the southern cape to a clump of rocks or islands, known by the various names of Rebels, Banister, and Levantados, a line of shoals or breakers. By this means two channels are created, the southern one of which is known as Half-moon Passage (Media Luna), but this is only available for small vessels.

The northern passage will admit vessels of the largest size, and is capable of being easily defended, as from the islands or rocks of the Levantados to the shore of the mainland the distance is little more than a mile.

In olden times great difficulty was experienced in entering this bay, and some very serious wrecks have occurred; but now the bay is so well-known that no danger is experienced in making this harbour.

Banister Islands received their names from an Englishman turned pirate, whose vessel was attacked by two English frigates in 1690; but carrying his guns and crew ashore, Banister compelled them to retreat in a damaged state, though his own vessel was sunk.

Attention was first called to this bay by the freebooters, who, extending along the north coast of the island, and finally overrunning the peninsula of Samana, established in this bay their place of rendezvous.

As the French gradually acquired a permanent hold as successors to the buccaneers on Tortuga and the west end, the Spanish authorities became alarmed and made efforts to hold it; and finally, in 1756, a number of inhabitants were brought over from the Canaries, and they were given plantations and live stock with which to begin a settlement. This effort was so badly sustained, that the place languished until, in the revolution of St Domingo, a number of French refugees sought safety here, and established themselves, creating some sugar estates.

On the uniting of the whole island under Boyer, these people left, and the coloured population from the United States came.

The French always laid much value on the possession of this part, and England was at one time extremely anxious to secure it, being, as it undoubtedly is, the key to the southern passage of the Gulf of Mexico.

It will be seen that, difficult as is the entrance to this famed bay, it is yet sometimes more difficult to leave it without the aid of steam; for sailing vessels cannot make their way out, unless with the land-breeze blowing, and often the sea-breeze blows so steadily that it is impossible to get out for a long time. Should, however, a great harbour be established here, this objection could be easily overcome by the use of steam-tugs.

Every authority, as well as practical investigation, serves to confirm the belief that Samana Bay and its surroundings is a spot particularly adapted by nature to be a grand arsenal or navy-yard for the power that owns it.

The peninsula, though not very extensive, will afford

occupation and nourishment to a large body of agriculturists in the raising of fruits and vegetables, and in the culture of the coffee, cocoa, and cocoa-trees, to which the hills are well adapted. Sugar-cane can be produced upon the plains, while the timber is abundant for the purposes of commerce and shipbuilding.

The great valley of the Vega Real, drained by the Yuna, with a current of four miles an hour, will pour into its lap an inexhaustible supply of agricultural products and precious woods; and wherever and whenever that spot may be selected for a city on this noble bay, under a sound Government it is destined in the future to be the great commercial port of this part of the world, rivalling even Havana or Vera Cruz.

Although there are reports of abundance of coal on the peninsula, investigation does not verify them, for the specimens that have as yet been discovered are simply the common lignite, of comparatively little value. The captain of the *Tyler* informed me he had tried it in his furnaces to no purpose.

The experience of residents and the records of authorities prove that, in a general sense, this district is very healthy, and free, ordinarily, from epidemics. On the low lands, or where the mangrove-trees prevail, there is always more or less of the "calentura," or slow fever of the country, which, perhaps, under certain circumstances, may terminate in bilious typhoid, or even yellow fever; ordinarily it is, however, a trifling affair, soon conquered with a little attention.

Samana is esteemed both a hot and wet place, there being the usual rainy season, with frequent showers in the dry season, while the thermometer ranges at midday as high as 90° in the shade, though at night and early in the morning throughout the year it descends as low as 70°. This temperature is, however, always rendered more bearable by the constant breezes that prevail.

It is curious to read, in the works of the writers of

different nationalities, the harmony that exists in their sentiments as regards the importance and character of Samana Bay ; but especially is this true of the French. A writer in 1861, at the time of the proposed taking possession of the island by Old Spain, writes: "We are particularly interested in maintaining the liberty and security of Hayti. This country yet owes us fifty millions of francs, that the invasion of Spain will jeopardise. Our interests are greater in the St Dominican question. The Haytians regard France as a second mother; the men of colour who preside over their destiny *belong to our country by their fathers, as they belong to Africa by their mothers.* The advantages, strategetical and commercial, of Samana Bay, have solicited for a long time the regards of maritime nations. This basin, so magnificent, where one can enter only by a channel of a mile wide, would be able to contain all the fleets of the world."

Estaing, in 1764, undertook to found there a great establishment. Louis Philippe even, in accord with the recommendation of various French naval officers, had the intention in 1846 to establish a great arsenal there, but this was frustrated by the English alliance. St Remy, in speaking of it, says: "Samana Bay is one of those maritime positions that is encountered but in two or three places in the world. It is not only the military key, but the commercial key to this part of the world."

On our arrival at Samana Bay we found that the visit of the United States Commission had created great excitement among the people, the members of which had pursued their investigations in every direction, and then left for St Domingo city.

Following their example, we steamed out of Samana Bay, and it was not long before we passed Montaña Redonda (round mountain), that marks the southern point (Cape Rafael) of the bay, being prominent from its strong resemblance to a sugar-loaf.

SOUTH COAST—LOS LLANOS.

From here to Punta Espada (Sword Point), the shore presents the aspect of a series of declivities covered with verdure, but apparently (as in fact they are) uninhabited.

Cape Engaño marks the most eastern point of the island, and we are now in what is known as the Mona Passage, the name given to the channel which divides St Domingo from Puerto Rico. In the middle of this passage are two small islands known by the names of Mona and Monita (Monkey and Cub).

Mona, the larger of the two, is about seven miles long and two wide, and was given to Diego Columbus by the Spanish rulers in 1512; and at one time is said to have been fully under cultivation, but now it is uninhabited.

The course of the steamer being now entirely changed, she heads almost due west, and we pass the Island of Saona, once famous in the annals of the Jesuits as a place where they held exclusive control over fertile fields. It is as large as the Dutch Island of Curaçoa, and said to be infinitely more fertile, though now desolate and unproductive.

Spread out before us we have a splendid view of the entire coast line of this southern shore, beyond which, stretching far away to the interior of the island, where they are met by the misty hills and mountains, lie those wondrous prairies or plains of which we have heard so much by their names of "Los Llanos" or savanas.

These occupy the whole extent of the south-eastern part, beginning at the Ozama on the west, and terminating at the eastern end of the island.

Far as the eye can reach stretch these vast plains, covered with long grass, with here and there clumps of trees, an occasional house or hut only to be seen; while in the far distance is the continuation of the Cibao range of hills, which divides these plains in two.

This is the country spoken so enthusiastically of by St Mery as being so well adapted to sugar estates; and they remind me, by their extent and character, of the vast sugar plains of Cuba, which teem with luscious wealth. These are now occupied but by the roving herds of cattle and their attendant "hateros" or herdsmen.

In all this district there are but two villages of any importance—the one, Higuey, being at the eastern end of the island, on the river Yuna, which empties into the Bay of Higuey.

This town is renowned because of the "Virgin of Alta Gracia," to which superstition attributes astounding miracles. It was founded as far back as 1502, by John of Esquivel, and has always been a place of importance in this part of the island, though to-day, like all Dominican towns, it is a straggling, irregularly built place.

The other town, Seybo, is situated at the foot of the mountains, nearer to the north and centre, upon the right bank of the river of the same name. It is not, however, the original town as founded by the Spaniards, but was settled a century ago by the farmers of the vicinity, who met there to hear mass.

From the left bank of the Ozama to Cape Engaño stretch these vast plains, comprising an extent of country near sixty leagues in length, containing 700 square leagues of land, of which more than 600 are in plains, comprising a body of the finest agricultural land in the world, and being watered by many rivers of various sizes. The products of this section are shipped at the romantic port of Romana on the coast, which is capable of being made into a good harbour for the extended agricultural products of this part.

All the inhabitants are a fine class of people, free and independent, though of different shades of colour; the majority being the native brown or creole white. I shall not forget the impression made upon me by the sight of some 600 of these people, who, hearing the United States Commissioners were at St Domingo city, gathered together from every direction, and marching up from their homes many weary miles, gathered in the great arsenal square,

Meeting in Arsenal Square.

with the flags of the United States and Dominica unfurled at their head.

After they had rested from their long and hot march, they were drawn up in a hollow square by the colonel who had charge of them, and a priest (their padre, as they called him), who seemed to have great influence and weight with them, made them a stirring address, amid much enthusiasm, in which he said that they would now, perhaps, have an opportunity of joining a great nation, in which the people were identified with the cause of progress, of intelligence, and of industry; it remained for themselves to say what they would be when that time came, as, if they were possessed of the above qualities of the people of that great nation, they would be equal to any one there. All were equal; there was no distinction of colour, no slavery, no tyranny; nothing but freedom and protection from a strong Government, which would bring peace and order into their beautiful island, and, with their consent, protection to industry and security for property.

For himself, he said, though he had been a Spaniard, Puerto Rican, Dominican, and always their padre (here the entire multitude with much respect uncovered), he yet hoped to call himself an American.

Three cheers were then given for the Dominican banner, and then three more for the American, which were given with a will, when the men broke ranks and took to the shady side of the wall for rest.

I seized hold of the colonel, who was a weather-beaten, swarthy-looking man of medium height, with grizzly moustache, who told me he was about fifty-six years of age, and that he had served in the army forty-six years of that time in various grades; that Baez was his chief, to whom he was devoted, and he would go just where the President told him. If he (Baez) was for annexation, so was he, and he knew it would be a good thing for Dominica, else Baez wouldn't propose it. This was the most refreshing and frank explanation of views I had met with from any one.

Alas! for those earnest people; they know little of "politics" as understood in the United States.

I wandered among these men, asking them questions about their habits, hopes, and experiences; and from all I heard but one sentiment—discontent at the present condition of affairs in the island, and hope for the future, that a connection with the United States would give them peace and security.

Most of the people seemed to be poor and badly dressed, but none lacked energy, and all expressed a desire for profitable work, some even asking if the prospect of a railroad through their country would not afford means of gaining money.

Although many of these men had marched that day

some eighteen or twenty miles through mud and under a hot sun, they contented themselves with a frugal repast of a roasted plantain or bit of jerked beef, their beverage being the water carried in the water-bottles by their sides, many of them with their pet gamecocks carried on their shoulder or under their arm.

Physically, these men are as fine a lot as I have ever seen, and while lacking even the elements of education, they are by no means deficient in natural intelligence.

On this plain, which we have been describing, the cattle of hundreds of owners pasture in herds, being annually collected, counted, and the young branded.

In the dry season it is customary to burn all the grass, the cattle taking to the timber, which is scattered at intervals in groups that look as if they had been planted by the hand of man, resembling great parks; near them are springs of water or streams, in whose vicinity grow various shrubs, upon which the cattle browse. In these groves the weary traveller is glad to hang his hammock and recuperate himself from the effects of the mid-day heat.

A Weary Traveller.

CHAPTER XII.

"A holy gathering, peaceful all;
No threat of war, no savage call
For vengeance on an erring brother."

ST DOMINGO CITY—*The United States Commission—First Impression of the City—Visit to Baez and his Cabinet—Historical Notes of the City—Its Present Condition and Appearance—Trade and Future Prospects—Schools—The Mausoleum of Columbus—Dominican Amusements—San Carlos and the Exterior of the City—The Harbour as a Port—Well of Columbus—Mahogany Trade—Labourers.*

IT was the early morning of one of those perfect days with which one only meets in the tropics that we came in sight of the famous old city of St Domingo. It does not make much of an appearance as regards size and grandeur when viewed from the sea south of it; yet, seen this beautiful day, with its gaudy-coloured roofs and ruined age-stained and picturesque towers, it presents a quaint and attractive sight, though a very different one from the splendid approach to her younger and richer sister—Havana.

A queer old place it is, and as we come up to its harbour, formed by the mouth of the river Ozama emptying into the sea, we cannot help imagining ourselves back ages ago. As we look at the ancient walls and turrets that tower high above our heads in passing through the narrow channel to the harbour, we almost fancy we can see the Spanish adventurer of the fifteenth century bringing his arquebus to "ready," as, dressed in the quaint costume of that time, he stands prepared to challenge us with his "Quien viva?" (who comes there). And, indeed, it requires no great stretch

SANTO DOMINGO CITY.

of imagination to picture thus such scenes, for here is seen no hand of progress on these old hills, which Nature has changed more than man. Would that we might truly answer to the challenge of the sentry—Here comes the spirit of American institutions, to bring peace and good-will, progress, enlightenment, and improvement to this beautiful but impoverished, depopulated, and hard-used land.

Here we found the members of the United States Commission busy in seeking that information they were sent out to obtain; and never was a nation more earnestly and honestly served than by this body of experienced gentlemen, who, without hope of reward or profit, and at much inconvenience to themselves, earnestly and conscientiously availed themselves of every means and opportunity to seek the truth about the affairs of the island.

In these efforts they were immensely assisted by the energy and intelligence of the correspondents of some of the most prominent newspapers of the United States.

First impressions of such a place as St Domingo city can-

The Ozama—Ruins of Columbus' House.

not fail to be novel and strange. From the time of landing

at the quay, entirely deserted of shipping, to the moment when, having secured quarters in the spacious saloons of a Government palace, the traveller has a chance to collect his thoughts, every moment brings a new, interesting, or funny sight.

Gaily-coloured walls, with dirty negroes sunning themselves against them; narrow streets, with solid-built houses, whose immense doors and spacious windows contrast forcibly with their limited height of only one or two stories; broad-brimmed-hatted horsemen on small, compact, quick-moving horses, contrast with the dusky urchin who, naked of everything but a shirt, bestrides an immense straw-saddle on the back of a very diminutive donkey,—all serve, with hundreds of other noticeable things, to strike the stranger, and impress upon him the fact that he has exchanged his Saxon associations of order, cleanliness, and precision, for the peculiarities of Spanish tropical life.

Knots of men and women, mostly coloured, and busy in talk, are scattered about the quay or in the small open places called "plazas;" odd-looking stores, with still more odd-looking assortments of goods, are entirely open to the gaze of the passer-by; while in the market-place are noticed the same peculiarities observed at Puerto Plata, only on a more extended scale. Go where one will, however, every one is cheerful, polite, and communicative, while the dusky "fair ones" presiding over piles of strange, unknown tropical productions, are merry, while obliging even in giving information.

Such are the sights that to-day first greet the traveller in the city that at one time was famous for its magnificence.

The day after my arrival I called at the palace to pay my respects to the authorities and present my letters of introduction. I was received by Mr Delmonte in the most cordial manner, and presented to President Baez, the Secretary of State, Mr Gautier, being present. They were all extremely affable and kind, and had rather a practical joke, though of a pleasant nature, at my expense; for on my happening to let drop a Spanish word, the President laughed and said—"I must talk to them all in Spanish, as it was too *hard work* for him to talk English, and Mr Gautier did not understand it, and therefore we should get on finely as one family." We had some pleasant words together, and I left feeling that my first had been anything but a formal call.

President Baez is a courtly, pleasant man, of medium height and agreeable appearance. He is just fifty-seven years of age, and would never be taken for other than a Spaniard were it not that his hair, as he turns his head, shows just a little of the character of the hair of the African. He speaks French as well as he does Spanish, but English only tolerably well. He seems perfectly frank. With the easy air and manner of a thorough man of the world, he impresses me as a perfectly upright man, and that seems to be generally the impression made.

Baez.

The accompanying portrait of him is a very good one, though somewhat younger than he now appears. The portraits circulated representing him as a black man are utterly false.

Mr Gautier, the Secretary of State, is a man of about forty years of age, rather bald, with thin black hair, small, piercing black eyes set well in his head, and with a noble brow that bespeaks intellect. He is rather reticent; but, as he speaks no English, it may be for that reason, interpreters being awkward mediums. I found him conversing in Spanish agreeable, but precise in his expression, as though he weighed carefully each word, and his entire head resembles somewhat the first Napoleon as depicted in pictures.

Minister Delmonte, who has charge of the public instruction and education, is a medium-sized, spare man, with a quick, nervous action, speaking English very well. He is very cordial in his manner, and seems honest and straightforward. In fact, as far as I have seen Baez and his Cabinet, judging from several interviews I had with them, my impressions are extremely favourable, and though prepared by articles in the newspapers of the United States to take a rather prejudiced view of some of these gentlemen, I confess I was entirely converted to the opinion, held even by the enemies of President Baez, that he is a remarkably talented man, earnest for the welfare of his people and country.

St Domingo city, the oldest existing settlement in the New World, humble as it is to-day, is yet a place of great interest to the antiquarian or artistic traveller.

Its early history is enveloped in a cloud of romance, but from which have been sifted the following facts.

When the Spaniards were originally settled at the town of Isabella on the north coast, one of their number, Miguel Diaz, having a difficulty with a servant of Don Bartholomew Columbus, stabbed him, as he thought, to death, and fearing the consequences of his act, fled into the woods, and finally wandered to the south side of the island, where, entering the domain, on the banks of the Ozama, of one of the native princesses, the latter eventually became enamoured of her Spanish guest, and it is even said they were finally married.

Diaz appears to have become somewhat tired of this princess after a while, and longed for the presence of his countrymen; and his wife, noticing his melancholy, and hoping to make him better satisfied, proposed to him to bring his companions to that region, telling him also, as an inducement, of the gold to be found in the vicinity of the river Jaina.

Diaz, big with this news, appears to have sought the vicinity of Isabella, and while loitering about there, learned that the man whom he supposed dead was still alive; and thus feeling it safe to return, entered the town and made known to Don Bartholomew Columbus the news of the gold mines of the Jaina. Bartholomew immediately took steps to verify this fact, and finding it true, received orders from his brother the Admiral to found a town in the vicinity.

The spot selected was on the high and commanding bluff on the left bank of the river Ozama; and here, in 1494, August the 4th, was founded the new town, to which was given at first the name of New Isabella, but which was afterwards exchanged for that of St Domingo, in honour, as some writers assert, of the day (Sunday) on which the town was first established, and, as others again assert, in honour of the father of Columbus, who was called Domingo.

To this place, in 1496, all the inhabitants of the original town of Isabella removed, and it soon became the capital town of the island. Columbus himself seems to have visited it for the first time on his return from Spain in August 1498, two years after its foundation.

Here the town remained, the houses principally being constructed of wood, until 1502, when Ovando came out as Governor to succeed Bobadilla.

The fearful hurricane foretold by Columbus was the cause of its removal to the other side, for in that storm the place was entirely destroyed, and Ovando then determined to change its location to the other or right side of the river.

This appears to have been a great mistake, and Charlevoix says it was only done because there were already there the habitations of some Spaniards; and it is undoubtedly lower than the other bank, and is frequently enveloped in the vapours of the river, which are created by the sun driving them before him—no small thing in a humid country. In addition to this, the opportunity was lost of always having a supply of fresh water, while in the new city the people had to rely upon their cisterns, because the water of the Ozama is brackish many leagues from its mouth.

The new town made rapid progress from the fact that a number of the inhabitants built up houses on speculation, which drew to the place many of those arriving from Spain *en route* to Mexico, who, finding such a substantial well-built city, settled down there.

The Governor Ovando intended to bring the water of the river Jaina, nine miles off, into the town, and a part of the aqueduct was even constructed, a slab in the principal square still remaining to show where there was to be a fountain.

Oviedo, the historian of the time, in describing St Domingo says, "that as touching the buildings, there is no city in Spain, not even Barcelona, so much to be preferred as San Domingo. The houses for the most part are of stone—the situation is much better than Barcelona, by reason that the streets are much larger and wider, and without comparison straighter and more direct, being laid out with cord, compass, and measure. In the midst of the city is the fortress and castle, and such houses so fair and large that they may well receive any lord or noble of Spain with his train and family, and especially is this true of that of Don Diego Columbus."

Although, from that day to this, the city has experienced many changes and reverses, its general plan is much the same, and many of the old landmarks are still standing. Some of the buildings in the vicinity of the Cathedral having a very odd and venerable appearance.

The form of the city is that of a trapezium or quadrilateral figure, whose four sides are neither equal nor parallel, being about 1100 yards long on the east side towards the Ozama, nearly 1000 yards on the south side

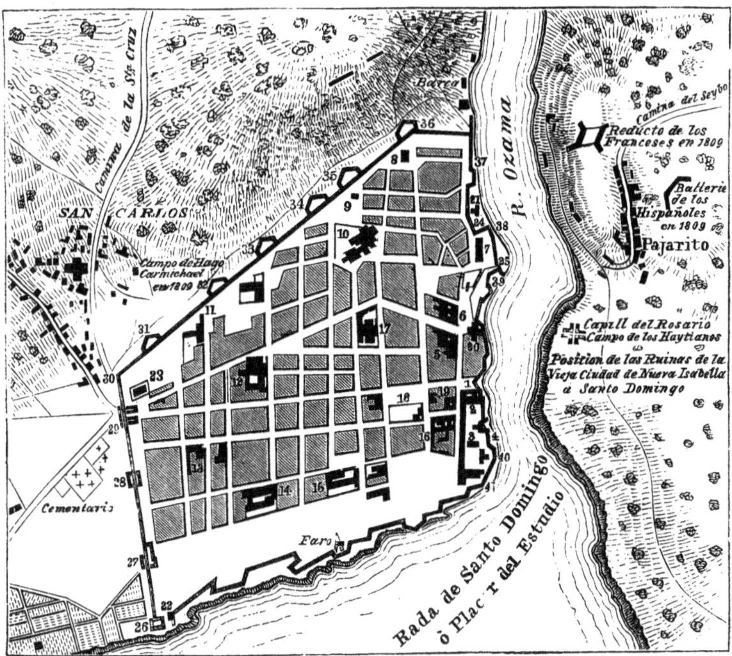

ST DOMINGO CITY.

1, 2. Barracks.
3. Powder magazine
4. Signal tower.
6. Government palace.
8–16. Churches.
10. Ruined monastery (San Francisco).
17. General hospital.
18. Cathedral.
22. Slaughter-house.
24–29. Gates.

bordering to the sea, and 1900 on the west side, and north toward San Carlos.

The circumference of the town is about 4500 yards, the main street running from the principal square to the land gate or Puerta del Conde.

The very walls of the east side of the city are washed by the Ozama, while on the south, the shore ends abruptly in bold rocky cliffs, against which the surf violently dashes; upon the edge of this cliff extends an old useless parapet, inside of which is a wide ample space originally used as the "Paseo" or promenade of the townspeople, but which now, overgrown with grass, appears silent and neglected enough.

The outskirts of the city are composed of rather un-

Old Part of St Domingo.

attractive frame or semi-clay huts, roofed with palm or straw; while in the interior of the town the houses are, many of them, solid and imposing. They are built in the old Spanish fashion, usually of one story in height, seldom over two. A wide entrance with immense folding doors opens into the hall, which conducts into the patio or court-yard, around which are the quarters and offices. The same lack of glass in the windows, and the use of iron bars, seen in Cuba, are universal here; while the quietness of many of the old streets in the upper part of the town reminds one of a city of sleepers. In the streets leading up from the wharf, and in the vicinity of the market-place, more life is seen, and the architecture of the stores and houses, if not so imposing, is more modern.

The whole city seems to be built upon a solid limestone

formation, sloping somewhat in the direction of the river, which makes its drainage easy, but appears to limit the supply of water. This is obtained principally from cisterns, that are placed upon the flat roofs, and to which the rain water is conducted by the pipes from the different roofs.

The walls of the older houses are very solidly constructed either of stone or the material known as mamposteria, a mode of architecture somewhat similar to that of Cuba. The method of making these walls is simple and economical. The glutinous earth of the vicinity is taken and mixed with lime, and sometimes, as in Cuba, with powdered stone; frames of planks are then made in the desired form, and these are filled with layers of this composition, sand and lime being added. The whole is then moistened with water, well pounded and kneaded, and allowed to dry, when the mould being withdrawn, leaves a firm solid wall, which, on exposure to the air, becomes hard as stone. Even the walls of the city are built in this way.

Business Street.

With the exception of the old churches, there are few really imposing buildings in the city, the government buildings, except for their solidity of construction, having nothing striking about them, though their style of architecture, peculiar to Spanish America, strikes the novice at first as somewhat grand, from the balconied piazzas supported on pillars of solid construction.

The general business of the city appears very limited indeed, and there are only one or two really large and extensive stores with general assortments of goods. But there is always a certain amount of amusement to be obtained by the stranger in trading among these old Spanish towns. The perfectly easy, leisurely way in which negotiations are conducted, the amount of chaff and compliments exchanged even in the most ordinary purchase, is somewhat astonishing to people of the Anglo-Saxon race; and it becomes, after a while, quite a pleasant amusement to have a seller name some ridiculous price for an article, just to see to how much one can finally reduce it.

In fact, it is a question if St Domingo city, under any circumstances, will ever become a great business place, in its present locality at least. The opposite bank is undoubtedly a more desirable location for a modern town in every respect; besides which, there are so many places in other parts of the island having greater advantages, that the general commerce of the island will hardly seek this as its port, however large its local trade may become.

Even its chance to be the capital of the island will, I think, be disputed by the interior town of Santiago, which, situated in the centre of the island, in the midst of a superb agricultural country, with ample water communication to every part, will have, with the assistance of the railroad, the controlling power in the island, becoming almost a second Chicago.

The principal trade of St Domingo city is confined to the shipping of mahogany, dye, and cabinet woods, which are brought down from the interior, as well as the hides from the cattle in the Seybo district, but this entire trade is limited in amount.

On the opposite side of the river the shore is well adapted for the erection of wharves for a large city, there being there a natural levee. On the hills above is a little village known as Pajarito (little bird), containing a few inhabitants only.

I was much amused, however, while strolling through the place, by a visit to the village school, which was simply a thatched hut with earthen floor, where I found a number of children, of both sexes and of all colours, seated on stools around the room.

Between each pupil I was astonished to find a gamecock attached to a sort of perch; and on my asking the children for an explanation, they said, "Oh! they belong to the schoolmaster, who fights them on Sunday." This functionary was out, but I afterwards met him, and found him

A Dominican School.

to be an intelligent coloured man, highly amused at my surprise at such new means of education, he explaining by a shrug of the shoulders and the remark, "Cosa Dominicana."

On Sunday we went to the grand Cathedral to hear the

morning service, high mass being performed by the Vicar-General; and though the worshippers were not large in numbers, they comprised all classes and colours, the female sex being predominant. The chanting of the priests was accompanied by an orchestra, principally stringed, and

The Mausoleum of Columbus.

small in number, that was placed in the choir, which is constructed in the centre of the church, a mulatto with strong nasal accent acting as leader of the vocalists.

The Cathedral, the most interesting building in St Domingo, is in its interior a grand old church, with pillars and arches and crypts and altars innumerable; and as we view its vast extent we can readily believe the accounts of the various historians, who give such glowing relations of its splendours in ancient days. Its exterior bears the marks of its great antiquity upon its form, not only in the weather-stained walls, but in the quaint architecture.

This old church was particularly interesting to me as

having visited the last resting-place of Columbus in the Cathedral at Havana, I had now the opportunity of seeing his first mausoleum in the New World; for it was here that his remains were brought from Spain, as well as those of his brother Don Bartholomew.

It seems extremely curious, and well illustrates the lethargy and decay of Spain, that, in 1783, when Moreau St Mery, a Frenchman, visited the city, it was a matter of absolute doubt and uncertainty as to the resting-place of these remains; and it was only through his exertions they were positively found to be there, in a leaden coffin, which had been walled up in the Cathedral; and even then it was not ascertained to a certainty in which coffin were the bones of Columbus himself. Another one was found at the same time, containing those of his brother Bartholomew.

This edifice stands facing the public square, and is built of solid stone, Gothic in architecture, and has a nave and two wings. It was begun in 1512 and finished in 1540, being constructed after the model of a church in Rome; and has withstood the shocks of all earthquakes—a proof either of the strength of its walls, or else the weakness of the shocks of the earthquakes, that once or twice in two or three hundred years have visited this island.

The church is entered by three large doorways and two porticoes, these being the most striking part of the building, massive and imposing in appearance, and richly carved originally, although now worn with age.

To mount upon the roof, one ascends by a spiral staircase built of stone, and from the roof a good view of the city is obtained; and it was upon this that cannon had been mounted in defence of the town, there being even a bomb-shell still remaining in its wall, fired by the English when attacking the French in possession of the city in 1809.

The city at one time possessed a large number of church organisations, being, as it was then, the principal arch-bishopric of the New World. When they were all in full operation, there were two or three monasteries, two nunneries, several hospitals, and a number of parochial or

Cathedral Door.

minor churches. All, or most of them, are now either extinct or gone to such decay as is sad to witness.

Many of these institutions, but particularly the Cathedral, were rich in gold and silver ornaments and decorations, but of which they have been despoiled at different times, principally, however, during the occupation of the French.

Desiring to get information about religious and educational matters, we called upon the Vicar-General, and had a very pleasant interview with him. We found him in one of his rooms, close by the Grand Cathedral, and in its courtyard, in fact. He is a short, stout, full-made man, with full black beard and moustache, sparkling black eyes, and full round head and face. As he sat before me I could not help thinking he was the very picture of a jolly Dominican friar, particularly as the close-fitting skull-cap, with a funny little button on top, gave him a very comical appearance. He informed me he had only lived here a year; that there was a seminary, primary school, and college, all under the care of the Church. The schools contained altogether some three hundred pupils. In the college there is a night-school for the poorer class, who are ambitious of knowledge, and of whom a certain number are gratuitously instructed at the expense of the Town Council; while others are admitted, that can afford it, at the rate of one dollar per month.

Our conversation with the Vicar-General was very full and entertaining, and his views of annexation very frank. I asked him how he liked the idea of it. He replied, "At present there is only one Church here, and that is the Roman Catholic; but if annexation comes, there will be others."

"Yes," I replied; "but then you must remember that you will have ample toleration for your Church."

He laughed cynically as he said, "But I have to tolerate others too."

I answered, "You have only your own Church, with a very small number of members; in the United States your Church is a very powerful one, and has a great many members; don't you, therefore, suppose that your numbers will be increased, and your church revenues improved by annexation?"

"Frankly, señor," said he, "it really don't make much difference with me either one way or the other. I like Rome better than I do here; it is sometimes so hot for me in summer; but I tell my people, when they ask me about it, they must remember that they cannot do with the United States as they did with Spain; once annexed they cannot get out."

In the building occupied as the seminary there are various classes under instruction by brothers of the Church, and some few refugee Cubans acting as instructors. A school of medicine is established, and the principles of physiology and medicine taught; lectures being given, while we were present, upon osteology, illustrated by the human skeleton.

We were exceedingly charmed with our visit through the seminary, which we made after seeing the Vicar-General; for though most of the classes were limited in numbers of pupils, we were treated with a courtesy that seems to be an instinct with these people and their children. In every case, on entering the room, the pupils, as well as their instructors, immediately arose, the latter coming forward, and in the kindest manner volunteering all the information we wanted.

What a change, however, from those early days in the history of the city, when its celebrated university gave pre-eminence to its citizens over those of all the towns of the New World, by the liberal education extended them, the renown of which became so great, that the city itself received the name of the "Athens of the New World!"

Another old landmark of the dead past of this historic town is the building known as the "Castle of Columbus," being the house built upon the margin of the west bank of the river by Diego Columbus, the son of the Admiral, while the old town of St Domingo was still upon the eastern side of the river. It was built very solidly of stone, and surrounded by an enclosure to protect him from the attacks of Indians. Afterwards, when the town was removed to the other bank, the house was completed, the ramparts of the town running down to it, and one of the gates immediately under it receiving the name which it bears to-day from the house of Colon. It has now gone to decay and ruin; but yet makes a picturesque and interesting point for the visitor to St Domingo city,—the illustration in a previous page showing it in a better state of preservation than it is to-day.

As we desired to satisfy our curiosity with a view of the Dominican cockpit, we paid a visit there in the early afternoon. The place was crowded, the pit being only a small place or circle of about fifty feet radius, much humbler than those of its Cuban neighbour. We mounted up to the top seat, by means of a ladder, for a standing place; but on Damion Baez, the brother of the President, perceiving us, he very kindly offered us seats below in the select part; but, as we only wished to stay a few moments, we declined his offer.

A cockfight seems to be the same all the world over as it is here, in Cuba, or "in Jersey." Much as we may disapprove of such exhibitions, particularly where representatives of the Government are present as patrons, I must confess I would rather "take my chance" with these people in their cockfights than with the roughs at a dog-fight in New York city, or a prize-fight in the ring; for I hold that none of these exhibitions represent truly "the people" of any of the places in which they may take place; and I am free to say that I have heard the best of Cubans, as well as Dominicans, speak of the cockpit with abhorrence, and hope for its abolition. The customs of a people, however, are not to be changed in a day, whatever time may effect. We saw but one fight, and then left, our interest being soon over, as our curiosity was gratified, and the noise of the audience, as they in their excitement screamed out their bets, was deafening.

This being the first day of the carnival, the streets all the afternoon were filled with maskers and mummers, who at this season have much liberty allowed them; but with it all, in the two or three days to which this privilege extends, we heard of no disorderly conduct whatever. It was in strong contrast, as we turned from one of these processions of merrymakers, to meet another making its way along the plaza; but it was a procession of a very different order —a funeral, which, with its four-wheeled canopy trimmed with white, and drawn by one horse, was carrying to its last resting-place the remains of an aged citizen, whose friends on foot formed the funeral cortege. In either case, very, very humble, and so different from the rich displays made in the great city of Havana, of which St Domingo may, in fact, be said to be a very small and cheap edition—inferior in every respect except in its natural advantages.

Long years of adversity and revolution have impoverished the country, killing all enterprise, deadening every energy of its people, and destroying every sense of security, so that if the capitalist should feel tempted by the numerous rich openings offered by the natural advantages of the country, he is deterred by the lack of confidence in the Government's power to resist the cabals and attempts of a lot of political vagabonds, who, seeing only in turmoil and trouble a chance for themselves to rob and appropriate, are ready on the slightest pretext to take up arms. Thus there being no commerce of any moment, and little production, the revenues of the Government are limited, and are not sufficient to meet the expenses. No improvements take place; communication by land from one town to another is at times utterly impossible, and only at intervals by mule and horse-back. The result is, that every class is poor, and feeling this, a sense of shyness is manifested to strangers by the better class not natural to their desires or traditions.

Although there is much talk about the unhealthiness, I cannot find that St Domingo city is ever anything but healthy; for, from the old historians down, every writer speaks of its healthfulness. I do know that since we have been here there have been but two funerals—one of them being the above; in fact, they have a joke here, saying "People die only of old age."

Certain it is that during our stay here the climate has been delightful, the nights being fresh and cool; and I am told there is no change in the summers, except that the days are a little hotter. Before day throughout the year a blanket is required in sleeping.

Our thermometer since we have been here at the palace has hardly varied a degree each morning, showing an even temperature each day at five o'clock A.M. of 64°, while at mid-day it has not gone over 85°.

I was constantly reminded of the pure air of Trinidad de Cuba, said to be the healthiest place in that island; and though St Domingo city is not situated upon a high mountain, as is Trinidad, it yet seems quite as cool and salubrious, owing to the fresh breezes from the hills prevailing at night, while those from the sea prevail during the day.

For a winter's residence for invalids, this city could be made a very attractive place, and would offer a fine field to enterprising hotel-keepers to establish houses, either in or out of the city, for the accommodation of those desirous of escaping northern winters. At present there is no hotel worthy of that name; but the stray traveller will be well taken care of by inquiring for "Monsieur Auguste."

Riding up over the hills outside of the town, we get fine views of the harbour, which is comparatively small, being formed by the confluence of the Isabella and Ozama rivers, which by their junction form a Y. Each of these rivers receives in its course the tribute of many others of less consequence, and of a very great number of streams and ravines, brooks and springs. Both of them take their rise in the mountains lying to the north-west of the city, and meet about three miles above it. The anchorage in the port itself is deep enough for vessels of any size, and it is a perfect landlocked harbour, the banks in some places being as high as twenty feet. The river for nearly three miles is about twenty-four feet deep, with a bottom of soft mud or sand. The present obstacle to it as a port arises from the fact that at the entrance there is a rock which prevents vessels drawing more than eighteen feet of water from entering; but this could easily be removed by blasting. In the time of the floods, some idea may be formed of the volume of water coming down the Ozama from the fact that the sea, at some distance from the river's mouth, is entirely discoloured by its muddy waters.

As we sit upon the hill looking down upon the city, it

has a strange appearance, with its red-coloured roofs and age-stained walls, those of the old Franciscan monastery, covered with vines and moss, being prominent in the foreground, just behind the bastioned angles of the northern walls.

Taking a bridle-path, we rode almost around the city, parallel with the walls, which are, in fact, as old as they look, having been erected as far back as 1506 by Nicholas Ovando, of whom such great deeds are told in the ancient Spanish chronicles. These walls are about eight feet thick and ten feet high, the revetment being of hewn stone, and the scarp cut in the solid rock. There is no

Old Franciscan Monastery.

glacis, while the bastions are very small, except those at the four angles, which are larger; the one at the south-west angle, known as La Forsza, built by Ovando, being in good preservation, though now beside it is the city shambles. Above the city, on the hill, stands the old town of San Carlos, as old as St Domingo itself, being perhaps better known to the readers of Irving as Ileignes. The ground, however, is the only antique portion of the place; for the houses are all modern, built of wood, of generally the most humble description, and the only striking object is the ubiquitous church that crowns the eminence.

There used to be an immense amount of ordnance at St Domingo city, but most of it was carried away by the English in payment of assistance rendered by them to the Spaniards against the French.

As a fortified city it would seem to be a failure, for the hill San Carlos commands it; and unless this place was fortified with advanced works in connection, no amount of money expended on its walls would prevent the city from being rendered untenable. This was practically illustrated by General Carmichael, when he took the city with his troops upon this hill without firing a shot.

Continuing our ride, we reached the Well of Columbus, on the left bank of the Ozama, deriving its name from the reputed fact that Bartholomew Columbus himself is said to have built this well. At all events, it is a very old structure of stone, with a quay or wharf parapeted of the same material upon the river, while standing against the hill-side is a double-arched structure, in the centre of which is the well or cistern, quite deep, and having in it delicious pure water, of which many of the vessels avail themselves.

Upon the quays, between the well and the city walls, we found large quantities of the woods of the country, such as lignum, fustic, ebony, iron-wood, and mahogany, together with dye woods, being weighed in large scales preparatory to shipment; and it makes quite a busy and strange scene, with the background of wooden booths of the roughest description, where the workmen regale themselves with "san cocho" (a stew), bad rum, cakes, &c., the end of the quay being devoted to the sale (wholesale) of fruits and vegetables.

The workmen or labourers seem to work steadily and earnestly enough, even in the hot sun, to set at rest the doubt whether these people will work even if they are paid; for here, where their wages are regularly paid by foreign houses, there is no trouble in getting labour.

To these landings come the country people from far up the river Ozama, in their strange boats, a canoe dug out of huge trees, which, propelled by its one man occupant, probably comes forty or fifty miles to bring a couple of hundred plantains, not worth perhaps more than thirty or forty cents a hundred; or perhaps the "canotero" brings down a more valuable freight, in the shape of two or three bits of mahogany, the average size of which is about three feet long by two square, the value of each piece not exceeding $8 to $10 here.

CHAPTER XIII.

"The plantain and banana's luscious fruit
In circled clusters load the curling shoot;
With golden bloom the nectared orange glows;
With spicy custard soft anana flows;
The juicy melon fills its netted mould;
And the crowned pine perfumes with fragrant gold."

VICINITY OF ST DOMINGO CITY—*Natural Caves—The Caves of Santanna—The Boundary Line—Beata and Alta Vela Islands—Neybo—Salt Mines—Sugar Plantations—Azua—Ocoa Bay.*

IT was with a good deal of amusement to ourselves, and gratification to a group of natives looking on, that a party of us gathered together one fine morning, prepared for a ride through the country lying in the vicinity of the city. Our horses had been gathered from various sources, though none of them, with their original equipments and their freely-costumed riders, would have passed a "dress parade." Two or three of us particularly presented a ludicrous appearance,—a robust western major insisting upon taking the smallest horse, while the doctor was more particular about the size of his saddle than the quality of his mount, the others being selected pretty much at haphazard.

Much to our gratification, however, our equines proved better in quality than in appearance, for size is no criterion of goodness in a St Domingo horse, many of those of the medium size being wonderfully endowed with powers of endurance and rapidity of movement, the gait being similar to that of the Cuban horses, a sort of rack or amble.

The land to the west and north of the city is rather rough and rocky, but after that it changes in character, and becomes very pretty, though for some distance out the country is somewhat level, and the soil of a rather reddish clay.

In old times the vicinity of the city was noted for the beauty of its gardens and the charms of the places of "recreo," or country-houses, which most of the wealthy citizens possessed; but to-day these have all disappeared, and one only meets with the ordinary "finca" or truck garden or farm, though along the sea-coast some pretty places have been established.

Strange to say, however, in all St Domingo, where nature is so prolific in every fern and fruit and flower, man seems to care very little about its cultivated beauties, and it is the rarest thing to find even an humble attempt at a flower-garden, be it in town or country. The explanation for this invariably given me by the people, on my asking why they did not have them, was, "What is the use? just as soon as we had one made it would be destroyed in another revolution."

St Domingo Ferns.

Most of the Antilles are noted for their caves or subterranean formations found in them; and St Domingo shares largely in this peculiarity, for they are to be met with in every part of the island.

On the east bank of the Ozama, some two miles distant from the village, there is a curious cave known as a "Cueva de Agua" or water-cave, where there is to be seen a natural lake formed in a rocky cavern, in which are many stalagmites of curious form.

The most noted of these caves, however, are those of Santanna, reputed to be one of the places of resort for the aborigines of the island, who came here to worship their zemes or gods.

To this cave our party directed its way, after having made the circuit of the town; and passing out by the western gate, and in front of the large cemetery, which lies bare and desolate just outside the city walls, we soon reached the thick scrub-covered rolling plain beyond the city, till, striking a bridle-path directly through the woods, we were protected from the sun by the dense foliage, which, meeting just above our heads, formed in many places a natural arch, under whose protecting shades we seemed as though shut out from the world, while turns in the path gave us lovely vistas of palms, and cocoas, and graceful flowing vines, and blossoming bush, that were charming; while the aroma and fragrance of the vegetation, on which still clung the morning dew, was especially delicious. Here, too, we met with the hedge of maya, upon which was now ripe the small yellow fruit, which, eaten sparingly, acts as a gentle purgative. At one of the houses, after we had ridden some distance, we picked up our guide, a negro boy, who, with only a pair of pants on, was drawing water, his back exposed in all its nakedness to the hot sun, which he did not seem to mind. Coming to a high fence, which we could neither go over nor let down, we actually took the difficulty by the horns; that is, we rode our spirited little horses, after a small fight, slap through the hedge of the prickly maya, without their being the least the worse for it.

And then we descended a narrow road through green fields to a shaded path that descends suddenly to the

Entrance to Cave.

entrance of the cave, which is composed of a double archway, the division being formed by grotesquely-shaped pillars of corallaceous rock, one of the arches permitting ingress of mounted visitors. Around these grew the thick tropical vegetation, the parasitical plants pendant from the branches of the trees giving an exceedingly graceful appearance to the entrance.

Being mounted on the largest horse of the party, I found it necessary now and then to stoop in my saddle in

CAVES OF SANTANA.

order to prevent knocking my head against the roof, and I calculated from this that the cave was in its lowest point, from roof to floor, some seven or eight feet high.

This entrance forms a sort of double saloon, passing through which we came into a rocky amphitheatre of perhaps three hundred feet or more in diameter.

The sight was indeed a strange one, the amphitheatre having all the appearance of having been at one time a lake, the walls of which were formed of the same peculiar rock, massed together in grotesque strata and strange forms, at the base of which, round the entire circle, were the apertures known as the caves; above, the clear blue sky, unusually brilliant in colour, while upon the upper edge of the amphitheatre was the luxuriant vegetation of this island, giving grace and beauty in every conceivable form and colour to the scene; the graceful tendrils of the vines entwining themselves around the trunks of the towering trees, whose thick and umbrageous foliage served to throw a tempered light into the cavity, the open floor of which was covered with masses of rock of varied form, thrown together in wild confusion. The mosses, and ferns, and herbage, that crept and grew over and in every crevice, added to the wild, strange, and beautiful scene.

What gave a still more interesting, and, if I may so express it, weird appearance to the amphitheatre, were the long, innumerable roots of the trees upon the verge of the rocks, which looked exactly as though they had originally taken root in the earth, which, having afterwards been washed away, left these same roots gathered together in bundles of from ten to thirty in number each, which, growing downwards, had finally taken root in the substrata, looking, as they hung relieved against the gloomy background of the caves, like so many woody pillars.

We entered several of these caves, and discerned naught

but gloom and owls, which our feeble candles served barely to disturb. While these caves are extremely interesting as showing the freaks of nature, they have neither the brilliancy of the crystal caves of Bellamar in Cuba, nor yet the grandeur and extent of our Mammoth Cave in Kentucky. Yet withal there is such a weird look about the shapes of the pillars and the forms of the walls in their different degrees of obscurity, that it makes one expect to see appear some strangely-formed demon or wild-looking hermit, inquiring by what right his solitude is disturbed by beings from a far-away western world.

The fact that some idols have been found in these caves is cited as authority for their having been used by the natives either as a place of worship or burial; for when a cacique died, his people opened and dried him by the fire, that he might be preserved entire. The body was then laid in some cave, together with his arms, and frequently his favourite wife attended him. This cave, it is said, was thus used.

After leaving the caves, we made a considerable detour, in order to get an idea of the agricultural interests of this part of the island; but we found comparatively little reward, for the amount of products are limited to the plantain, some garden vegetables, with a small amount of tobacco.

Tamarind.

A tropical shower coming on, we sought shelter under one of the most superb trees I have ever seen—a noble tamarind, of immense size, whose foliage, growing somewhat like that of the horse-chestnut, was so dense that we were perfectly protected from the downpour of rain. These trees always remind me of our locust-trees, though so much larger, and the grouping of the leaves with its fruit in the branches forms a most graceful natural feature.

It always seems to me that nature in St Domingo stands a constant reproach to the inhabitants for their supineness and indifference to improving their condition. For one is constantly led to think what might be accomplished by man's energy in a country where nature does so much.

From St Domingo city westward to the Haytian border there is not a single town of any importance, though there are several villages of considerable size scattered at intervals throughout a section of country comprising some of the finest agricultural lands in the world, capable of supporting a large and industrious population, and where the climate is as salubrious as in that of any other part of the globe.

The roads, like those in the rest of the island, are hardly worthy of the name; but there is a fair bit of road from St Domingo city to the river Jaina in the west, available in good weather for carts, though pack animals are generally used—the traveller invariably going on horseback.

Moreau St Mery, who seems to have personally and most thoroughly examined all this district of country from St Domingo city to the Haytian line (at the time of his visit, 1784, in possession of the Spaniards), speaks in the highest praise of the character of the soil, the salubrity of the climate, the abundance of wood and water, and the advantages of numerous harbours on the coast.

Having determined to penetrate to the interior of the island and the north-west, and being informed the southern side was similar, in most respects, to those parts of the north which I proposed to visit, I was forced to decline the services of one of the natives of this section of the country, who offered himself as guide, with a strongly written recommendation. Here it is, as also the portrait of the individual, as characteristic of his class, in case any future traveller should need his help:—"Manuel Seybano knows all the country about the upper Nigua and Nizao; one of the best mountaineers I ever saw—when he is sober—and good as a circus when he is drunk—a type of man rarely found out of the backwoods; a noted pig-hunter, and if the pigs are not wild, 'poco importe,' if he does not get caught himself; spends about half his time in the woods, and the other half in the calaboose for making mistakes between wild and tame pigs (*i.e.*, those with or without ear-marks)."

Manuel Seybano.

As St Mery's notes have been verified by later authorities and the personal investigations of members of the United States Commission, it may not be amiss to give here a general account of the principal points of this section.

Beyond the province of St Domingo on the west, beginning at the Ocoa river, and extending to the boundary line, lies the famous district of Azua, comprising within its limits the communes of Azua, Neyba, Barahona, San Juan, Las Matas, Banica, &c., most of which lie in the section marked in the map as the debatable ground, and comprising some of the finest parts of the island, but now in a disorganised state from the constant irruptions of the Haytian borderers united with some refugee Dominicans, who, banded together under General Cabral, a former Dominican leader, keep the country to the west of Azua in a state of suspense similar to that of our Indian frontier.

The western border of the Dominican territory begins, as will be seen on looking at the map, on the south bank of the river Perdenales (Flint river), flowing at the west side of the high mountain range known by its Indian appellation of Bahoruco.

These mountains, rising majestically from the Dominican lines, face with a gentle slope the sea nearly to the south-west, opposite to the shore of which is the small island of Beata.

Valverde says that these mountains are extremely fertile, and possess a lovely climate ; and quotes as an illustration that a Spanish officer, being up there in pursuit of fugitives, had tents erected for his party, which he covered with cabbage-leaves, so large was their growth.

This situation, where everything seems to bespeak mines of gold, and where gold-sand is found in the water, was a great resort for the Spanish and French negroes, where they formed themselves into an unconquerable body, and committed depredations on the surrounding country.

All along this shore going east are many coves, where vessels of moderate size may enter, and particularly Eagle's Cove, where it is said ships may approach near enough to be fastened ashore. Here is met the most southern point of the island, Cape Beata, and opposite it lies the little island of the same name, famous in times past as the great resort of French privateers, they being eventually driven from thence by Admiral Cowley. Columbus saw this island in 1498, and took shelter in its passage from a storm in 1504.

Some six miles to the south-west of Beata is the now famous island of Alta Vela (Big-sail), so called by Columbus in 1494, on account of its height and form, which at a distance resembles a vessel under full sail. The land on the island rises to the centre, and is covered with wood; but it has more lately been occupied as a guano-island, with the expectation of procuring large quantities of that fertiliser. An engineer, however, on board the steamer, whose services had been engaged there, informed me that as yet the quantity of guano was very small, it having only been found in pockets in the rock, and that his services were engaged to run the engines in the new occupation of salt-making.

Continuing north from Cape Beata, the first bay of importance is Neyba, into which empties the river of the same name, that has its source in the above-named mountain, and which waters a fine extent of country. That looking west was all formerly occupied by the Maroons or runaway negroes, being originally the famous province of Xaragua.

In the early days of the conquest these slopes were devoted to the cultivation of sugar; and St Mery, a practical planter, computes that in the two plains adjacent to this coast there could be established over 250 sugar plantations capable of employing in his time over 50,000 negroes; while in the plain of Neyba, watered by that river, 150 more plantations could be profitably established.

The river Neyba having several mouths, that run through low grounds or marshes, the Bay of Neyba is not so good a port for this section as the Barahona, a little to the south; but this is capable of being made into a good harbour, and it is said Toussaint had commenced to establish there an important town when the arrival of the French put an end to his plans.

All the country lying to the east of the curious lake called Enriquello is known generally by the name of the Plain of Neyba, which is pretty generally fertile. Near the little town of the same name is situated the famous mine or rock of crystal salt, which is generally used by the people in that vicinity for curing their provisions. The salt is said to have the peculiarity of becoming much heavier on being exposed to the air; and it is said that the natural reproduction of this mineral is so rapid that quite a large hollow will be filled up again in the course of the year.

To the north, on the Neyba, lies the fairy valley of St John, or San Juan, noted for its great fertility in all time and the salubrity of its climate, while more lately it has been the seat of Cabral's raids.

In old times the whole of this district comprised the province of Maguana, under the control of the chief Caonabo. The town of San Juan is an old place, and has suffered many reverses, having shifted its location at various times.

To the north is the town of Banica, which, originally founded by Ovando in 1503, is now held by the Haytians. The whole of this beautiful valley of St Thomas, as it is called, possesses a superb climate, being an elevated district, and well adapted to raise cattle, sheep, wheat, and all the products of the temperate zone.

And now we come to the famous commune of Azua, which always seems to have been a favourite part of the island, and has been noted for the luxuriance of its sugar-cane, its fruits, and the salubrity of its climate.

Almost identical in its peculiarities of soil and vegetation with the district of Monte Cristo in the north-west, Azua seems always to have been a more settled part, probably from its lying in a milder region, and being upon the great southern route, in old times, from the Spanish to the French capital of the island.

The old town of Azua was founded in 1504 by Diego Columbus. He gave it the surname of Compostella, in honour of Gallego, commander of the order of Santiago, who had a habitation in the neighbourhood, its present appellation being the old Indian name.

This is the district which first produced in the most

prolific manner sugar for the Spaniards—the cane being noted as producing for six consecutive years full crops without care or renewal. In fact, to-day cane is shown in bearing said to be seventy years old.

But sugar alone is not the only excellent product, for every fruit and vegetable is remarkably perfect in this region, the orange especially being noted for its flavour.

The present town is situated on the road from San Juan and Neyba to St Domingo, and is some two leagues distant from the Bay of Ocoa, one of the most famous ports on the south coast, and in which Columbus took shelter from the great storm.

The old town, where Hernan Cortes was town-clerk before he started out on his adventurous career, was destroyed by an earthquake in 1751. This terrible event led the sea up to the very town, when it was abandoned.

Like all other Dominican towns, it is now a straggling collection of one-storied houses, built of palm-leaves, straw, and poles, gathered round a wide open space honoured with the name of "plaza;" and aside from the fact that it has been the home of the Baez family, who own large properties in the vicinity, there is nothing to attract the traveller at present.

With railroads, and capital, and immigration, this would probably prove a district agriculturally of the first importance. In this case the Bay of Ocoa, with its port of Calderas, being splendidly adapted for a great marine rendezvous, would prove a formidable rival to St Domingo city.

All this district to the west of Azua has suffered much from the various revolutions and incursions which seem to have selected this province for their inception; but now, happily for the rest of the island, these little "unpleasantnesses" are pretty much confined to one locality. To thoroughly understand the cause of these, we shall have to study a little of the history of St Domingo since it became a republic.

CHAPTER XIV.

> "Spain, watching from her Morro's keep
> Her slave-ships traversing the deep,
> . . . . . .
> With bitter hate and sullen fear
> Its freedom-giving voice shall hear."

The History of the Dominican Republic, including the Spanish Possession.

RETURNING to the period when the Dominicans separated themselves from Hayti, whose people had revolted against its chief, President Boyer, we look in vain in the annals of the time, from 1843 to the present, for any period of six consecutive years of peace and tranquillity for the inhabitants of the Spanish part of St Domingo.

Nothing but conspiracies, revolutions, and civil wars mark a period of some sixteen years, in which Hayti, by constant incursions, added to the troubles of her neighbour. In absolute despair, it would seem, of securing tranquillity in any other way, one of the Dominican chiefs ceded in the most arbitrary way to the Government of Spain the island over which she had formerly had extreme control, by right of discovery and conquest.

Immediately upon the giving to the breeze the flag of freedom by Duarte, the whole people of the Spanish part were in arms; and it was declared free of Haytian rule in a formal manner February 27, 1844, a day that has ever since been kept sacred as the birthday of the Republic of Dominica.

Carlos, surnamed Riviere Herard, who had succeeded Boyer in the direction of affairs in Hayti, receiving news of this insurrection, marched by the southern route in March 1844, to attack the Dominicans, as they now called themselves, with a force of 15,000 men; but being opposed by General Santana near the town of Azua, he was entirely defeated, March 19, and forced to retreat, reducing to ashes on his way that town, a fate to which it has since become well accustomed.

About the same time a similar expedition was sent into the interior region of the island, the Cibao; but meeting with a like fate, it was compelled to retreat; and, following the example set by Dessalines, the country through which the army marched was laid waste with fire and sword.

On the declaration of independence, a temporary Government had been formed under a "Provisional Junta Gobernativa;" and there were two divisions in the island—the north with Duarte at its head, and the south with Santana for chief.

On the 10th July, however, Santana—who, covered with the laurels gained in his victory over the Haytians, had marched into the capital—was on the 12th proclaimed supreme chief of the new republic; and in the following November, delegates from all parts of the island having assembled at San Cristobal, a constitution was formed and confirmed, Santana being elected by the spontaneous vote of all the towns of the island President.

Santana, it appears, was an humble planter, who had been living a quiet life in his native district of Seybo, but called into action by the affairs of his country, he seems to have acted with great decision and bravery; and being possessed of much landed wealth, is said to have used it freely in the service of his country. Without being either brilliant as a lawyer or a soldier, he was possessed of good sound sense.

It would appear that he resigned his office in 1848; but Zimenes, his successor, playing into the hands of Soulouque, the latter was induced to make an incursion in 1849 with 4000 men against the Dominicans.

Santana being called upon to assume command of the troops, met the enemy at Ocoa, April 21, 1849, with only about 400 men, and succeeded in defeating Soulouque's army utterly. For this he received the name of "Libertador;" and Zimenes being declared unfit for his position, Santana, forcing him to resign, restored peace and tranquillity to the republic, acting under the title of Dictator. But he became unpopular from not securing the recognition of the United States; and in 1849, Buenaventura Baez was elected President of the republic by a great majority of the electoral votes,—serving out his full term, it appears, with great honour to himself and advantage to the country, the republic being now recognised as having a political existence.

Hardly had Baez taken his seat as President, when he was waited on by a deputation from the Cibao district, bearing a petition signed by the most prominent men of all classes, asking him to open negotiations with the United States for the purpose of annexation.

Baez does not appear to have favoured this at the time, and advised its postponement till a future day, assuming that the slavery existing in the United States made it inexpedient for a country so many of whose citizens were dark-skinned to ally itself thereto.

No one can blame him for this, knowing full well, as he did, that his own status in the United States, as regards colour, would be hard to define; while in some parts of the South he would have been placed on a par with the field-labourer of the plantation. It would appear he was persistent in maintaining these views until he saw that it had become a matter of necessity, and was decidedly the wish of the entire people of the republic.

It really does seem as though for a few years the Dominican people enjoyed a season of rest and improvement. The country was out of debt, the money in circulation, consisting of paper issues, had a value fixed by the Government; some attempts were made at organising an army and navy, stores and munitions for which were duly purchased; while, more important than all, a mediation was obtained, in which Great Britain, the United States, and France united in securing peace from hostile neighbours.

As the time for a new election drew near, Baez, who had identified himself with the party known as the clerical party, became unpopular with the people, who, it appears, thought more of the State than of the Church; and in consequence, in 1853, Santana was duly elected President.

There does not seem to be any reason to suppose that Baez acted in any improper way, or committed any act against this decision of the people, as he appears to have retired quietly to his estates in the vicinity of Azua.

Santana, however, either mistrusting Baez, or jealous of the reputation he had acquired, seems to have acted more in keeping with the character of his former position as Dictator, rather than as President of a free republic; for he decreed the banishment of the ex-president from the island, to which decree Baez appears to have yielded quiet submission.

In order to settle the status of the clerical power, Santana also made the Archbishop take the oath of allegiance to him as a power greater than the Church.

On the 25th of February 1854, a congress of revision met in the capital, and confirmed the constitution of 1844, Santana promulgating the same as President of the republic on the 27th, making a speech at the same time on the happy state of affairs existing.

Although in the early part of this term Santana seems to have been very popular, and succeeded in repelling another attack made by the Haytian ruler Soulouque in 1856, notwithstanding the mediation that had been formed, yet it would seem that administrative power was not one of his gifts, and affairs in the island became very unsettled; the credit of the Government was lost, and public opinion became so well fixed as to his incapacity for government, that he himself was compelled to confess his inability to control any longer its affairs; and, therefore, resigning his office, he retired to his place in the Seybo province.

Curiously enough, however, he seems to have mistrusted the future, and made such preparations in retiring, by taking ample supplies of ammunition and arms, as would enable him, if he saw fit, to take an active part in future events if they should not prove to his satisfaction.

It is stated that a movement that he made towards leasing the Bay of Samana to the United States was the real cause of the discontent against Santana in this term, particularly as this feeling was fostered by the representatives of foreign Governments, who, in fact, protested against the consummation of the treaty, which had been prepared by the agent of President Pierce. The change in Government put an end at that time to these negotiations.

Baez at this time was out of the country, but all parties pretty generally seem to have united in requesting him to return and occupy the presidential chair, Santana himself even using his influence to induce the diplomatic corps to make use of their position to induce Baez to return, which, after several refusals, he finally concluded to do, taking his seat February 1, 1857.

Hardly had he been installed in office, when attempts at insurrection in various parts of the island were made, all of which were put down, until there arose a more formidable one in the region of the Cibao, of which the large and flourishing town of Santiago is the capital.

This place, the centre of the tobacco trade, controlled principally by foreign merchants, and with a population more largely composed of whites and active, enterprising coloured people, has always had jealousy existing among its people against St Domingo city, as being the capital of the island, it being contended that Santiago, laying aside the question of antiquity, has greater claims to hold that position.

Here, then, a strong feeling, fostered it is said by the English agent, existed against Baez, which finally assumed the form of an irresistible rebellion; and he was driven in 1858 from the island, going to Europe to look after some private matters.

We have here the first appearance in the active affairs of the island of Jose Maria Cabral, the intimate friend and schoolmate of Baez in former days, but latterly his political rival. He was with Baez at this time taking part in the various encounters of the rebellion against his authority, and remained for a time on the island after Baez had left; but his connection with that officer made him such an object of suspicion and persecution, that he, Cabral, found it convenient to depart also.

Santana, who had taken an active part against Baez, was again called upon to preside over the affairs of the Government, and it was through him the island passed eventually back to the Spaniards.

Unable to preserve peace among the factions of the island, without means or resources for its government and improvement, set upon constantly by the Haytians, who on every occasion and under every pretext sought an excuse to war upon the Dominicans, and regain possession of the whole island for themselves, Santana, it would seem, disheartened with affairs, and believing that some strong power was necessary to preserve the individuality of the Dominican territory, suddenly, and almost without consultation, either of the people of Dominica or their rulers, threw himself into the arms of Spain, giving up to its authority, in May 1861, the entire possession of the Spanish part of the island.

It is a very difficult matter, judging at this day from the chronicles of the times and the conflicting statements of friends or enemies of Santana, to form the proper estimate of his character; but it is something to say in his favour that, up to the period of the Spanish annexation, he appears to have been to a great extent the idol of the population; and even now the traveller frequently hears from the older people sentiments of the warmest admiration for the "Lion of Seybo," as he was called.

Nominally the President at different times, he was, in fact, the dictator of the island, whose will was supreme law. His power over the masses of the people, it is said, was extraordinary; and he did not hesitate to punish the most noted chiefs of the island.

Many people may blame him, and do, for his desire of annexing the island to Spain; but knowing what we do now of the Dominicans and their history, we can afford to look with greater leniency on this act, in the belief that, feeling the need of means and protection from a strong power, having had experience of the selfishness of the different leaders in their party quarrels, utterly ignoring the welfare of the country, and having a watchful foe like Hayti ever ready to avail herself of the troubles and dissensions in the island, he acted the part of a patriot and statesman in ceding to Spain the possession of a territory which had been identified with the glories of her past history.

Charity will concede as much, we think, to a man whose memory to-day is revered; who, while alive, was always honest, and who, for himself, never despoiled the public treasury. Valiant without a rival, he was the first to hasten to battle, and his breast was the first presented to the balls of Haytian enemies. He gained with justice from his admiring countrymen the appellation of "Libertador de la Patria."

In manner, Santana is said to have been rough and brutal, though, according to some authorities, he would be better characterised as determined.

Santana seems to have been really desirous of annexing the island to the United States; but in this, it is said, he was frustrated by the threats and opposition of the French Consul-General at Port-au-Prince, Maxime Raybaud. He then offered it to France, and finally to Spain, sending for this purpose General Alfan to make the offer.

That the people of St Domingo were not generally consulted in this movement there can be no doubt, and even in some of the cases where an effort was made to consult their wishes, a decision was given against this action.

The whole scheme, it is said,—and appears to have been,—was a private one of Santana's, who, calling together the commanders and governors of the different districts of the republic, informed them he had opened negotiations with the Spaniards to incorporate into their monarchy the Dominican republic; and gave instructions how they were to treat the people in regard to securing their votes.

Many of those who gave their votes testify they were not aware to what extent this plan of incorporation was to be carried; and it is even stated that Santana himself was deceived eventually by the Spaniards. This may be believed if we read the treaty made between the two authorities, which seems just and reasonable enough, if its provisions had been fairly carried out, which they were not.

This treaty embodies as follows:—

1. That the industrial freedom shall be preserved without the power of slavery being re-established.

2. That the republic of Dominica shall be considered as a *province* of Spain, and enjoy the same privileges.

3. The services of the greatest number possible of the men who have been of importance in the country since 1841, particularly those of the army, shall be recognised and have preference in appointments.

4. That as one of the first measures, the Spanish Government shall recognise the responsibility of the paper circulating in the island as money.

5. That it shall recognise as valid all acts of the Dominican Governments that have succeeded one another in the island from the birth of the republic.

Spain denies that there was any previous treaty made for this incorporation, claiming that it was the spontaneous act of the people.

Facts, however, do not corroborate this, for it appears the measures of the Spanish Government were taken with due deliberation, while the *people* of St Domingo were taken by surprise. In the circular sent by Santana to the governors, it was stated that Dominica was to be considered as a province of Spain. When the affair was consummated, and the treaty came to be signed, it was found that this was meant to be considered as a *province beyond sea*, to be governed as were Cuba and Puerto Rico.

It will be curious to watch the opinions of the press in Spain as an exposition of Spanish sentiment and policy on American affairs on this St Domingo question; and we find the *Cronica* of 1861, speaking of the "unexpected demonstration" in St Domingo, accounts for it on these grounds:—

"Fear of their enemies on the border, who wish to possess their territory; mistrust of the United States in its aspirations; that, instructed by the lack of success of the republics of the Continent, they have hopes of sharing in the *same benefits as Cuba and Puerto Rico*, and that they want to be permanently governed. Tired of its own independence, and afraid of the encroachments of the United States, it seeks our protecting power. And *with this island stretching its right hand to Puerto Rico and its left to Cuba, we commence a new system, giving us the control of the Gulf.*"

Nevertheless, they were a little fearful that the United States would interfere with this occupation; but that Government being busy with its own rebellion, took no steps against it, but eventually recognised the transfer.

They claimed that "the principal service that St Domingo can render us, is that of preventing the North American race from getting a footing too near Cuba."

A weak opposition only was manifested in Spain against this project, some of the papers stating, in order to create a feeling against it, that yellow fever constantly prevails in St Domingo, and Le Clerc's expedition was cited as an illustration of the fatal consequences that might be anticipated for the Spanish soldiers in taking possession.

This charge was met by the assertion, "that while it is true that the Antilles are subject to this fever, it is also certain there are portions never affected by it, and among these is St Domingo, in which not a single Spaniard who has gone there has lost his life from it, but, on the contrary, all live happy and contented."

This transfer was consummated by Santana inviting the population of St Domingo city to meet in the cathedral square to witness the incorporation with Spain.

Two war-steamers had been sent by Spain to Calderas harbour, and a number of Spanish officers had landed at St Domingo, without visiting any other parts; and on the day of this incorporation these two vessels of war came up abreast of the city.

From daybreak of the 18th March 1861, signal was given of the solemn proclamation of the union of St Domingo, numbers of people circulated about the streets, and at six A.M. the "plaza" was peopled by numbers of all classes, and a short time after began to arrive the troops that had constituted the garrison, *all without arms.*

General Perez, chief of the capital, arrived with his staff, while senators, officers, and some persons of distinction were present.

General Santana made a speech from the balcony of the court of justice, informing the people what was to be done, and announcing, in accordance with the expressed wishes of the people (?), the alliance with Spain.

Two prominent chiefs, who had heretofore manifested their opposition to the scheme, were by some means induced to remain tranquil, and though present, they, with the people, seem to have remained quiescent, offering no sign either of dissent or approval.

The secretary of General Santana read the act of incorporation, as follows:—

"In the very noble and loyal city of St Domingo, on the 18th day of the month of March 1861, we the undersigned, met in the Hall of the Palace of Justice of this capital, declare, that of our free and spontaneous will, in our own name and that of those who have conferred the power upon us of acting for them, solemnly proclaim the Queen and Lady the excellent Isabel II., in whose hands we deposit the sovereignty that until now we have exercised as members of the Republic of Dominica. We declare equally that it is our free and spontaneous will, as well as that of the people, who by our presence in this place we represent, that all the territory of the republic is annexed to the crown of Spain, to whom it belonged before the treaty of the 18th February 1855, in which her most Catholic Majesty recognised as a sovereign state that which to-day of its spontaneous will the people to it return this sovereignty. In witness of which," &c.

Notice was at once sent to Governor Serrano at Cuba, and immediately troops to the number of 3000 poured in from that island and Puerto Rico, until further levies from Spain arrived, the whole number reaching eventually some 6000 men.

But it must not be supposed that the incorporation went on thus smoothly all over the island; on the contrary, though I find records of documents purporting to be the will of the people of San Juan, San Antonio de Guerra, Pedro de Macoris, Baya Guana, Monte Plata, Savana la Mar, and Seybo, signed each by the governor or commandant, the parish priests, and one or two of the prominent officials, as representing the will of the people, yet I do not find any record of the general popular will at such places as Azua, Puerto Plata, Mocha, Vega, Santiago, and Monte Cristo.

On the contrary, I even find that at Macoris (San Francisco de) an attempt was made by the people of that town to dispute this action of the Government; but the governor of the place, putting a cannon in position on the plaza, opened fire on the people, who were thus dispersed.

Some time after, when troops had been landed at Puerto Plata, the ceremony of exchanging the Dominican for the Spanish banner took place, in presence of these armed bodies.

"Spain began her rule with fair and generous promises, but they were not fulfilled. She mistook entirely the temper of the Dominican people. She forgot that they were freemen, and had virtually been their own masters for three quarters of a century."

So far from keeping close to a liberal reading of the terms of the treaty, no sooner was she assured of her possession of the island, than the promises to her "most favoured" province were forgotten. In place of the improvements promised, and the appointment of Dominicans to office, hordes of officials came from the two slaveholding islands of Puerto Rico and Cuba, and were placed in authority over the heads of free citizens, many of whom, from their colour, they professed to look upon as no better than bondsmen.

A machinery of Government was established, oppressive and intolerable, for which the people were expected to pay, and calculations were made as though based upon an immense revenue, to be derived from a country flourishing in agriculture and commerce, and with a numerous and well-to-do population—just the reverse of the actual condition of the island. It is stated that the entire expenditure of the republic for the year preceding the Spanish annexation was but $241,347, while the estimates for the year 1863, remitted to Spain for approval, amounted to $4,476,000, and this to be applied to the administration of a territory some 20,000 square miles in extent, containing less than 150,000 inhabitants.

The same policy that ruled in the slaveholding island of Cuba was endeavoured to be reproduced in St Domingo, and though some of the wiser and more enlightened minds of Spain protested against the folly of endeavouring to make a free people retrograde, the policy was persisted in, until it brought its own reward.

Let us see what the Spaniards themselves say in their press.

"But if in this incorporation Spain proposes nothing else than a vain display of authority, if she seeks nothing more than a means of satisfying a horde of hungry agents, who hope to prosper at the expense of the country," &c.

"The Cabinet of O'Donnel could not accept the reincorporation to Spain of Dominica, in order to condemn it to the same rules that were prevalent in the Antilles."

At no time, while the Spaniards were in possession, was there perfect peace in the island. At St Domingo city, where were the principal headquarters of the officials, tranquillity and contentment, arising from the flow of Spanish gold, seem to have prevailed up to the very hour of the departure of the Spaniards; but in the other parts, especially in the Cibao and the north, great discontent prevailed.

Hardly a month elapsed before numbers of the Dominicans opposed to annexation, who had gathered together in Haytian territory, promoted an insurrectionary movement. Geffrard, who had become the ruler of Hayti, on receiving news of the Spanish incorporation had protested against it, in which he was also joined by the representatives of France and England. Issuing a proclamation, in which he put forth doctrines that seem to be those of the present rulers of Hayti, he held that "from the moment when two peoples inhabit the same island, their destinies, by sympathy or attempts of the stranger, are necessarily united. The political existence of the one is intimately allied to that of the other, and they are bound to guarantee one to the other their mutual safety."

The negro population, fearful that the restoration of European power in the island would bring a return of slavery, sided with the Dominicans, claiming "that the proposed organisation given to the Island of St Domingo defrauded completely the people of those hopes they had for the future in their change of Government."

With these views, the movement of the Dominicans sheltered in Haytian territory was encouraged; and at the head of this party was General Cabral, who had united with him several other prominent chiefs, among them General Sanchez. These, marching upon Santiago almost before the Spaniards had time to take possession, proclaimed a republic.

Santana, who had marched to Azua on the appearance of opposition, from thence despatched General Alfau to the Cibao, where he was successful in putting down the republican movement, capturing nearly all the leaders except Cabral, who made his escape into Hayti, wounded and sick.

Most of these prisoners, comprising the very best of the youth of the Cibao, were murdered in cold blood; and though for the time this had the effect of putting an end to any future attempts at rebellion, the fire of independence only slumbered, awaiting the slightest breath to fan it into flame.

So heavily, however, did the Spanish rule weigh upon the people, that small revolts were constantly occurring in different parts of the island, and it seemed impossible to secure peace; though it is stated that, with great nobility of character, the Dominicans did not at first revenge the cruelties perpetrated on them by the Spaniards, but even returned their prisoners on parole.

Oppression, however, became so strong, that a general desire for freedom prevailed throughout the island, but particularly in the Cibao region, of which Santiago was the capital, where the Spaniards had, in the Fort St Louis, their principal headquarters.

So serious did this feeling become, that the Spaniards seem to have become alarmed, and a general amnesty was declared to all, whether they had acted in opposition before annexation or in rebellion since.

It was too late; the smouldering fire was not to be entirely quenched, especially with such rulers as General Buceta in command of the Cibao district.

Stained with every crime, this man had been expelled as a criminal offender from Spain, but had at first been given the command of Samana, being afterwards removed to Santiago, where his greatest pleasure seems to have been in seeing how much he could torment the people over whom he was placed. He ruled with an iron hand; and the accounts of his brutality and cruelty are something frightful, testified to, as they were, in my presence by priest and layman, man and woman.

Although representations were made to higher authority asking for the removal of this Governor, no notice whatever appears to have been taken of them; and he retained his position until at last the people, worn out with his cruelties and oppressions, as well as those of other officials, broke into open rebellion; and at the mountain Capotillo near the village of Dajabon, an humble farmer, a countryman named Cabrera, raised the banner of revolt.

This man, utterly illiterate, not even knowing how to read or write, placed himself at the head of sixteen men in August 1863, and descended into the plain of Monte Cristo, where he was joined by Pimentel, Luperon, and others, who took possession of the small village of Savaneta.

Here they were joined by a large body of Dominican refugees from Hayti, who, crossing the frontier, united their forces, then marched upon and took Dajabon, Guayubin, &c.

A Spanish column that was despatched from Santiago to meet them was dispersed with slaughter, after being ambushed. General Buceta himself was left alone, and only by good luck made his way back to the city, where he assumed command, troops having arrived to support him.

About 2000 Dominicans, however, marched down and took possession of Puerto Plata, but the arrival of the vessel of war *Isabel II.*, which landed a force under cover of her guns, compelled them to evacuate it.

From this beginning spread rapidly throughout the island the war against the Spaniards, who, so far from accepting this action as the wish of a free people, looked upon it as the action of revolted slaves.

As the Dominican people have been reflected upon for their apparent readiness to accept the dominion of Spain and then throw it off, I have, in order to be perfectly impartial in the matter, sought my information principally from Spanish sources; and I shall here quote the remarks of the Spanish press when the news came of this rising in St Domingo.

After acknowledging that the island was not unanimous in favour of annexation, the *Cronica* says, "Now that it is done, the only way to pacify it is to leave the people as free as possible consistent with its subjection to Spain.

"Give to the Dominicans political liberty, economy of government, and peace, and in a few years its population will increase; and so far from being a charge to us, it would be a source of revenue for Spain.

"In St Domingo there only needs labourers for agriculture, for industry, for the arts; it needs a great immigration from Europe if it is to prosper; it is a healthy country, a virgin country.

"The responsibility of the O'Donnel Cabinet is not in having accepted annexation, but in not having secured it, converting it in their hands into an element powerful and beneficial for Spain."

And when the pride and ire of Spain was roused by the further news that came of the probability that the insurrection could not be subdued, "Let us promptly quell this insurrection with all our forces, and this done, let us *restore to the Dominicans those rights and privileges of which we have robbed them.*

"The Duke of Tetuan began by attacking in place of respecting existing customs, first of which was the religion that for forty years had been tolerated.

"The Archbishop Monijan had hardly arrived when he ordered the Protestant churches to be closed. Before the annexation an interment cost $60, after his arrival it cost $500.

"They have deprived the islanders of office, some of the most prominent men having been removed, and they have inflicted upon the island a horde of rapacious officials.

"This was the error; people that have once tasted of liberty, before resigning themselves to lose it, prefer death. They should then have respected the franchises and liberties of the Dominicans, without taking into account the rule that governs for the other of its Antilles. In fact, the Island of St Domingo, in place of gaining, has lost."

So positive, however, were the Spaniards in their determination not to relinquish the island, that in April 1864, in the Cortes, the Minister, President of the Council, said "they would fight in the Island of St Domingo until they triumphed, calling forth all their resources, since they would not permit an atom of territory to be alienated from Spain."

But it is amusing to read, when things became desperate, how some of those very writers who had previously been loudest in praise of St Domingo now saw fit to depreciate it, and so wrote: "The people, accustomed to a solitary life in the woods, can, owing to the lack of roads and population, maintain a constant guerilla warfare. There are Dominicans who cross entire leagues of earth *leaping from tree to tree*, without touching the ground with the soles of their feet; and, born in this climate, they do not suffer from the fevers that attack the European who risks his life in their woods."

I have neither the space in this volume nor the inclination to detail the horrors of this war, that continued until 1865, in which every atrocity which the human mind can conceive was committed; and the details of some of the acts of the Spanish officials show that, while they have not forgotten the example of crimes perpetrated in this very island by their bloodthirsty ancestors, the civilisation of the present day has done nothing towards softening those instincts engendered by the blood of these same ancestors.

I well remember, being in Cuba at this period, how the blood was chilled by the accounts we received from the neighbouring isle of St Domingo; and the inhabitants of the former beautiful isle little thought then that in a few short years these same scenes of Spanish cruelty and oppression were to be enacted on their own shores by their tyrannical masters.

So general became this revolt against the Spaniards in St Domingo, that many of those who had finally accepted the government of Spain were now heartily opposed to it, and in rebellion against its authority.

Among these, General Baez, who had taken the oath of allegiance, and had visited Spain, where he was made a General of Division, was found.

General Cabral, who at first had revolted, as we have

seen, but afterwards recognised the sovereignty of Isabella, having, through the intercession of Baez, been pardoned, and taken the oath of allegiance, united with Baez in efforts to succour their country, taking refuge in Hayti, where they sought help from Geffrard, even offering him, it is said, a portion of the Dominican territory at present comprising part of the province of Azua.

Suffice it to say here, however, that the Spaniards, being eventually compelled to leave the island, they left it as near as human hands could make it a waste of desolation; and the traveller to-day will find hardly a spot in this beautiful land that does not bear testimony in a ruined town, well-filled graves, or a desolated household, of this last epoch of the "Time of the Spaniards."

It was a bitter pill for the pride of Spain to be compelled to relinquish her hold upon the island; and the press was free in its denunciations of those who, by their acts had brought about this state of affairs.

"And the Archbishop of St Domingo, who is now at Toledo—what has he done? We must be severe, for the greater the rank, the position, and the power, the greater the responsibility. He went there filled with old-fashioned ideas of the time of the Inquisition; he found Protestant chapels, he wished to shut them; he met with Protestant families, he wished to expel them; he encountered people legitimately married by Protestant ceremony, he wished to separate them. To paint the harm this great imprudence has done is impossible."

At last, by an act of the Cortes, March 3, 1865, the island of St Domingo was declared free again, Spain protesting that in 1861 she had only listened to the voices of the Dominicans in asking for annexation, as she did now for separation.

But even before the Spaniards took their departure, a quasi-form of Government had been effected; for in August 1863, after Buceta had been defeated at Santiago, the town burned, and he compelled to withdraw into the fort, the Dominicans marched down to Puerto Plata, and there proclaimed the new republic, with Pepillo Salcedo as its first President. But he, being suspected of collusion with the Spaniards, was overthrown by General Polanco, who was proclaimed President; until Pimentel, whom we have already seen among the first to take up arms, following this example, headed a movement against Polanco, and he became President, and remained so at the time of the departure of the Spanish troops. And thus, by a series of events peculiar to St Domingo, before it had ceased to be part of a monarchy it had already been three times a republic.

Pimentel, who seems to have been only a simple farmer, blessed with good common sense, but no education whatever, joining the patriot forces with no other object than to benefit his country, became by force of circumstances its chief.

Santana, meanwhile, the former great leader, who had been made Captain-General, but had resigned his position and retired to his farm until the rebellion broke out, when he offered his services to the Spaniards, had just died in St Domingo city, without having gained any reward for his efforts to settle the country—dying, in fact, it is said, from sorrow and mortification at seeing the cruelties inflicted on his countrymen by the very men whom he had aided to bring into it.

A strong feeling at this time was manifested in favour of annexation to the United States. When the Spaniards left, Pimentel, however, found he had a rival in General Cabral, who, with the military chief Manzueta, was at the head of the troops of the south at the capital; and as soon as the place was evacuated, they availed themselves of the absence of Pimentel, then on the frontier resisting an attempt of Salnave to overthrow Geffrard, to march into the city and proclaim against Pimentel.

The latter, when he heard of this new aspirant for President, tendered his resignation; and Cabral was proclaimed Protector by the voices of a few hundred people gathered in the plaza at St Domingo city, being incited thereto by the friends of Cabral, August 4, 1865.

The rest of the island seems to have known nothing of this new movement, and the entire district of the powerful Cibao seems to have been entirely unconsulted; but this is the way Governments are made in this famous island. A few hundred people gather together, and shout "Vive Cabral!" "Vive Polanco!" and the fortunate chief called declares himself the Government.

Cabral, however, who, it appears, had made use of the plea that he was acting for Baez, did not remain long undisturbed; for the people, finding out his desire to become their ruler, grew restless. A decree was then issued by Cabral calling for a Congress to elect regularly a President, and form a constitution. On the 25th September 1865, the Convention for framing a constitution met after eight days had been passed in electing members. During this delay, General Pedro Guillermo organised a movement in the Seybo province; and a party formed at the town of Higuey. Taking for their watchword, "Cabral, Manzueta, and Baez," they marched to Seybo without opposition; but arriving before the walls of the capital, they were denied entrance by the people (though it appears Cabral was willing enough to allow them to enter). He, however, went to San Cristobal to raise troops to oppose this movement, leaving Pimentel in the city, who, entering into league with Guillermo, pronounced for Baez as President.

It must be understood that Baez was not in the country; but in almost every movement that had taken place in the island, the eyes of the people seem to have searched out Baez as the only man who had the ability and disposition to govern them honestly. Even Santana had stated that he made the Spanish annexation in order to have Baez as Governor of the island; and no sooner had the war of the Spaniards assumed a favourable aspect, than Salcedo, one of the revolutionary chiefs, had written to Baez, praying him for his country's sake to come and assume control of the Government.

Guillermo, being permitted to enter the city, assumed command; but the Congress refused to recognise his authority, claiming that Cabral, as Protector, represented the Government until a President was regularly appointed. By an article of the constitution it was provided that Congress should appoint the first President, and they, it appears, were decidedly in favour of Cabral; but Manzueta, acting in connection with Guillermo, both of whom professed to represent the wishes of the entire island, and not that of the capital alone, walked into the congressional halls, and announced to the members, drawing his sword at the same time as a weighty argument, that they *must* elect Baez as President, which it appears they did; and there seems no reason to doubt that this was really in accord with the wishes of the people, with whom Baez was now particularly popular, as being the advocate of the doctrine of universal suffrage.

A commission was formed in October 1865 of some of the most prominent citizens, for the purpose of proceeding to the neighbouring island of Curaçoa, and inviting General Baez to come and assume the reins of government. Although I do not find that Baez used any efforts to bias public opinion, yet the desire at this time appears to have been unanimous throughout the island that Baez should be called to be President. Even Cabral solicited appointment as one of the commissioners, and Pimentel and other prominent chiefs pronounced decidedly for Baez. But it was only after repeated efforts that Baez finally concluded to accept the invitation, and in forming his cabinet, Cabral received the appointment of Minister of War, while Pimentel was made Secretary of the Interior.

In December 1865 a new constitution was formed, but this only lasted until the following April, when it was set aside, and the constitution originally adopted under Santana in 1854 substituted for it.

Cabral, it appears, is a man who has always had ambitious projects for himself, desiring positions which he has not the ability to fill. Born in St Domingo, he was partially educated in England, where he passed several years of his life, when, returning to the island, and becoming mixed up in its military affairs, he gained considerable experience in the practical duties of war-making on a small scale. A tall, raw-boned mulatto, of much bravery, he was well calculated for a guerilla leader; but in the administrative duties of Minister of War he seems to have fallen into his proper place of a mere cipher; and becoming disgusted with his position, he, under plea of ill-health, sought a refuge in Curaçoa; and from there, with a certain General Valverde, began his machinations to overthrow Baez. In this they were joined by Pimentel, who, claiming that the change of constitution was a farce, attempted to provoke insurrections against Baez, and incited the people of the Cibao to rebel.

Baez, in this case, appears to have behaved with great magnanimity, for though he had Pimentel in his power after his treason, he does not seem to have treated him harshly; and finding that Cabral had sought refuge in Hayti, from whence he designed making an attempt on St Domingo, he sent him word that, in order to save bloodshed, he, Baez, would resign his position, and Cabral could come and take it.

This conspiracy against Baez, it appears, united together Pimentel, Cabral, and Valverde, the pretext they used being that Baez had altered the constitution; but it is evident there were other more truthful reasons to be found in their individual ambition and jealousy of each other.

The words of Baez himself perhaps give the best idea

of matters at this time. "There are documents in circulation proving that I was called back to the country, in which documents the names of Cabral, Pimentel, Manzueta, Garcia, and others, almost all those who appear in the revolutionary ranks, are prominent. I have in my possession a large number of letters from all the generals—perhaps one or two may be excepted—congratulating me on my return, and offering me their services.

"Notwithstanding this, within the five months that I have been in power, I have had to face as many rebellions; and let it not be said that they have been provoked by measures taken by my Government, for the first one broke out a few hours before I took the oath.

"Wearied with fighting against factions, and wishing to prevent civil war, as soon as I had knowledge of the last insurrection in the Cibao, I sent General Pimentel to those provinces, but he was not able to fulfil my wishes or avoid bloodshed. The people of their own free will preferred to fight, and Cibao is to-day the theatre of civil war, which I behold with sorrow, and desire to stop. . . .

"You will inform him (Cabral) that I am by all means determined to leave the Presidency for a more capable or more fortunate person."

Baez, therefore, with some of his adherents, left the country and went to Curaçoa, while Pimentel, the emissary of Baez to the people of the Cibao, and who had traitorously deserted his cause, entered the city of St Domingo with Garcia and Luperon, and in August 1866 they formed a triumvirate.

As all these men were Cibaoyens, it was not long before there was a jealous fear against them in the capital, the inhabitants of the south believing they would remove the capital to Santiago; and Cabral, availing himself of this feeling, used it to secure his own election as President; but he seems only to have been made the puppet for more designing men, and the country during his rule seems to have been constantly in trouble, and no improvements made.

Such was the strait to which matters were reduced, that Cabral endeavoured to lease the Bay of Samana to the United States for two millions of dollars; but as his Government would not give entire control over it, the matter fell through for the time, until, in 1868, Pujol was sent to Washington by Cabral to renew the negotiations, and it was stated that affairs had become so desperate, he must offer Samana to the United States.

Baez, whose friends were then heading a movement to overturn Cabral, issued a proclamation against this attempt to transfer the soil of the republic; and the reader curious in such matters will find in the Appendix three proclamations all under identically the same heading, but showing how ideas are likely to change under various circumstances.

In March 1868 Baez again became President of the Dominican republic, and the people apparently were so glad to welcome him back again, that they offered to make him Dictator, which very wisely he declined; but he still remains the President, evidently to the satisfaction of the people, a few only of some ambitious leaders desiring for their own purposes to throw the country into a state of revolution.

Cabral meanwhile has been constantly on the Haytian border, making petty inroads with a force of all the vagabonds of the country, not large enough to accomplish anything of moment, yet quite large enough to keep a peaceful people in a state of unrest and anxiety.

Baez, since his new inauguration, finding what was the unanimous wish of the people, seeing what were the great necessities of the island, has, I believe, been earnest and honest in endeavouring to bring about annexation to the United States; and whether he is not wise in this, I leave the intelligent reader to judge for himself from the foregoing facts.

As the Dominican Secretary of State said to me, "St Domingo wants a strong Government, which we cannot have so long as she remains isolated and exposed to the attacks of Hayti and the conspiracies of ambitious chiefs. With annexation to the United States we hope will come peace, immigration, capital, roads, and the development of all the interests of the island."

Thus, with persecution and bloodshed, and in frequent revolution, has the present republic of Dominica been born.

It is in theory a constitutional republic, the government of which is divided into three branches, the executive, legislative, and judicial.

The first consists of a President and Vice-president, elected by an electoral college for a term of six years, with a difference of three years in the time of their election. Both of these officers are ineligible to the presidency on the following terms.

The President appoints a Council of State, consisting of a minister of public instruction, of the police, of the interior and of agriculture, of public works and commerce, and of war and marine. On one of these four ministers the duties of minister of foreign affairs devolves at the will of the President.

The legislative branch of the Government consists of a Senate elected by the primary assemblies, and has two members for the city of St Domingo, two for Santiago, and one for each of the other provinces and districts—nine members in all.

These hold office for six years, and may be re-elected.

Each province and district has a governor, and each parish and military post has a commandant nominated by the executive, and responsible to him.

The towns are governed by ayuntamientos or councils, elected by the primary assemblies for three years, and are constituted of as fine a body of intelligent, educated men as can be found in any similar organisation.

Each town or commune also possesses an alcalde, a sort of justice of the peace, who is appointed during good behaviour by the President, and I am happy to bear testimony to their high standing.

The laws are administered by a supreme court sitting at the capital, and there should be minor courts in all the different provinces or districts; but, from the state of affairs existing in the island, these cannot be said to be now in operation.

One of the greatest curses to which the island is subjected is the great number of petty leaders which the frequent revolutions have brought into existence. Many of these men, with no other qualification than that of personal bravery, and having a number of followers who look upon them as their chief, presume to hold themselves subject to any leader who will look after their individual interests.

Holding the rank of general, the numbers of their command would not in many cases amount to a corporal's guard; and yet they receive pay, and wield a certain power, entirely disproportionate to their actual influence for good, though for bad it is incalculable.

Some of these generals are actually possessed of such crude ideas, that the author was asked by them what would be their rank in the United States in the event of annexation; and he was considerably amused at seeing the dubious expression that overcame their countenances when told it would be the proud one of "citizen," with perfect liberty to go when and where they would—to work.

CHAPTER XV.

"Here trees for ever green adorn their shoots
At once with blossoms and with ripening fruits—
Fruits that with fragrant nectar richly flow;
Here all the flowers through every season blow."

JOURNEY OVERLAND—*Organising a Party—Our Route—Crossing the Ozama—Tropical Forests—Lunching "al fresco"—First Night Experiences—La Tosa—San Pedro—Natural Farm—Bad Roads—Apartments—The Country People—Rough Experiences—Grand Scenery—Sillon de la Viuda—Serico—Ride to Cotuy.*

ONE of the most curious things in connection with St Domingo is the astonishing ignorance of many inhabitants in reference to localities which they have not visited. I have met men who for years had lived on the island in one place, who gave me the most ridiculous and exaggerated accounts of other parts, of which they had only heard. Thus, on the north coast, they spoke to me of the Cibao region and the interior town of Santiago as though it were a matter of the greatest and almost insuperable difficulty to visit them: and the word "Cibao" carries almost as much mystery to the ears of the modern traveller as it did to Columbus when he confounded it with Cipango. When, at St Domingo city, it was proposed to cross the island by land, people seemed to think a man must be either crazy, or that he expected to derive some mysterious benefit from such a trip; and we were mysteriously told the trip was almost an impossibility, and accompanied with unheard-of dangers and risks. When it became known that one of the United States Commissioners intended to penetrate into the interior, and ascertain for himself the opinion of people there, heads were gravely shaken, and remarks made about the safety of trusting himself amongst the people of that region.

The Government authorities were, however, very kind in offering every assistance, and advising the trip to be taken; and having made up my mind individually to "do" the island as well as possible, I was only too glad to accept Mr Commissioner White's invitation to join him in his trip across to the north coast. A party was therefore organised, consisting of the Honourable Andrew D. White, United States Commissioner, Professor W. M. Gabb, Surveyor to the Geological Company of New York, Doctor H. B. Blackwell, of the *Boston Press*, and the author of these pages; and our preparations were made in such a manner as would lead one to think we were about to start upon a tour in the prairies.

Horses were fitted out with M'Clellan saddles and equipments for riding, while others were prepared with immense straw panniers (macutas), in which to carry supplies; servants were engaged; while, almost of more importance, strong canvas hammocks were secured for each of us.

Early, therefore, on the morning of the 21st February, our adieux having been said the previous day, we gathered at headquarters, blankets, cloaks, and umbrellas strapped to our saddles, while our general wardrobes had been bestowed in the smallest possible kits to place in the panniers.

Shades of dignified pompous officials! what would ye have said to have seen this distinguished emissary of a great nation (only outdone by his followers) so lost to the "convenances" of official position as to wear his pants inside his boots, a fireman's shirt without collar enveloping his person, while on that head from whose piercing orbits were to go the rays that should carry yea or nay to this aspiring island, was placed a most undignified, natty-looking, but perfectly comfortable "wideawake"?

The guerilla appearance of the rest of the party, however, was redeemed by the eminently respectable appearance of the venerable-looking "Doctor."

But, vamous señores; we are now out over the hills of San Carlos, where we stopped for a few minutes to organise more perfectly our cavalcade, and from which old village we had our last view of St Domingo city.

A beautiful sight indeed on this fresh, bright morning in February, with the atmosphere as clear as ether, the sky as blue as cobalt; and there at our feet the historic, sleepy old town, its moss-covered walls and vine-clad towers, with the graceful palms shooting up from walled courtyards, making a strange, yet beautiful and interesting picture, to which the bright blue sea, with its foam-crested waves, formed a sparkling, spirited background.

Putting spurs to our horses, we soon got over the intervening four miles that separated us from the ferry by which we were to cross the Isabella, an arm of the Ozama, the river upon which St Domingo city is located.

The road up to this point had been fair enough, running through ordinary rolling land, tolerably well settled with the small huts of the negro or the better one of the white inhabitant; the land being chiefly covered with scrubby vegetation, groups of palms, and the "platano" plantations, upon the products of which the inhabitants principally rely for meat, bread, and vegetables. This, being a coarse kind of banana, with a dry, mealy flesh, is either boiled or roasted.

Our first arrival at the ferry seemed to make no impression on the negro boatmen on the other side, for they appeared in no hurry to bring their flat boat to our assistance, until the energetic "cussing" of the Professor, accompanied by the waving of an official document and the shout of "official service," served to startle them into coming over for us—the ferry-boat being a huge flat boat, and the machinery the ferry-rope. The river here was more than fifty yards wide, perfectly clear, running swiftly between low marshy banks; but immediately after crossing, we made a steep ascent up a muddy, rough path to higher land, where, striking the main road, we continued our journey, our way being almost continually through the woods, which, though interesting to us from the strange appearance of plants and trees, it would not be so to describe. We were glad, therefore, when, at noon, the sun being hot enough even to

Crossing the Isabella.

penetrate the thick foliage on the road, the announcement was made of our mid-day resting-place.

This was upon the banks of a small fresh-water stream, known as "El Yuco," whose limpid waters furnished us the fluid for some cold rum-punch, concocted of the sour orange (naranja agria), picked from overhanging trees, the juice of which, incorporated with some native (Dominican) rum, made a most capital punch. This was our first camping-out experience; and, if the party is to be believed, no such repast had been ever enjoyed before as was this frugal meal of "sardine" sandwiches and cold punch.

The propriety, however, was suggested to Mr White, of trying some of that champagne that had been, according to the newspapers, so liberally furnished among the Commissioners' supplies, and which would serve to lighten our loads in more senses than one; but we were informed he had seen none of it; and I am sadly compelled to acknowledge there was none on this trip.

To complete our grandeur, we were supplied with music by a peripatetic musician, who, with a companion, happened to come up while we were lunching, and who, in return for hospitality extended them, favoured us with some music (?) from a huge guitar he carried, and which, being the only baggage he had, enabled him to travel from the one end of the island to the other without difficulty.

Musician.

Being recuperated, we were again on horseback, picking our way through the muddy road of the forest, in which, from time to time, our ears were saluted by sharp reports as though of pistol-firing; these came, however, from the higuero, or, as we call it, the "sand-box" tree, the fruit of which resembles somewhat that article, being a tomato-shaped corrugated fruit, which, becoming dry, is, by the heat of the sun, caused to explode.

Sand-box Fruit.

These explosions take place only at mid-day, when the sun is intensely hot; and their reports are at times quite startling.

After some miles of riding we came out into the open, upon beautiful savannas, which, though somewhat more rolling, yet bear the generic name of "Llanos" or prairies; and which would seem to have been thrown here by nature as natural farms, for the land was of the very best deep black soil, covered with long, rich grass; while here and there were belts of timber.

A Natural Farm.

The country reminded me much of the Minnesota bottom lands, except that here the horizon was bounded by beautiful views of cloud-capped mountains, to whose very feet rolled these magnificent plains, all ready for the hand of the husbandman. As evening was now drawing on, it was deemed advisable to select a place to rest for the night, particularly as some of our party, not being accustomed to horseback riding, might suffer from a first ride of twenty miles, and especially over such roads as we had had.

This we did, stopping at La Tosa, as the estancia (farm) was called, being a simple negro-house, with one or two out-buildings, all constructed in the rudest manner, the farm occupying a little knoll in one of the above savannas, while back of it was a belt of timber, through which was a small stream of clear water. As we had ridden on quite rapidly, we had to await the arrival of our pack-horses, pending which all hands laid themselves out for a siesta upon the blankets and ponchos we spread upon the ground, and we were soon oblivious, even of the calls of hunger, until the noise made by the arrival of the train awakened us to the fact that it was the hour for supper, which meal with us, on our journey, usually meant dinner too.

Alas! for all human hope, our joy at the arrival of our train soon was turned to grief, for one of the stupid brutes, not knowing the valuable nature of a part of his cargo, attempted, while the panniers were still upon him, to refresh himself with a roll on the grass, whereupon, the large glass demijohn that contained our entire supply of rum was utterly smashed, and that precious fluid escaped. Our grief was great, and we were only restored to good-humour by the indignant manner of Simon, who had just arrived with the balance of the train, being gravely told by the "Professor" that his horse was so tired he had been stood up against the house, but unfortunately had lost his balance and fallen over.

Simon, our muleteer, never liked to have any remarks passed upon the quality of the horses he furnished us, though, in truth, they were none of the best.

However, the Professor and I, being old campaigners, soon had our preparations made, with the assistance of "Francisco," for the disposal of the various edibles we had extracted from our cans of preserved vegetables and meat, and such was the effect, that no sooner was supper ended than some of the party immediately took to their hammocks for rest, which, in the case of the Commissioner, was soon consummated by sound slumber, in spite of the trifling inconveniences of hat, clothes, and boots.

Have you ever swung in a hammock, dear reader? If not, I assure you there is a new sensation in store for you. In St Domingo it is as much a part of the republic as the people themselves.

Those we had were made of stout canvas about six feet long and five wide; at each end are a number of cords at regular intervals, which, fastened thus to the hammock at one end, are united in a huge knot at the other, and to this a strong cord being attached, the hammock can be slung to a beam or attached to a ring in the wall, and thus be suspended in the air like a huge bag. It is a great institution, and I believe has been introduced since into the States by every member of the party.

Our first night was troubled with those pests the fleas, and they had even no respect for the august body of the "Commissioner;" for that high priest of Cornell was discovered late in the evening filling his shirt with pulverised camphor, said to be a sure preventive.

The Professor and I, protected by the clouds of smoke emitted by our pipes, and in which we had indulged while trying to restrain the Doctor from some fearful witticisms, fared rather better; but, notwithstanding these little inconveniences, including the advent of a stray dog into the hut in search of some friendly bone, we all managed to get a good night's rest in this our first night's camping-out in St Domingo.

The day was yet young when we turned out of our bags, the Doctor and I going down to a neighbouring brook to be invigorated by a bath in the cool waters of a limpid stream.

The dew lay heavy on the luxuriant grass; and as we passed through the woods, the air was fragrant with the odour of the rich vegetation, while the oranges in large numbers hung with their golden cheeks wet with the morning dew. The air, too, was quite fresh and bracing, as it nearly always is in this island of an early morning.

Selecting a little spot in the stream formed into a natural pool, we enjoyed the clear, cool freshness of the water, which a short distance above us came bubbling over mossy rocks; in fact, the whole scene might have passed for some little bit in the Adirondacks, had it not been that an immense tree fallen across the stream was covered with the parasites and plants peculiar only to the tropics.

Meanwhile the Commissioner, as became his custom on the journey, had called the family and some neighbours together, and extracted from them their views about annexation, and the condition of the people in the vicinity.

The master of the house was a fair type of the people who are pretty generally scattered throughout the island as the country people (paisanos), and who constitute pretty much the agricultural class. Those of a lighter colour, or white, are more apt to be found as hateros or herds men, raising cattle, and are a brighter, more intelligent class.

Old Negro.

This old negro had a wife and two grown-up sons, and lived on a farm of about 200 acres, the only building of any account upon it being this dwelling, which was one of the simple palm-houses of the country, containing only

PARASITES.—A ST. DOMINGO BROOK.

two rooms. He raised a few cattle and grew some cane, coffee, and a few fruits, without much trouble, and without the slightest system in his labours.

Upon asking him why, with so much land and such apparently comfortable means, he did not have a house and a garden, and improve his place, he told the same story we had so often heard of revolutions, and raids, and forcible enlistments. He stated, also, he had previously had a fine house, and had the means to build one now, but that he with the rest of the people were discouraged by the unsettled future.

His sons seemed to be willing enough to work at $6 per month, and spoke with some interest about the possibility of a road being made that would require the labour of the young men. But I am afraid, in long contracts, the "dias de fiesta" would either interfere with the work, or else the principles of the labourers would have to suffer.

In the saddle again, we rode for some eight miles over some superb rolling prairies, capable of being made into the finest sugar-plantations. The day, clear and bright, fairly sparkled with the purity of the atmosphere—an every-day occurrence here, however, except in the rainy season of May and following months.

Again we struck the Ozama river, the same that we had left deep and dark at St Domingo city, but here swiftly rushing along over its gravelly bed, its waters clear as crystal, tempting the wearied horseman as he fords it by its cool, refreshing look and taste.

Riding through this valley of the Ozama, we find the country almost entirely unsettled, although the land can be had for the asking; but the population is sparse, and rarely do we see a house, though a rough wooden cross stuck up at the side of some hardly discernible path tells the wearied traveller that, on following the trail, a habitation of some kind will be found, it may be a few yards or a mile away.

Traversing now a heavily-wooded country, through which the merest apology for a road is found in the simple clearing out of the underbrush and the cutting down of the trees that may happen to stand in the direct line, we came out upon a level tract or savanna known as La Luisa, which, covered with long tall grass, is similar to some of our Illinois prairies, though much more beautiful and diversified, and upon the surface of which lies here and there the water which, from frequent rains, is so abundant all through this part of the island.

Exactly such savannas I have seen in Cuba turned into

A Native Hut.

splendid sugar estates, the land ditched and dry, while the water was carried into well-constructed reservoirs or conducted to the mills.

Although a tropical shower was passing over our heads, we were more tempted by the umbrageous shelter afforded by the foliage and branches of a noble mango-tree than that of a dilapidated native hut, at whose principal and doorless aperture stood, in the most indolent of positions, its lazy proprietor, who, with ample leisure, would, it appears, esteem it lost time to repair his roof, although the material was at hand; and yet a site and land for which many of our people would give thousands, even the wretchedness of the cabin adding to the picturesqueness of the scene, for behind it waved the graceful palm and cocoa trees, with the broad-leaved banana, that gives such richness to all this tropical scenery, while furnishing the principal sustenance of the people.

"What's the use?" the owner replies to my question why he don't put things in order; "it would only be ruined in the next revolution."

Our noonday siesta finished, a short ride brought us to our resting-place for the night, the habitation of one Jose Gervase, at San Pedro, who received us in the most hospitable manner, placing at our disposal "apartments" for the night.

As we rode up, the women were working underneath a thatched roof, which had only a few stout poles to support it, being otherwise entirely open; and this was the continuation of the hut or house proper in which the family lived.

Our hammocks were soon slung under this roof, as there were always some of the party ready for a swing in this most fascinating of resting-places. It being Washington's birthday, it was determined to celebrate it by a *grand dinner*, as fitting to the representative of the Great Republic; with what success may be imagined, when I mention that the *menu* was in accordance with our service of (tin) plate, and the "omelette au-ron" a success.

I will say nothing of the speeches, owing to the fact that what would have proved the "event" of the evening was slightly marred in its solemn effects by the advent of a friendly pig between the legs of the speaker.

But I think the American people would certainly have been amused, if not astonished, at seeing the perfectly republican simplicity of its representatives, as they sat on upturned barrels or ends of logs, looking like a lot of guerillas in bivouac.

In the midst of our hilarity came the vesper-hour, and immediately our host and his family fell to their prayers and evening hymn, with such evident earnestness, that, though we had, out of respect, immediately uncovered, we yet, moved by such evidence of simple but honest piety, bowed our heads in reverence also.

Although sleeping in the open air, our slumbers were of

Apartments.

the soundest, and the sun was well up when we were stirring about, awaiting our chocolate before starting, during the preparation of which much information was elicited from the people; and it was with a hearty "Happy journey and God be with you, señores!" from the master, that we took our departure.

Five miles riding brought us to the foot of the mountain range bearing the general name of Cordillera, which, towering up here into an altitude of some 3000 feet high, bears the euphonious appellation of "Sillon de la Viuda"

VIEW FROM SILLON DE LA VIUDA.

(Widow's Saddle), to the south of which are the sources of the Ozama river.

Over grassy slopes and rough defiles of now hard clay, except where here and there some mountain stream trickling down keeps the path moist; up wooded hills, upon which are seen every form of parasite, whether in its incipient form of a mere bundle of grass upon the branch of some tree, hanging in strange woody ropes or graceful festoons, or framed into sturdy many-trunked trees, we ride; now holding hard with knee and braced-in stirrup, or almost embracing the horse's neck, one hand firmly grasping a lock of the mane to prevent sliding back, we gain the mountain top, where, dismounting, we fasten our horses, and then pushing our way through the bushes, we come out upon an abrupt, sharp point upon the very ridge.

And this was the "Widow's Pass," and there the great mountain heart of the island, with the towering Yaqui peak soft and distant!

What a sight was then laid out before us, unrolled like some huge topographical map, only with every point marked in bold relief by Nature's own hand, so there could be no mistake about hill or dale, mountain or valley.

Steep down rose the extreme points and tops of the trees of the mountain below us; beyond that a high mountain slope, and then descending slopes, and valleys covered with forest, with now and then a bright brown patch of the savanna land; while in the distance rolls back into hazy eternity the dark-blue hills in various shades of indigo, blue, cobalt, and, where the morning sun glints on them, the most delicate violet tints, the tops of the highest hid away in cottony clouds. But words fail to paint a scene like this, where even the pencil cannot portray its beauties, needing, as it does, the colouring of a Church or a Bierstadt.

This pass is a defile so narrow, separating the north from the south so effectually, that a handful of men might dispute the passage with an army.

Here the Spaniards, in early days, offered to make a stand against Dessalines, when he attacked their lines to drive out the French; but the latter had no faith, and would not trust them with arms, else that desolating march might have been prevented.

Descending the mountain, we reach a stream of clear running water, into which the Doctor and I, warm and muddy, rushed to get our baths, the first we have had in what might be called a St Domingo stream. Mr White, although envying us our enjoyment, declined bathing, from the fact that Admiral Porter had cautioned him against

Sensitive Plant.

bathing in these streams. Many of the authorities of the island give this advice also, and, perhaps, under certain circumstances, of hot sun or heated body, it would not be wise to enter the almost ice-cold water; but our experience has taught us (including since the Commissioner), that when the clothes are slowly removed, and the body cooled before going into the water, no evil results are experienced. On the contrary, in the early morning we have found great benefit from it, to say nothing of the immense refreshment of such a bath after a long day's ride.

Very pleasant enjoyment it is to thus pull up at mid-day and enjoy even the frugal meal that may be called lunch, breakfast, or dinner, when, spreading a poncho upon the rich herbage, a siesta forms a pleasant finale to the lazy toying with that wondrous creation of Nature, the sensitive plant, whose tender petals seem to fold themselves up even at the breath of man.

Our afternoon journey of this day was not soon to be forgotten, for we all had deep experience of St Domingo mud on the roads, which were almost impassable.

The Professor led the way through one quagmire; but the author, coming next, turned a little aside, and in went his horse up to the girths in sticky, pasty mud. Spurrings and lashings, answered by wild efforts on the part of the horse to extricate himself, only served to fix them deeper in the ditch, until the horse, infuriated and frightened, seemed ready to fall over on his rider.

"Jump for it!" shouted the Professor; and jump I did, plump over my heavy boot-tops into the mud; but throwing myself forward to the solid ground with the reins still in hand, succeeded, with whip and shouts, in pulling my now unburdened horse through to *terra firma*, where he stood trembling like an aspen, the only question between us being which was the muddiest.

The Commissioner and the Doctor, profiting by my sad example, wisely made a detour through a short bypath in the woods, and came through without mishap; but we were all glad enough when the Professor turned aside into the very bed of a stream in preference to taking the road, and following up its course, we had sure, gravelly bottom, even if it was at the cost of being occasionally splashed with pure water. That wild, strange scene I think none of us will ever forget, as, pursuing our way, we rode through a narrow bottom-land, in the centre of which was the little stream, over which and our heads would sometimes meet and entwine so thickly the branches and foliage of the trees on its banks, that sunlight was entirely excluded; and then through openings in the bushes we caught a view of groups of palms and other strange trees in the meadow, while rising directly behind them were the hills covered with the gigantic forest trees, over which had grown the most dense and graceful hanging canopies of the morning glory, making a scene in which it would appear that Nature herself had draped and festooned the sides in honour of the representative of progress embodied in the modest person of Commissioner White.

At last we strike the road again, and then bursting out

Royal Plain.

from the timber upon the open ground, we get our first view of a part of the far-famed Vega Royal (Royal Plain). It appears that the name "Vega Real" was given by Columbus himself originally only to the level country lying between Samana and Monte Cristo; but as new villages sprang up, the word in its meaning became more contracted, being applied to the land at or near the place called La Vega. Now it means all that level tract lying between the Monte Cristo range and the Cibao or Cordillera ranges of mountains, extending west from Samana to the Haytian frontier, near Monte Cristo.

In this immense valley are comprised the best agricultural lands and the principal towns of the island, including Cotuy, Macoris, La Vega, Mocha, Santiago de los Caballeros, Guayubin, and Monte Cristo, and though there is abundant tableland, it must not be imagined it is all flat prairie soil, for even many of the prairies are very rolling in their nature, while ranges of hills break up the level at various points. But here to-day in the "Vega," in the "Cibao," as it is indiscriminately called, is the principal agricultural wealth of the island; and though thus far on our journey we had met with few houses, we began to find, as we approached the region where the character of the country changed so much, more signs of cultivation and habitation.

We had some peculiar experiences of the weather of this island, for though the day was bright, we were constantly subjected to a series of showers, none of which lasted over ten minutes, and then it would be perfectly clear, until we really all became tired of being fooled so often, and vowed neither umbrella should be hoisted nor poncho put away. In one of these pleasant showers the temptation of making a picture of the Commissioner was too great to be resisted, and it was deemed so characteristic, that I promised it should form the subject of my dedication page. Crossing a number of savannas, we reached at length the banks of the Cevico river or creek, which we quickly forded, and rode through a grassy, green avenue lined with palm, cocoa, and banana trees, into the village of the same name, where we put up in the usual fashion at the hut of a negro citizen. Cevico is simply a congregation of thatched huts around an open space called a plaza; and the statistics of the town are complete when I state there are fifteen houses and seventy-five people.

We were received, however, by quite an historical old personage, Severino Gonzalez by name, who, a light-coloured mulatto, and now eighty-nine years of age, had been a captain in the army of the celebrated Dessalines.

Severino Gonzalez.

But his manner of receiving us at his door was simply superb, and would have befitted a prince showing us into a splendid palace, instead of the humble. earth-floored, thatch-covered hut of which he was the owner. With his blanket wrapped about him in Roman toga-like folds, he, with quiet dignity and a magnificent wave of his hand, said, "My house is at your disposition, señores." My regret was only equalled by my chagrin when, after pouring out my thanks in my best Spanish, the Professor slyly said to me, in homely but forcible phrase—"Dry up, old fellow; he 's as deaf as a post."

In this house we found the family principally consisted of females, the daughters of the most opposite coloured complexions; for while one was black as ink, possessing withal a graceful figure, the other was one of the finest-looking yellow women I had seen, with straight hair and superb black eyes, her form answering in its proportions and grace to a sculptor's model.

Orders were immediately given to gather the people of the village together before our departure in the morning, in order that the Commissioner might hear their views.

Bright and early, therefore, next day came a perfectly black negro with more clothes on than most of those we had seen.

He informed the Commissioner that he was the "Commandante," and leaving that gentleman to digest the information, he retired to an inner room with the aforementioned good-looking young woman; and after some time had elapsed, reappeared in a clean suit of clothes, a Colt's revolver in his belt, and a brown felt hat bound in white on his head, the whole suit forming a happy contrast to his dusky face, which, I must say, gave one the impression that he would willingly "knife" you for a ten-cent piece. Seating himself in a hammock, he in an extremely consequential manner was proceeding to give us an idea of his great importance, when he was abruptly cut short, and told to allow the people to come in, as the Commissioner wished to see them, and not the dignitaries.

The "Commandante."

A number of all classes then came in, to whom Mr White made an address, and they showed themselves very enthusiastic at the idea of having perpetual peace given them, some being affected even to tears; and it was with hearty "God speed you!" that we took our departure as soon as the interview was over.

We had fourteen miles of the roughest riding to do that I have ever seen in my life before we reached Cotuy, over roads that were not roads, up steep slippery banks of clay, and down rocky declivities that in places were so narrow, and gave such dangerous footing, that we were compelled to dismount and whip our horses down, picking our own way by holding to branch and bush with our hands, while our feet were constantly treading air. Well may every one exclaim and pray, "Give us roads!" to which we say "Amen!" most heartily.

A sorry figure we cut, as, nearing Cotuy, we were met by the Commandant, a very black darky, who, in spotless linen suit, put us quite to the blush for our mud and travel-stained appearance. However, we were escorted into Cotuy to the house of the alcalde, who had prepared for Mr White's party—Mr Gautier, the Secretary of State having, we found, sent a courier on in advance to advise the authorities of his needing care and quarters. This house was an humble affair, though as good as there was in the village, it being simply of one story, divided into three parts, with a thatched roof; these three parts formed the rooms, the one on the left being that in which the alcalde held his court, the centre being the living-room, while the third part was redivided into two small rooms, one the shoemaking shop of his son, the other a bedroom appropriated to Mr White's use.

As we had left Cevico at early morning without any breakfast except a cup of coffee and a roasted plantain, we were nearly famished on arriving at the alcalde's, and a suggestion was made that he should give us something to satisfy us while our people prepared a more substantial meal. Bless the dear old man's heart! In a twinkling we had a dish of fried eggs with onion and garlic seasoning, served in cassava bread, moistened with warm water, and a dish of rice. Bread we had not, there being none in the town; but do you think, *lector mio*, we held back on that account? No, sir! to use a homely but apt phrase, "we went through" those dishes, and I had the satisfaction of helping the august Commissioner himself to the last egg. Ye pampered officials at home! think how your devoted servants suffer in a strange land.

Seriously, however, four days roughing it in St Domingo mud, woods, and roads, had made us ready for anything at meal-time. Tired as we all were, we had to receive the calls of one or two of the high public functionaries, and particularly the Commandant, a perfectly black man, and the fastest talker I have ever heard in any language; but after much talk, Mr White excused himself on the plea of fatigue; the officials took the hint and left us, but not yet to slumber, for to such an extent is hospitality carried in St Domingo, that when a stranger of importance arrives in a town, the band of the special locality proceeds to serenade the new-comer. However pleasant such a compliment might be to the tired traveller, even if performed by Strauss' band, yet it was a little too much for our feelings when a "din infernal" was made outside the house by the village band, consisting of a big drum and a little one; and so exasperated were our drowsy feelings by the noise, that it was promptly ordered to clear out, even the expected douceur (through ignorance, however) being withheld—"Cosa Dominicana."

CHAPTER XVI.

> "Through citron groves and fields of yellow maize,
> Through plantain walks, where not a sunbeam plays;
> Here blue savannas fade into the sky,
> There forests frown in midnight majesty."

COTUY—*Its Appearance, History, and Location—The Yuna River—An Old Church, and Novel Mode of Advertising—A Village Cemetery—A First Regular Meeting to Receive the Commissioner—Courtesy of the People—Swimming a River—The "Royal Road"—Hu-man-i-cu—Old Cocoa-Trees—Domestic Institutions—Woman's Rights—Reception at La Vega—The Town and its History—Hospitable Attentions—The Only Steam-Engine—The "Grand" Cathedral—An Official Breakfast—The Famous Hill Santo Cerro—Superb View of the Vega—The Old Town of La Vega—The Valley of Constanza—A Paradise—Arrival at Mocha—An Attractive Town—Pretty Girls—Handsome Cemetery—Eloquence of the Commissioner, and some Plain Talk.*

ONE and a half miles from the river Yuna, in the centre of the savanna, lies the old town of Cotuy, one of those originally established by the Spaniards, being distant from St Domingo city some eighty miles, and equally distant from the town of La Vega to the north, and the bottom of Samana Bay, thirty-five miles.

Situated formerly a little farther to the north, it was known as La Mejorada, or the Privileged, but eventually received the name of "Las Minas," because it was located in a district noted for its mines of gold, silver, copper, and iron.

It was a flourishing place soon after its foundation by

order of Ovando in 1505, and some of the mines were worked up to 1520, when the scarcity of workmen was beginning to be felt. When the mines were closed by order, this town began to experience the same results that affected all the others, and became almost extinct.

The modern town is a very humble place indeed, consisting of about two hundred houses and less than a thousand inhabitants. It is principally built around the plaza or square, which forms the centre of the town, the houses

Plaza and Old Church, Cotuy.

being of the usual framed, thatch-covered style peculiar to the country.

The population, as far as we could learn, were principally interested in raising pigs; but the country throughout this region is famed as a fine country for growing tobacco, coffee, and cacao.

Under favourable circumstances there is every reason for its becoming a large town, situated as it is on the banks of the river Yuna, the largest navigable river, with one exception (the Artibonite), upon the entire island.

This river, taking its rise in the rocky hills of the valley of Constanza, runs pretty generally due east, and passes within a mile and a half of Cotuy, and thence continuing its course through the great plain of the Vega Real, it finally, by various mouths, empties into the Bay of Samana, thus in its course running through an extent of country some 200 miles in length.

It is fed by innumerable streams, and at present is navigable for boats some forty miles from its mouth to Almacen; but canoes have no difficulty in ascending as high as Couty, the usual depth of the river being even in the dry season several feet, the width from 150 to 200 yards. It would not be a difficult matter to improve the channel in such manner as to permit of flat boats being floated down; and in this event, Cotuy would become the agricultural shipping-point of the great extent of country in its vicinity.

Ten o'clock having been appointed by the Commissioner as the hour for the official reception, we occupied ourselves, after rising, in paying our respects to the village curé, visiting the old church and the village generally.

We were much interested in the padre, a man of many years, and who, though born in Catalonia, Spain, had lived here nearly all his life, and "a better country I never want," he said, surpassing even his native province in healthfulness. He was too ill to accompany us, but we paid a visit to the old church, that had been standing many hundred years, and bore over the main door a crack caused by the great earthquake of 1842.

A more poverty-stricken, cheerless church-interior I never saw; built of stone, many parts had gone to decay without effort at repair, while the whole place had a damp, earthy smell, which, with the humble bier standing in an alcove, served to remind us of a charnel-house.

As showing the utter simplicity of the religion of these people, we noticed there was placed in the curtained niche of an alcove a wax figure, nearly life-size, of Christ bearing the Cross, which of itself was horrible; but in the midst of other decorations, of bits of gold-paper and paper-flowers, a highly-coloured gorgeous label had been taken from a vermicelli box and pasted at the foot of the figure of Christ.

If this label had been in some foreign tongue, it might be supposed that it remained there in utter ignorance by priest and people of what it was; but there it was in Spanish, as fine an advertisement as I ever saw, that Farrell and Son, Barcelona, made fine vermicelli for soups.

Walking through the town, we saw nothing to interest us; but, having a theory that the living are best judged

Cemetery at Cotuy.

of from the manner in which they treat their dead, I walked out to the village cemetery on the outskirts of the town, which was a very humble, simple affair indeed. A lot enclosed by a fence made of withes, a wooden portico under which was a simple door with a cross in white paint marked upon it, served as the last resting-place of the villagers, the graves of whom were marked by no elaborate monument, but usually a simple cross of wood.

23

Returning to our quarters, I found the people were already gathering for their interview with the Commissioner. They were from all sections and of all colours; and the room not being capable of holding them all, they crowded in at the windows and doors, anxious to get a glimpse of the man who was perhaps to decide their future.

The Commissioner in a few well-chosen phrases explained the nature of his mission; and when he appealed

Meeting at Cotuy.

to them for their desires of annexation, there was no mistaking their earnestness as they shouted, "We wish it."

It was a remarkable sight to see, in this humble habitation, these men, different in language, customs, and even complexion, earnestly invoking the representative of the Great Republic to give them that liberty with which they were familiar in name only, and for which many of them had been struggling all their lives.

One man, a tall swarthy fellow, whose feelings got the better of him, could not restrain his enthusiasm, but stretching himself to his full height, raised his hands to heaven, and exclaimed, " With body and soul, God knows, for myself and for all this people, we want it and hope for it " (annexation).

It was with a good deal of pleasure that at an early hour next day we took our departure from Cotuy; for though we had been well treated by its people, one gets soon tired of a place where there is absolutely nothing to do or see; and the dusky Commandant seemed desirous of making the most of us, as such an event as the arrival of a distinguished stranger was extremely rare in these parts.

He therefore deemed it his duty to see us safely on our way, and, mounted on a fiery little horse, seemed proud to display his horsemanship, for which all Dominicans are noted.

In an humble way these people, with true courtesy, did all that lay in their power to honour the "passing guest;" and if I seem to speak lightly of their appearance and habits, it is in no spirit of ridicule, but as a mere matter of truthful description that I see them as " ithers see us."

At last we arrived on the banks of the main river, the Yuna, a branch of which we had crossed soon after leaving Cotuy, and here we found that our pack-horses would have to be unloaded, and swam across, while their cargoes were taken over in canoes, we ourselves being under the necessity of half-swimming and half-fording the river with our horses.

The river was quite wide and with a swift current, the shores low and gravelly, as was the bed of the river; but we all managed to get over without accident, except the writer, who, with his usual luck, managed to secure two good bootsful of water.

The negro boatmen were very skilful in getting over without loss our cargoes and horses. This was done by means of a cotton-wood canoe, a large ceiba-tree furnishing the material, the canoe being simply the trunk of one of these trees hollowed out by fire and axe.

In this a perfectly nude negro stood with a long pole and pushed his way over; the horses, having their halter straps held by another negro, swam after the canoe, which was allowed to drift with the current of the stream, while

"Camino Real."

the negro poled its head to the shore—an amusing as well as exciting scene.

Leaving behind us the Yuna and its branches, we came out into a beautifully shaded road, with grassy surface, traversing which for some miles we reached the bank of the stream where we made our noonday halt.

Our afternoon ride was still over level country, now savanna, now wooded and slightly rolling, until we struck the "Camino Real" or royal road, a great wide avenue in the forest, though now in fearful condition, but bearing evidence that at one time some attempt had been made to make a regular highway, for still standing on each side were the "royal palms" planted for shade in regular lines, which gave an imposing and graceful appearance. But the roadway itself was filled with mud and water, the ground worn into ridges and gullies, resembling our corduroy roads, only, in lieu of the timber, the ridges were of earth baked hard by the sun.

This is caused from the fact that the animals traversing this road put their feet in the same place as those gone before, and these gullies, becoming soft, fill with water, and get deeper and deeper, so that the traveller pursuing this route feels his horse stepping into these gullies, and over the ridges with a motion like camel-riding.

Some hours of this fatiguing work made us very thankful when we at last arrived on the banks of the Jaina, a branch of the Yuna, where we were enabled to refresh ourselves with a swim in its clear and swift-running stream about twenty yards in width, and over our saddle-girths in depth.

A pretty savanna with the romantic Indian name of Hu-man-i-cu, was our stopping-place for the night.

Here we were hospitably received at one of the best houses with which we had met among the country people, quite a large cabin in the centre of several acres, enclosed with the pretty and luxuriant hedge of the maya or prickly aloe, while palms and cocoas gave shade to the house.

Around us were fine views of the distant mountains, which towered high above the tops of the neighbouring forests. Our hosts seemed to be people of the better class, the husband, however, being away in the calaboose under charge of sticking a knife into a man at a dance a few evenings before.

His wife took it very philosophically, as being quite a "cosa Dominicana," and she appeared in many respects quite an intelligent woman, her colour being what we should call brown, though two of her children were quite black.

Well-to-do as these people appeared, there was not an article of crockery (if I except one it would not be polite to mention) in the house. Everything usually made of such material was here fashioned out of calabashes, cocoanuts, or gourds; and yet there was every variety of bowls, cups, and ladles, all scrupulously clean and highly polished, in the cupboard, which had its place in the corner under the name of "La Fuente," and of which the lady of the house appeared very proud.

"La Fuent ."

The "Doctor," a strong advocate of "woman's rights," having engaged my services as interpreter in a conversation carried on with the wife, was anxious to have her opinion on the subject; and I was highly amused when she said, with a good deal of vim, that "women had no business with such matters; that if they attended properly to the duties needed in their domestic circles, their husbands would manage other matters for them." She was decidedly in earnest when she said "there could be but one head to a house—that was the man;" all of which the Doctor put down to a gross state of ignorance.

Like her more favoured sisters elsewhere, however, she preferred the town to the country; it was more cheerful and lively, and she could have more "bailitas" (little dances).

Here I saw some fine specimens of the cocoa or chocolate tree, one of them being pointed out as twenty-five years old, and still profusely bearing fruit.

This product alone would make St Domingo a flourishing and wealthy island, if the inhabitants, feeling assured of the future, chose to turn their attention to its cultivation; and it would be a difficult matter to compute the amount of wealth to be acquired in an island where, without trouble, its plains can be filled with cattle and cane, while the hills, even to their tops, produce so readily the cocoa and the coffee. If there were no other products, if the immense wealth of minerals and fruits, and other products so easily cultivated, were left out of sight, and only the first-named produced, there is wealth enough here for millions of people to live in ease and comfort, who are now struggling with starvation in less favoured countries.

The Cocoa.

Three miles from Hu-man-i-cu, the other and even more difficult road from St Domingo city, known as the Jaina road, joined the one upon which we travelled; and a few days previous Professor Blake of the United States Commission had passed that way with his party.

We reached La Vega, only a few miles' ride from our night's resting-place; and entering a beautiful avenue, bright with the evergreen grass of this always verdure-clad island, we were met on the outskirts of the town by the Governor of the province, Jose Rodriguez, the Commandant of Arms, and about fifty of the most prominent men of the place and vicinity, all well and clean dressed men, white, black, and coloured, and all well mounted on the active, spirited horses peculiar to the island.

The fine horses and equipments, as well as the bright, clean appearance of the riders, put us quite to the blush, as, on our tired, mud-splashed horses, and with personal attire rough, dirty, and careless, we received their salutations. I have never been more agreeably disappointed in my life than I have been in the people of St Domingo. No matter what the shade of colour, from the time that I landed at Puerto Plata to the moment I left the island, I saw nothing but the most natural and graceful courtesy exercised, not only towards all strangers, but also to each other.

And here we might have thought we were going to be taken to the most superb palaces and entertainments, judging from the manners of these men, who, making no pretension, placed with true politeness before us such accommodation as they had.

Escorting us to our quarters, the guard doing us honour as we passed the plaza, we were safely bestowed in the house of the village padre, who, vacating the premises, as we afterwards found, left the house and servants entirely to our party, furnishing our meals and attendance without a single command on our part, or chance to make any recompense, even at our departure keeping the attendants out of the way, so that we should not settle with them.

Interchange of courtesies here ensued, accompanied with

hearty hand-shaking and good wishes from the people. Appointments for official receptions being made for next day, we were left to enjoy the luxury of getting baths and clean clothes, of which we stood much in need after our journey.

The balance of the day being left unmolested to wander where we pleased, we availed ourselves of the opportunity to stroll through the village and the outskirts. One of the most striking objects was considered to be the remains of a steam-engine, said to be the only one ever put up in the

The only Steam-Engine in St Domingo.

island, and certainly the only one I saw or heard of in my travels. This we found lying on the banks of the river, utterly useless and broken. It had been brought out from the United States by the village priest, Padre Moya, who had it put up; and an American, named, I believe, Jordan Lancaster, from New Jersey, engaged to run it. Logs from the neighbouring hills were sawn, and afterwards floated down the Camou river; but the Spaniards left the mill ruined, as they did everything, when they departed the island; and there the boiler still lies, a fitting emblem of dead progress in an island where there is ample field for the remunerative working of thousands of mills and engines.

The present town of La Vega is situated on the river Camou, one of the tributaries of the Yuna, and at a short distance only from its right bank.

It lies in the centre of a beautiful savanna, which in

La Vega.

form is nearly round; and is almost completely surrounded by hills, the town being to the north of the Cibao range, which it faces.

It owes its foundation to the destruction by an earthquake of the famous old town, founded by Columbus, of Concepcion de la Vega, which lay some six miles to the north and east.

It is laid out in a regular manner, the streets crossing each other at right angles, in the centre of the town there being the usual plaza or square, near which is the only building of any importance in the village, the church.

The houses are principally constructed of wood, though

of a much better class than those in the majority of the towns, some of them being quite respectable frame-houses. The remains are still to be seen of ruined stone houses, showing that, at some previous time, the place deserved its name of a substantial city; but lying in a plain as it does, and seen from the outskirts, it has anything but an imposing appearance, although its natural location is lovely and perfectly salubrious.

The town receives its name from the great valley in which

La Vega Cathedral.

it is situated; and the province of which it is the capital is noted for its superb lands for grazing and the production of coffee, cane, and tobacco.

Strolling through the town, we found there were some primary schools in the place, and well attended; but the amount of business carried on seemed limited enough.

Judging from the church, it was evident that more had been anticipated for La Vega than it had been enabled to fulfil; for an immense church or cathedral had been begun on an extremely grand scale for so small a place, but was not able to be finished owing to want of funds.

A very imposing structure in design, with pillared arches and solid walls of stone, it had been roughly roofed in, leaving the rafters and a portion of the unfinished wall unplastered. Yet there was the usual amount of tapers and flowers, only the limited number of worshippers were lost in so great a place.

Our party was entertained at a state breakfast, given by the village padre, who, a native of Corsica, had been educated in France, and we found him to be a highly polished and cultivated man.

We enjoyed our entertainment much, meeting the principal men of the village, all of whom were white, and as polished and intelligent a set of men as could be met under the same circumstances anywhere, while the material on the table was only excelled in its cuisine by its profusion.

I must confess we were all much astonished at finding the unanimity of sentiment existing in this region, after what we had heard; and while there was some difference of opinion in reference to the present rulers of the island, there was an entire and hearty sentiment desiring annexation to the United States.

A still more extensive general meeting of the citizens and people was held when breakfast was over, at which speeches were made; and, our adieux being said, we rode off, escorted by the Governor and a number of others, being joined also by the padre, who, with his robe tucked up around him, and mounted on a spirited little horse, challenged any of the party to a race, which he would doubtless have won; but our whole party increasing their gait after fording the river, we were soon on our way to Mocha.

But, six miles from La Vega, we were to see a spot in which we were more interested than any place on the island, and of which we had received what we deemed

THE VEGA REAL FROM THE SANTO CERRO HILL.

fabulous accounts. This was the famous hill "Santo Cerro" of Columbus.

The road we were travelling was very romantic and beautiful, though rugged; and suddenly leaving it, we began our ascent over a very narrow and stony path, that led up almost perpendicularly above the tops of the trees, on what seemed a mere knob of rock.

Still continuing, we found we were ascending an isolated hill, and as we cleared the trees of the lower surface, we began to get superb views of parts of the Royal Plain.

We were none of us, however, prepared for the sight we beheld, as, reaching the very top of the hill, we found spread out before us in every direction the whole extent of the Vega Real, the famous Royal Plain of Columbus.

The spot upon which we stood was the famous Holy Hill, noted in the history of the island as the place whereon was worked a great miracle in favour of the Spaniards.

It is related that Columbus having erected a cross upon this hill, the Indians in vain attempted to cut it down and to burn it. Struck with terror, they perceived the Virgin sitting on one of the arms of the cross, and the arrows they shot at her returned to pierce their own bodies (?).

Notwithstanding that "every Spaniard would have a piece of this cross," there was left enough (so say the chroniclers) to take to St Domingo city, where it was covered with silver filigree, and, under charge of the priests, was produced at the Cathedral, to help to sell indulgences and perform fresh miracles.

Upon the top of this hill, which forms a level plateau, stands a plain wooden church, originally founded by the Brothers of Mercy; and upon the very edge of the hill stands a large wooden cross, overgrown with vines, to perpetuate the memory of the original cross, I suppose. Back of the church there is a small village containing a few inhabitants; but it is said, in former days, when the Holy Brothers had formed this hill into a hermitage, there were beautiful gardens all over it, where were produced fruits only grown in temperate zones, but which, from the height of this hill, found a congenial atmosphere.

But historic as is this old hill and its surroundings, it afforded us the greater gratification of seeing, I might say, the whole island at our feet; for there, far below us, to the right, to the left, lay the thousands and thousands of leagues of the noble, beautiful plain famed in and out of the island as the Vega Real. In front of us, looking north, and stretching away until lost to sight, lay, hazy, grand, and majestic, the Monte Cristo range of mountains, extending almost to Samana, the bay of which, with its waters blue and hazy, or glittering in the sun, we could perceive like a spot in the distance.

From the base of the hill whereon we stood to the mountain range, lay quiet and peaceful the vast level plain, broken here and there by the silver ribbon of a stream, or the curling blue smoke that served to mark the location of some hut or pueblo;—such a plain as that seen from Catskill, New York, or the Dyke, in England, on a clear day; yet the very opposite in its character, for here were seen no rich fields of grain, no pretty farmhouses or neat villages, showing a careful and successful agriculture.

No; here was seen naught but nature,—beautiful, it is true, but wild, uncultivated nature,—where the palm, the cocoa, and hundreds of forest groves held undisputed sway over this superb expanse of land, where, with labour and capital added to intelligence and industry, it could be made to bloom into a perfect flower, fruit, and vegetable garden.

It may seem too practical amidst such scenes, but I could not help wishing there might soon be seen the smoke of the locomotive on the projected railroad, that would bring access, civilisation, and culture in its train to this superb region.

Descending the hill, we bade adieu to the padre and his

friends, and, accompanied by the Governor, we proceeded on our journey. A short distance from the base of the Holy Hill he pointed out to us the clump of stones that marked a portion of the site of old Concepcion de La Vega, to which the plain gave its name.

Here, too, with this spot the pen of historic romance has been busy; for it is said this is the spot where was first celebrated in America, in a formal manner, high mass, upon which occasion officiated the famous Father Las Casas; and every place in the vicinity is connected with Columbus.

In 1493, Columbus having received an account of the mines of Cibao (literally stony or rocky ground), came himself to verify the report; and upon this occasion, when crossing from Isabella, *via* the Monte Cristo range, he discovered this plain; when so struck was he with its extent and beauty, that he named it " Royal."

Constructing in 1495 a fort at La Vega, he was enabled, it is said, to defeat, with his brother Bartholomew and the small number of troops with him, 100,000 Indians; and this post became the foundation of the city of Concepcion de la Vega, the city being built on the very spot where Guarionex, cacique of the kingdom of Magua, had resided.

The other fort established in the Vega by Ovando in 1504, and known as Magdelina, was placed at what is now known as Macoris.

Owing to the fact of the mines of the vicinity, and the town being made a bishopric, it soon became an important place; but in 1564 an earthquake overthrew the whole town, and the ruins, up to within a few years, it is said, were plainly visible, the earth in some places remaining half open, leaving exposed to view the roofs of buried houses. The place is now, however, overgrown with rank vegetation.

In the time of the original Spaniards it was the chief place from which they emanated on their forays, and here it was that Roldan's mutiny was brought to a focus; while at the time Bobadilla came out, Columbus received here the news of his arrival.

In later years, so absolutely had the country gone to ruin, that the pass used by the Spaniards of that time to visit the mines of the Cibao became unknown, and it was not for many years that it was rediscovered.

Strange to say, this very pass, leading then, as now, to the valley of Constanza, is little known, and yet the latter is famous as being in one of the most delightful parts of the island. It is said to be some five leagues in circumference, is fine and well watered with delightful springs. The pasture is good for all sorts of cattle, and from it one can descend on the other side to the fairy valley of San Juan already alluded to. It is stated that horses become particularly excellent here, while sheep and goats thrive amazingly. The situation is so cold, that during eight months of the year thick blankets are necessary on the bed, and in the hottest season meat keeps sweet several days.

On the highest part of the neighbouring mountains there is often a slight white frost, and in the valley fire is often desirable for comfort towards evening. This was formerly a famous country for wheat; and those who have succeeded in penetrating to some parts of this mysterious valley, state there are yet people residing there who are white, the women having even fair hair, and blue eyes similar to the Biscayans.

It was my intention to have penetrated into this unknown country, but being unable to secure a guide, I was compelled to believe the assertion that it was to-day impenetrable, and that, in fact, for many years it had not been traversed by white men.

In 1864 the Dominicans were pursuing the Spanish troops through the valley from La Vega to Hincha, and their general, Esteban Rocas, was compelled, in order to effect his retreat, to cut a way through this section over mountains and precipices, and this for infantry only, it being impossible for a cavalryman to pass. For this reason, as was pithily explained to me, "No one knows anything about it, since a Dominican would rather go two or three days without eating than on foot; he wants his horse, and will not visit places except he can go on horseback and make a figure." I confess to having a good deal of sympathy with them on that score since traversing their country. Sir Robert Schomburg endeavoured to penetrate it, but was unsuccessful, though it is said Colonel Henneken was more successful. And yet this is part of the country to which even Columbus gained access.

The sierras bordering it are very high, some of the peaks being from 7000 to 9000 feet in height; and it is believed by all the natives, from the nature of the quartz rock, that there is abundance of gold.

I am led to believe, from what I was told, and what I have seen of the vicinity, that this valley is similar in character to those in eastern Cuba in the region of the Yateras, which, from personal experience, I can testify to as being superb in climate, salubrity, and soil.

And so, thinking of the far-away past and the almost unknown present of this beautiful land, we continue our journey to Mocha, passing through a tolerably well-settled country, upon each side of the road being the various agricultural places known as "fincas" "estancias" "ynjenios," or "canuco," all meaning smaller or lesser farms, where tobacco, corn, and plantains are grown, or cane-sugar and molasses rudely made, while coffee is left to grow almost wild.

In the bracing air of evening we came in sight of the beautiful town of Mocha, as it lies nestling in a plain at the foot of the great hills, and we now began to feel the immense difference between the temperature of the coast and the hill country, as these elevated plains and mountains are called.

Here again we were met by the Commandant, a remarkable-looking man, and unmistakably a white gentleman; and, of course, there were a thousand apologies made by these more than courteous people for the accommodations offered us; but we really had no cause of complaint on that score; and we were glad, after our pleasant evening meal, in company of some of the prominent men of the place, to bestow our wearied bodies in our ever-present bags.

With such a day as we awoke to, there was no lingering in one's bed, and so, bright and early, we were out and about, drinking in new life from the glorious atmosphere of this region.

Mocha is an active, thriving town in the great plain, about twenty-five miles to the north of La Vega. It is situated in the heart of a country noted for its productiveness over all other parts of the island, the tobacco and coffee of the locality being famed for its abundant growth and good quality; and from what I saw of this region, including Santiago, I believe, in case of immigration into the island, this section will become the chosen spot.

The population seems to consist more largely of pure white people than any place in which we had been, and the general character of the town and its people seemed, after a short acquaintance, to be of a superior nature.

The streets are well paved; there are many stores with a fair assortment of goods, and apparently doing an active business. The houses are mostly built of stone or the concrete of the country; and from the careful condition in which they are kept, the town, with its abundance of blue and white paint, presents a clean and gay appearance. Altogether I was reminded of some of the pretty and flourishing villages of Cuba.

The town boasts of a good-sized church of stone, covered with a corrugated iron roof, and it presented a more cleanly and thriving appearance than any church in which we had been; while the cemetery at the end of the main street was

MOCHA.

a remarkably handsome place, both in its construction and its locality; for situated upon the very brow of a hill, it overlooked the lovely plain, beyond which, in the distance, the many ranges of hills formed a charming background.

We were quite surprised to find not only two-storied houses in the town, but even some that had garret windows, a degree of civilisation we had not yet met with in the island.

And here, I may say also, we saw the first really beautiful women whom we had met; and the sight of two lovely looking girls at one of the corner windows, with their

Mocha Cemetery.

brunette complexions, rosy cheeks, lovely eyes, and rich dark hair, was too much for some of our party, who, putting themselves at the feet of the young ladies (figuratively *à los pies de V. M.*), were rewarded by their very gracious smiles and "gracias."

Here again Mr White was called on to address a large crowd of these earnest people, who had congregated at the town-hall to hear about the possibility of their becoming "Americanos."

Eloquent as he always was, and fired by the earnest, longing looks of the men of these strange assemblies, it was a rather trying ordeal to go through to be compelled to stop in the midst of an eloquent peroration to allow the interpreter to translate it to the audience; and Mr White was fortunate in having at his service Professor Gabb, whose long residence on the island has rendered him familiar with the colloquial language of the people.

All it is necessary to say here about these addresses in various parts of the island is, that they were extremely practical and to the point; and though these people heard some very "plain talk" about themselves, and what they would have to expect as part of the American Union, the remarks of Mr White were everywhere received with honest appreciation.

CHAPTER XVII.

"Earth, yield me roots!
Who seeks for better of thee, sauce his palate
With thy most operant poison. What is here?
Gold! yellow, glittering, precious gold!"
—*Timon of Athens.*

FROM MOCHA TO SANTIAGO.—*Improved Roads—Fine Lands—Reception at Santiago—First Sight of the Yaqui—Description of Santiago and the Gold Regions.*

WE had now been eight days on our journey, almost constantly in the saddle, traversing a country which may be said to be almost a primeval wilderness. Up to our arrival at Cotuy, and from thence to Mocha, the country was so sparsely inhabited, that houses by the roadside were met with but rarely.

Almost without nourishing food, exposed to the sun, and occasionally wet by the sharp tropical showers that went as quickly as they came, yet we were all in fine health and good spirits, notwithstanding the prognos ications of the evil-minded; and it was, therefore, with keen appreciation for the beauties of the road that we started on our journey of fifteen miles from Mocha to Santiago, the famous city of the "Cibao."

Mounting our horses, and accompanied by a brilliant escort, we left behind us, early in the afternoon, the pleasant town of Mocha, with its gay appearance and pretty girls; and striking a continuation of the Royal Road, we found we were in a much more thickly-settled country.

The road was wide, shaded, and pretty generally dry, though here and there we came upon some ugly places, through which we had to struggle and stick in the pasty mud.

The soil throughout was of the richest, blackest loam, similar to the splendid lands of Mississippi; while on each side of the road we found the habitations of a much better class, and the farms or plantations on a larger scale; yet with all there was a perfect absence of systematic labour and agriculture.

One of the places pointed out to me as an "ynjenio" or sugar-place, was possessed of a fine lawn in front of the house, shaded here and there by the most superb specimens of the royal palm, while fine cattle were browsing on the grass; the house itself, commodious but plain, being only one story in height, of wood, and painted bright red.

Inquiring about land values, I was told the house and over a thousand acres of good cleared land, capable of raising cane, coffee, cocoa, cotton, and fruits, could be bought for about $5000 in gold; a grand speculation with a stable Government assured.

We soon had signs that we were approaching a prominent town, for we constantly met the "requeros," or mule-trains, on the way, with loads of tobacco to the principal depot, Santiago.

Then we passed whole fields of guava growing wild, acres of broad-leafed tobacco, corn, and other productions, while groves of the "ramon" tree, upon the leaves of which horses and cattle feed as though it were grass, met us at every step.

Some distance out from Santiago we were met by General Cacerees (the reputed son of Baez, whom he very much resembles), the commander of the military district, accompanied by no end of governors, commandants, generals,

THE RIVER YAQUI.

and others, all assembled to receive and do honour to Commissioner White. Mounted as they all were on fine horses, they presented an animated sight.

Presentations and congratulations being over, the cavalcade wended its way towards the famous "City of Gentlemen," of which we caught a glimpse when we were yet some distance off.

Riding apart a little from the road, I was taken by one of the officers to the edge of a bluff, and there, far below

Vicinity of Santiago. Tobacco Train.

me, rolled the wide, swift-running, but now rather shallow, Yaqui river, the famous gold-river of Columbus, which, running through the heart of the island, drains some of its most fertile plains, the limits of which end abruptly, and in many cases precipitously, on the Yaqui. This river, known by its various names of Yaquey, Yacki Grande, takes its rise in the mountains near the Peak of Yaqui, and in its course extends some 200 miles, emptying finally into Manzanillo Bay. Having a number of tributaries, it waters and fertilises a vast extent of country, and from the nature of its banks could easily be formed into a vast canal. So winding is its course, that Columbus, crossing it several times, believed he had met with as many different streams, and accordingly bestowed various names upon it.

After many windings in the road, we came in sight of Santiago, high up on a plateau, its abrupt cliffs and walls giving it the appearance of a regularly fortified place, as at this point the town itself was not visible.

Descending to the river bank, and then mounting up a steep hill, we enter this queer, ancient, and historic city, bearing still about it, with its ruined walls and grass-grown streets, vestiges of its antiquity, relieved only by the fresh new houses of stone and plaster that have in later days been built.

A house having been prepared for our reception, we were soon comfortably bestowed in the most modern well-built house with which we had yet met, but, like most all Spanish houses, having its saloons over the stores and warehouses of the ground-floor.

During the whole evening numbers of the most prominent men called to pay their respects to the Commissioner, and appointments were made for the next day for the public meeting with the people generally.

I had read of the beauty of the moonlight nights in St Domingo, but up to this time we had had no fair specimen; but I confess the opportunity we now had of enjoying one of those beauties of the tropics was superb.

The house in which we were located was upon the highest part of the plateau, the windows, like all those of this country, large and opening to the floor, so that swinging in one's hammock you could look out on the beautiful scene before you, the white walls of the house looking even more white in the pale light of the moon, while by contrast the shadows were deeper and more mysterious, and stretching away beyond were the gently rising hills that finally ended in the mountain range which almost entirely surrounds the town, forming as it were a vast amphitheatre. A beautiful scene indeed, with the evening air pouring in fresh and pure; and, with the fatigues of the day upon us, it was no very difficult matter to slip away into the land of dreams.

"Santiago de los Caballeros" is one of the most ancient towns in the Island of St Domingo, and to-day really the most important in every respect. It received its name, St James, in honour of an order of knights in Spain, and was founded in 1504, owing to its vicinity to the

Market Square of Santiago.

famous fort "Concepcion de la Vega," and its being about half way between that place and the port of Puerto Plata.

As has already been shown in the earlier chapters, it has at various times been subjected to attacks from the early French and buccaneers; it has been burned down by fires;

it has been shaken down by earthquakes; and more lately utterly destroyed by Dessalines, and by the Spaniards when they left the island.

It is situated on the right bank of the Yaqui river, in a savanna that extends to the very edge, being nearly surrounded, as above stated, with hills and mountains; and from its frequent destructions, it possesses now no building worthy the attention particularly of the traveller. It is built, as usual, around a large plaza or square, in which is held the market, the largest and most busy one we had seen, where it was a most amusing and instructive sight to stroll and see the country people with their products of every variety for sale.

The streets are quite straight, and pretty generally run at right angles to each other, the houses in the main part of the town being almost entirely constructed of stone, while in the outskirts they consist of frame-work or the usual palm-thatched houses of the country; and for this reason, seen from the hill at the back of the town, and looking across to the opposite bank of the river, the town presents a rather irregular appearance.

It lies in the very heart of the finest agricultural region of the island, and is about 160 miles from the capital, with which it has little or no commercial intercourse, its port proper being the town of Puerto Plata, though in former days, when Monte Cristo was an organised port, its traffic principally went there, as the roads there are better, and easily accessible even for carts, while that to Puerto Plata is something fearfully difficult, and at times almost impossible, even for animals, the only means of transport.

The climate is undoubtedly the finest in the island, the place being noted for its salubrity, and it now possesses a population of about 8000 inhabitants, largely composed of whites, the majority of whom are as intelligent and polished as can be met with anywhere.

Being situated in the heart of the tobacco region, San-

SANTIAGO.

tiago is a place of active business, and controls this trade, many of the merchants being simply the agents of the foreign houses established at Puerto Plata; and this influence, principally German, controls this part of the traffic of the island.

The tobacco raised in the vicinity seeks this place as its depot, where it is packed on the backs of mules or horses, and, in charge of the teamsters who specially follow this calling, is despatched to Puerto Plata, whence it is shipped to Hamburg.

With the proposed railroads to Samana and to Monte Cristo, Santiago must become the great trading centre of the island, if not the capital.

In addition to the agricultural products of the region of which it is now the capital, Santiago has been, and probably always will be, the centre of the great mining interests for which in all time the island has been famous, but which have never yet been attempted to be developed.

About these mines there appears to be no really reliable information, but the geological survey now being carried on by Mr W. M. Gabb in the interests of a New York company will throw great light on this subject, especially if a work proposed by Mr Gabb, and for which he has had ample opportunities from his position of gaining materials, shall be published. It will not, of course, be to the interests of the company to make known all they know about such matters, but in general terms, I may state as Mr Gabb's opinion, that gold occurs scattered over a large part of the north flank of the central range of mountains (south side of Cibao), and also on the upper waters of the Jaina river. The gravel is rich in quality, but the quantity is too small over any given area to make it of great value. It might be placed on a par with the class of mines known in California as Chinese diggings, and will not pay a white man's labour.

Gold quartz veins abound higher up the mountains,

above all these "placer" deposits, but their quality has yet to be ascertained. That they bear gold has been proven by direct examination, and by the inferential proof that the gravel deposits derive their gold from them.

Iron occurs in paying quantities only in one place, the Maimon river, a south branch of the Yuna, about a hundred miles from Samana Bay. It is superb in quality and the position of the deposit with reference to work, but the transportation and demand questions are too much for it now.

Coal prospects are bad, such as are found being of poor quality, and appearing only in two or three inch veins.

Professor Blake, the geologist to the United States Commission, who traversed the island from St Domingo city to Puerto Plata, reports superficially that "for the greater part of the distance between the Jaina river and the Vega Real, we traversed a gold region comparing favourably in its indications of the metal with the gold regions of Georgia and the Carolinas.

"Some portions of this region along the Jaina were anciently worked, in a rude and imperfect manner, by the Indians and Spaniards. Within a few miles of the ruins of the ancient city of Buenaventura, but on the opposite side of the Jaina, there are ancient pits and mining shafts, partly filled up and overgrown, known among the people as 'Puits de los Indios' (Indian wells). It is evident that the miners, whoever they were, followed the bed of a ravine to its head, and then sunk pits at intervals, probably at the prolongation of the placer, and excavated the gravel between them, in the same manner as California miners 'cayote' their claims. There are doubtless some hill deposits along the Jaina that would pay to work, if water can be delivered upon them without too great an outlay.

"There is no lack of water in adjoining streams, and there is sufficient fall or drainage for tailings. . . .

"There is no doubt that there is a gold region of considerable extent and promise in the island, but I did not see anything to excite great enthusiasm regarding the deposits, or to encourage the expectation of immediate large returns from mining operations there. There is enough, however, visible to justify the labour and expense of carefully prospecting the ground. The rocks are very similar to those found in all gold regions."

Of iron ore he says, "There is abundance all along the route of brown iron ore, but it is questionable whether it is sufficiently pure to make pig iron."

I may say here, that people pretty generally state there is gold in abundance throughout all this region, but that it needs tranquillity to work it out scientifically, although, even in a rough way, it pays the ordinary labourer to wash it out.

We were informed of some Americans who had been in the interior for two or three years, but they being very close mouthed, nothing was known of their operations more than that they occasionally came down for provisions, which they paid for in gold. We saw specimens of the grain gold that had been gathered, and it is the same that, having been assayed at the United States mint, showed a fineness of 0.946.

I was also informed by a prominent and reliable physician of Santiago that many of the country people always have more or less grain gold in their possession, and that there was one woman in particular who every Saturday came into Santiago to sell a certain amount of gold, which, from its form and its nearly exact quantity, proved the regular result of a week's washing.

So much for modern investigation. Yet both history and tradition have given important facts on this subject; for as Lyonnet, who was twice sent out by the French Minister of Marine, in 1809 says, "Not a single country unites within itself a greater variety of mines. Nature has left nothing to desire in the mineral region; gold in the part of Santiago, and in the region of the Cibao; silver is common in the vicinity of Puerto Plata and Neyba; a quarry of marble at some distance from St Domingo; there is also clay for pottery, porphyry, alabaster."

We have it on record by Columbus himself that the Indians paid a tribute in gold on this island; and Oviedo, who is deemed a reliable historian of the events of his time, has even illustrated his description of gold-washing with

Gold-Washing. (Oviedo.)

drawings of the natives at this occupation, the process appearing similar enough to that of pan-washing to-day.

In the first voyage of Columbus, when his ship struck on a rock at La Navidad, it is related the cacique sympathised with the great Admiral so much, that, among other things, he presented Columbus with a mask, of which the eyes, the ears, and the nose were made of solid gold.

When the mines of La Vega and the Cibao had been in operation some time, the discovery of those at San Christobal or Buenaventura (good luck) was made, and

Bartholomew Columbus, going there in May 1496 to examine them, established a working party.

Although as early as 1499 these mines are spoken of as being in decadence, it is yet on record that in 1502, according to Oviedo, two men, Garay and Diaz, found the most wonderful nugget of gold which has ever been discovered in any mine; it weighed 200 ounces, and was valued at 3600 dollars of the time. Romance even accompanies this statement; for it is related the lump was first discovered by an Indian woman in the service of the two above named, who were so delighted that they killed a pig to roast, upon which to feast their friends, serving it up on this same "grain" of gold for a dish, and of which they boasted that their Majesties had never dined off so rich a one. Unfortunately it was lost in that gale predicted by Columbus, it having been purchased by Bobadilla to send to Spain in the fleet.

Walton in his time states that the poor people at a rivulet close by, after heavy rains, continue to wash the sand they collect in a small calabash, obtaining often an ounce a day; the small particles, he says, being dislodged by the mountain torrent from the great mine, the old vein of which is now fallen in.

But it was the famous mines of the "Cibao" (the Indian name for a stony country) which were the first that afforded specimens of the riches of the country, and yielded them the most treasure; and these were situated in the centre of the island near La Vega and Santiago, bordering on the river Janico; while in the mountains that enclose the valley of Constanza were large veins of a productive nature, large particles being washed down by the rains.

Muñoz states that Columbus wished to satisfy himself of the richness of that region, and accordingly, in March 1494, made that famous march by the Gentlemen's Pass (Puerto de los Hidalgos) into this region, when he was presented with gold-dust and gold in grain by the cacique, two of these latter, it is said, weighing more than an ounce.

Walton states that in the south, at Guaba and at Bahorico, several persons clandestinely enriched themselves without ever making use of a tool, the maroons, who at that time occupied that section, procuring all the necessities they wanted with the gold they brought down to the villages with them.

I find it stated that in 1502, although the working of the mines temporarily ceased, it was not from lack of results, but only from the difficulty of obtaining labour since the order portioning out the Indians had been revoked.

In 1505, however, the Governor Ovando, who, it is well known, had pursued a policy opposed to this order, made his peace with the King by sending home as his share from the mines of La Vega and Buenaventura alone 460,000 escudos of gold per year, a sum large enough to make the court wink at his transactions. But it must be remembered also that, in addition to this, Ovando carried on the government and made expensive improvements out of the revenues of the island, and as the cane had not yet become productive, we must suppose the yield of gold was large.

This is corroborated by Herrera the historian, who alludes to the gold from the mines as amounting to over 460,000 dollars per annum in those days, and that not counting the grain-gold surreptitiously appropriated.

Peter Martyr, who had also good opportunities of knowing, says, that besides silver, copper, and iron, the mines produced, in his time, 500,000 ducats of gold.

Even as early as 1502, as much as 240,000 crowns of gold were minted at the old town of La Vega from the mines in the Cibao; and the town of Cotuy, in those days, was generally known by the name of "The Mines," from the fact that there were so many miners living there, and working the mines in its vicinity. Santiago, it is said, was also at one time inhabited principally by goldsmiths.

When we remember that all these above-named sums were abstracted at a time when metallurgy was almost unknown, and the loss excessive, we can imagine what must have been the original richness of this part of the island; and it remains yet to be seen, by practical explorations and workings, if these are exhausted.

Some authorities state that in 1511 many of the mines were abandoned from want of labourers, and because the working of the cane had become so profitable. That there must have been foundation for all these statements, it is given as a fact that, in Ovando's time, the receipts of gold received in Spain were so large, that the news spreading among the people, there were not vessels enough to take out the emigrants desiring to go to St Domingo.

In 1530, when the decay of St Domingo had already begun, I find the President of the Royal Court remitting to the Emperor, as his share of one-fifth of the mines, $10,000 in gold and fifty measures of pearls, at the same time advising him that they had discovered in the island a very beautiful mine of silver and several mines of iron; the latter being judged, in Spain, better than that of Biscay, although these mines were never worked.

Permission coming from the Emperor to work these silver-mines, so much silver was extracted, that permission was also granted to coin reales (ten-cent pieces) of the value of those in Spain.

As, however, the wondrous wealth of the mines of Peru and Mexico became known, interest seemed to be lost in those of St Domingo from various causes, principally, we may suppose, from lack of labourers, until, in 1543, all work ceased; and by a royal decree Spain ordered that all the mines should be closed, the execution of the order being intrusted to an armed force, while the civil officers visited each spot and denounced the most severe penalties on those who should attempt to work them.

But when the island had reached a state of almost

absolute decay, there yet seems always to have been more or less ore of various kinds taken out; and I might cite here facts from Charlevoix, personal investigations of St Mery, of Soulastre, of Walton, and of Valverde; but, to use the words of the latter, "To indicate all the places where are to be found the mines of St Domingo is impossible, because many have not been discovered, and the memory of others has been lost that were worked at the beginning. The island contains, however, ranges and forests where only the montero or fugitive negro have penetrated; mountains, it can be said, where human foot has never trod, consequently there are many to discover." But all these authorities give place and date to gold mines and discoveries.

As, however, I have fortunately succeeded in seeing the report made by the Commissioner, Juan Nieto, sent out by the Spanish Government in 1793, and who, from being the mineralogist to his Majesty, is entitled to confidence, it will be best to accept his statements concerning the mines of the island, showing not only that there are very valuable mines in the island, but where they are. The reader will find it in the Appendix.

It is only by thus gathering our information from various sources and periods that we are able to form any idea of the real nature of this wonderful island. Among other authorities, I may quote an article from the "Annales de Chimie," by Guyton, who says, "It had long been supposed that platina was found only in the gold mines of Santa Fe and Choco, in Peru. Twenty years ago there was a report that some had been obtained from a ferruginous sand in St Domingo; but apparently the examination of this was not executed so as to give decisive results, since it has not been published. What Mr Percy submitted to the inspection of the Institute in February 1810, leaves no doubt of the existence of this metal in St Domingo, eastern part. It exhibits precisely the same characters as that we have seen from

Spain. It is found principally after heavy rains in the sands of the Yaqui river, at the foot of the mountains of the Cibao."

If the theory be true that all these islands constitute the ridges of one vast chain, of which Cuba and Porto Rico are a part, it is only natural to suppose that the same veins of ore found in one will be in a greater or less degree found in the others; and though there is no regularly opened mine of copper in St Domingo, yet the signs are that there is abundance of that metal; and we need only refer to those wonderful copper-mines of the "Cobre" in eastern Cuba to be satisfied that this ore does exist, in paying quantities, on these islands.

Having thus gone, at some length, into the mining prospects of the island, we need only again refer to Santiago, to say that, notwithstanding what had been said about the strong anti-annexation feeling existing there, we were not able to discover much of it. Strolling about frequently alone, in stores, and among the people, and in the market, I confess I was much astonished to find the sentiment so generally diffused among a class of people, especially those who, one would think, to look at them in their listless positions, cared about nothing but being let alone. Yet eyes would sparkle and faces brighten as they spoke of having a strong Government. The secret may be explained, perhaps, by my experience with a fine-looking old yellow woman in the market-place, to whom I said—

"Well, old lady, you don't care about annexation, I suppose; you look comfortable enough?"

"Yes; I want it too, more than anybody."

"How so?" I asked, noticing that she looked very sad.

Her eyes filled with tears as she said, "Now my old man 's gone, I want my boys home from soldiering." And this seems to be the case with most of the womenkind, as they complain that, with constant attempts at revolution, there is no surety for the men remaining at home.

At the public meeting accorded to Mr White, the *élite* of the people of the Cibao were present; and I was struck by the fine forms and intellectual heads of most of those present, comprising members of the Church, law, medicine, and the leading native merchants.

Eloquent as Mr White had been in placing before the people whom we had hitherto met the nature of his mission, he seemed to be more than ever impressed with the responsibility resting upon him, especially as here were represented the intellectual men of the island, capable of taking any position demanded of them by society.

Referring to their sad history, to their revolutions, and to their position (or lack of it) as an independent state, he compared their past with their future, in case they were admitted as a part of the American Union.

Comparing the condition of the island as he saw it with what it had been described to him, he expressed the immense pleasure he had received in their beautiful land, and spoke feelingly of the wealth and happiness that would be produced naturally by their alliance with some strong power; and he hoped, for their sakes, it would be with the United States. Explaining fully the nature of our Government, he cautioned them, if they did not wish to become citizens of the United States, it was now time to express their views, which they could all do there openly or meet him in private; but that they must remember, that once part of the United States, there could no longer be tolerated discontent and uprising against their rulers; that a means was provided and a term prescribed when officers could be changed, this power being always in the hands of the people; and that, if they earnestly and honestly wished to enter the American Union, and were accepted, they would have the satisfaction of knowing that, while they thus became Americans, they would none the less remain Dominicans, a name of which they seemed so proud.

These remarks were received with great and evident satisfaction, and every one, at the conclusion of his speech, rushed forward to take the Commissioner by the hand, the rest of us coming in, also, for an occasional "shake" from some enthusiastic "man and brother."

CHAPTER XVIII.

"Delightful change! how cool the breezes blow,
And fan the sickly moisture from my brow!
The lungs confess their balm; no more the same,
Lightness and vigour renovate the frame."

FROM SANTIAGO TO MONTE CRISTO—*The Puerto Plata Road—Fording the Yaqui—Its Bottom Lands—The Vega again—A Dangerous Insect—Polite "Guajiro"—Tobacco Culture—A Dry Country but Fine Climate—The Amina and Mao Rivers—Some Tropical Habits—Swimming the River at Guayubin—A Faro Bank and Hotel—Multiplicity of Generals—A Long Ride through a Sterile Country—The Agave Species—Monte Cristo—Left Alone on the Island—Manzanillo Bay—The Country South of the Yaqui—The Uninhabited Region—Crocodiles and Iguanas.*

WHEN our party reached Santiago, it was found that, owing to arrangements with the other Commissioners, Mr White would not have time to accomplish himself all that he desired, in visiting both Puerto Plata and the land lying to the north-west of Santiago up to Manzanillo Bay and Monte Cristo. As both the Doctor and myself had already visited Puerto Plata, the Commissioner requested us to make this journey overland, and report to him at Monte Cristo, while he joined the ship and came up by sea; which arrangement being acceded to, our preparations were soon made, we retaining two of the peons (servants), with the necessary stores and horses, while the balance of the party accompanied Mr White.

General Cacerees, learning our intention, with great

kindness furnished us with letters to all the authorities in the districts in which we expected to travel, ordering that every facility should be shown us for prosecuting our journey; and as our projected trip was to within a few miles of the Haytian border, on which there was constant fighting, it will be seen the orders might prove of good service to us.

The region we were about to visit is famed throughout the island as being, so far as climate and healthfulness are concerned, a perfect paradise, the only requisite lacking to make it a Garden of Eden being a more liberal supply of water.

On the morning, therefore, of March 3, an hour or two after Mr White and his party left us, we took our way out of Santiago; and fording the Yaqui river, which is the same stream we afterwards find at Manzanillo, struck the broad wide road that leads all the way to Monte Cristo, and which is said to be the only continuous road in the island upon which carts can be drawn.

We found the road dry and dusty, the soil composed of a whitish clay, and then red gravel and clay, but it was wide, free from mud, well shaded, and bordered with timber, and could, with a little care and expense, be made into a most excellent waggon-road for transporting to Monte Cristo the produce that now seeks Puerto Plata as an outlet.

Travelling this road for about eight miles to where it turns off towards Puerto Plata, we found the country so uninteresting and unsettled, that we determined to try the south bank of the Yaqui, as being less known and more interesting, for though a longer route, it runs in and near the fine bottom lands of the Yaqui.

Following, therefore, a small creek, we struck at its mouth the main river, whose banks at this point were quite low, the river being about 100 yards wide, running swiftly over a gravelly bed; but the current was so strong, that we had to change direction and ride our horses directly against it, thus making a long sweep across the river, our guide remaining upon the shore and pointing with his finger the direction we were to keep. Striking the other shore, we turned our horses' heads on the now south bank, and continued our course through low bottom lands well wooded, and which, much to our surprise, we found to be well settled, principally by negroes or mulattoes, who busied themselves in the raising principally of tobacco; the field of plantain, it being understood, is always as necessary an adjunct as the roof of the house, for it is upon the "plantano" that the Dominican countryman lives.

We found the people along this section generally quite poor, indifferent, and without much aim or hope for anything, except just to live. Occasionally we could find some intelligent person that showed more signs or desires for improvement. They were all, however, exceedingly kind and communicative to us. We find nowhere the orange tree cultivated, nor any of the finer bananas, while the coffee and the cocoa and cacao are left to grow wild or by accident.

It was the same old story.

"Would not all these things grow?" we ask.

"O yes," is the reply. "I suppose they would if they were planted."

"Why don't you grow them then?"

"What is the use? Who wants them? There is no market for them, and we don't want them. We have all we need without the trouble."

Yet all these alluvial lands were rich in soil and forest growth, and the tobacco alone that could be raised would amount to an enormous sum, for these lands are of that low, moist nature that fine tobacco requires, and similar to those in the famous "Vuelta Abajo" of Cuba.

Riding for some seven miles along this bottom land in a fair road bordered on each side by the most luxuriant vege-

CACTI COUNTRY, NÉAR MONTE CRISTO.

tation, we met with no settlements until we came to Platanay, which was simply a congregation of frame huts in an open savanna, the population apparently consisting of women and dogs.

Our afternoon ride brought us up into the higher land, away from the bottom land, and we soon had evidence of the dry nature of the climate of this part of the island in the parched, hard nature of the soil; for though of apparently good clay, it was baked so hard by the hot sun as to seem like stone, the country being almost entirely uninhabited, except when we came out upon some savanna-like place such as Platanay. We had been having, even in the bottom lands, signs of the cactus in many forms, but now we found them coming almost exclusively, the short (espargato) thick kind, with its broad prickly leaves, being even eaten by the cattle. As the sun was getting low we increased our pace, entering upon one of the strangest bits of land with which I have ever met. In many places the path wound up by some strangely formed fissure or chaotic abysss, that at a distance looked like rock, but on near approach proved to be clay, that from long dryness had split and cracked and crumbled, while upon the level plain every variety of the cactus was met with, growing in weird and strange confusion, and giving with their strange forms and cold grey colours, with here and there a dwarf tree, from which the dry moss hung down in strange festoons, a spectral, gloomy character to the landscape.

As the shades of night quickly fell, we came upon a rude out-of-the-way cemetery, which, it would seem, had been fittingly placed here; for this purgatory, or city of the dead, was a subject worthy of Doré's pencil. As the gloom of night closed over us, we felt we were not in the most enviable position, for, riding fast, we were far ahead of our servants or guides. We knew not the road, and we knew our resting-place for the night must still be some distance off, with no water near, either for ourselves or our horses.

The moon, however, coming out from behind the clouds, enabled us to see the road or path, or rather one of many; but luckily taking the right one we kept on, occasionally passing through some wide, level plain, upon which stood the tall rank grass, burnt dry by the sun, and upon which we saw, now and then, cattle, large and fat, feeding.

This is one of the peculiarities of St Domingo. Traverse these vast savannas in mid-day, and you see not a living thing; but as soon as the sun goes down, you find coming out from bush and wood and tree, cattle, horses, mules, and goats, while you look in vain for the house of the owner. With an amount of sense which the stranger would do well to imitate, they sleep in mid-day.

It is my belief, that in this one article alone, the people could make themselves rich by raising beef and hides to send to the northern markets, if there were any facilities for doing so; for cattle have always increased so fast here, even without care, that a hide at one time was worth more than the whole carcass, and this too only six days from New York markets, with meat at fancy prices. And there is really no drawback to this, or why herding should not be carried on as extensively here as in Texas.

Sometimes a large fly similar to the cantharides, when an animal is wounded seizes upon it, and fastening itself to the sore deposits there an egg, which afterwards breeds into a maggot that gnaws and widens the wound, and finally deprives the animal of life.

I have seen a cow that otherwise was perfect, having torn the flesh of its hind leg, was being gradually killed in this way; there it lay without being able to move any distance, the insects having actually burrowed into the bone, and yet no one thought of attempting a cure, although the wound was like a window, so easily could it be looked into.

But meeting a "Guajiro" who was returning from water with his cattle, we were informed as to our correct road, and putting spurs to our tired, thirsty horses, we rode rapidly until about two hours after sunset, and after passing several dry brooks and cañons, we came out upon a level plain, which, by the appearance of the grass and the cattle, we judged produced water, and making our way up to the only house in sight, we discovered we were just above the Yaqui, on high table land, where, finding we would be allowed to swing our hammocks, we made ourselves as comfortable, pending the arrival of our peons, as we could.

A "Guajiro."

The people with whom we had stopped were more than usually intelligent. Both the man and the woman were mulattoes or natives, though they claimed to be white, and both could read and write. They were much in favour of annexation, and spoke of the benefits the country would derive from it. Their business was to raise tobacco and graze cattle, which, notwithstanding the drought, they said grew fat and strong feeding on the leaves of the espenosa, a species of cactus.

To my inquiry why an intelligent man like him did not raise better tobacco, and improve the quality of it, he replied: "What 's the use? Good, bad, or indifferent, the merchants pay just the same price for it; there is no market to go to except Hamburg, and Dominican tobacco has always had such a bad reputation that no higher price can be had there for it. If we could go into another market where, when the grades are sorted, a better price would be paid according to quality, it would improve us and our crops."

Although it was very dry here, as they thought it, yet they could always raise two crops a year, one of tobacco, the other of corn. As for the low country, he said he could not be induced to change, the climate up here being always so good, in which his wife coincided. We found the night quite cold enough even with two blankets in our hammocks, but the morning air when we arose was superb, fresh, and bracing, and as we came from our bath in the Yaqui we were prepared to believe all that had been said of this paradise of a climate.

For months and months it never rains a drop, and two years ago for one whole year it never rained. This is unusual, for they have their regular rains almost every day in July and August, and in the winter, what they call the "Northers," it rains December, January, and February.

Leaving here at an early hour of the morning, we soon came to the Amina river, a pleasant, rapid-running stream, and after striking into some bottom lands we came to another rapid stream, the Mao, both of which empty into the Yaqui. Both of these we forded, the banks in each instance being low and well timbered, the bed of the stream being small, clean stones. Penetrating the woods we came upon a plateau, upon which was placed the straggling village of Mao, an assemblage of a dozen or so native houses, inhabited by mulatto-coloured people and some negroes. The invariable reply to our question, "What do you raise here?" was answered by "Tobacco, sir."

"Won't fruits grow, and cane, and coffee, and cocoa?"

"Oh, yes; only we don't raise them."

"Why not?" I ask.

"Quien sabe, señor." (I don't know.)

We make a detour, get lost in the bottom lands by the river bank, stumbling in our way over quite good-sized tobacco patches and plantation fields, and finally, being gone about six miles out of the way, we were piloted by a native Dominican, he having the kindness to ride out of his way at least a mile to show us our right road.

The aspect of this part of the Vega Real is very peculiar and changeable; as you strike the main stream of the Yaqui everything is of the most luxuriant nature, palms and vines, and forest trees, covered with the various species

The Vega Real.

of the orchid, shade a surface thick with grass or green-leaved bush.

Going some distance away from the river, or perhaps between two streams, usually emptying into the Yaqui, though now dry, the plain stretches out before you, covered with stunted vegetation which seems dying from thirst; while as we noticed in the distant mountains of the Monte

Cristo range it was constantly showering, but those showers did not, strange to say, extend beyond the summit; and this I afterwards discovered to be an actual fact, that while the north side is receiving abundance of rain the south is as constantly being parched up by drought.

The new road to which we had been piloted we found was the "Real Camino," which, in this case, means something, it being a wide, dry mud road, with a sterile tract of land on each side, which seemed to be burnt up by the hot sun and the lack of water. They talk about the burning suns of the desert, but I think it would be hard to rival this midday sun of Dominica, for the road was utterly devoid of shade: there was no grass upon which to feed the horses, and no water for mile after mile. With my pocket-handkerchief wrapped around my head Dominican fashion, a huge palm-leaf hat on top, and my umbrella raised, it seemed utterly impossible to avoid the rays of the sun; so, thinking the quicker I was out of it the better, I put spurs to my horse, and, leaving the Doctor to take it

Gigantic Cactus.

more slowly, I galloped on for shade, grass, and water. Hot and hotter it seemed to me as mile after mile I rode quickly on. Nothing but dry sterility; not a house, not a human being to be seen anywhere, and not an animal even, except a stray comical-looking jackass now and then; while, to make matters worse, every brook I came to was dry as a bone, and "earth, earth everywhere, but water none." I looked at the cactus in its varied form, many species of which were perfectly gigantic, or the beautiful aloe plant, with its fresh green leaves and tall-stemmed flower, and wondered how they stood it and lived, when, happily, just as I was beginning to despair, I discovered ahead of me a clump of trees, with a few cattle under them, and riding up, my eyes were gladdened by the sight of a shallow, clear running stream, well shaded by dwarf trees, and some few of a larger growth, but no grass of any kind. Here were gathered a number of horses, mules, and cattle, all standing quietly beneath the trees to keep out of the hot sun. My horse was soon tethered after watering, and hoisting my umbrella, I made a shelter of it in the sandy bed of the stream, stretching myself with intense relief for a siesta, taking care to have my revolver in convenient distance in case of accident, and then was lost in sleep until disturbed by our party, an hour afterwards, just arriving.

Here is where the newcomer fails in adapting himself to the climate, and often brings upon himself sickness and suffering; for in place of following the example of the natives, the traveller from the north comes here full of energy and life, and imagines he can stand anything, and so, perhaps, he can for a time; but he will eventually find that a wise Providence prescribes the life he ought to lead. Thus a man, wishing to work or travel, should be out and about at five o'clock in the morning, and at ten or eleven should shelter himself from the meridian sun until two or three, when the cool breezes of the afternoon have arrived, and thus he can easily accomplish quite as much and with more comfort than in the north.

Thus learning from experience what we had been frequently advised of, we remained until the strong afternoon breeze set in, and then started for Guayubin, a small village upon the Yaqui, where we were to stop for the night.

Night overtook us before we entered again the rich bottom lands on the river; but, as the moon was bright, we were rather glad to continue our journey over a country that offered us nothing in the way of scenery, soil, or inhabitants.

Arriving, however, on the banks of the Yaqui, we found a small settlement, and were informed we would have to canoe the river ourselves and swim our horses, and that the boatmen were on the other side. However, we rode directly to the river bank, which we found to be some fifteen feet high and steep, and here we sat and stood for nearly an hour waiting for the ferrymen, who seemed to be carousing on the other side. Our shouts moved them not. I bawled to them that, being in a hurry, we wanted to cross, at which they seemed to be much amused; even my shouts of "official business" and "government service" were of no avail, until they deemed it worth while, after an hour of this work, to come across for us. A man may be pardoned if, under such circumstances, he uses strong language; and I am afraid though ours was good Anglo-Saxon, it could not be found in the Shorter Catechism.

One of the men, we found, was inebriated; but, as they both seemed to understand their business, we allowed them to unsaddle our horses, which they led down to the river bank, where was a large dugout or canoe. In this were placed our saddles; we stepped in also; and one negro, taking the paddle or pole, placed himself at the stern, while the other, taking the halter straps of the two horses in his hands, placed himself at the bow. Then there was a row, the horses pulled and backed, and the canoe rocked and turned till I thought we should get a bath also; but finally, with shouts and pulls, the horses were got into the water immediately over their heads. Then the swift current took us, steered by the paddle; the horses snorted, and plunged, and swam, their heads being supported by the negro in the bow; every few yards we came to a sort of bay or shoal, on which the horses were allowed to get their footing, then another push and a swim, and so on to the other side. Here, a few yards from the shore, we had to saddle up, as the canoe could go no farther; and, mounting our wet, tired horses, we rode up the bank, where we found a guard drawn up, this seeming to be an advanced post. A few words to the sergeant and the use of the General's name gave us rapid directions for the village, which place we soon found, much to our gratification. Having a special order to the General of the district, and asking for his house, we were shown to the centre of the town, where we found a low, one-storied house of two rooms, well lit up. Dismounting, we showed our letter, and was told the General was not there, but would be soon. The brother of the General then came forward, and he was informed we needed shelter for ourselves and food for our horses. The house was placed at our disposal in which to hang up our hammocks, the poverty of the place, he said, not permitting him to offer other accommodations. Wet, tired, and hungry, we tied our horses and entered. The first room had a billiard table, upon which some persons were playing, while behind it, in the corner, was a faro bank surrounded by players. Turning from this room we were ushered into another one, where already two hammocks swung and a bed was placed. We were too tired to be critical, and the offer of some hot punch made of eggs, rum, milk, and nutmeg, not only mollified us, but furnished us what we needed in the shape of meat and drink, as we were by this time accustomed to short rations.

The General, Don Frederico Garcia, accompanied by several others, soon made his appearance, and apologised for his inability to treat us better, but was profuse in his offers of assistance. He seemed to be a fine, frank, manly fellow, quite handsome, and every inch a soldier in his carriage. He immediately presented us to his friends, whom he also honoured with the title of general. This made about the sixty-fifth general we had met with since we had been upon the island; but, as yet, never a company of soldiers had been seen. Ah! well, it is only "cosa Dominicana," I suppose.

Our baggage having arrived, and hammocks hung, we excused ourselves on the plea of fatigue, and tumbled into our bags, where, happily, we were oblivious of everything. Bright and early the General came to see us, and finding us determined to start immediately, kindly gave us a dragoon to show us the road and take us to his (the General's) father's, half-way on the road to Monte Cristo, where we were to breakfast; and swallowing our coffee and bit of bread, we were soon *en route*, following the river for some distance; then leaving behind us the fine tract of bottom-land in which Guayubin is situated, we were soon again upon the dry, hard soil of this upper country, that appears only fit to grow cacti or browse goats, innumerable herds of which we met on our road.

A sharp ride of three hours brought us to the house of Don Ambrosio Garcia, the father of the General. Here upon a knoll, standing a little way back from the roadside, was the plain but commodious dwelling-house, without a blade of grass, a tree, or even a piazza to shelter the occupants from the sun; but such a magnificent site, and still more superb air, made amends for this; and the kindly way in which Madam received us and bade us welcome was extremely pleasant. Breakfast was soon prepared for us, to which we did ample justice. We had hardly finished it when Don Ambrosio arrived, and welcomed us to his house most cordially. He had just come in two hours from Monte Cristo, our destination.

Perhaps if the isle of Dominica were peopled entirely by such men as the two Garcias, father and son, it would to-day be something in the political world; for here was one of the most pleasant, intelligent, courtly men with whom we had met. His grandfather was an Englishman, his mother a Spaniard, I believe; but, at all events, he was a warm advocate for annexation, which would be the salvation of the country, in his opinion. He had owned this land for a lifetime, and would not change it for any place in the low country. The wife, who had been born and bred in Santiago, was of the same opinion, on account of its extreme healthfulness, good roads, and purity of air.

Don Ambrosio talked about the dryness of the soil and the scarcity of water, and then took us out to his canuco or farm, to show us the orange, the pea, the bean, the tomato, corn, pumpkin, squash, a number of native fruits, and, like a small tree, the cotton plant growing upon what he and others called sterile soil, because, forsooth, without machinery, or wells, or cisterns, or even the simplest agricultural implements, it did not grow the cane, coffee, and cocoa, all of which require more or less water.

I asked him, did he ever plough the land? He replied, he had never had a plough, and didn't believe there was one on the island (which was true enough); but that, if he had, he could make his land very valuable by turning the soil in the rainy season. This, he said, was very irregular; but they generally had plenty of rain throughout the year, though at times it was very dry. Professor Blake and Major Macgrue, old Californians, have since told me that all this district, from what they have seen, resembles very much California; and that, with irrigation, this would be first-rate agricultural land for any and everything. But even now there are two things that can be grown there that are invaluable. I allude to the cotton plant, which, in place of being a simple bush planted from the seed each year, is here a tree, growing two and three years, which

The Cotton Tree.

needs only to be trimmed and pruned to produce a large yield of the finest cotton—quite equal, some say, to the sea

FLOWERING ALOE.

island; and not only white in colour, but of the kind known as Nankeen.

The other article is that of the "Cabulla" (Foucroya Cubense of botanists), a species of agave, from the fibres of which they get an article of hemp, of which most all the rope on the island is made, and which, being mixed with "sisal" hemp, makes splendid rope. Both of these grow naturally without care on this dry land, and with care and cultivation could be made to flourish in extensive plantations.

All of this apparently sterile region is the home of the cactii, of which I counted more than a dozen species, while the family of agaves are seen in an immense variety; and we found specimens of the aloe in flower, with a stem over fifteen feet high,—the most superb specimens we had ever seen.

Don Ambrosio speaks of the disputed ground partly in possession of the Haytians, as being the garden-spot of the island, extending across to Azua on the frontier. While he described the entire valley of the Yaqui as consisting of a fertile stripe of alluvial lands adjoining the river, thence a high rolling plain extending on both sides to the base of the mountains; the lower portion of the rolling plain, capable of irrigation, and with irrigation capable of producing every species of tropical vegetation, especially sugar-cane.

The southern slope of the northern hills is generally dry for about fifty miles from Monte Cristo; but the north side of the southern range is very fertile. All of these dry lands are, however, especially valuable for cotton. Of course, during the wet season, the whole character of the country is changed; everything then becomes bright, fresh, and green; and this is about equal to our summer and spring, occurring in April, May, June, and July.

Notwithstanding these dry seasons, the cattle, horses, and mules do extremely well, for the region is remarkably healthy, and the former, when there is no grass, eat the espargato.

Refreshed with our rest, including a siesta in the hammock, we left late in the afternoon the house of Garcia, where we had been so hospitably treated, and started on our journey for Monte Cristo, some twelve miles off, in a country of the same character we were now in.

As the sun was just preparing to set into the horizon, we mounted the ridge that separated us from the sea, and then bursting on our view was a superb scene indeed. From the high point on which we stood the road descended into an extensive plain, broken a little to the left by a low hill, beyond whose crest could just be seen the roofs of the houses in the village of Monte Cristo, the land stretching down to a sandy, level coast; to the right, the plain, through which a small stream of brackish water ran, extended to a bold, high hill, known by its various names, La Grange (the Barn, given it by Columbus), and the "Morro," and which, making into the sea in front of the town, formed, with another strip of abrupt land, the promontory, inside of which was the spacious bay of Monte Cristo, in which now rested only a few fishing boats, where, in times gone by, rode merchant vessels from other climes.

Descending the hill by a winding road we entered the little village, that is all that remains of the once populous, large, and important town of Monte Cristo, now simply the depôt for receiving mahogany and other woods from the neighbouring country, to be shipped in small schooners to Puerto Plata, whence it goes to the European markets. Here we were hospitably housed in the warehouse of a German merchant, there being no hotels of any kind.

We had hardly reached Monte Cristo when we found the *Nantasket* coming into the harbour with Commissioner White on board, and after remaining only long enough to get some fresh provisions, and take the Doctor on board, she steamed out of the harbour *en route* for home *via* Hayti.

MONTE CRISTO BAY.

Although I had intended to investigate the island more fully than the others, it was not without considerable regret that I saw my companions take their departure, and leave me to pursue my journey alone; for the pleasant intercourse of the Commissioner and the Doctor had made very agreeable a journey through these tropic wilds, that would otherwise have been only interesting. But the Doctor did his best to leave me in a cheerful frame of mind, as I saw the last of him (shallow water preventing stepping from shore into boat), perched upon the shoulders of a stalwart sailor, his pockets filled with fruits of various kinds, a bundle of native hemp in one hand, while the other held carefully a superb specimen of the aloe flower, his umbrella protruding from under his arm.

And so our pleasant party was broken up; the many days of rough, hard journeying over, and the pleasant talk we had at our jolly mess all done; and I left to pursue my further investigations all alone.

Although the present town of Monte Cristo is a place of comparatively little importance, not being an open port, and the population only a few hundreds, it has in its time, as previously mentioned, in the past history of St Domingo occupied a prominent place, and one, as we have said, likely again to be occupied, in case of an improvement in its affairs.

It is stated to have had at one time a population of 26,000, with its houses well built of stone, while upon the prominent points around were quite considerable forts, not a vestige of which now remain.

In the time when the Yaqui also emptied its waters into the bay, there was no difficulty in obtaining fresh water, whether for the inhabitants or for the shipping that then frequented the port.

From the fact that this source is now changed, Manzanillo has become more of a place of shelter for vessels, although there is yet in that bay no town, and it is more than probable that, with its natural advantages, it will become a formidable rival to Monte Cristo.

Both of these places, however, are the natural shipping points of an immense and superb tract of country lying to the south of them.

Monte Cristo is likely to prove an important point in the island, if ever the enterprise and energy that American annexation shall bring sets in; for this is the most accessible point from the interior of La Vega and Santiago, and, with a road made over which waggons could go, all the tobacco that now seeks a market upon mule-back by the fearful path down the mountain to Puerto Plata would come here for shipment. A hundred thousand bales of tobacco even now find their way to market each year, upon which a tax of two to three dollars per bale has to be paid for transporting it the small distance of sixty miles—a business that in old times was done here at Monte Cristo.

Twelve miles west of Monte Cristo is the superb harbour formed by the Bay of Manzanillo, with clear water, the bottom at sixteen fathoms being seen. It is a bay equal, or even better, than Samana, though perhaps not so extensive, being five or six miles wide, and seven long, having also small arms and coves. In places the water is so deep that vessels can anchor with their bowsprits touching the shore.

The shores are well wooded, the red mangrove predominating, from which it is presumed the reputed unhealthiness of the place arises.

There is abundance of rain there, and the great river of Yaqui, which runs by Santiago, naturally empties into this bay; but at present a lagoon is formed, caused by obstructions, sand, snags, &c., that have formed all the way down from Peladero. This lagoon extends for about eight miles square, and is gradually working its way back to the interior, covering up the low wooded lands in its vicinity, and thus forming the lagoon, in which abound innumerable fish; and here also the "cayman," for which the waters of the island are famous, makes his home.

Manzanillo Bay lies in a direction from north-west to south-east, and extends into the island a distance of about ten miles, and has emptying into it a number of streams be-

Cayman.

sides the Yaqui, the principal one of which is the Massacre, or Dajabon, famous for its pure water.

The water of the Yaqui is also exceedingly pure, and the lagoon or lake formed by it has an average depth of five or six feet, but the channel varies from eight to fifteen feet; so that steamers might easily find their way through it, were it not for the old logwood forests through which the river passes.

Forcing one's way through the water-plants and swamp-timber, you at last come in sight of the river Yaqui itself, nearly 250 yards wide at this point, with its waters so clear that the fishes and caymans in it can be distinctly seen.

Originally the Yaqui emptied into the bay at Monte Cristo also, as it had two mouths, but it has now become dammed up, as above described; but it is considered feasible to open the channel again, which would give fresh water to Monte Cristo, and restore the fertile lands in immense quantities, now overflown by the lagoon. It is said that the river can be made navigable for flat-boats and small stern-wheelers all the way to Santiago.

Residents in this vicinity state there is a natural change going on at this mouth of the river, which in a few years may throw it back to its natural bed, leading out by Monte Cristo, for the various channels are now being entirely closed up by the numerous trees and obstructions that the river carries down, and which form what is called in Dominican parlance a "balza" or bay, similar to those formed in the Mississippi, and which throws the natural course of the river into the woods on each side.

Both sides of this river, from the lagoon up to the Maguaco, are covered with logwood tracts, in width from one to three miles, the wood being of good quality, straight and thick; and it is said that, working it economically, and cutting down only the trees of larger growth, eight to ten thousand tons may be annually extracted from this quarter, as the trees grow very fast. The difficulty in exporting this article at present is the distance required for transportation, which, with the workmen's wages, makes the expense too great.

All the lands south of the Yaqui bordering the river, from Manzanillo to Guayubin, are extremely fertile, and a number of small settlements are scattered throughout the section. Tobacco, wax, and honey are produced in abundance; but the two latter, from the want of cooperage and easy conveyance, are not at present valuable as products, though immense quantities could be exported.

The "sierra," or range of mountains that extend from the southern boundary to this section, and that run nearly parallel with the Yaqui river, furnish abundance of mahogany of the finest kind.

This grows in "manchas," as it is called, or clumps of from fifteen to twenty trees close together, while for some distance no other mahogany-trees will be found; and it is according as these trees are more or less convenient to water or means of transport that they are cut down. For this reason, at all accessible points mahogany has become somewhat rare, but in the interior, even at short distances in the impenetrable forests, there is abundance of this valuable wood, together with fustic, lignum vitæ, ebony, and many other valuable woods hardly known.

Our hardy lumbermen from the Middle and New England States, with their experience and sawmills, would find a mine of gold in all these timbered lands of St Domingo, some of the most precious and choice logs having at times sold in England as high as £100 ($500).

The present mode of getting out this timber is very rude. A merchant, for example, buys the right, at a trifling sum, to cut down in certain tracts all the mahogany he can find. Then with a party he penetrates into the forest, and at the most accessible point selects his trees, which are cut down, and divided into various pieces, according to the mode of transportation, which in every case is exceedingly difficult; if by water, then the logs are larger, but most generally oxen are used to haul the small pieces through the woods, and this done, even then it has to be often recut into smaller pieces, easy to carry on mule-back; and it is no uncommon sight to see, in the woods or on the road, trains of these diminutive animals each with a small square piece of mahogany in the straw panniers carried on each side.

Sometimes the wood is so heavy that, in water transportation, it sinks; and again, the mud is so deep, it cannot possibly be hauled further, and is therefore left on the road to decay.

All of this territory that I have been describing is known

The Iguana.

as the "Despoblado" (uninhabited), as, being near to the Haytian frontier, it has always been a desolated ground, although some of it comprises the finest land in the island. The soil is rich enough to grow sugar, coffee, rice, and tobacco on all the levels; the hills furnish the wood, while in the savannas the cattle can be raised in large quantities, the guinea-grass growing as high as the knee of a man on horseback.

The cayman on all these rivers is said to abound, while the famous "iguana," a species of the lizard family, not only abounds, but is said here to become dangerous from its great size, some of them reaching five feet in length.

A resident described them to me as being "more audacious than the cayman, though not to be compared in length or strength with the latter. Anyhow, I do not care to meet them on foot, as they turn round like a snake; while a man is all right in the face of an alligator, whose only fearful weapon is his tail—the claws and teeth only work afterwards; but this cussed old iguana jumps about like a dog, and can turn round ten times in a minute." Its flesh, however, is eaten as a great delicacy, the example having been set by the early Spaniards, who described it as a serpent, and at first refused to touch it; but the "Adelantado" (Bartholomew Columbus) being enticed by the pleasantness of the cacique's sister, Anacaona, determined to taste of the serpent. But when he felt the flesh thereof to be so delicate to his tongue, he fell to without fear,—an example which his followers seeing," &c.

I saw here some of the largest terrapins with which I have ever met, and they are found in abundance in the waters of all parts of the island. Listening to the account given by a merchant, over a barrelful of them, of the mode of their capture, I laughed incredulously, and said it was equal to St Mery's story of the dogs of the island, who, wishing to swim the rivers, and being afraid of the caymans, place themselves at some place on the bank, and there yelp and bark, until seeing they have drawn all these monsters to one place, they (the dogs) start off to another point as hard as they can go, and there safely swim across.

"Not only," said my friend, "can I vouch for the truth of that story, but I will add that the mules often resort to that artifice, too, to get across the rivers; and I have seen them do it." Such being the case, I am bound to believe his account of terrapin-hunting reliable, more especially as I had ocular demonstration that the terrapins were caught.

These gather together in the shallow water under the crocodiles or caymans, as they rest with their backs exposed in some sunny place in slumber.

The negro women, who by the by have not the slightest fear of the cayman, knowing this, seek these sleeping monsters, and gently tickling them on the belly, cause them to turn over, when the women quickly seize the terrapins beneath.

CHAPTER XIX.

> "Favoured of Nature, Eden of the seas!
> Where beauty, health, and plenty join to please!
> Clime of the sun! yet fanned with cooling air!
> Brighter than summer, yet than spring more fair!
> . . . Let industry secure
> Wealth to thy plains, and commerce to thy shore!"

THE NORTH COAST LINE FROM MONTE CRISTO TO PUERTO PLATA.—*Lack of Water—Advantages of Irrigation—Tobacco Preparation—Dominican Soldiers and Haytian Battles—Country Hospitality—Used-up Horses—Fresh Start—The "Puerta de los Hidalgos"—Bottom Lands of the Coast—Impromptu Cooking—Old Isabella—Laguna—Domestic Economy—A Long Ride—Played-out Horse—The Road from Santiago to Puerto Plata—The Requeros—Rough Accommodations—Bad Road to Puerto Plata—Arrival there and Departure.*

WISHING to examine the country lying between the Yaqui river and the coast, and extending from Monte Cristo down to Puerto Plata, I took my leave of the former place, and making an early start, began my journey in that direction, although I had many misgivings about my horse and those of my attendants, which, from their long and arduous journeyings, and the poor food with which they had been supplied, showed signs of giving out.

Strangely enough, although corn grows in abundance at the least two crops in the year, it is with the greatest difficulty the traveller can in most places purchase enough grain with which to feed his horse, and he is therefore compelled to trust to the guinea-grass, or avail himself of patches of corn planted simply for fodder, no attention being paid to the grain. Thus the poor animals are worked and starved to death, never being groomed or attended to, and in many cases it is simply their hardy natures that saves them from a miserable death.

For the first twenty-four miles my road was the same as that by which I had come, namely, from Monte Cristo to Guayubin. Traversing it in daytime, I was better able to see the country, which, as I have before stated, is generally very dry, very little settled, and called sterile, though, from what I have already written, it will be seen that all that it needs to make it fertile is a simple system of irrigation.*

About twelve miles out I met our friend, Don Frederico Garcia, the commandant and governor of the province, on his way up to Monte Cristo, and thence to the frontier for a little scout against Luperon. He was accompanied by quite a number of distinguished (?) generals and others, all mounted on horseback, to whom I was introduced with much formality. We had some pleasant words together; and on bidding them good-bye, I saluted General Garcia, hoping that his desires might be soon gratified, and that then we could both shake hands as "Americanos." "God grant it," he said, "and you must embrace me as your friend and brother anyhow;" whereupon, spurring his

* While in England, it has been the good fortune of the author to meet with Lieutenant Woodward of the Royal Engineers, now acting as Assistant Commissioner of Irrigation in the Island of Ceylon. From him I learned that many parts of that island are similar to those of St Domingo, but that by a simple system of irrigation thousands of acres of land that had been considered as worthless and sterile have been rendered fertile and productive, by bringing the waters of the various rivers over the land at certain periods.

This has been easily accomplished by erecting dams in the various streams, which, being filled during the season of high water, have been flooded upon the land in the dry season.

This system could be easily adapted to St Domingo, where there are no lack of watercourses; and so naturally adapted are their banks and the nature of the country through which they pass, this could be accomplished at a very trifling expense in comparison with the immense value of the lands they would thus bring under luxuriant cultivation.

horse close to mine, he threw his arms around me and gave me a most hearty embrace.

Now as "Frederico" is a fine-looking, handsome white soldier, this little ceremony was not so bad, but when General ——, a stalwart jet-black negro, pushed his horse up to mine, and said, "Yo tambien (I also), sir," I confess I felt a little weak in my patriotism, but still allowed him to give me a good square squeeze, taking care to avoid the threatened embraces of the rest of the party, on the plea that my horse was a little weak and tired, and I must hurry on; so with more hand-shaking and hearty good-byes, we parted the best friends in the world.

My poor horse, fatigued with his constant journeyings on the island, was utterly overcome before I reached Guayubin by the heat and thirst, which latter he was entirely unable to allay from want of water the whole of this distance. On arriving near the bottom lands of the Yaqui, he was so utterly used up, that I had to dismount and lead him a mile or so to the house of Señor Rodriguez, to whom I had a short note of introduction, where, by the assistance of one of their people, he was conducted slowly to a watering-place, where he was able to cool his mouth, now parched almost to dry leather, while I availed myself of the opportunity of taking a short siesta in the ubiquitous hammock, pending the arrival of my escort, which I had considerably outdistanced. As all of Rodriguez's family were away, I sent my "peons" on to Guayubin, only a mile or two farther, to order my mid-day meal, and see if it were possible to procure fresh horses, as all of those I had were almost entirely knocked up.

At this house I had the chance to study their primitive way of preparing the tobacco for market and for domestic cigar manufacture; it is of the most rude and simple nature, the tobacco being merely run over while dry, and piled up in quantities enough to fill a ceroon, without regard to colour, perfection, or quality of leaf, all being stowed indiscriminately in a pile inside the matting. Yet, with care, the tobacco of St Domingo can, I believe, be made as valuable in the marts of commerce as that of Cuba. Some of that I smoked in the uplands of the interior was quite as high flavoured and good as that of the best Vuelta Abao, and doubtless, if care were used in its curing, large quan-

Lizards.

tities would be equally good, that are now only passable, from negligence or ignorance in preparation.

Having refreshed myself at Guayubin, I found I could not be supplied there with fresh horses.

The secretary of the General, however, who, though a negro, seemed to be master of several languages, advised me to go on a few miles farther to a place called "Villa Lobo," where there was a superior "Coronel Commandant," who might be able to furnish me a dragoon and horses, and to whom he wrote me a note of introduction.

Starting off my escort, therefore, slowly, I gave instructions to my guides where to meet me, and their gait being so exceedingly slow and tiresome, I set off alone at a more rapid gait, in order to see more of the country by daylight.

It is a peculiar feature in this island that everywhere in the dryest sections the moment you come near a water-course or river the whole aspect of the country changes from dry sterility to that of the most luxuriant vegetation; so that the traveller in these dry regions usually tells his approach to water by the gradually-improved appearance of the vegetation and soil. Thus it is around Guayubin in every direction, for near it are some of the best lands on the island, while the town itself is situated on the finest bottom lands bordering the river, where everything grows of which it is possible to conceive.

Leaving again the town behind me, I found, as I gradually travelled on, the country to fall somewhat back into the dry and sandy nature of the soil about Monte Cristo, though here and there I came across patches of tolerably good land.

Not a soul did I meet nor a living creature did I see, as I rode on mile after mile, if I except those lively little fellows the lizards, which, of every size and colour, constantly in their quick nervous manner crossed my path, or rushed from their hiding-places in the grassy paths of the woods, alarmed by my horse's feet.

Night soon overtook me on my lonely road, and I was not sorry to join company with three wild-looking soldiers, as they informed me they were going the same road—two of whom were on foot, the third being mounted on a diminutive jackass, with the rations and arms of the party. I kept company with them for some time; but thinking to make time, and having received instructions about my road,

I continued on, until, in entering a woody defile, it became so dark that I mistook the white, gravelly bed of a dry stream for the road, up which I rode some distance, over rocks, jumping trees, and struggling against branches overhead, until I finally brought up against the precipitous bank; but the moonlight coming to my assistance, I discovered my mistake, and retraced my steps to the point where I had lost the road, being guided thereto by the songs of the soldiers, who had come up and were passing on ahead of me. I soon rejoined them, and was amused and interested by their accounts of soldier-life in St Domingo, and the general service of the army. There is one thing to be said about these Dominicans, and that is, they could, with drill and discipline, be made the best of infantry soldiers, for they think nothing of starting off and marching their forty-five to sixty miles per day, day in and day out, apparently without any fatigue, and on food that we would not think could keep body and soul together. As I rode alongside the mounted one, the two footmen kept always ahead, singing at the top of their voices some Dominican refrain, which seemed to enliven their weary journey.

They gave me some amusing accounts of their fights with the Haytians, and seemed to hold them in great contempt, as they (the Dominicans) did not hesitate to attack with the odds against them of sometimes five to one. At the time I considered this as braggadocio, but I was credibly informed by a Haytian general that this was absolutely the fact, as the Haytian people were not fond of fighting, and they dreaded the machete of the Dominican soldiers, a sort of sword with which all Dominicans of the lower ranks are armed, whether they are soldiers or civilians.

An eye-witness described to me, in amusing terms, one of these fights, in which the two parties approached each shouting with all their might; then the Haytians would fire in the air, thinking the noise would scare their opponents; but the latter, drawing their swords, would rush in, and compel the Haytians to seek covert, and thus sometimes a whole day would be spent by these people, to the number of several hundreds, without any one being hurt, and yet it would be called a great battle, each side claiming a victory.*

Machete.

Coming to a halt in a narrow path in the woods, the party informed me that, turning a little to the left, I would come to the place of which I was in search; and bidding me good-bye, they started off, leaving me under their instructions to find myself in front of a large house in an open savanna, before which was blazing a large fire, and about which were gathered a number of soldiers. Inquiring for the commandant, I found, with my usual luck, he had gone back from whence I had just come, but that his wife was there. I asked for her, when, from a crowd of women at the door, there arose one who said she was that lady. Handing her the note and telling her my needs, she remarked that she could not read it; that there were no horses, but that I was welcome to make myself as comfortable as I could. As the prospects were not very attractive for a long stay, I thanked her very kindly, and having the address of a well-to-do planter in the neighbourhood, I hired a guide to show me the way to his house, leaving word with my peons to come up with me.

"Villa Loba" I found to be a large scattered settle-

* The author happened to be near a place where there was a skirmish in which Luperon, with a party of some ten men, came very near being captured, being compelled to take to the woods, several of his party being killed or captured, as was also his horse and equipments with private papers. The whole number engaged on both sides was not over twenty-five men, and yet I saw in the *organ* of Cabral, as well as in some American papers, an account which purported to be that of a tremendous battle, in which, of course, the "Patriot" party were the victors.

ment on some very excellent land, most of the smaller huts being occupied by negroes, while the larger places, or "canucos," were inhabited by well-to-do whites or mulattoes. In a short time I arrived at the house I was seeking, the moon happily serving to show us our road, over which it was only by beatings and spurring of the guide and myself that my now utterly used-up horse was conducted.

No sooner had I arrived and made my wants known, than I was invited in the most hospitable manner to dis mount, enter, and make myself at home, my poor horse being immediately looked after. On entering the house, I found it to be a substantial wooden building in the usual fashion of the country, with several rooms, the main one being filled with quite a number of women of all ages, busying themselves by candlelight in shelling the native white and red bean, or "frijole," of the country. Of course my advent created great interest, and they chattered and worked at a great rate until the arrival of my peons and horses put a finishing touch to their curiosity, and they all prepared to clear up the room, that I might swing my hammock and make myself comfortable for the night.

I found all of these women kind, bright, and intelligent, with a natural dignity and refinement quite surprising in people of their habits and situation, and the younger people I found could read and write, while several books of poetry in Spanish, and one or two illustrated French magazines, showed some disposition for and power of knowledge.

Here it was decided that my present horses were utterly unfit to prosecute the long and tedious journey I had before me to Puerto Plata, and I therefore made my arrangements to discharge my guide Simon and the horses that had come all the way with us from St Domingo city, my host making arrangements to send me in the morning with his brother and two horses to the old town of Isabella or Laguna,

NEGRO HABITATIONS.

and everything being ordered for an early start in the morning, I was soon, after my long day's journey, sound in the most refreshing of slumbers in my hammock.

I found in conversation with my host that, like all these

Primitive Sugar-Mill.

places, tobacco was the principal product, with the "platano" for food; but that everything could be grown easily in the way of sugar-cane, coffee, and chocolate, to say nothing of hundreds of smaller fruits and vegetables. I saw, on examining his sugar-mill, that it was of the rudest description, a simple "trapiche" or wooden mill of three upright rollers of wood, worked by a one-

Sugar-Boilers.

horse power, the juice being conducted in a rude wooden trough to two small open-air boilers or pans of rude construction, not holding, either of them, over ten gallons of juice, and from this there was manufactured a limited quantity of rum and syrup for home consumption; and these were actually the only kind of sugar-mills I saw in operation in any part of my journeyings in St Domingo.

These people, though probably of the most intelligent country class, seemed to have no idea of improved labour, of beautifying places, of increased comfort, or of solid, substantial, nourishing food. They have never seen any better, they know no better, and I doubt if they desire better, unless example is set before them.

I asked my host, as politely as I could, so as not to give offence, for the amount I was indebted to him for his hospitality, the food of my horses, &c.

"Señor," said he, "I am a plain man; I know nothing of the customs of the world, and how a stranger should be treated as he deserves; but I do what I know and feel. I have no account against you. There, you see, is the broad public road; it comes very near my house, from which you can always see it. Whenever you come this way, and you want food and shelter either for yourself or your horses, believe me this house is yours just as much as it is mine, and you are welcome."

So with a hearty shake of the hand, and laughing good-byes from eyes and lips of the bevy of women at the door, I rode off in charge of the brother of my host, with many "God speeds" and "Pleasant journeys."

And this has invariably been my experience of the country people of St Domingo. Quiet and inoffensive, devoid generally of education, unaccustomed to the ways of the world; yet they have always shown themselves hospitable to a fault, as far as their means would permit; and their natural intelligence and instincts are so good, that any one would be quickly undeceived who took them for fools, while readily receiving a lesson from them in quiet good-breeding.

Puerta de los Hidalgos (Pass of the Cavaliers).

Our road led through a beautiful rolling country, gradually ascending in its general tendency, being well wooded, with occasional open lands ; but the entire country being well adapted, I should think, to cane and coffee.

There are two roads leading from this section over the mountains to the coast, one farther to the west, and the other the famous pass of Columbus, the "Puerta de los Hidalgos" (Pass of the Cavaliers), so named because when Columbus penetrated to the interior of the island, he came by this route, then the only one known; and this was so difficult, that in order to permit their horses and supplies to be got through, the young cavaliers went to work, and with their own hands removed the rocks and cut away the underbush to open a passage ; and in honour of the energy manifested by these young soldiers, it received the above name. It was the first-made road in the New World, and, as we found by experience, a fair type of the mountain roads of St Domingo.

Soon after leaving Don Antonio's, we had struck a gradually ascending country, until we gained the mountain side, and struggled up nearly to the top. Here a rocky path, that looked as if it might be the bed of a mountain torrent, offered us the only means of descent; and this, the guide informed me, was the famous pass. Slipping and scrambling, now almost lying down on the horse's back, or again hugging his neck, we managed to get down somehow ; but the excitement and the grandeur of the scene repaid me for the apparent danger.

The sides were mostly precipitous, while huge masses of rock lay scattered in wild confusion here and there in our path, which was covered on each side with trees and bushes, some of the former of enormous growth, the branches frequently meeting above our heads in such a way as almost to exclude the light of day. Through this wild path we came to a turn in the road, which exposed to our view, above the openings in the trees, the blue ocean of the north coast. This was a peculiar sight, for standing as we were upon the top of the mountain, and looking over the vast extent of forest that intervened between us and the coast line, it curiously enough brought the blue waters of the sea apparently in a line with the tops of the trees, thus leading one almost to believe the intermediate space was some vast hollow inside of an immense embankment.

The range of mountains upon which we now were are known as the Sierra, and run parallel with the coast, being of limestone formation, and with rather a scarcity of water, offering no attraction to the miner. From its summit we now gradually descended by a rough road almost to the sea-shore, to the house of a countryman. We had passed mostly thus far a highly uneven, wooded country, fairly watered, until now we were on the bottom lands along the coast, where we met with plenty of natural clearings on the hillside or in the bottoms. Most of these were occupied by settlers, growing tobacco, coffee (wild), the plantain, and a great deal of fine cotton—fine staple and good length. One of these places presented quite an American appearance, the house having piazzas, and the first grape-vine-covered arbour I had seen on the island. The soil everywhere was of the best black loam, unmistakable in its richness, and capable, as all the inhabitants told me, of producing everything in the shape of vegetation.

All the people of this section devote themselves principally to the tobacco culture, paying no attention to cattle, though they own large numbers of hogs. These are allowed to run wild and take care of themselves, and this they have learned to do to such an extent, that every spot where there is anything planted has to be surrounded with a strong fence of withes to prevent their entrance. The woods are full of these strange-looking animals, generally tall, gaunt, and wiry, quite savage in their nature; and, as they rush out on the traveller as he rides through the forest, might easily be mistaken for the peccary. The flesh of these constitutes the only meat used by the people of this section.

Wild Hogs.

At our stopping-place for our mid-day meal, I was compelled to fall back upon my own resources, as the guide knew nothing of cooking any of the stores I had for that purpose; and the bright-eyed hostess of the house where we stopped having apologised for having nothing to offer, and her culinary experience being confined to boiling or roasting a banana, or frying a piece of pork, looked with interest and astonishment at my successful operations for a meal, until, overcome by her curiosity, she exclaimed, "Dios, señor (Lord, sir), but you are a good cook!"

The sun was well above the meridian when we started for our night's destination—La Laguna, a settlement just the other side of the old site and Bay of Isabella, famous as the first place settled on the island by Columbus. Our road still lay in the bottom lands of the woods, the main road now and then being crossed by wide open swathes in the underbush running down to the seaside, used for roads by the mahogany-cutters in hauling down the huge logs of that wood, fustic, and other valuable woods, with which all this tract of country we passed through abounded. Many of these pieces of wood we saw left half buried in the mud, some of the heavy rains having made the paths so muddy that it had been impossible to get the logs to the coast for transportation and shipment. All of this cutting is done with the rudest of implements, no saw whatever being used, and the pieces being simply hewn into rough logs of a size suitable for transportation.

This shipping of mahogany is quite a business with the coast people, as they haul or float these logs down to some convenient bay or inlet, where small vessels or lighters convey them to the larger ports for shipment abroad; and in some cases, where the size of the bay permits it, the large vessels themselves come up and load directly at the port. All of this soil of the bottom lands appears to be of the richest kind, resembling much the bottom lands of the Lower Mississippi, and equally favourable, I should say, for the cultivation of the cotton crop.

Timber of every kind was met with in this region, some of which was of immense growth. One tree that we saw, called by the natives "Higo," had projecting from its trunk, higher than a man could reach, some twelve huge buttresses, and such was the spread of these, that a good sized tree was growing from between two of them.

The parasites "Haguey" and "Cupey" we met with in

Parasitical Vines.

great number, both in the form of the newly-grown vine and the more matured tree, while the palm of every species was seen at every step. A new fragrance saluted my nostrils in the most delicious of odours arising from the millions of a small flower growing on a bush, and called by the natives "Aroma," resembling much in its odour our lilac, though the aroma is more delicate, the flower being of a small yellowish red colour. A pretty star-shaped flower that grew in profusion also attracted my attention, the guide calling it "Doña Anna." Late in the afternoon, as we were within a short distance of the old settlement of Isabella, I was tempted by its historic associations to turn aside from the road and see what remained of it. There was absolutely nothing to repay me for my trouble, the place possessing no natural beauty, and the few ruins remaining having no particular form or meaning, being mostly covered with running vines and thick vegetation. With much difficulty can be made out where has run originally a small village street. Still it was something to see a place that was the first settlement of Europeans on the American continent, a place hallowed by the memories of association that Columbus' actual presence gave to it, and the few stones lying in mixed heaps perhaps having been parts of walls holding up the roof under which he himself may have sat.

In such places the tarantula frequently makes its home; and here for the first and only time I saw one of those horrible-looking spiders, whose numbers and bite have been so much overrated; for I was told, and found it to be the case, they are not often met with; and if they do occasionally succeed in stinging some careless person, their bite is only painful, and never dangerous.

The place to-day is as it was when its settlement took place, remarkable for its unhealthiness, a great deal of the "calentura" or fever of the country prevailing there, which, from its situation, I should judge could not be otherwise, as it is upon the side of a small river emptying into a small bay, the shores of which are low and somewhat marshy.

Tarantula.

Night overtook us before we came to the settlement (a very scattered one) of Laguna, and I had the misfortune to find also that the planter at whose house I had expected to stay was absent with all his family, and, at the suggestion of the guide, we pushed on a mile or two farther to the house of another planter, making our way through dusky ravines and thick-foliaged covered paths, fording also two or three streams, until, tired and sleepy, we were gladdened by the sight of lights in the house of our destination.

This I found to be a large wooden house, set back from the road in a large savanna, around which was the usual fence of the country, with—remarkable to me, as I had not seen one before in all my travels—a large double English gate, that opened and shut in the good old-fashioned way, instead of necessitating our taking down about twenty poles to get into the enclosure. The occupant of the house was a South Carolina mulatto, who had long lived out here, and was now engaged in trading with the country people for mahogany and other woods, and though he spoke very disparagingly of the habits of the people, he himself set no different example to them in his person and habits, for his establishment offered nothing cleanly or attractive in its interior or exterior arrangements. His wife was swinging in a hammock, sick with the fever she told me, but he said she was only "playing off;" and judging from my after observation of her lazy, filthy ways, I should judge he was right.

What perfectly helpless, useless people these women are, many of them! They seem to be so utterly ignorant of everything a woman should know. Their housekeeping amounts to nothing; their cooking, simple as are the viands, is vile, and they appear to do nothing but loll in hammocks and smoke cigars. However, I have been too long in Dominica to be particular; and my hammock being swung, I am soon in the land of dreams.

With morning comes the announcement that one of our

horses is knocked up, and I must hire another one, which has to be sent for to some distance; so, availing myself of the time, I proceed to the river (Isabella) bank, and have a most delicious bath in its clear, swift-running waters, finishing which, I become interested in the food question, as nearly twenty-four hours have elapsed without my eating anything.

"I have nothing," was the reply of my host to my question about food, "except plantains and slapjacks to give you." Now slapjacks are very well in the abstract, but when they are offered a hungry man as the subsistence upon which to prosecute a long and tiresome journey, they are bad, in point of fact. I therefore suggested that I had some remaining stores that might be turned to account if he had wherewith to cook them. He had the means, and they were at my disposal to cook to suit me, and thinking this was the safest way to avoid being poisoned by boiled lard, garlic, &c., I became immediately "chef de cuisine."

I think my readers would have been astonished at the way my material was converted into a Dominican stew; for rice, sardines, pickled salmon, canned tomatoes, stale bread, peas, claret wine, vermicelli, pepper and salt, and sauces all went into the soup-kettle, with what result I leave them to imagine, when I say that, after disposing of the soup from this "olla podrida," and eating a large quantity of its more solid material, the balance was disposed of by every man, woman, and child on the place, who were called in to partake of the most luxurious feast they had ever seen; in fact, my guide was so overcome by his share in the disposition of the viands, that he informed me confidentially I was the best cook he had ever seen, and that "American (?) cookery pleased him much."

God help us, though! A man, to travel in this country and keep his life, needs to be a little of everything, and for these people any good "square meal" would be as a new era in their lives.

The horse arrives; he has one eye and a sore back, but his four legs appear good. I have no choice; I must reach Puerto Plata before next day, to meet the expected steamer, and I am told, with sharp riding, I can get there by midnight, the distance being about forty miles. My guide swears it is impossible; I cannot reach there until late next day; the road is infernal, and that if I want to break my neck, all right, go on; but he wishes to preserve his. We have much talk, and finally start together. I leave him behind on the road until my horse becomes indifferent to the spur, through weakness, as I think. I try coaxing, no use; kicking, no go. I lead him, he makes me pull him; and, becoming desperate, I lie down and go to sleep until my guide rejoins me. I curse him and the horse, he laughs, and says it is an old trick of the horse, he is lazy, and my spur not sharp; tells me to mount, and hands me a switch, and, presto, what a change! I have just time to say "Good-bye—to-morrow in Puerto Plata"—and off I start; and sure enough I never laid eyes on that guide again until next day I found him, late in the day, inquiring for a mad American, who, he was afraid, had come to grief on the road.

Played out.

And yet that was one of the most enjoyable rides I had in St Domingo, as far as the country was concerned; for beautiful fields, deep, thick woods, good grassy slopes of road, succeeded by rocky precipices and mud paths, followed each other in rapid succession. Now I would be galloping through some magnificent sweep of tableland, over grassy paths that led by a tobacco, plantain, or coffee patch; now I would be slowly picking my way down to some rapid river by its stony and precipitous bank, the rapid but clear waters of which had to be forded, sometimes saddle-flaps deep; then again I pulled up at some negro "bohio" (hut) to inquire my way—one thing never ceasing, and that was the movement of my switch either upon the body of the horse or before his eyes, the effect being good in either case. Before striking the Puerto Plata road I counted no less than ten rivers or turns of rivers that I had crossed, the water, without exception, being sweet, clear, and cold, and their beds usually gravel or small stone; the banks, in many cases, being exceedingly precipitous. The principal one of these, and that I crossed several times, was the Bajabonita or Isabella, whose waters, though swift, were

On the Bajabonita.

generally shallow, though, from the nature of its banks, it

will be seen, in the rainy months, it can become like most others, very deep. In all of this north coast tract of country, from its rich soil, its fine climate, abundance of water, and general capacity to produce every tropical plant, I should say it was the most desirable part of the islánd, being exposed daily to the refreshing northern trade-winds.

Once or twice I managed to lose myself in the multiplicity of the woodland paths; but I was always set right in the kindest manner by the simple natives, whether black or coloured. I must confess, however, their ideas of distance are limited, or very hard to extract from them. For example:—

"How far is Puerto Plata from here?"

"Whew!" and a long whistle.

"Is it more than a league?"

"Yes, sir."

"More than two leagues?"

"Oh, yes; more, sir!"

"Carajo! is it five, then?"

"Well, when you have travelled five leagues you are pretty (cerquita) near it."

Then I get mad, perhaps, and say, "Is it one day or two days' journey from here?"

"Oh, no, sir; only three hours' ride," which is, perhaps, equal to twelve miles; but that is the way all distances are judged on the island, so many hours from one place to another.

As night draws on, I find myself entering the main road running from Santiago to Puerto Plata, just below the high point known as Altamira (High View). The scenery is grand in the extreme, though wild and picturesque; great hills stretch away on every side, upon the tops of which are gathered the heavy clouds that forebode a tropical rainstorm, while even yet the sun is setting in magnificent glory. The road itself is fearful; a mere ravine of melted clay, with rocks of all sizes tossed about apparently in volcanic confusion. Long trains of mules, laden with tobacco and fruit and solid bits of wood, can be seen here and there struggling, or falling, or picking their way down the road, the air made lively by the sounds of the requero (teamster) as he curses, directs, or implores his animals.

Now it is a shout of "Bur-r-r-o" ("Oh, jackass!"), with a whack of his stick, or perhaps a scream at the top of his voice of "Ca-val-yo" ("You fool of a horse!"), accompanied with imprecations, as the animal, staggering under its heavy, awkward load, struggles from a bed of mire up to its very belly, or slips and falls upon some great rock; the tune being entirely changed into that of a lively refrain by the swarthy driver as he and his mules strike some little bit of road barely passable and level.

This is a ludicrous picture, looking at it in our way, to see these long trains of animals, many of the horses not as large as a good sized donkey, come struggling under their heavy loads through the mud, attended by a swarthy, tall, Indian-looking fellow, in a broad-brimmed-hat, shirt, and pants, and with a machete (sabre) almost as long as himself strapped about his body, its curious scabbard hieroglyphically marked, ending in a turn or twist similar to a lobster's claw; but on these little horses, and with these strange men, come one of the greatest sources of the wealth of this island. These requeros are a special class, who devote themselves to the carrying trade between Puerto Plata and Santiago. They are a wild, rough set in their manners, and many of them said to be very wealthy; but all living a frugal, hardy life, and, without exception, honest and reliable. In Puerto Plata, merchants told me they thought nothing of calling to any one of these men passing the door, and handing him a roll of money, say, "Give that to So-and-so in Santiago." "Write the direction," would be the reply, and the exact money never failed to be properly delivered.

Nevertheless there is fitting occasion here for the intervention of the Society for Prevention of Cruelty to Animals, for these patient beasts are most shockingly treated, beaten almost to death when wearied with their heavy loads, or having their rude pack-saddles placed upon backs that are so fearfully raw, a fresh palm-leaf needs to be laid on, even to bear the hitching of the saddle.

Darkness and the pouring rain overtake me together half way down the mountain. My guide and baggage are miles behind, and will not probably be up in the rain to-night. I, however, struggle and fall and blunder on, trusting to the good sense of my horse to carry me through the dangerous places; but at last, after sundry mishaps, I follow the advice and example of the "requeros," who have halted their teams to await either moonlight or day-break.

Seeing a house by the side of the road, I ride up and say—

"Buenas noches" (good night).

"Good night, señor. Dismount."

I explain how I am fixed, and am invited to enter and make myself as comfortable as I can.

The same old story—a rude house on splendid land—a canuco of tobacco and plantains—not a thing to eat or to drink, in fact, and I look around for a place to sleep. Around three sides of the house runs a wide bench, upon this, one after another, the occupants spread their beds of undressed hides, and in a few moments are snoring.

I ask for a hammock, which luckily they have, and in which, with hat, boots, and clothing still on, I throw myself, covered with mud, to get a night's rest.

Day breaks, gloomy and damp. My horse unfed, except from browsing on the short grass, stands, wet from head to foot, more dead than alive, while I, "faute de mieux," make my breakfast off an orange and a cup of coffee—all that my shelter affords.

Saddling up, I am soon on the road again, and the sun

CONUCO OF PLANTAIN AND TOBACCO.

coming out, dispels the rain and gloom. All Nature smiles above and around; but in my path, running water, mud, broken rocks, and swollen streams, make it a narrow and crooked one indeed; team after team I pass, all on their way to Puerto Plata — horses, mules, men, and women covered with mud; the men barefooted and in shirts and pants; the women in a simple gown, which, rolled up pannier fashion on their persons, shows more of their form than decency requires.

At last, from the mountain side, I get a view of Puerto Plata and its lovely bay far down in the plain below. Visions of a hotel rise up before me—dreams of a breakfast "a la fourchette" come quickly in my mind, to say nothing of anticipated delights in sporting once again "store clothes;" and so I whip up my now nearly dead horse, until, attempting to pass a dangerous-looking quagmire, my horse rebels—whip and spur no use. Then two little negroes rush out, and caution me not to go there, as I can't get out. They point to another place that looks even worse. I try it, but my horse refuses it, even under pressure of spur and whip.

Now, "horse sense" is considered good the world over: I have a great respect for it. Therefore I dismounted, fixed the reins to the cantle, and leaving my horse to his own judgment, I whacked away at him, until, becoming desperate, in he plunged at the designated spot, which proved to be a slough of liquid mud, breast deep. With fearful struggles he went through to the other side, while I picked my way on foot through the prickly hedge, congratulating myself on not having absorbed in my trousers and boots quantities of Dominican mud.

Never did town look so charming in my eyes as did Puerto Plata that day, and it was truly a haven of rest to me in the days I passed there preparing my mails for the steamer, after whose departure I took passage in the Dominican man-of-war for Monte Cristo. This man-of-war is simply a large fore-and-aft schooner, carrying a gang of thirty-five men, with one brass six-pounder gun, which the captain frankly told me he was afraid to fire off, fearful that it would "burst," or open the seams of his vessel. However, we had a pleasant sail up of eight hours from Puerto Plata to Monte Cristo, keeping only a short distance from the shore, and affording me an opportunity of seeing the character of the coast of the interior of the country through which I had previously passed.

Point Isabella.

Cape Isabella now loomed out low and sharp against the high wooded walls that formed its other shore. Entering the Bay of Monte Cristo in a strong gale under foresail and jib, we found a United States steamer, the *Yantic;* and as soon as we anchored, Captain Carpenter was good enough to send a boat for me, and I was soon on board with a large mail-bag of letters for the officers and crew, to enjoy once again a Christian dinner.

CHAPTER XX.

> "The image of the jest I 'll show
> You here at large."—*Merry Wives of Windsor.*

JOURNEY TO HAYTI—"*Cosa Dominica*"—*Dauphin Bay*—*Poor Accommodations*—*Tropic Night at Sea*—*A Cuban Horror*—*Cape Haytian from the Sea*—*First Experiences in Hayti*—*Haytian Officials*—*Value of Haytian Currency*—*Advantage of being supposed a United States Commissioner.*

ON the afternoon of the 27th of March, finding there was a small schooner to sail that night for Cape Haytian, though nominally for Turk's Island, I engaged passage in her.

Matters were all arranged, baggage fully prepared, and the authorities notified of our intention. I was fortunate in having for my *compagnon de voyage* a Cuban revolutionist, a colonel in the insurrectionary cavalry, who, having come up with me from Puerto Plata, was to accompany me to Hayti, and thence he was to go to Jamaica.

Our passports and papers were pronounced all right by the commandant at Monte Cristo, who, with a thousand offers of service, and profuse promises that we could count upon him under any circumstances, bade us an impressive good-bye—this was about five o'clock in the afternoon.

But greater enterprises have sometimes failed through

smaller means than the lack of a cart (*vide* the saving of Rome), which came very near being the cause of our plans failing.

At seven o'clock, being all ready, we desired to have our rather extensive baggage taken in a cart down to the schooner's boat, some distance from the village ; but upon sending for the cart, were informed that no vehicles were allowed to go through the town from sunset in the evening until daybreak in the morning.

Of course, we thought this was a mistake as far as we were concerned, and accordingly sent word to the commandant (the same above alluded to) that it was for us and our baggage that the cart was desired.

Word came back that it was against orders, and no cart could be permitted to pass, contrary to these instructions, through the village.

Our host, a well-known merchant, and friend of the commandant, went himself to explain. It was no use, he returned unsuccessful.

By this time we were boiling angry. Here was a man who, a few hours before, had vowed he would do anything in the world for us, and now refused even to let us have a cart, and to him I had had friendly letters, and official letters from the authorities, too !

By Jove ! it was too much. And still having in my possession a document from the Governor to "all authorities," ordering them to assist me, I "went for" the commandant, found him with a crowd in a beer-shop, and calling him out, asked him what this all meant. He vowed again he would do anything in the world for me, but this he couldn't do, as it would cost him his straps.

"Do you see this paper ?" I asked, flirting my order in his face ; "and do you not know its contents ?"

"Oh, yes ; but I dare not give you the cart."

"I do not ask it, sir," I said ; "I demand it. And do you tell me that, with this order, sent by your superior, who is directed by his superior, the President of this island, that you, a subordinate, refuse to obey it?"

"Well, sir, it would cost me my position."

"Never mind your position. Will you obey it or not?" I growled at him.

"Well, sir, I will give you the cart, but it is I that will suffer. I do it on my responsibility, and I am willing to do anything to serve you." But here I cut him short, upon which he directed the officer of the guard to accompany us to the boat with the cart—"Cosa Dominica!"

Getting on board the vessel, we found her to be a small fore-and-aft schooner, manned by a captain and three men, all Jamaica negroes, speaking English, the cargo consisting of twelve oxen, which completely filled the small hold.

The night was clear, and though the breeze had not yet sprung up, anchor was quickly weighed, sails set, and we slowly dropped out with the current from the Bay of Monte Cristo, the last hail being from Captain Carpenter of the *Yantic*, as we passed under her stern, wishing me a safe passage.

Now, although no open war is declared between Dominica and Hayti, yet such are the relations existing between them, that no vessel is cleared from the ports of one to those of the other. Consequently, although it is perfectly understood by the authorities where this schooner comes from and goes to, her papers specify that she sails under the English flag for Turk's Island.

Only a few days before, however, a young American merchant, having business in Hayti, had chartered a small boat to take him up to Cape Haytian, or the "Cape," as it is called, some United States despatches being sent at the same time. When the boat arrived, however, at the Cape, the owner was taken and imprisoned for several days, being finally set free, and told to return to Monte Cristo, with the remark, that the next time he brought American despatches he would be hung. However, we are slowly drifting along on the now still ocean, not a puff of air being felt, and so we go below in hope to use the pigeon-hole of a cabin for sleeping. Vain hope! At any time it is small; but now, with the heat and the stench from twelve oxen coming through the partition, we are driven on deck.

Here we tried to sleep on the narrow space by the companion-way, but our attempts were unsuccessful; and while dozing I was constantly threatening to roll off into the sea; and notwithstanding the captain assured me that I would wake up before "touching water," we finally amused ourselves with conversation.

Long hours my Cuban friend and I passed in talk about his island and its revolution, with the prospects of its continuation and success, from which I gathered their prospects were never better, and, without any immediate chance of the revolution ending, it still was rather increasing than decreasing, and likely to be prolonged for years in the section of the island of which they are now masters.

Seeing that I was familiar with his country, he confided to me many details of the revolution; but one account he gave me that still placid night, with the stars looking gently down upon the same calm waters that washed his own sunny isle, I shall not forget.

The Colonel had been sent, when quite a young man, first to England and then to Germany to be educated, studying in both these places, and finally in France. Possessed of large means, he had returned to Cuba and entered largely into business just before the breaking out of the insurrection, in which he took part of his own free will, leaving his father, an old man of many years, on the plantation, and indifferent to the cause.

After long, long months of absence of toil and fighting, the Colonel, it so happened, was passing in the vicinity of his father's house; and halting his troop at a distance, not wishing to compromise his father, he himself sought an interview, which he succeeded in obtaining; and on taking his departure, with a curious presentiment, he asked the old man's blessing.

Joining his troop, they rode on to their camping-place, in which they had hardly been installed when a messenger, an old servant of the Colonel's, arrived to say that the Spaniards having shortly after followed the Colonel to his father's house, had accused him of holding communication with his son.

The old man, while disowning any improper motives, acknowledged his son had been there and received his blessing; and the Spaniards, infuriated at this news, set fire to the out-buildings, and told the old man they would kill him.

On receiving this news the Colonel, with his troop, rode as fast as their horses could carry them; but arrived at the plantation too late, only to find——

"What?" I asked, as soon as I saw the relator had recovered from his emotion.

"The out-buildings burned to the ground, and in the hall of my father's house, the old man lying with his skull split open, and his grey hairs soaking up the blood!"

Then he told me how he and his troop, having each taken a solemn oath, followed up that party day after day, occasionally capturing a straggler, until, by a successful ambush, he succeeded in capturing the whole party, some fourteen in number, with their officer.

"What became of them?" I inquired.

"Having hung them to as many trees, we passed our sabres through their bodies, and left them to serve as warnings."

Tired out watching for the breezes that came not, we selected the softest planks on deck and turned over, rather than in, to sleep.

Daybreak found us still off Manzanillo Bay, "a painted ship upon a painted ocean," for not a breath had we of wind: and this was provoking indeed, for the Cape is only sixty miles from Monte Cristo, and the voyage is usually made in a few hours, we having expected to reach there by daybreak; and not a mouthful of food of any kind was there on board that we could possibly swallow.

As the sun rose the wind sprung up a little, and we slowly gained headway, drifting rather than sailing, within sight of another of those beautiful bays for which this island is famous, that of Dauphin Bay.

Dauphin Bay.

This, it is said, is one of the most beautiful ports in all St Domingo, being able to contain a great number of vessels, closed as in a basin—the entrance being gained by a canal only a quarter of a league from side to side, which, at the bottom, opens into two wide bays, where are several islets, close to which there is water enough to careen vessels; these also can anchor close to land. The bottom is good everywhere. There is also a river emptying there, which, though deep, is brackish.

This bay is on Haytian territory, having upon its shores a fort known as Fort Liberty, which forms a frontier post.

About eleven o'clock the trade-winds blew fresh and strong, and our little boat flew over the waters like a bird, until the prominent hills of the Haytian shore that marked the location of the Cape grew bolder and bolder, and we could even see the white walls of the town on the very edge of the sea.

Twelve o'clock found us running close in to the shore, examining with eager interest the walls of the old Fort Picolet at the very entrance of the bay, until a short time after found us at anchor directly opposite the custom-house wharf, with mind intent on shore and breakfast.

Alas! vain hopes. It was the hour of siesta; offices and stores were closed, and no officials were seen.

We proposed to go ashore on our own responsibility, but to this the captain would not consent, as he was liable to

Cape Haytian from the Sea.

a fine, telling us we must wait patiently until two o'clock, when the officers would be on board.

To us, with hungry stomachs, the minutes seemed like hours; but at last—oh, happy sight!—there put out from the captain of the port's office, a mile up the beach, the customs boat. Nearer, yet nearer came the boat, until, about opposite the custom-house, it put in there—right

30

under our very eyes, and this, too, after our waiting nearly two hours!

Ah! dear reader, did you ever hear any real, right-down honest swearing? If not, then you should have been on board our schooner that moment. We had barely recovered our breath when the boat at last came off to us—a boat big enough for the cutter of a frigate, with the crew of a lame negro, a small boy, and a half small boy, while in the stern, in the shelter of a torn rag tied to a broken pole, sat two young, gaping fellows, with sallow complexions, who we were told were the officers.

The sarcasm of my remark to them, "That their breakfast must have been a good one, they were so long at it," I am afraid was lost upon them, as we hurried into their boat to be pulled up to the landing of the afore-mentioned captain of the port. Here we were received by another pallid specimen of humanity in the shape of an old, weazen-faced, dried-up official, who, with a slow and stooping gait, pottered around, until, reckless with hunger and rage, we howled at him to hurry up his movements, as we were nearly famished. I thrust my passport in his face; he asked me my name; I told him to read it; he said we must wait for his secretary; we swore we

The Nondescript.

wouldn't—we wanted our Consul and our breakfast; until, poor man! frantic with indecision, he commenced writing our names down on stray scraps of paper, and then calling a nondescript sort of youth, who happened to be passing by, bade us go with him to the "General de la Place."

If ever there was murder near being committed, it was upon that youth that morning. Up one street and down another in the hot sun, by piles of ruins overgrown with vines, through streets that looked as if there were no sound habitation in them, until, hot, hungry, and savage, he brought us back to within a square or two of whence we started, to the office of the government interpreter; where, thinking this was a ruse for fees, we vowed we could talk every language under the sun, and didn't want his services; but the captain of the schooner it seemed did.

Then that youth made a sign to follow him again, but I laid my hands upon him and asked him "Did he wish to live any longer?" He bowed a scared assent, and muttered something like "General de la Place;" but I made him understand his only hope consisted in getting us there by the shortest route. He "lived the other side of the town," was his reply.

Yes, I should think he did, that mahogany-coloured, bald-headed, spectacled, wiry old cuss, with his begilded old swallow-tailed uniform coat; and he might just as well have gone up to the top of the mountain with his office as far as we were concerned, for we couldn't have been more nearly dead than we were when we arrived there.

He was a courtly old fellow, I will say that for him, this "General de la Place;" and I was so far mollified by his gentlemanly manner as to address him an appeal in French that he would facilitate our progress as quick as possible, as we had not partaken of food for twenty-four hours.

"*Tou' d' suite, monsieur*," was his reply, smilingly given. After a few questions and some notes by his secretary, a spectacled old negro, the General bowed us out, our troubles being over, as we thought, until we heard this old hypocrite say to the guide, "Bureau of Police."

Utterly overcome at this, I supported myself against a wall, and glaring upon the uniquely costumed guide, I insisted upon knowing exactly how far we had to go yet, and in what direction. If there was any more places besides the "Bureau of Police" to visit, I declined positively to go, unless they took me as a criminal to one of their prisons, where, in any event, they would have to "feed" me; but, as a free and mighty American citizen, travelling in a country at peace with my own nation, I pro-test-ed.

It will hardly be believed, but that youth grinned! Yes, I repeat it—actually grinned in my face, and muttered, "Republique (?) d'Haiti," as he pointed to himself. By Jove! I wish he had been, for I think then and there the glorious Republic of Haiti would have become utterly extinct, never more to be found upon the school-maps to puzzle the brain of our young (and some old) scholars as to whether it was a separate island or not from St Domingo.

The "Bureau of Police" looked more like a horse-stable, with its dirty guardroom and rusty old muskets, and dirty, ragged negro guard.

The "chief" and his aide, coal-black negroes clad in blue denims stiff with starch, received us, asked us impertinent questions, which I cut short by poking my passport at him. He laid it on the table, leaned over it, examined it, turned it over, and then fell to studying it for some minutes, after which he looked at me and said—

"Your name?"

"You have it there before you," I replied.

"What's your business?"

"To get your *vise* on that passport, and something to eat, as quick as the Lord will let us," I responded, at the same time informing him I was an American citizen, as that paper showed, and if there was any more delay I should place myself under the protection of my Consul, and let him attend to my business.

The chief fell to studying the paper again, but finally ejaculated, "Half-a-dollar," at which the captain of the vessel protested, telling me it had never been exacted before, bût I however put the money down, on which the "chief" handed me my document.

This was a little too aggravating, and therefore I remarked, "Eh bien, mon ami, you have read my paper, for which I make no charge; but for this half-dollar, you must earn it by giving me your autograph, or a stamp, or a seal;" to which he muttered, "Mais oui," "Mais oui;" and having examined all the others, he scrawled some hieroglyphics over them and declared we could go.

"Anywhere?" I ask, "no more officials to visit?"

"Non, non, monsieur."

"Le bon Dieu soit benit!" we utter and leave.

"To the hotel," we savagely say to the youth with the "casquette de-paille."

"It is closed, busted—there is none," is the reply; at which imagine our "pheelings," O sympathising reader!

From the previous day up to noon of this day, not a mouthful of food; from noon up to evening waiting on these officials, and yet no food—and now no hotel!

Happy thought! To the Consul, whom luckily we find at home. He immediately sallies out with us to hunt up at a billiard-bar-room and café a place where we could be entertained (?) after a fashion—where they owned just one bed, and this I magnanimously gave up to my companion, as I still had my trusty hammock, which I was permitted to hang in an arch of the courtyard, where the

Consul left us to "go through" that landlord's bill of fare from beginning to end.

Haytian Waiter.

"What will you have?" he asks.

"Everything, anything, beer, bread, fruit, cheese, bring it all at once;" and no Haytian before or since has appeared so charming as did the attendant as he promptly complied with our command.

Our *menu* for dinner was composed more leisurely and in a better frame of mind; but revenge is sweet, and my slumbers were sound that night. Why? Because, just as I was rolling myself up in my bag, the landlord asks, "*Are you a United States Commissioner?*"

"Bother! No; good night."

"Well, the authorities think you are, and *have doubled the guards to-night.*"

"*Ah! mais bon soir, voisin.*"

"The Paris of the West Indies." Well, it may have been in times gone by, but to day it can hardly be entitled to that name, unless on account of its ruins. With a class of people like the old polished French planters of the "ancien régime," this town may have possibly been all that the historians say it was, for as far as nature is concerned the place is lovely indeed. The good God has done everything for it; but now, with these semi-barbarians, it has been for years retrograding in civilisation and improvement.

As a panacea for the evils of my first day in Hayti, I awoke to find myself suddenly a millionaire. Yes, it is the truth; for in one day I was transformed from "an humble correspondent," with a few hundreds in good solid gold, to be a "commissioner" with $200,000 at my control. But let me explain.

My first act on rising on this magnificent morning of my second day in Hayti was to adapt myself to the custom of the country and ask for a "cocktail." I got it; I drank it. I had no fault to find with it, for it certainly was well fabricated.

"How much?" I asked.

"Thirty dollars, monsieur."

I start back horror-struck. Thirty dollars for a drink! I see it. I am a poor, miserable American, disowned by his Government, in a foreign land, and these barbarians know it, and now they want to swindle me. But the old spirit of '76 comes strong upon me, and I get reckless. I vow I will not pay it; and drawing from my pocket a silver coin of the realm of America, value ten cents, I declare it is all the money I have.

To my amazement the mild barkeeper says, "I haven't the change, sir."

Ah! I begin to see it; and with a princely air I say, "Oh! keep the change," as I walk to the door in a dignified manner; but once out, I walk, yea, I run. Where? To my bankers, upon whom I have a letter of credit for a few hundreds. I present the letter.

"Do you want it all now, sir?"

"Yes," I say, in a careless, easy manner, "if convenient." (I think I see now the cause of the peculiar twinkle in that clerk's eye.)

"It will take us some time, sir, to get it ready. Please amuse yourself for half-an-hour or so."

So I kick my heels against a large box of American soap. I whistle; the minutes go by; I light a cigar and stroll out to the door; it looks like business, for many carts are gathering around the square. I stroll on the quay, and am stopped by a dirty-looking negro with a club, a shirt, and a portion of pantaloons, who says, "You can't go there!"

"Who are you?" I ask.

"One of the guard."

I am scared; I back out, and attempt to slip around the corner, where I hear shouted at me—

"Que bagage ta?"

I turn, I tremble, my knees bend, for there, mounted before me (to be sure, the donkey is very small, even if it has large ears), is a mighty warrior in cocked-hat, with befrogged and gilded swallow-tailed coat, cotton pants (nigger stripe), and though he has no shoes, he wears a spur: therefore I know he must be a general, for his sword is large. I salute with respect (I missed being a general once myself), when I hear a laugh and the remark, "Don't lose time on that fellow; he's only a guard." Mortified, I attempt to cross the street; it is blocked up with mules and donkeys heading one way. I turn down another street; it is the same. I think this a nice active place for business, and turn into the street leading to my bankers'; it is filled with donkey-carts, drays, mules, and horses with panniers and carts drawn by bullocks. I think this must be an unusual day in business, perhaps a market-day.

"What does all this mean?" I ask of a sable cartman, in my best French.

"Ca—oo—dee," he replies.

I try it again.

"Que bagage," is the response. Now, as I haven't any baggage with me, I am at a loss to know what it means, when happily an English-speaking person steps up and says, "I guess you don't understand creole, and these fellows don't speak French." I ask him then what all this means. He replies, "It is the United States Commissioner drawing a draft in Haytian money, and these carts are to load up with it."

"Why, that is funny," I replied; "I thought I was the only strange American here, and the Commissioners had all gone home."

"No; this one got in last night from Monte Cristo."

"Oh, dear!" I began to feel so queer that I just had strength enough to fall in at the door of a café, and say "Beer!" (You know everybody drinks ale here, or, as it is called, "beer.")

Thus strengthened and encouraged, I sought my bankers, and asked, as well as the crowd will permit, "Is that ready?" They call me into the private office, and ask, "Now, what are you going to do with all this money? Where are you going to put it? Because we have a large warehouse here, and will store it cheap for you."

"Oh, oh!" I begin to think my mind is going, but yet gasp out, "What does all this mean?"

"Why, don't you see? You present your draft, and say you want the money. Now, the only money they have here is the paper money of the country; it is to-day worth $400 in paper for $1 in gold, and if you draw your $200,000, it will take all these carts and mules to carry it; and if you will be advised by us, you will leave your draft here, and draw the money as small as possible, as you want it; therefore let us send these carts away while you take 'a beer.'"

I took the beer.

CHAPTER XXI.

"All heroes are alike: the point's agreed;
From Macedonia's madman to the Swede."

CAPE HAYTIAN—*The Paris of the West Indies—Population, Commerce, &c.—Ruins of French Civilisation—Beautiful Views—Fear of American Encroachments—Duplicity of Officials—Arbitrary Government—Trip to Milot—Scenes on the Road—Arrival at Sans Souci—Strange Treatment—Polite Officials—"Taking" the Citadel—Cristophe the Emperor—Horrible Cruelties—Views of the People—Return to the Cape.*

THE town of Cape Haytian is to-day, though one of the oldest towns on the island, a city of ruins. Settled originally by the "filibusters" from the Island of Tortuga, it would seem as though fate had decreed that it should be the objective point of the raids not only of foreign "filibusters," but of native enemies also.

First settled in 1670 by the buccaneers, its history shows a sad record of mingled progress and ruin, of great riches and extreme poverty, and finally of devastation by God and man.

This is the original "Guarico" of the Spaniards; then Cape Francis of the French; more lately Cape Henry, after Cristophe; and now usually Cape Haytian, though known simply as "The Cape."

Lying at the very foot of some noble mountains that stretch boldly out into the sea, and form a prominent landmark to the mariner, it is to-day, approaching it from

TOWN AND BAY OF THE CAPE.

the sea, a lovely spot, as first seen from the deck of a vessel.

A deep curve in the coast line forms a fine bay, upon which rests the gaily-coloured walls and roofs of the town in a long, narrow plain, running from the coast back to the verdure-clad hills, which form such a superb background to the picture.

Across the bay, and opposite the town, stretches away a vast plain, that ends only at the base of a range of mountains that nearly mark the boundary line between Dominica and Hayti, and the view in every direction is charming in the extreme. The town has been at one time an extremely well-built city, with houses entirely of stone, well-paved streets, large public square, and fountains and churches, grand and innumerable, and of the highest character of architecture, bearing even to-day traces of having been the handsome place that St Mery describes so minutely as existing before 1789.

Before the revolution that separated the island from France, this town had become the centre of commerce, and such was the degree of luxury and refinement to which its inhabitants had reached, it was everywhere spoken of as the Paris of St Domingo.

Its misfortunes began in 1793, when it was burned in the troubles among the revolutionary chiefs; again by the French fleet; and that old Turk, Cristophe, also laid it in ashes. For many years it struggled along in improvements, and many handsome houses and buildings were rebuilt, until in 1842 the terrible earthquake that visited the island laid almost the entire city in ruins, burying under its walls thousands of persons, while whole families were swallowed up, and became extinct in the catastrophe. The country people came in crowds into the town and gave themselves up to pillage, plundering the houses and the inhabitants without hesitation; and when remonstrated with, they with imprecations remarked, "It is our time now," and their numbers were so great, that no general resistance could be made to their maraudings.

To-day the street parallel with the sea is tolerably well built, mostly with large and substantial storehouse dwellings of the foreign merchants, and throughout the town substantial stone dwellings and wooden buildings are mingled promiscuously with the ancient ruins.

A more romantic place for the artist's study it would be

"Bord de Mer."

hard to find; and one can traverse square after square of crumbling ruins of stone, can walk through narrow paths that once have been stately streets, and see on every side arches, pillars, balconies, groined walls, and niches over which is growing and running the luxuriant vegetation of the tropics, while in the interior of courtyards, and what have once been halls and saloons, many finished in marble or solid stone, are growing the full-aged cocoa, banana, palm, and other trees, and in and about some of the public squares are ruins of noble churches and convents, even yet beautiful and majestic in their decay.

Of the inhabitants, the larger portion are black—jet black; and then come the mulattoes of various degrees of colour, a few native whites, and then the foreign population, by which latter class is mostly transacted the commerce of the place, which consists in exporting coffee and logwood, and the importing of provisions, dry goods, hardware, soaps, &c., a large portion of which come from

A Mercantile House.

the United States, particularly the common dry goods—the whole of the country people being, in fact, clad in the blue denim of the Amoskeag Company of New England.

Many of these foreign merchants live in a very great deal of style and luxury, occupying generally the rooms over their warehouses, many of which, those especially in the upper part of the town, are very handsome, solidly-built establishments, showing at once what the cities of this island would become if there were peace and a safe government.

What the great bulk of the black population does for a livelihood I was unable to find out, for they were principally occupied in "loafing" while I was there, though a great many of the women keep small stores for the sale of fruits, notions, &c.

The only active workers that I saw were those along the shore engaged in loading and unloading vessels, and these seemed to be as quick and steady in their labours as any one could desire; and as they are paid promptly by the foreign merchants who employ them, I am led to believe that a good deal of the inertness of the people of this island is simply owing to the uncertainty of being paid.

This seems always to be present to the mind of the Haytian of the lower class. I have had a fellow carrying my trunk on his head stop short, and turning to me, say, "You pay me? You *sure* you pay me?"

Again I have seen them, when I asked a service of them, shake their heads dubiously.

"Why, I will pay you for it," I would say.

"Will you, then? Well, pay me *now*, and I 'll do it." And doing this, I had no reason to complain.

But, from tradition and experience, these poor ignorant people seem to have a bad opinion of the white man, to whom they still apply in a general sense the term *méchant* (wicked).

As a type of the way in which they work at their ease, I was struck with the process of building a house two stories in height. Part of the second story being already built, one of the workmen seated himself in the scaffold of the upper window, and received the bricks thrown to him *one* by *one* by the man below, still another one being ready to take them from the hands of the first and lay them down for him. It would be a nice calculation to know how long it would take, at this rate, to build a three-story brick-house.

The town is an extremely interesting one to the casual traveller fond of historical researches, and the natural beauties of the surrounding country are so great, that many beautiful rides can be taken on horseback in the vicinity.

One of these, to a place called Marchegal, is particularly interesting, affording an opportunity of seeing a large portion of the town itself; and then, mounting up by a lovely road on the mountain in rear of the town, affording a superb view of the plain, and the town with its bay, the plain

Old French Place.

beyond, and the mountain range still further off, upon one of the peaks of which can be distinctly seen the celebrated Citadel of Cristophe.

From this old place of Marchegal can be obtained some idea of what this country was in its civilised days; for here may yet be seen stone terraces, stone walls of solid architecture, drains of mason-work, stone baths, and remains of beautiful gardens and improved agriculture; all, alas! now sunk in ruins.

A few days' sojourn will exhaust the attractions of the

city; but half a day's journey from the Cape, towards the Dominican frontier, lies, in a charming valley, the little village of historic fame known as Milot, celebrated as the residence of King Cristophe.

If the reader has ever heard anything at all of Hayti or its history, he will have heard of this celebrated negro, and the wondrous palace of "Sans Souci" he built for his royal dwelling, while on the mountain is the equally famed "Citadel."

Before visiting the island I had read of these wondrous places; and in my various travels in St Domingo, whenever "The Cape" and Hayti were mentioned, these places were spoken of as something fabulous, that were well worthy of a visit.

As no travelling is allowed in the island without passes, I called our Consul to my assistance, and determined to visit these places; and he was kind enough to make application to his friend, the General of the province, Alexis Nord, for a permit for me to visit the Citadel and Sans Souci at Milot, which was apparently granted. Here it is, translated from the original, forcibly illustrating *free* Hayti, a regular written document on a printed form:—

*Liberty.** *Equality.* *Fraternity.*

No.——

REPUBLIC OF HAYTI,
CAPE HAYTIAN, 31st March, 1871,
68th year of Independence.

Nord Alexis, General of Division, Aide-de-camp of his Excellency the President of Hayti, and Commandant of the Department of the North.

Permit to Mr Hazard, American subject, to go to Milot, accompanied by a guide, to attend to his business. *He is recommended* to the kindness of the authorities.

NORD ALEXIS.

Meanwhile some friends, hearing of my intention, decided to make up a party to accompany me, and invitations were given by them and accepted, without it being stated particularly that I was to be of the party, which was composed principally of foreigners.

* The italics are the author's.

It will hardly be believed, but when it was known that I was to be of the party, they all backed out, because I was an American and reputed Commissioner, and my company was not deemed safe. For such is the state of fear in which the country is kept, and so arbitrary are the acts of the Government, that foreign merchants even do not feel safe, and, therefore, are careful not to compromise themselves in any way.

Pleasant company is always agreeable; but still I was determined not to lose my trip, notwithstanding the lugubrious accounts given me of the danger I ran; so, casting about, I began negotiating for a guide and a horse.

The first appeared in the person of "William," a graceful native, accomplished in the languages of English, creole, and broken French. Hardly yet accustomed to the currency of the island, I was somewhat taken aback at the sum he required for his services, $2000 (£400); but with the aid of pencil and paper and a close calculation, I made out the net amount would just be five dollars of real money; so he was at once engaged.

William.

All efforts proved fruitless to hire a horse for myself, though the guide was more fortunate; and I was compelled eventually to accept the offer of one from a friend. Then William failed me: first it had been the horse; then he wished to indulge himself in a spree; then he appeared before me in a costume that foreboded rain; until, tired of delay, I named the hour at which I should start with or without him; but I finally succeeded in getting off, quite late one afternoon, with my guide, both mounted, and he carrying my hammock and some few stores.

Out through the north-eastern gate we rode past the sentry—who, on my asking him a question, politely replied, "Give me a dollar!"—to a broad, hard road, bounded on one side by the savanna, while back from the other rolled beautiful ascending land to the very mountain, while all along were the usual one-storied wooden-houses—the land, although in such close proximity to the city, being generally uncultivated.

Just outside the city gates, beside the public road, where thousands and thousands of people are continually passing, is a large potter's field, where diseased cattle are taken and left to die and rot, while in the same place is put the household furniture of those who die of yellow fever.

Passing by this lot, you see the whitening bones and skeletons of defunct animals, and tables and chairs, and even mattresses, left there intact to impregnate the air with the seeds of contagious disease, when a simple bonfire of the articles so infected would remove the revolting sight and prevent all danger. But such is sanitary law in this enlightened (?) Republique d'Haiti.

"William," I discovered, had some difficulty in keeping up with me, so I awaited his arrival, and then discovered he was very drunk, being constantly tumbling from his horse.

In explanation he endeavoured to convince me that it was the "fool of a horse," that would not keep in the road; but ordering him to go ahead of me and lead the animal, it was very quickly seen which would not keep straight.

However, we made progress, though a slow one, and for the first few miles I was struck with the great difference in population between Hayti and Dominica; for while in the latter part you rarely meet any one in the road, here were crowds of negroes, men and women, on foot and on horseback, all going to or from the city with produce or supplies.

The road, too, was a hard gravel-and-sand road, perfectly practicable for carts and vehicles; and three miles out we came to a solid stone bridge over a small stream,

Squatters in Ruined Places.

the parapets of which were in ruins, though the causeway was good. I ask, "Who built it?" "The French," is the reply. They don't built bridges now-a-days.

For some distance our road ran through rather a barren tract, and then turning off, we struck most beautiful prairie land, only cultivated here and there with the plantain patch, while on the sides of the road grew thick the logwood originally planted by the French for hedges.

Or, again, we passed fields of what looked like bushes or scrub timber, so thick was it, and which I found was the coffee, left to grow wild and be choked up with rank vegetation. A sad, sad sight, too, were the ruins of gateways and houses with which we met at almost every step. All of them were of the most solid kind of masonry, the gate-posts in many instances being of solid stone and of carved work, while the houses gave signs of having been large and stately mansions; but all, all were crumbling to decay.

It required no great stretch of imagination to picture this section of country before the Revolution, when this whole plain, with its handsome houses, superb plantations, and well-kept hedges, presented the appearance of a vast and beautiful flower-garden.

I found the country well cut up by good roads, that originally appeared to have been solidly constructed with stone, and ditches were in many places dug on each side, while stone culverts and drains gave evidence that at one time civilisation had had some share in the improvement of the country.

I was particularly interested in seeing this; for often I had thought it would be impossible to make roads or keep them in order in such a country as Dominica, and here I had new evidence that it was not only possible, but easy to make and drain good roads.

Constantly before us in the turns of the road we saw the blue hills of our destination, seeming almost to recede as we advanced, conspicuous, however, on one of which were the sheer walls of the Citadel.

Night was closing in on us as we struck a more fertile country, where the cane was cultivated in large fields, and where occasional groves of coffee were met with in uncared-for luxuriance. More than this, too, we passed for miles through groves of the guava, whose yellow fruit, just ripening, filled the evening air with the most fragrant, delicious, almost suffocating perfume.

Now, in almost every direction, we saw the glow of fires in the different fields; and it needed not to ask the cause of this, for the night air was heavy with the odorous fumes of the cane-juice, which they were boiling in their rude way to make sugar and rum.

Then a tough bit of road, and we began our ascent by a rocky road on the mountain or hill that intervenes before reaching Milot; but directly we descended again, and there, calmly lying in the moonlight, was the village of Milot in its beautiful plain, while beyond it were the gloomy hills of the Sierra, as a background to the immense walls of the far-famed palace of Sans Souci, that even in the night were remarkable in the grandeur of moonlight and deep shadow.

We asked at several houses for shelter, but there seemed something wrong, as no one was inclined to grant it, a proceeding very unusual in these regions.

Finally I ask for the Commandant, and am directed to the quarters on the hill. I ask for the General; he is away, but his subordinate comes forward and asks what I want, though he seems to know already that I am an American. He says he has no quarters. I tell him he must find them. He says, "My orders don't call for that" (he hasn't looked at them). I tell him he had better read them. Says he can't, but will see the General's secretary; and we start out to hunt him up, until I tell him, "Never mind; get us into any house."

He insolently says he can if I will pay, which of course I tell him I expect to do. Meanwhile one woman, more hospitable than the rest, says I may swing my hammock in her house if I like, as "she loves the Americans; they saved her life." Considerably puzzled, I dismount, and when our arrangements are all made, I get from her that a messenger came up before me to say that an American was coming up to "take" the Citadel. I laughed heartily, until it was explained that they were afraid that I came to make plans of the fort so that we could come and take it.

I went to my bag for the night, laughing at the idea these people had of the Yankee nation, and was roused up at an early hour in the morning by my guide, who said the subaltern had sent word that I must get up at once, see the town and the palace, and go about my business, as my order permitted nothing else.

Pretty mad, I sent him my compliments, requesting him to visit a place not in the Arctic regions, and, turning over, went to doze again.

When I awoke, I found the General had returned, and sent me a courteous message that he was sorry he had not been there the previous night, as he would have furnished me comfortable quarters, and requesting me to call on him as soon as convenient.

Breakfast over, I went up to his quarters, and found him to be a perfectly black, ordinary negro, but speaking pure French well. I showed him my order, and told him I wished to visit the historic Citadel.

This he said I could not do. I quoted my order to him, and we had some angry words together, ending in my telling him I should hold him responsible to his superior for not complying with instructions.

Then at last it all came out—the vile duplicity of these people and their rulers; for this very Alexis Nord, after apparently complying with the request of the Consul, had sent a messenger on ahead of me to give other instructions.

Naturally, I was pretty mad, finding, after my trouble and expense, the objects of my journey were only to be partially accomplished, and I took the liberty of telling "the General" some views I had about savages. I had, of course, no right to find fault with being kept out of any place, particularly a fortress, for every Government has a perfect right to exercise its own judgment in admitting strangers to such places; and had I been the only foreigner to whom was refused this permission, it would still have been far from me to find fault.

PALACE OF SANS SOUCI (MILLOT).

But this was not the case, as I understood the Citadel had been quite frequently open to the inspection of foreign visitors ; but of the deception practised, and the discourtesy shown to the Government of which I was a citizen, I think I had just right of complaint, though I have since learned that no nationality is exempt from these petty displays on the part of Hayti. However, I made the best of a bad bargain, and started with a guard to view the principal object of interest, the "Palace Sans Souci," and a superb palace it must have been in its time. Imagine a long, narrow, lovely valley clothed in verdure, shut in by high hills, and ending at one end in a gently-rising knoll that blocks up the narrow ravine between two grand high mountains, the precipitous faces of which seem the walls of a natural fortress, and you have an idea of the natural location of the palace.

The palace of Sans Souci was constructed by Henry Cristophe, the King of the North, upon the brow of the hill of the village of Milot, then an old sugar estate. The site was well chosen, because there was a superb view of the valley below and the hills around, while it (the palace) was imposing and grand. Its original plan was primitive, but was successively increased, and thus its architecture is irregular. There was a *rez-de-chaussee* or basement, then a second story and a belvidere, or look-out, from which superb views were obtained. Upon the right was the throne-room, and below was a circular church used by Cristophe and his family; upon the left was the terrace of Caimito, so named from a large tree of that species that overshadowed it. Then some large dwellings for the officers and secretaries, while adjoining these were solid buildings for sheltering the many carriages and equipages of the King. Behind the palace were large gardens filled with flowers, fruits, and vegetables, while water ran down in cascades from the neighbouring mountains. Ranged above the main palace were buildings used as storehouses, arsenals, barracks, &c., for the military, while printing-offices, the mint, and offices added to their extent and number.

Most of these buildings are still standing, as well as the solid stone steps, the esplanade, the courtyard wall, with its ponderous gate-posts. Although the earthquake of 1842 ruined them to such an extent, they have never since been occupied; yet, seen as they are to-day, with their historic associations, their magnificent natural site, the extent and majesty of their architecture, the traveller is well repaid in making a special visit to them.

Besides this palace of Sans Souci, Cristophe had other magnificent places throughout his dominions, bearing the various names of the "Queen's Delight," "The King's Beautiful View," "The Conquest," "The Victory," "The Glory," &c. Most of these were sugar estates, others were cotton plantations, but all lying in this most fertile and beautiful plain of St Domingo and Hayti, known as the "Artibonite." But here at Sans Souci was the favourite place and residence of the tyrant King Cristophe; and as long as a stone of these walls shall stand, so long will there be a monument to one of the greatest savages and murderers that has ever disgraced God's earth.

The history of this man and his rule in Hayti seems like fabled romance, and is too long for me to give here, but a few facts may not be uninteresting.

For fourteen years Cristophe, originally an African slave, ruled here at Sans Souci, where, seated on a throne placed under the before-mentioned caimito-tree that shaded the terrace, he held court. His officers and people dared not look upon his face, but knelt before him as slaves, and with a wave of his hand he consigned immediately to the dungeon or death any of his subjects who displeased him.

Did he want a carriage built or an article made, he would have brought before him the artificer.

"How long will it take you to make one like this?" he would ask of the now trembling mechanic.

"Three months," perhaps would be the reply.

"If in two weeks it is not here before me, finished, you will be thrown from the precipice," was all that Cristophe said, and the man was taken away. It was at this palace that Cristophe died by his own hand.

To show the character of the man, a short time before the revolution broke out against him, he had had an attack of paralysis, from which recovering somewhat, he had himself put in a rum-and-pepper bath and rubbed by his attendants. This made him feel so much better that he ordered his people to be assembled, and then appearing before them on the terrace, he was so stupefied that he fell upon his knees in the attitude of supplication, and had to be carried in.

Then came the news of the revolution against him at the Cape. He saw his fields of cane burned before him under his very eye. Then came the revolt of his favourite troops; and seating himself in the gallery of his palace in a dressing-gown and curious hat he wore, he made pass before him all the troops of his guard: to each one of them he gave a dollar to go and fight the rebels.

Meanwhile he was seated on the esplanade with his two daughters near him, when word was brought him that his guard too had deserted him. Rising up, he bade good-bye to his wife and family, and withdrawing to his chamber, blew his brains out with a pistol.

The officers and people of the palace immediately sacked it of all its precious valuables, while his wife and daughters, enveloping the body of their father in a hammock, fled to the "Citadel" above.

This "Citadel," it is probable, has had more to do with making Cristophe infamous (as well as famous) than anything else. It was constructed originally by the French upon the chain of the mountain "Bishop's Hat," a height of several hundred yards above the level of the sea. Begun in 1804, it was not finished until 1820, for there was always being executed upon it new labour. Such was its height that, standing upon its walls, one gets dizzy; and from thence were thrown into the valley beneath thousands who had incurred the enmity of the King; so that it came properly by its name Grand Boucan. Such was the cruel treatment of the labourers employed upon it, who worked without pay and very little food, that 30,000 persons are said to have perished in its construction.

The walls of the fort are built upon the solid rock itself, and are from fifteen to twenty feet thick, and of great height, being built of masonry or solid stone. There were several batteries of the largest kind of ordnance placed one above the other. Here in this citadel were the arsenals and storehouses of the King; and the accounts given of the quantities of provisions, of gold and silver, and precious things stored there, seem fabulous, were there not on record the names of those who became rich at its sacking. The commotions of nature have utterly ruined this once formidable place, and naught remains now but the ruins to show the immensity of the place and its conception, and even these are guarded with jealous care by the authorities from the eye of the stranger.

Prince Saunders, the agent of Cristophe in England, gives the following information of these places in the time of his master:—"The Citadel Henry, that palladium of liberty, that majestic bulwark of independence, that monument of the greatness and of the vast combinations of a Henry, is built on the lofty summit of one of the highest mountains in the island, whence you may discover to the left the island of Tortuga and the reflection of its beautiful canal; in front, the gentle risings, with the city of Cape Henry, its roadstead, and the vast expanse of ocean; on the right, La Grange, Monte Cristo, the city of Fort Royal, Manzanillo Bay, and the surrounding hills.

The eye is gratified with the prospect of the beautiful plain, and the magnificent carpet of verdure spread before it.

"The position, fortified by nature, and to which art has added all its science, with casemates and bomb-proofs, has secured it from being successfully besieged, while the mouths of the cannon overtop the elevation of the high ground, and command the adjacent territory, affording protection to the whole north."

He describes Sans Souci as a town "likely to become the capital of Hayti." "Ravines have been filled up, mountains levelled, and public roads laid out. This superb royal palace, its sumptuous apartments, all with inlaid work, and lined with the most beautiful and rarest tapestry, . . . all these combine to embellish the retreat of a hero. . . . I know it to be the intention of our King to have the rotunda of his palace in the Citadel paved and lined with quadruples; such a novel species of apartment will reflect a precious drapery, and be without a parallel in the world."

My visit to this wonderful place I shall never forget, and returning to the village, I gave orders for our start. Availing myself of the time, I rambled through the village, entering into conversation with the people, and to my inquiry, "Why do you dislike the Americans so much?" I was invariably told that the Government had informed them the Americans wanted to come and take their lands and make them slaves and work. I am very certain that many of these people were much enlightened before I left them, but they were hardly able to realise my last words, that we had freed our slaves, and were now educating them.

Having no idea of being detained on the road by the slow movements of William, I determined to start back alone, as I was now familiar with the road, and notwithstanding his warnings that a present shower would end in a violent storm, I left him to convey to several of the natives some of the home truths about their condition, and putting spurs to my horse, I reached the Cape safely, after an extremely hot ride, much to the surprise and gratification of my friends, who I really believe had felt seriously alarmed about me, as it was currently reported I never would reach the Citadel, and, in point of fact, owing to the trickery of the Government, I did not. Before I left the Cape, I was known as the American who had attempted to "take" the Citadel, one rascal having the impudence to make a sign of throat-cutting in pointing me out.

As I had the intention of going overland to Gonaives, the Consul had asked for a letter for me from the authorities, one of which, similar to that given me for Milot, was furnished by Alexis Nord, the other, purporting to be a recommendation to the authorities at Gonaives, was given into my hands sealed, and, in all probability, had my plans been carried out, would have been duly delivered to its address.

On my return, however, I found such difficulty in getting horses, that I decided to avail myself of the chance to visit the entire north coast of Hayti in the American steamer *Port-au-Prince*, which runs regularly from New York to this island every month. For this reason my letter to the authorities at Gonaives could be of no further use, and with so much talk and so much duplicity on the part of the officials, I confess my suspicions were aroused, and my curiosity excited as to the honesty of its contents. Therefore, after I left the island, it being still in my possession, I took the liberty of opening it; and here is its literal translation, upon which, I think, no comment need be made, as it speaks for itself, simply stating, however, in justice to myself, that never, as far as I know, did I give hint or intimation to any Haytian that I had ever had anything to do with a United States Commission. It is more particularly valuable, however, as an exposition of the sentiments that seem to pervade the breast of every Haytian, no matter what his status socially, who has not been out of the island, that the acmé of perfection has been reached by Hayti and its people, from which happy delusion it would seem almost a pity to undeceive them, were it not that the world generally, and they particularly, will be benefited by a critical examination.

Liberty. *Equality.* *Fraternity.*

REPUBLIC OF HAYTI,

No.—— CAPE HAYTIAN, April 2, 1871.

68th year of Independence.

CHAVANNES, General of Division of the armies of the Republic, Provisional Commandant of the Arrondissement.

To the Commandant of the Arrondissement of Gonaives.

GENERAL—Monsieur Hazard, one of the members of the American Commission sent to the eastern part of the island, has been here some days, coming from Monte Cristo, in order to go to Port-au-Prince, for which he is furnished with a permit from the Commander of the Department North.

As we ought to prove our independence, preferring rather to bury ourselves in our ruin than to annex our country that we have gained at the price of the blood of our forefathers, and *as we are at the level for which God has created us, men equal to all men in any part of the world,* I have not need, General, to *recommend* for this stranger all the regards you should have for him, in order that, on his return to his own country, he may be able to defend us from the "sauvagerie" of which very often we are accused.

It is with these sentiments, General, I salute you in the country (*en la patrie*).

CHAVANNES.

Sorry am I to confess that I cannot conscientiously make this defence, and, in fact, I have been, like most persons who visit Hayti, utterly disappointed in its people and government; and the candid and impartial traveller, friend of the black race though he be, must feel, in visiting this island, that its people have not yet solved the problem of self-government; for though their constitution seems to be good enough, it is yet so unwisely administered by those in power, that the country has simply been, since Boyer's time, a country of revolutions, at the history of which it will be well for us to glance, in order to properly understand the condition of its affairs to-day.

CHAPTER XXII.

"This country, which for twenty-seven years has never ceased to be in a state of revolution, caused by the ambition of those without occupation, who have seen in this way a means of making money, or of repairing their bankruptcies in the changing of Government officers, *has need of a reform, moral and political.*"

LE CONTE.

HAYTI FROM THE DEPARTURE OF BOYER IN 1843 TO THE ADVENT OF SAGET IN 1870.

IT would be neither interesting to the reader, nor possible in a volume like this, to detail the acts or history of every individual who appears prominent in the annals of Hayti from 1843 to the present time.

Eminently a country of factions and of revolutions, happily for the world at large, Hayti's political status has in no way affected the rest of mankind. Nevertheless the philanthropist cannot but regret that, while the history of the rest of the world shows a wonderful record of progress, civilisation, and enlightenment in the past thirty years, she alone stands a warning, in her present condition, of the evils resulting from a lack of all these. The excuses given by the party that overthrew Boyer, "that he had remained stationary for twenty-five years, that he had not given education to the people, and that he had maintained the military system, which retarded civilisation and aided to violate the law," are just as applicable to-day. The impartial writer hardly needs to rely upon his own judgment to form an opinion of Hayti and its people, for so numerous and so frank have been the confessions made by many of these literary patriots, that it is not a very difficult matter to select what is really the truth, and that may be found embodied in the words at the head of this chapter. General Le Conte, who within a few months has himself become a martyr to this fever of revolution, and paid the penalty of failure, was the author of these words, and, perhaps, as a real Haytian, a descendant of the famous Dessalines, as good a judge of his people as can be found.

Numerous causes of discontent, however, added to the action of Boyer in paying indemnity to a Spanish man-of-war, created the insurrection against him in 1843, at the head of which was General Herard Riviere, a mulatto, an ignorant soldier, and a man, it is said, without the slightest political knowledge or experience; but he was supported by a body of young men, who believed themselves justified by the excuses given above in overturning one Government without having prepared plans for another.

Many of these young men were well instructed; some had been educated in Europe; but the largest part of them, and they the most noisy and demonstrative, had been ruined by their debaucheries. They wished, therefore, to rebuild their fortunes, and, with the vanity peculiar to the Haytian, shine in the first rank.

Hardly, however, had Herard been installed at the head of the Government, when he was compelled by the condition of affairs in the Dominican part to march to the frontier, and while absent, revolts broke out among the blacks, and several candidates were proposed as President; but Herard, returning at the head of his army, with the assistance of some friends, effected a *coup d'état*, by which he was made President, and subsequently, in January 1844, confirmed for life.

The pen tires in transcribing the names of the Haytian Presidents, they were made so fast, after the spirit of revolution had once begun its career, and the eye finds no period of peace or tranquillity among this people on its page of history.

The revolution of Hérard, begun with great promises, soon weakened under the excess of zeal of its promoters, who it is said had deceived the country, and the people were again in revolt, wreaking their vengeance and hate on the innocent as well as guilty; and from that time to this, the spirit of revolution seems to have taken such hold, that the Haytian takes it in with each breath of air. For several years immorality and corruption joined with revolution in demoralising the country. Individual governments, or those of party, succeeded one another in shorter or longer intervals, according as the character of the chief was more or less strong and absolute; but the people have never had a voice in the election of their chief ruler, for some bold chief or some party, having the control of an armed force, imposed its candidate upon the people, who, too timid to act otherwise, accepted him, while hoping and waiting till some more fortunate one should have his turn.

Thus (says Leconte) the laws have never been observed in Hayti, and their violation is the most natural thing in the world. The leaders demand their execution, but in order to facilitate their personal interests, or those of their favourites, devotion to the country in Hayti goes for nothing; it is the devotion to a leader or individual that is the act of virtue.

Thus Hérard, becoming unpopular, was deposed by the people, and fled to Jamaica, and an old negro, named Guerrier, was appointed his successor; but he did not live long enough to have any effect, and dying in 1845, soon after his election, he was succeeded by Pierrot, a still older negro, some seventy years of age. Nothing of any importance seems to have occurred during his term, which was short, but a vast waste of money, induced by a system of rewards to military chiefs, and an army was, at great expense, kept up, and constant incursions made upon Dominican territory.

In the spring, however, of 1846, another revolution was inaugurated by the nomination of General Riche, a man sixty years of age, to the Presidency, Pierrot retiring disgusted to private life.

Riché made some efforts to improve the condition of affairs, his term being a great advance on that of his predecessors, and some attempts were made at general agriculture; but the revenues of the island were principally absorbed by the army, and it is said that out of five million dollars revenue, three millions were expended for that purpose.

After the fall of Boyer, some of his ministers had assisted his successors with their counsels, and the Ardouins, Dupuy, and others were thus found aiding Riche; Dupuy, a man skilled in affairs of state, it is said, being his chief councillor; and although petty revolts were occurring all over the island, he was enabled to maintain his position for a short time.

But the same causes which tended then to demoralise the country and unsettle its people are those that render it a hotbed of revolution to-day. The bankruptcy of its treasury, the ambition of aspiring chiefs, the hatred of disappointed ones, and the want of any regular system of commerce and agriculture, with the incubus of an army living in idleness and eating up the substance of the land, must have their effect.

Riché dying in 1847, the senate and the country were divided as to his successor—two competitors being in the field, Generals Souffran and Paul; and in order to get out of this difficulty, Senators Ardouin and Dupuy named Faustin Soulouque, and, on his being proposed by the President of the Senate, B. Ardouin, he was declared chief of the republic.

Soulouque had been born a slave, and was at eighteen

years of age a slave of General Lamar, who took him for his "aide-de-camp," from which he was slowly promoted until he became a General.

He was superstitious, illiterate, and a member of the secret order of Vaudoux. A fine-looking mulatto of about sixty-two years of age, though appearing much younger, he was excessively vain and fond of admiration.

Without the slightest political experience or knowledge, Soulouque, believed to be a man without decision, will, or fixed views, was thus selected by a coterie which, having governed pretty much the country through his predecessors, expected to find in him the easy tool or lay figure with which to work.

The majority of the people, astonished at first at this nomination, that took the country by surprise, remained indifferent, and some of the most prominent men, laying aside their prejudices, determined to yield the new official their support for the sake of the country.

But it would appear that if Soulouque had nothing else to recommend him, he had at least a will of his own, with some administrative capacity, which quickly made him independent of his electors.

On making this discovery, these men, it appears, were much chagrined, and endeavoured to unite all the coloured and mulatto influence by turning Soulouque into ridicule, and finally conspiring against him.

Soulouque, however, threw himself into the arms of the blacks (always spoken of by the mulattoes as the ignorant blacks), and a terrible and bloody struggle of caste ensued, April 16, 1848, in which he was the victor; but it was only through the interference of foreigners that more horrible deeds of murder and bloodshed were prevented.

Soulouque now created an empire, as it was called, and in August 26, 1849, declared himself Emperor, under the title of Faustin the First, appointing a number of his followers to titles of nobility, to which has been, and always will be, attached a certain amount of ridicule, though the names bestowed on some were simply those of the districts to which the French themselves had given the name of Limonade, Marmalade, &c.

For twelve years Soulouque reigned in the most absolute manner, like a tyrant it is said; but it is also related of him that, though without instruction, he was sincere and honest. At all events, adopting the motto, "I am the state; my will is the law," he made himself felt throughout the country as its ruler, and thus prevented any attempt at conspiracies against him.

Ambitious to bring the whole island under his rule, he made several attempts against the Dominicans; and a favourite oath of his was, that he would exterminate the rebels of the east as so many hogs; but, as we have already seen, these attempts were unsuccessful.

"Let us rejoice," he said; "we await the future, when a time shall come when the people will say, 'What a beautiful epoch was that of Soulouque!'"

But even this happy (?) reign was troubled by such a practical matter as payment of a debt; for the French forced the Emperor to hypothecate one half of the customs duty (treaty of May 15, 1847) towards paying the debt due them, and of which not one single payment had been made from 1843 to 1846.

Notwithstanding all this regal splendour, it does not appear the masses of the people were either contented or happy, and the Haytian phrase "Yet another revolution," was to be illustrated by Fabre Nicholas Geffrard, one of Soulouque's generals, who, in 1859 at Gonaives, raised the banner of revolt.

Loaded with debts occasioned by play and libertinage, it is said Geffrard personally carried very little weight, but announcing himself as the representative of a chief named Paul, who was much respected by the people, and who had already raised the banner of revolt in the west and south, he was soon supported by large numbers of the discontented population; and Faustin the First was compelled to leave the glories of his new empire behind him, and take refuge in Jamaica, where he was soon to be followed by Geffrard.

The latter, however, soon came out under his own name, offering the people a democratic rule, with free and liberal institutions, of which he declared himself the champion; and no sooner did he feel assured by the strength of his followers, than he declared himself President of the republic, and the empire fell.

Some of the portraits made of Geffrard are not very flattering; he is pronounced a hypocrite, a shallow man, making great pretensions; as extremely dishonest and devoted to libertinage, keeping a number of mistresses, and aiding by his own example to demoralise not only the young men, but in seducing the young women from virtue.

From the first his rule gave no peace or satisfaction to the country. An attempt made to assassinate him resulted in the death of his daughter; while his entire rule was not free from executions and assassinations, many women even suffering death.

Born of a mulatto mother by a black father, Geffrard, it is said, availed himself of this circumstance to ingratiate himself with both parties, now claiming with the blacks that he was of them through his father, and in the same manner he claimed a position with the mulattoes.

It was during Geffrard's rule that the Spaniards, then in possession of the eastern part of the island, threatened to bombard the town of Port-au-Prince. The Haytians, it appears, had committed, as was their frequent custom, some raids on the frontiers, carrying off horses and cattle; and the Spanish authorities immediately demanded reparation, which not being granted, a fleet was sent to Port-au-Prince, and a demand made on Geffrard for some 40,000 dollars, as also that the Spanish flag should be saluted. Forty-eight hours were only allowed for a final decision. Geffrard protesting he would not comply with the terms, and the Spanish commander being equally obdurate, it was only through the influence of the diplomatic corps that the latter consented to leave the sum to be settled by arbitration, Geffrard, under protest of force alone, consenting to salute the Spanish flag.

Nothing, however, it appears, could make Geffrard popular, and being well aware that there must be a change, he wisely decided to take French leave of the country, and with a large amount of public funds he made his escape to Jamaica.

Succeeding Geffrard came Sylvain Salnave, a plain honest soldier, who, supported by the army, was sustained by the great mass of the people, especially the blacks, who made him President of the republic; but, with the best intentions, he appears not to have conciliated all parties—the aristocracy, as the mulattoes are called, being opposed to him.

Duly elected by the Constituent Assembly on the 14th June 1867, he entered at once into the discharge of his functions, which by the same Assembly were prescribed to terminate in May 1871; and the constitution at present in force was then promulgated, the customs laws passed by Soulouque, and slightly revised by Geffrard, being enforced then as they also are at present. This constitution, which "the Haytian people proclaim in presence of the Supreme Being, in order to consecrate for ever its rights, its civil and political guarantees, its sovereignty, and its national independence," is undoubtedly a good one, and, if fully carried out in all details, quite sufficient to make happy and prosperous any people living in a land so highly favoured by nature as Hayti.

This constitution, amongst other articles, provides that "the Republic of Hayti is one and indivisible, essentially free, sovereign, and independent." The territory and the islands that belong to it are inviolable, and cannot be alienated by a single treaty or convention. The territory is divided into departments; each department is subdivided into "arrondissements," and each one of these into "communes," all of which are determined in their number by law. All Haytians are equal before the law. They are all equally entitled to civil and military offices, dependent on merit alone. There is no distinction of birth, order, class, or colour. The liberty is guaranteed to every citizen to go and come, remain, &c., without being arrested.

Yet to-day it is a common occurrence for the military to take young boys and men from off their mules in the public streets, even though they may be household servants with their employers present, and pack them off to the army, without asking permission, or the recruits having any redress. "No law shall be *ex post facto* in its effects." Yet no change in government has ever taken place that the upholders of the previous recognised stable authority have not been murdered, imprisoned, or exiled—Salnave as we shall presently show, being the first victim. Three powers form the government—the legislative, the executive, and the judicial; and each power is independent of the two others. The legislative power is exercised by the Senate and the Chamber of Communes, forming together the National Assembly. The President of the republic is the executive. The Chamber of the Communes is composed of the direct representatives of the people, elected by the primary assemblies of each commune; this chamber elects the senators. The President of the republic is elected by the National Assembly for four years, and no one can be re-elected but after an interval of four years.

Notwithstanding this constitution and its rules, and a President who seemed desirous of conforming himself to it, a war-cry was soon raised, and again this island was given up to revolution, murder, pillage, conflagration, and bloodshed, when "blood flowed in waves, and fortunes were utterly swept away, whole families being compelled to flee to Jamaica and St Thomas, with only their jewellery to furnish means of subsistence."

Salnave sustained himself with varying success against the revolters, who committed every crime, maiming and torturing their prisoners, young girls being violated, while women and children were ruthlessly murdered.

In Port-au-Prince, where Salnave was finally held besieged by the "Cacos," as the new party was called, crowds of distressed people sought the various Consulates for safety; and though Salnave proclaimed they would be attacked if affording this shelter, many persons were protected, though even foreigners were not safe from the wrath of parties until English and American men-of-war sailed into the harbour and covered the town with their guns.

In November 1867, Chevalier, one of Salnave's generals, deserted him with a large body of troops, and joined the rebels; and the Cape falling into their hands, two of Salnave's war-steamers were captured, leaving him only one, the *Terror*, at Port-au-Prince.

On the 18th December, three rebel vessels entered this harbour at night, and, through treachery, captured her without a shot being fired.

The news of this capture aroused the city, when it was found that General Brice had landed 1500 men, and the town was to be attacked. Salnave, finding the town had been partially set on fire, retired with his friends to the grand palace, a handsome stone edifice, where it is said he was making his preparations to leave, as also to resign his position, when the town was bombarded by the vessels in the harbour.

One of these, the *Terror*, had its guns under charge of the only practical artillerist on board, a young American named Hall, and he, under threats of taking his life, was forced to point a gun upon the palace, which he did with such precision, that a shell burst in the throne-room, the most magnificent in the palace, but then filled with a large quantity of powder, which exploding, immediately blew up the entire building.

Salnave, who was just mounting his horse to seek protection at the American minister's, escaped, and took the road to La Coupe (Petionville), on the heights above the town, which latter was only saved from total destruction by the crews of the English men-of-war. In the ruins of the palace five hundred men perished. Brice being now in command of the town, despatched the *Terror* to bring Nissage Saget, then at Arcahaye, to the capital, and on his arrival ensued still further scenes of horror, many prominent men and officers being proscribed and murdered.

The English Consul had persuaded Salnave to retire, and he sought shelter on the frontier, endeavouring to make his escape to Dominica; but he was captured by that high-toned patriot Cabral, January 11, 1870, who, surrendering him to Saget, received, it is said, $5000 in gold.

Meanwhile hundreds of people had sought the protection of Mr Bassett, the American minister, who occupied a country-house some two miles out of the city; and at one time there were over a thousand persons, men, women, and children, on his ground, being fed at his own expense, and though demands were made by the new authorities for the lives of these poor people, Mr Bassett declared, at immense risk to himself, that on the score of humanity his flag covered them all, and not a hair of their heads should be touched. All honour to him! for his efforts were successful in saving thousands of lives, though he himself was shot at on the public streets.

When Salnave was brought into town, a prisoner, and wounded in the left hand, he was escorted by some two thousand soldiers to the court-house, and there tried by a military court, of which General Lorquet was president, on the charges of cruelty and bloodshed since the time of Geffrard, firing the town, and treason.

His trial lasted three hours, and he was pronounced guilty, sentenced to death, and twenty minutes after taken to the steps of his own ruined palace, and there shot to death.

On the 29th May 1870, the present incumbent, Nissage Saget, was named (it cannot be said elected) President for four years, and still remains at the head of this free and orderly republic of Hayti, whose citizens have reached, "at the price of the blood of their forefathers, that level for which God has created them, men equal to all men in any part of the world." God help the world if this were so!

The reader looking over this chapter will perhaps think I have exaggerated these events of Haytian history. I wish I could say I had; but, on the contrary, I have been so astounded at the records written by Haytians themselves, that I have endeavoured to soften the details I found there, lest I should be accused of this.

But is Hayti to-day any different, and does it promise any better future? Alas! no; that is indeed a blank.

What is this experiment of "self-government," so described by some over-zealous or badly-informed people? Do they not know that at present there exists in Hayti another of those military despotisms for which the island is famous; that passes are required by the country people to come to town; that the only police are soldiers; and that not a year goes by unaccompanied by revolution and bloodshed?

Do they not know that there are no general means of education, or of communication, except by roads ordinarily fit only for animals, most of which even were originally made in the time of the French; that bridges going to decay are not repaired; that there is no general system of agriculture, and absolutely no manufacturing of any kind; that positively there is no freedom of opinion of any kind, and that neither foreigner nor native dare express their honest views, if they are not in accord with the Government? Do they know that this Government is bankrupt, its coin depreciated to four hundred dollars of paper to one in silver; while France threatens it for a settlement of its claims, and Prussia has been forced within three months past to forcibly seize Haytian war-vessels in settlement of her claims, only too glad, doubtless, to strengthen her hold upon an island whose principal trade she monopolises, whose merchants are principally composed of her citizens?

Do they not know that the men of the island exist upon the industry of the women, who are really the only labourers; and that, furthermore, at least two-thirds of the population do not speak any language recognised by the civilised world; that there is not a town on the island not remaining in ruins more or less caused by their revolutions?

Again, do they not know that, with acres and acres of splendid sugar-cane, there is hardly a steam-mill; that, with a soil especially adapted by nature for coffee-raising, there cannot be said to be a dozen coffee estates in the island, and that even the coffee, which, left thus in its wild state, grows in such abundance that it cannot all be harvested, is in the marts of commerce valued as an inferior article, not from any demerit of its own, but from the fact that the people are too lazy to clean and prepare it properly for market?

I could here quote many paragraphs from Haytian writers themselves showing how conscious they are of their own shortcomings, but space does not permit me; yet I cannot refrain from quoting a few passages from the works of their most celebrated historian (Ardouin), who says: "In general the people of Hayti are capable of industry; a thousand means besides those of agriculture are offered to them to arrive at a state of great prosperity, but they do not avail themselves of them. In the towns, where there is a surplus of inhabitants, there is no lack of labour, but few of the workmen acquit themselves well in their tasks. A great part remain idle, and indifferent to the happiness that depends upon them; they like better to vegetate than live honestly by labour. The youth of the country give themselves up to foolishness and frivolity, and to that idleness which is the mother of all vice. The crime most frequently committed is theft, and the greatest number of the criminals are the young."

"Another consideration comes from the natural union of the men with the women without any tie of marriage, and the number of children by one father having different mothers, creating irregular and irresponsible families and ties."

Quoting from a late article in one of their papers (*La Gazette du Peuple*, April 6, 1871), the editor says: "For sixty-eight years, from which dates our existence, what have we done? Nothing, or almost nothing. All our constitutions are defective, all our laws are incomplete; our custom-houses are badly administered, our navy is detestable, our finances are rotten to the base; our police is badly organised, our army is in a pitiable state; the legislative power is not understood, and never will be; the primary elections are neglected, and our people feel not their importance; almost all our public edifices are in ruins; the public instruction is almost entirely abandoned."

Yet, not satisfied with her own position and the regulation and improvement of her own people and affairs, Hayti presumes to interfere with her neighbour, Dominica, furnishing the disturbers of its peace with assistance, in order to create an impression that the people of that part do not want to join the American Union.

God forbid, that the annexation of this part of the island should be thought of by us for one moment, even though Dominica becomes one of our States; for the people of that part, humble as they are, are years ahead of the mass of the Haytians, and it will take years of missionary enterprise and instruction to prepare them for the blessings of civil liberty as enjoyed by us.

Perhaps to-day no nobler enterprise could be undertaken by the United States than the annexing, settling, and improving St Domingo, in order that, in time, the influence of its new civilisation might, by example and its spreading influence, develop among its dusky neighbours a desire to share in the blessings and advantages which it is the boast of Americans that American institutions bring.

It is this fear, I truly believe, with which the authorities of Hayti regard Dominican annexation to the United States, for they know well enough that their safety and control exist only so long as the masses of the people remain sunk in ignorance and sloth.

It was during these negotiations Hayti became alarmed, as she always has done at any effort made by a foreign power to get control in the island; and she assists with arms, men, and munitions the rebel Cabral, who is so conscious himself of his position that he even entitles a newspaper (purporting to be his official organ, but which is printed by Haytians at Port-au-Prince) *Revolutionary Bulletin;* and Luperon, who is simply a robber chief, was maintained likewise; and so patent to the whole world was this aid rendered by the Haytian authorities, that the records of the United States Consulate at Cape Haytien bear the copies of the protest of the energetic Consul at that place (a coloured man) against this improper and illegal action towards the United States.

But perhaps the best illustration of the absence of true wisdom and statesmanship in the government of Hayti is its treatment of the outside world, an example of which is the following, from the report of the United States Commissioners, three gentlemen eminent for their learning, statesmanship, and philanthropy.

HAYTI.

The Commissioners, of course, felt a deep interest in the experiment of self-government which the blacks are trying in Hayti. They certainly wished it all success.

They could not understand how any new and close relations between St Domingo and the United States could affect that experiment otherwise than favourably. They felt that it would be unjust to our Government to suppose that it contemplated any action injurious to it. They had too much faith in the virtue of our institutions to doubt that the form established of similar institutions in a neighbouring land must act favourably upon republicanism and progress in Hayti. The only force to be exerted would be a moral one, the force of example. They knew of no valid claim which Hayti had against St Domingo, nor of any rights or interests which could be endangered by the extension of our institutions over the western end of the island. Nevertheless, they desired to give to the Government, and to intelligent citizens, an opportunity of stating their views.

Moreover, they desired, in the most friendly spirit, to make the same observations and study of Hayti and its inhabitants as they had made of the Dominican Republic. They intimated to the President and his Council their dispositions and desires. They stated even that they should be glad to be put in the way of ascertaining what were the claims of Hayti upon St Domingo, and what were the views and wishes of the Haytian people with respect to any changes that might be brought about in the neighbouring republic. But they received no encouragement to pursue their inquiries. They asked verbally, and through our minister in writing, for permission to explore the interior of the island, but this was met in a spirit equivalent to a refusal.

They contented themselves, therefore, with taking such testimony, and gathering such information upon matters bearing upon the question of annexation, as they could without giving offence. In reviewing the whole field of their investigations, looking to the interests of both divisions of the island, they are firmly persuaded that the annexation of St Domingo to the United States would be hardly less beneficial to the Haytian than to the Dominican people. This benefit would arise first from the example which would doubtless be afforded of a well-regulated, orderly, and prosperous State, the great need of that part of the world, and which it has as yet never seen ; a second and more direct benefit would arise from the equitable establishment of a boundary line between the French-speaking and the Spanish-speaking nations upon that island, and its guarantee by a strong power.

This would end the exhausting border warfare which has been one of the greatest curses of Hayti as well as St Domingo, and would enable both to devote their energies thenceforward to the education of their people and the development of their resources.

Respectfully submitted,

B. F. WADE,
ANDREW D. WHITE,
S. G. HOWE.

To the President of the United States.

Naturally such a state of affairs as herein described must have its effect upon the character of its people, and thus the lower order of Haytians are utterly ignorant and illiterate. "They are improvident and thoughtless of the future, from a consciousness that their lands are held by a tenure often depending on the whim of an officer, and are, moreover, liable to the devastations of contending armies. They attend not to the increase of planting. The pruning-knife seldom checks the rank luxuriance of the coffee-tree, or the hoe extirpate the choking weeds. The first years of Haytian independence gave a gleam of prosperity, for the country was in that secondary stage of forwardness in which the French left it, and from which it has since gradually declined."

Of the better class and the leaders, the following from a prominent Haytian, who was very frank with me, gives this expression of his views and experience: "The greatest ambition of a Haytian is military glory; to become a general is the very pinnacle of his hopes, and to attain this, anything will be sacrificed. If the country be at peace, and he see no chance in this way to get in, he sets about getting up a revolution; this once attained, and successful, the victors take the spoils, until they, in their turn, have to give place to other successful ones. Meanwhile the country goes to ruin; the blacks do not work, because lazy and indifferent; the peaceable better classes remain as quiet as they are allowed to be, while a small party in power holds despotic control over the lives, hopes, and fortunes of the others, without doing anything to better either the country or its people. Consequently most of the business of the country is done by foreign traders, who, under the protection afforded by their flags, transact business, taking care, in return for the risks they run, to exact exorbitant profits wherever they can; even with this they have their privileges restricted, and, as a general thing, the Government is largely in their debt."

No wonder that Candler, the champion of the black race, who visited the island in 1840, and distributed books and tracts, was compelled, even in the then more favourable condition of the island, to say, "What a mournful exhibition is thus presented to us of the morals of Hayti! How earnestly must the friends of freedom and of good order in civil society desire amelioration in the institutions of the country!"

What would he now say?

CHAPTER XXIII.

> "Oh! whence, as wafted from Elysium—whence
> These perfumes, strangers to the raptured sense;
> These boughs of gold, and fruits of heavenly hue,
> Tinging with vermeil light the billows blue?"

COASTING THE ISLAND—*Passengers and Tropical Mode of Travel—Coast Scenery—Port de Paix—Tortuga Island—St Nicholas Mole—Bay of Port-au-Prince—The Town—Odd Appearance—Lack of Hotels—Suburbs of Port-au-Prince—Pretty Country-houses—Old French Places—La Coupe—Road-making—Haytian Soldiers—Feeling about Annexation—Noble Conduct of he United States Minister—Aiding the Dominican Revolutionists—Visit to the Interior—Sugar Plantations—Lake Azuey—A Swim in lieu of a Dinner—A Long Ride in Bad Weather—Departure—Gonaives.*

ON the morning of April 3, we went on board of the steamer, having bid good-bye to our good friends of the Cape, and found a large number of passengers already congregated on the deck, the majority of them being Haytians of various shades of colour. These people were mostly members of the Senate and House on their way to Port-au-Prince, where these bodies were just going into session. They seemed to be a well-behaved, polite set of people, several of the legislators being quite young men, while one of the senators was a venerable, corpulent negro.

The *Port-au-Prince* was a moderate-sized steamer, with accommodations for a sea-voyage of only about twenty passengers, but she had probably twice that number now.

But as the voyage around the island is a very smooth and pleasant one, the Haytians lived and slept on deck under the awning; in fact, I found it more agreeable myself to swing my hammock aft, and rest in that, than go below in the warm cabin.

Rather an odd sight, though, to see passengers on a steamer content themselves with spreading their mattresses and blankets upon the deck, and thus get their night's rest—men, women, and children being huddled together promiscuously.

The steamer is owned by a New York firm, and came out direct from that place to Cape Haytian, consigned to the American house of Murray, Price, & Co. The company has a subsidy of $40,000 per year from the Haytian Government, which I believe remains unpaid for two years past, for which subsidy the steamer carries a mail once a month, and also, free, the members of the Government and their families between the capital and the Cape.

The anchor is up, and off we go from this beautiful bay; but keeping close in shore we have the opportunity of seeing the lovely scenery of the Haytian coast; and nothing can be more charming than thus voyaging in these tropic seas amid such beautiful scenes, where, as in the present case, our company was pleasant, the ship agreeable, and its officers attentive.

I was much interested with the talk I had with the Haytians about themselves and their Government, and they all expressed much sympathy in the rude treatment I had received at the hands of the authorities, the Citadel story seeming to be familiar to them, and of which they professed to speak as a great outrage. They may, or may not, have been sincere, but at all events they heard some candid opinions from me.

These members expected a warm time in the Assembly with Saget, the President of the republic, as there was a dead lock between them on various questions, and one or the other would have to yield, else there would ensue still another of the many revolutions which are periodical on this island.

The greatest trouble affecting the present Government is to know how to run its finances, as the paper money now out has little or no value, and in fact there is nothing of value in the republic upon which to base credit, unless the customs are hypothecated. The greatest revenue is obtained from the export duty on coffee, which amounts to an enormous sum, but which kills the industry of the country, making the coffee so high to export to foreign markets that millions of pounds are left unpicked on the trees each year.

This I can readily believe, for as we sailed along the coast we did not see any signs of a thickly-settled country or of a general agriculture. Only occasionally we saw clearings on the hill-side that marked the residence of some settler; yet the country is beautiful in the extreme, and, as the Haytians on board told me, splendid coffee land.

Now we are entering a noble canal or passage formed by the island of Tortuga and the mainland, and upon the shore of the latter is spread out before us the little town of Port de Paix, presenting a pleasing aspect from the sea. It is a small place, with tolerably well-built houses of stone, a large church, and a public fountain; but the site of the town is unhealthy from the low, marshy nature of the land in the vicinity; but the country about it is said to be fertile in coffee, with forests of many valuable woods.

Its historic interest is centred in the fact that Columbus landed here on his first voyage, naming the place Valparayso, or Valley of Delight; it was also the dwelling-place of one of the ancient caciques; and the French, being driven from the island of Tortuga opposite, settled here, and gave it the present name of Peaceful Port.

Tortuga (or Turtle) Island, which forms the other shore

of this channel, is about nine leagues long and some two miles in its greatest width, and is apparently uninhabited and uncultivated, but the woods upon it are said to be very valuable. This island is noteworthy as being the original home of the famous "buccaneers," freebooters, or filibusters of the New World.

Haytian Coast.

Leaving Port de Paix, the character of the shore seems to change very much, and becomes more wild and barren, with occasional hills of the coffee, and late in the afternoon we came to the superb harbour and bay of Mole St Nicolas. This is the first place in the whole island where Europeans landed, Columbus entering the bay on the 6th of December 1492, and naming it St Nicolas in honour of the patron saint of that day. He gave it the name afterwards of Mole from its shape.

This place, called the Gibraltar of the New World, remained almost unsettled until 1764, but it was successively settled by French, Germans, and English, and at different times immense sums of money have been spent on its forts and walls, which, in the numerous attacks and revolutions from which it has suffered, have become in a great degree ruined and dismantled—Cristophe having ordered all the principal forts to be destroyed. The bay itself makes a fine picture from the sea, and ships of the largest size can ride out gales with perfect safety. The soil here is arid and poor, and produces in perfection only the grape and the fig. But the climate is said to be extremely healthy.

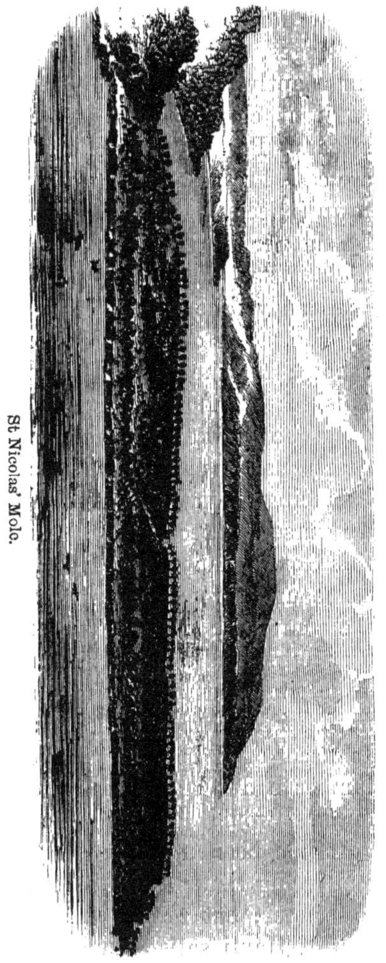

St Nicolas' Mole.

This port or bay is esteemed to be as valuable and commanding a place in the west of the island as Samana Bay is on the east, commanding as it does the channel between Hayti and Cuba, and probably, under any strong and stable Government, would become an important and strong naval rendezvous in these waters.

From this point the shores become very barren and

unattractive, were it not that nature assumes such strange shapes in the volcanic-looking rocks of the shore, or the terrace tablelands that look like artificial glacis. Then follows a forbidding-looking coast, hardly shrub or sign of vegetation to be seen; but the rocks rise up in level plains or ledges, that assume the form which entitles them to the name aptly bestowed upon them, "The Platforms."

Night closes on us as we enter the bay in which is situated Port-au-Prince, and which at daybreak all hands are called to see. A magnificent harbour and a queer old town indeed, are our first impressions, not much changed by further investigations; there also we find at anchor a little fleet of Haytian men-of-war.

A lively time we had of it, as we got into the dock, with the chattering of these coloured people, both on board and ashore; but the sight of the only wharf in the port nearly finished me; for, utterly broken and decayed, it was the only one allowed by the Government, and upon it were nearly naked negroes with sacks of coffee on their heads, balancing themselves on the loose planks, an exploit which we ourselves became quite familiar with. To show how this Government is conducted, this wharf has been supposed to be under repair by a friend for some time, who took the contract from the Government with the understanding that he might import the lumber for it duty free; at the same time the authorities also passed an ordinance that no other lumber should be landed within the city limits. It need only be said that, since that time, if all the lumber had been put upon the wharf that was imported for it, it would be as big as a mountain.

It had been my intention, on reaching Port-au-Prince, and seeing that part of the island, to have gone overland to Jacmel; but the experience of what I had seen of this part of Hayti satisfied me that I should not be repaid for my trouble.

As the steamer, owing to the intervention of the Holy

Week, would be detained in port some ten days or two weeks, I was only too glad to make my arrangements to proceed to the United States in her.

There being no hotel of any respectable kind in the town, I was glad to accept the kind offers of hospitality made to me by our minister and others.

Mr Bassett, the United States minister, lives most delightfully, about a mile out of town, on a hill overlooking the town and bay, affording a superb view in every direc-

United States Minister's House.

tion, while the place is charming in its luxuriant vegetation, having also a marble bath large enough for swimming, with water fresh and cold from the mountain stream.

This dwelling was originally built in 1849 for one of the many rulers of Hayti, the Emperor Soulouque; and though making no pretension to elegance, is a house perfectly adapted to a climate where one passes most of the time out of doors or on piazzas, of which this has an ample supply; and here, amid flowers, or shaded from the sun by awnings conveniently lowered on the porticoes, one escapes entirely the heats and odours of the town below, while favoured by ever pure and fresh breezes from the neighbouring mountains.

Near to Mr Bassett's are several other beautiful places, with terraced gardens, roomy and stone-built dwellings, and superb stone swimming-baths, in which the ladies of the families swim as well as the men. Most of these places were originally owned by the old French planters, and from them can be obtained an idea of the luxurious manner in which, during the palmy days of Hayti, the French planters lived.

I was particularly glad to meet these places, as showing me what a refined, energetic, and intelligent people could make for themselves in the way of beautiful homes and plantations in the St Domingo portion of the island, under a strong and stable government.

Some of my most delightful hours were spent enjoying the kind hospitality of Mr Bassett and his lady, sharing with them some delightful rides on horseback, both to the town as well as the neighbouring country. One ride of an evening I remember with particular pleasure, up the fine mountain road to La Coupe, a beautiful village at the top of the hill. The road all the way up was apparently dug out of the mountain side, solidly constructed like a turnpike, and afforded us most superb views of a lovely valley between the mountain ranges, and also of the town and bay of Port-au-Prince.

This was the only real attempt at a road in the whole of St Domingo or Hayti that I saw; but it was enough to show that no great difficulty is to be encountered in opening the whole island to good means of communication and travel.

Having arrived during Holy Week, we found business pretty much at a stand still, Holy Thursday being kept as

PORT-AU-PRINCE.

a close holiday by the people and authorities. I was much amused, while in the cabin of our steamer, by a visit paid by a coloured gentleman, who said he was the officer of the guard at the wharf, to the captain of the ship. This official stated he waited on him, the captain, to tell him that he must not permit any one to work on that day, as it was a holy day, and the authorities did not allow it. The captain told me to say that he had permission from the authorities, and that, in fact, work never ceased on board ship. My acting as interpreter engaged me in quite a long and amusing theological discussion with this august official, the disputed points of which were finally settled by our "taking a drink" together, which he seemed nothing loth to do.

Mr Hall, an American, who has served in our navy, being chief of artillery on board the Haytian man-of-war *Terror*, I gladly accepted his invitation to go on board of her, and a highly interesting visit I had. She is commanded by a Frenchman formerly in the French merchant service, and has several white officers, while her engineer and crew are all black. I was pleased most with the beautiful order in which Mr Hall had his batteries, the pieces of which were principally 10-inch Parrott guns, with one or two 11-inch Dahlgrens. The vessel was quite a large one, and seemed in excellent order, barring the crew, who, I thought, were rather ragged and dirty, which can be accounted for from the fact that only one suit of clothes is issued to them at a time by the Government.

Port-au-Prince, the capital of the republic of Hayti, is certainly an interesting town for a few days to the stranger, not alone from its being the principal town in the Island of Hayti, and curious in its architecture and appearance, but also from its historical associations.

The town was permanently established as far back as 1749, the convenience of its location to all the other points in the island, as well as its proximity to the most fertile plain of the island, the Cul-de-sac, being the principal reason of its present location.

Different portions of it were originally built at different times, but, like all the other towns of importance in Hayti, its original character has been very much changed by the succession of revolutionary fires and earthquakes to which, since the period of its settlement, it has been subjected.

The ground upon which it is situated has a rather abrupt descent from the hills around down to the edge of the sea. The streets, which are wide and of good width, run at right angles to this bay front, being crossed at regular intervals by others, which thus gives the town the appearance of being laid out with great regularity, for while on board ship in the harbour one can see these principal streets extending back up the hill some distance, except to the south, where the plain terminates at the foot of the range of mountains.

A Street in Port-au-Prince.

Directly in front of the town are several small islands, which tradition says gave their name to the town, from the fact that they were known as the Prince Islands, while far out in the bay are seen the hazy hills of the Isle of Gonave, which, with the point of land, Cape St Nicolas, really forms the harbour of Port-au-Prince.

This Isle of Gonave is said to be about forty miles long by nine wide, with valuable woods growing upon it, and a climate remarkably healthy, but it is to-day unsettled; its ancient name, familiar to Irving's readers, was Guanabo or Guanabano.

Bay of Port-au-Prince from the House of the United States Minister.

Port-au-Prince is reputed to be a very unhealthy place at times, much fever, both yellow and native, prevailing there; and if the theory of the prevalence of the mangrove-trees be true, it is easily accounted for, the shores and islands being covered with these breeders of pestilence.

Historians tell us that at one time the town possessed handsome, solid structures, including public buildings, fountains, churches, &c.; but if so, they have almost entirely disappeared, or left ruined walls to mark where they might have been, for to-day even the houses of the Assembly are of wood of most ordinary construction, while the

President's palace itself is only mediocre as an ordinary building. The ruins of the palace of Salnave are still extant, and show that they may have been a very majestic series of buildings, quite imposing in their architecture, while occasional fountains, the worse for age and neglect, show, in different parts of the city, attempts in ancient days to beautify the place.

There is yet, however, in existence an immense stone basin in the upper part of the city, originally built and still used for the purpose of bathing the horses of the town's-people, a degree of luxury of which no other city I know can boast.

To-day the lower part of the city has a good many fine warehouses, principally those of foreign merchants, who live on the second floors; but the great majority of the houses are built of wood, in the most nondescript, irregular styles of architecture. The market-places are mere open squares, and the church, though large, has nothing remarkable about it; but the streets, lined with their odd stores and contents, void of sidewalks, and filled constantly with people, present an odd and novel appearance.

There seem to be no sanitary rules whatever, and the only cleansing of which I heard was that of the city streets by the heavy rains and showers. In fact, quite in the city, and upon the open square, dead animals are taken and left to die and rot without hindrance from any one.

It being the Holy Week, with a great deal of show and ceremony going on, I had an opportunity of seeing a good many interesting sights, the military displays and Government shows being the principal ones.

The President and his staff made a great display in their brilliant uniforms, the former particularly, who, though a man over fifty years of age, was gorgeous in diamonds, feathers, and gold lace.

My admiration (?) for the soldiers was mingled with pity on account of the nature of their clothing, which, however brilliant in high-coloured braids and flannel ornament, must be awful hot for them in this climate, consisting as it does of our old army clothing. The people are, I understand, a little "down" on the Americans on this subject, it appearing that their uniforms were a lot sold at auction at Baton Rouge, at one of our Government army sales, purchased by a government officer in New York for about $6, and sold at $26 to the Haytian Government. This uniform is sarcastically called the Van Bockkelen uniform in Port-au-Prince.

Of course, the population are principally blacks, while the mulatto class constitute the principal aristocracy, to which are added the white French creoles, as also many of the foreign merchants, and at a social gathering all these will be seen in various proportions according to circumstances.

As many of the native coloured population have been educated in France, there are found a good many highly-cultured men, extremely courteous and gentle in their manners; and of some of the younger men, only a few removes from white, many may be said to be quite elegant in their dress and manners. Among the creole population one meets with extremely lively and agreeable women, many of whom are married to foreigners.

The old distinction of colour, however, exists even here, I am told; for the mulattoes pride themselves on being a different people from the blacks, while the latter sneer at the former as being neither white nor black.

I found a good many English-speaking people, and amongst them some coloured people who settled here years ago, established themselves in business, and are now doing well. I had many conversations with them, among whom there seems to exist a great difference of opinion about some things. For instance, some say annexation is the only salvation for the island; others say it would not do at all; and one individual, speaking of the annexation of St Domingo, said, "The time has not come yet for it."

"Why not?" I asked.

"Because the day that that takes place there won't be a white man left alive in the island." (? ! ! !)

Mr Bassett, our minister, I find, has made a great many friends for himself by the straightforward, manly course he pursues, and though naturally he does not please every one, yet he is extremely popular with the majority. Certainly, if Mr Washburne received so much praise for his course at Paris, what ought to be said of Mr Bassett's course here during the Salnave troubles, when nearly 3000 people sought the protection of our flag at his office and house, and where he, on the score of humanity, refused to allow a single person to be harmed by the excited revolutionists thirsting for their blood?

Standing alone at that time in his position, shot at in the public streets, and without the presence of a single American man-of-war to sustain him, he fed and cared for those people at his own expense, and though his course was sustained by the authorities at home, I am sorry to say the money he then spent has never yet been refunded—a nice encouragement for an official to assume such noble responsibility!

I picked up a great deal of curious information about the St Domingo business while I was in Port-au-Prince. I found the locality from which emanate all the proclamations of Cabral, and was permitted to take from the press itself, where it was being printed, copies of the paper, *The Dominican Flag*, or *Revolutionary Bulletin*, which purports to be printed in San Juan in Dominican territory, but which is made up here, as well in its accounts of imaginary battles and victories, as its truthful (?) sentiments of the "Dominicans."

The printer of this sheet laughingly told me he always took care to get his money for the printing and work; and that was the end of his business. I also had the pleasure of meeting the distinguished author of "Cabral's

Protest" to the Commissioners, who, on my quizzing him about it, laughingly replied, "Well, Cabral signed it, even if I did write it." This same party confessed to me that though it was his business to write against annexation, he was perfectly aware the people of St Domingo were unanimous in favour of it.

I was a little puzzled for a day or two to know how to get back into the country, as I was quietly informed no permission would be granted me, if asked for, by the authorities. As I had, however, a passport regularly viséd by government authority, I determined to take my chances and "go it alone." This was more easy for me to do from the fact that I had a letter to an American merchant here who owns a large sugar estate some distance back in the interior, and, as he was at his place, made my arrangements to pay him a visit.

Having found a horse to carry me and my traps, and having very luckily found a guide in the person of an engineer, who was going to the very place of my destination to repair some of the sugar-mill machinery, I started out of the northern gate of Port-au-Prince for the sugar place of La Selle, in the grand plain, of the Cul-de-sac, famous in all time for its splendid agricultural qualities.

Our road was a broad, level one, leading through an immense plain, the sides of which were bounded by mountains clad in verdure, and about which were heavy clouds rolling before us that promised rain.

This road, like all I have thus far seen in Hayti, was a perfectly good one, capable of being travelled in good weather by vehicles of every kind, though, with the exception of an ox-cart we occasionally met, all the travelling was on mule or horse back. The sides of the road were almost universally lined by the hedges of logwood, that had grown to such an extent as to be now a valuable article of export, while the coffee-tree was, as usual, seen here and there growing almost wild. The houses were of the most ordinary kind, constructed of the small withes or planks of the narrow woods of the country, and principally thatched roofs.

Countrywoman and "Piccaninny."

It being market day, we found the road filled with the country people on the way to town, some on muleback, some on foot, but not a cart of any kind did we meet. Most of those we met were women, some with immense straw hats on, others with baskets on their heads, and yet, again, some with nothing but a "piccaninny" stowed away on their backs by a cotton cloth wrapped about the waist.

All of the people, especially the women, were cheerful, and answered with a smile our "Bon jour, ma chère," often having a reply to offer. In fact, throughout my visit to Hayti, I was satisfied that the majority of the people are quiet, docile, and peaceful, and that it is only owing to their chiefs and party leaders that the men are so brutish, in many cases made so by their vagabond life as soldiers.

Ruined walls, houses, gateways, ay, even the remains of a bridge, met us at various distances out, marking the era of a past civilisation, which, alas! seems now to be utterly extinct; while the agriculture that had once made this island to blossom as a garden, with its superb coffee places and sugar estates, has now sunk into nothing; for the traveller beholds naught but the plantain patch, the wild coffee-field, or the small field of sugar-cane, whose product is principally used to make the drink, rum, or tafia, that has as much to do, as anything else, after the miserable Government, with the degradation of the people. After some hours of riding we came upon a tract of country in which we see "sugar estates" that have more claim to the name, for the houses and mills are larger and more numerous, and the extent of cane cultivated greater; but even of these the product is principally rum and tafia.

We found we had plenty of streams to cross, and farther on we discovered the rain-storm had been travelling ahead of us, tne roads being now heavy with mud and water, and as the soil is the same rich clay or loam that prevails in similar places in Dominica, we were not sorry, after a fatiguing ride of some fifteen miles, to find ourselves at our destination, just as night overtook us.

My letter presented, we were soon made welcome, and bestowed in comfortable quarters, our host entertaining us with his experiences of sugar-cane growing; and as this is about the only regularly organised place in the island, his remarks will give a more than flattering idea of labour and agriculture on the island.

He has under cultivation a thousand acres of cane, which is growing all the year round, for as fast as cut down it renews itself from the same stalk, no attention being paid to the weeding, hoeing, or care of the cane, as is done in Cuba.

His labourers are all blacks, all living on the place or in the vicinity, and his contracts are made with about thirty-five heads of families to do the necessary work, the average wages per hand being about twelve cents per day, and this he esteems expensive labour for the quality furnished.

He has little or no strong control over this labour, being compelled to humour the hands in great degree in their holidays, fandangos, and church celebrations. He has steam-engines, distilleries, and valuable apparatus, under charge of a coloured engineer, to whom he pays $12 per month, the whole place being in charge of an administrator, who receives a salary or interest.

Contrary to every other sugar-producing country, the mills stop every day; and when I ask if this is as profitable as running the mills night and day during the regular season, the reply is, "If I attempted such a thing my plantation would be burned by the people."

Although some $50,000 have been invested in the place, it yields, owing to the poor labour and the irregular system of agriculture, a rather slim return, and this is only in rum and tafia, little or no sugar being produced. Many of the neighbouring plantations that have no mills send their cane to this one to be ground.

A schoolhouse has been established on the place, and maintained at private expense, it being open to all the children of the neighbourhood; but such is the condition of the people, and the lack of interest they take in bettering themselves, that not over fifteen pupils attend the school.

In the morning early my host bade me good-bye, as he returned to Port-au-Prince, while I, with a guide, undertook a day's journey and return, to the celebrated Lake of Saumatre, which lies equally between Dominica and Hayti, some twenty miles from my stopping-place. The French name this lake from its bitter-tasted waters, and the Spaniards bestow upon it the name of Azuey, the line of demarcation between the two nationalities cutting it in two nearly equal parts lengthwise; and the waters are said to have the curious peculiarity of ebbing and flowing like the tides of the sea.

However, bright and early we started on our long and tedious journey, my guide being a coloured man from Philadelphia, formerly a servant in a family there, but for many years domesticated in Hayti, and by name Jerry.

Jerry was a bright, smart fellow, fond of study, and intelligent in the affairs and condition of the Haytians, and I was much the gainer in information from the day he spent with me; and as he not only speaks English but creole perfectly, he was of great service.

Our road still lay through a flat and uninteresting country, the soil of a sort of white clay in many parts, in others of dark rich loam, it being all well watered and wooded, the agriculture being limited to the cane, plantain, and wild coffee. The country was only sparsely settled by negroes living in the rudest of huts, with no attempts at gardens or improvements of any kind.

At some of the little settlements through which we rode we found parties of the men gathered fighting cocks, while at others the sound of the tum-tum or banjo gave notice of a fandango that was taking place.

In another place, as we drew near the frontier, in passing a large house with a number of men seated or standing about it, we were halted and directed to dismount, upon doing which we found it was the headquarters of the commandant, and a guardhouse near the frontier, and thus I expected to have had some trouble, as being an American, and having no authority to travel, I was liable to be interfered with.

I don't know how Jerry fixed it, but I do know the officer was very polite, inviting us to take a little tafia with him, and, very glad not to be stopped on my journey, I accepted his apologies with great pleasure.

Another hour's ride brought us, through woods and bottom-lands, to our first view of the lake, but both our horses and ourselves being in need of rest, we stopped at a small canuco in search of food and rest. Luckily for me, we had taken the precaution to bring a few crackers with us, otherwise we should have fared badly, for not a thing could we buy. Eggs they had none; fish, although the lake was full, they did not catch; oranges they did not grow; and thus, here in a land that ought positively to flow with milk and honey, it is impossible to get a mouthful of any wholesome Christian food.

I asked Jerry how these people lived, both here and on

"Uncles and Mammies."

the plantations, and he assured me the only food eaten by them—men, women, and children—was ordinarily a sweet potato or plantain, boiled or roasted, with a drink of tafia-rum, and that with this they constantly eat the sugar-cane. As a very great luxury they might very rarely eat a piece of salt mackerel or codfish, and if they happened to go to town, a small roll of bread would be purchased as a great luxury.

At different times there have been a number of American negroes brought out and located on the island, but in most cases bad faith was kept with them. In the case of those who came out with Redpath, many of them were deceived, and forced to work two days in the week for Government in order to contribute to the money for their passage out. Some of these old people quite amused me with their questions about "home," and many of them reminded me of the "uncles" and "mammies" of the Southern States.

These were a very different class from those I had met in Port-au-Prince, some of whom, quite intelligent people otherwise, carried away by their position as successful merchants, spoke rather contemptuously of their less favoured brethren.

One of the most singular things I observed was that here, on this side the frontier, with identically the same soil and climate as that in Dominica, tobacco was not raised, and was considered a great and rare luxury, while just on the other side the Dominicans raised abundance. So also with cattle; while there there was abundance, here there was none to be seen, except maybe a sheep or two, or perhaps a goat.

While our horses were feeding I endeavoured to get a siesta upon a palm-leaf mat that had been spread upon the ground for me. Vain hope! for in the branches of the cocoanut-trees in whose shade I was lying were some bee-hives, their occupants buzzing about; over and under me the fleas and mosquitoes fought as to which should have me in possession, while an occasional ray of the hot sun warmed me up into a state of tropical frenzy, until, desperate with my inflictions, I gave the order to saddle up, and Jerry and I were soon, after a rough ride of a mile, at the border of the beautiful lake of Azuey, where, in old times, sugar places and French civilisation made this a garden, now, alas! wild and uncultivated, even unmarked by such a sign as would show what had been, were it not for the piles of ruined walls and stones that marked a garden wall.

The lake is surrounded by steep hills, except on the southern side, where is a small plain, filled in days gone by with beautiful sugar places.

The water is clear as crystal, and looked very tempting to us after our long journey and unsuccessful attempt at refreshments. We hitched our horses in the woods, and going to the only favourable spot on the shore, found a small party of coloured females washing clothes.

I remarked, "It was a nice place to bathe."

"Oh! yes," they said, "very nice."

I suggested that we had some idea of going in.

They thought we would like it.

I began to "peel," apologising for disturbing them, which I did not succeed in doing, as they said, "Oh! don't mind us"—and Jerry laughingly exclaimed, "Oh! you needn't be so modest; they ain't afraid, if you are not."

Ah! *cosa d'Haiti!* But the water was good and invigorating, combining as it did all the elements of hot and cold baths—for there were springs of both all in a very small space. It may be for this reason I could not discover any brackish taste in the water, for which the lake is celebrated; but at the end of the lake, where there are some salt mines, this peculiarity may exist in a more marked degree.

The lake is a very pretty one, looking exactly like some of our Hudson River or Lake George scenery. It is about fifteen miles long and about eight miles wide in the widest part, being capable of steamboat navigation, it is said.

After we came out we were pleasantly informed there were crocodiles there, too, and I have to thank them for the respect they manifested to the person of the first American who had ever bathed there.

Heavy clouds warned us of an approaching storm, which finally broke upon the other side of the lake, and so we were soon in the saddle, hoping to outride the rain, which we succeeded in doing for an hour or two.

But finally it came upon us—a pouring, heavy rain, that came straight down, leaving no hope of keeping dry even with umbrella and poncho.

But why describe that long and weary ride home—the mud and mire, the water above and below, the swollen streams, the tired horses and riders, and the long, weary hours before we reached our night's destination, or the long and uninteresting journey over the same road next morning to Port-au-Prince? Suffice it to say that, with that last journey and the advent of the rainy season, I concluded that, having visited the most favoured parts, I had seen enough of the interior of Hayti, and glad I was to get back to comfortable quarters and civilised food in Port-au-Prince.

Next day, going on board the steamer that was to return me to the States, I found her, with a full cargo of coffee and logwood, ready to sail, a number of passengers having also engaged passage in her to New York.

A lively time we had getting off, for among the passengers were the American Consul and his wife, who, after a residence of many years, were taking their departure for good, their leave-taking of the town and its people being marked by the assembling on the wharf and steamer of all the principal people, black, white, and coloured.

Then there was a young belle, too, whose friends, with the "sympathy" peculiar to these people, gathered to take a last farewell; and as most of those were handsome young people of the feminine order, there were some of us quite sorry not to have such charming friends to whom to say good-bye in Haytian fashion (*i.e.*, kissing on both cheeks).

My farewell was of a different order, however; for as I

grasped the hand of a stalwart merchant, the last to go over the side, he said, "Remember me to H——; tell him Hayti hasn't changed for the better; that, bad as things were when he was here twenty years ago, they are to-day ten times worse." Alas! poor Hayti!

But now we are clear of the deck, tears are shed, handkerchiefs waved, and at last we are steaming over the beautiful bay to Gonaives, our last place to visit in Hayti. With placid sea and soft skies I find it more agreeable to swing my hammock on deck for the night than to go below in the cabin. Many of the passengers think as I do, and stretch themselves on deck, being protected from night dews by the awning; therefore we are all ready, when day breaks, to get the first glimpse of the little town of Gonaives, which, though situated in a beautiful bay, offers nothing very attractive in its landscape surroundings.

The anchor dropped, a party of us were soon ashore in the fresh early morning, being received at the landing by a German merchant, who acts as Consul for the United States.

Then we saunter through the great, wide, hot streets of the town, that looks as if it were originally intended to be a place ten times its size. We went into the large church filled with its dusky devotees; and while my devout companion says her morning prayers, I occupy myself in studying out the problem of the church architecture and decoration, and the authorship of some of the paintings upon the walls. Then a stroll through the market-place, with its country people dealing in small supplies; through the "Place," with its one tomb or monument to a defunct Colonel Somebody, and we have seen the entire town of Gonaives, and are ready to enjoy the hospitalities of the tasteful and comfortable mansion of the Consul, presiding over which is his charming wife.

Yet Gonaives is a place of some importance in the

commercial world, for here are shipped large quantities of the coffee of the island, of which that produced about Gonaives is said to be the very best. Cotton, too, is produced, and used to be shipped in large quantities, while, in the palmy days of Hayti, when there was an agricultural system, indigo in large quantities was an important product.

The town is situated on a flat, level plain, its name being the original Indian name, though the place was not really settled until about 1738.

The place is historic, as having been the port from which Toussaint L'Ouverture embarked in the *Heros* for France, never more to be actively heard of in the annals of the country; but here also was proclaimed the solemn Declaration of Independence that made the Haytians freemen; otherwise it is one of the most uninteresting places I have seen.

Again we are on board the ship, steering along the coast, which presents the same characteristics of rocky shore, verdure-clad hills, or curious tableland, forms that have entitled this part of the coast to the name of Platform; and as the shades of night are closing in, we see behind us the last point, as we head directly north, of the Mole St Nicolas; whereupon, with visions of the balmy days of a northern spring before us, we join heartily in the chorus ascending to those tropic skies, of—

"A wet sheet and a flowing sea,
And a health to the Homeward Bound!"

CHAPTER XXIV.

APPENDATORY.

> "Methinks I see my country rise,
> Her regal emblem now no longer a bird of prey,
> But spreading out her ample wing,
> A broad impartial covering,
> The weaker sheltered by the stronger."

GENERAL VIEW OF ST DOMINGO—*Some Reflections on its Future—Views of President Grant—Climate—Insects—Seasons—Lands—Emigrants—The Population and its Character—Finances—Concessions and Grants—Hints to Emigrants or Travellers—Dominican Manifestoes—General Statistics—Treaty for Fixing the Boundaries—Notes on the Mineral Products of the Island.*

IF the reader has accompanied me thus far, he will now have a good idea of the past history of St Domingo, as also its present condition.

If, in some of my descriptions of the people, I may have appeared more candid than perhaps good taste or courtesy would require, it has simply been that I might place distinctly before the world the actual condition to-day of this island and its people, and this with the sole view of benefiting them.

No one could be more astonished than was the author when, having carefully followed all the discussions in the

United States upon this subject, and having his mind filled with the denunciations of this island and its people (by political leaders for political purposes), he landed upon the shores of St Domingo, where, instead of finding war and bloodshed, troops and cannon, and a people controlled by mere force, he found instead everywhere the utmost peace and quietness.

Greater still was his astonishment when, reaching St Domingo city, the headquarters of the tyrant, the usurper, Baez, he found that person in peaceful occupation of the Presidential chair, or walking about like any other citizen, unattended or supported by the armed myrmidons that had been described as alone keeping him in place.

In order not to fatigue the reader, I have touched in my journeying very lightly on the sentiment of annexation to the United States among the people of St Domingo; but here I deem it a fitting place to testify to the almost universal wish of the people, high and low, to come into the American Union; and this testimony may be esteemed of greater weight when I say, that it was elicited, not only from the people in many a quiet talk, in dwellings and stores, in towns and villages, away from any official presence or influence, but also in the wilds and solitudes, where I heard but one cry, "Give us peace and safety, and good roads."

In the contest of politics against St Domingo annexation, some of our wisest and best men seem to have been led astray either by false information or through ignorance of the actual condition of affairs in that island, and some phases of this contest would appear ludicrous were not the results so serious.

Here, for instance, while a champion is wielding the weapon of defence in favour of the revolutionist Cabral, the latter comes forth and refuses to be defended in the following "official document," of which such fellows always seem to have a large supply, thus:—

GOD. *COUNTRY.* *LIBERTY.*

JOSE MARIA CABRAL, *General of Division of the National Armies, and Superior Chief of the Revolutionary Movement, &c.*

To the Honourable President of the Senate of the United States of America.

HONOURABLE PRESIDENT—The honourable Charles Sumner of Massachusetts, in his discourse upon the proposed annexation of the Island of St Domingo, pronounced in the Senate the 21st December 1870, says, with reference to my policy, "They have assured me that his policy (Cabral's) is to unite the two Governments of Hayti and Dominica, as they were before the revolution and war that lasted from 1846 to 1848 (?), terminating with the insecure independence of the Dominican part of the island."

The policy that the Senator Sumner attributes to me being that which neither my party nor I follow, I consider it my duty to protest, as I here do, against this part of the above discourse; and in doing this, I believe I have well interpreted the wishes of my associates, and fulfilled one of the sacred duties that have been imposed upon me as chief of a party. I have the honour, &c.

JOSE MARIA CABRAL.

NEYBA, *February* 18, 1871.

But this distinguished champion was not allowed to escape the wrath of the opponents of Cabral either; for the *Boletin Official* of St Domingo says, "Mr Sumner, the orator of the Senate at Washington, whose lips should never be opened except to utter political or social oracles in accord with his great reputation, . . . wounded in his self-respect, &c., runs as the wounded stag, and in his flight fastens deeper and deeper the dart that wounds him. The Commission will see that the lamentations of Mr Sumner are nothing but the ignorance of our history, and a means of discrediting the high and wise policy and the aspiration of an immense majority."

But having made ourselves acquainted with the past and present of this beautiful land, the question naturally arises, what will be its future?

Not only are the Dominicans and the Haytians interested in this question, but so is all the world, and especially the American people. The philanthropist, the statesman, the merchant, and the manufacturer, are all equally concerned in an island which, under certain circumstances, will conduce to advance the cause of civilisation and humanity, the extension of trade and the production of necessary articles.

Though, as an American, I should be glad to see our institutions carried into that island, and our great privilege of self-government bestowed upon the people of the tropics, yet I should be equally glad, for the sake of the Dominicans and the Haytians, to see their island allied to some progressive Government; and Germany has already a strong footing on the island in the hold her merchants have acquired on its trade and commerce.

That any Government would profit by this connection there is not the slighest reason to doubt; but to the United States, from their position, would accrue advantages and benefits that could come to no other nation; and these were perhaps never more clearly and soundly expressed by any statesman than by General Grant in his annual message when recommending the measure to national legislation. He said:—

"During the last session of Congress a treaty for annexation of the republic of St Domingo to the United States failed to receive the requisite two-thirds vote of the Senate. I was thoroughly convinced then that the best interests of this country, commercially and materially, demanded its ratification.

"Time has only confirmed me in this view. I now firmly believe that the moment it is known that the United States have entirely abandoned the project of accepting as a part of its territory the Island of St Domingo, a free port will be negotiated for by European nations.

"In the Bay of Samana a large commercial city will spring up, to which we will be tributary without receiving corresponding benefits, and then will be seen the folly of our rejecting so great a prize. The Government of St Domingo has voluntarily sought this annexation. It is a weak power, numbering probably less than one hundred and twenty thousand souls, and yet possessing one of the richest territories under the sun, capable of supporting a population of ten millions of people in luxury. The people of St Domingo are not capable of maintaining themselves in their present condition, and must look for outside support. They crave the protection of our free institutions and our laws, our progress and civilisation. Shall we refuse them? The acquisition of St Domingo is desirable because of its geographical position. It commands the entrance to the Caribbean Sea and the Isthmus transit of commerce; it possesses the richest soil, best and most capacious harbours, most salubrious climate, and the most valuable products of the forest, mine, and soil of any of the West India Islands. Its possession by us will in a few years build up a coastwise commerce of immense magnitude, which will go far toward restoring to us our lost merchant marine. It will give to us those articles which we consume so largely and do not produce, thus equalising our exports and imports. In case of foreign war it will give us command of all the islands referred to, and thus prevent an enemy from ever again possessing himself of rendezvous upon our very coast. At present our coast trade between the States bordering on the Atlantic and those bordering on the Gulf of Mexico is cut in two by the Bahamas and Antilles twice. We must, as it were, pass through foreign countries to get by sea from Georgia to the west coast of Florida. St Domingo, with a stable Government, under which her immense resources can be developed, will give remunerative wages to tens of thousands of labourers, not now upon the island. This labour will take advantage of every available means of transportation to abandon the adjacent islands and seek the blessings of freedom and its sequence, each inhabitant receiving the reward of his own labour. Porto Rico and Cuba will have to abolish slavery as a measure of self-preservation to retain their labourers. St Domingo will become a large consumer of the products of Northern farms and manufactories. The cheap rate at which her citizens can be furnished with food, tools, and machinery will make it necessary that contiguous islands should have the same advantages in order to compete in the production of sugar, coffee, and tobacco, tropical fruits, &c.

"This will open to us a still wider market for our products. The production of our own supply of these articles will cut off more than one hundred millions of our annual imports, besides, largely increasing our exports.

"The acquisition of St Domingo is an adherence to the Monro doctrine; it is a measure of national protection; it is asserting our just claim to a controlling influence over the great commercial traffic soon to flow from west to east by way of the Isthmus of Darien; it is to build up our merchant marine; it is to furnish new markets for the products of our farms, shops, and manufactories; it is to make slavery insupportable in Cuba and Porto Rico at once, and ultimately so in Brazil; it is to settle the unhappy condition of Cuba, and end an exterminating conflict; it is to furnish our citizens with the necessaries of everyday life at cheaper rates than ever before; and it is, in fine, a rapid stride toward that greatness which the intelligence, industry, and enterprise of the citizens of the United States entitle this country to assume among nations. So convinced am I of the advantages to flow from the acquisition of St Domingo, and of the great disadvantages—I might almost say calamities—to flow from non-acquisition, that I believe the subject has only to be investigated to be approved."

And it can be said that if this doctrine of Monro is to be maintained with any reason by the United States, it is hardly fair to the Dominicans to say to them, "You shall not come into our Union, but neither will we allow you to ally yourself with any one else." Other nationalities might naturally have something to say in this direction; for, as said the *London Times* (Nov. 29, 1869), on receipt of the news of an expedition starting from the United States to take possession of Samana, which was looked upon by some as a stepping-stone to Hayti, and from Hayti to Cuba:—"The commercial life that would be imparted by these movements can hardly be over-estimated; and hence, supposing them to be carried out with fairness to all parties concerned, they may be contemplated as full of promise in favour of an extension of British trade."

If it be the mission of England to colonise and settle (see parliamentary debates on Fiji annexation) the desolate spots of the world, it may be claimed for the United States that it is hers to encourage all aspirants for civil liberty in any part of the New World, and either by her protection or incorporation lend a helping hand to humanising all young peoples irrespective of race or colour.

One of the most curious features about St Domingo is, that although it is the fashion to-day to belie and be-little it, yet in all the authorities, from the time of its discovery to the present time, no matter of what nationality, there is hardly a writer who does not speak in the most glowing terms of this island, its climate, its scenery, productions, and the general natural intelligence of its people, and their gentleness and kindness of disposition under favourable circumstances. I am glad to bear testimony to the fact, from personal observation, that the masses of the people of St Domingo will compare favourably with those of Great Britain, Belgium, or France.

Canon Kingsley has been by some deemed romantic because, familiar as he is with the lower classes of his own country, and with the masses particularly of the London population, who live, in many cases, utterly ignorant of pure air, light, and warmth, he should wish that the beautiful but unsettled solitudes of the New World might be peopled by some of their number.

But the writer so far agrees with him that he wishes, in these days of international meetings, that some grand international organisation could be formed to transport those who have not the means themselves, to those parts of the western continent where a new field of health, labour, and riches would be open to the teeming populations of the old world, and no more favourable or desirable spot does he know than the beautiful Island of St Domingo.

While I do not wish to inflict upon the reader a mass of dry statistics, which he would probably never read, it is due to the full understanding of our subject that I give some practical information in reference to matters that have been much misunderstood, most of which I extract from the reports of the United States Commissioners, verified as it has been by my own personal experience and consultation of every available authority.

And, firstly, in regard to climate and health. The testimony of witnesses, the observation of the Commissioners, and the reports of special investigations, show that it is generally a healthy country. Emigrants easily become accustomed to the climate. On the coast, where hot weather prevails, care must be taken. Individuals from the Northern States, now residing on the coast, and engaged in cultivating plantations there, say they can labour with their own hands, and that white men may work under certain regulations as safely as in the United States. As a fair illustration of this, it may be stated that the greater numbers of those persons engaged in commerce are foreigners, from France, from England, from Spain, but more particularly from Germany, all of whom, with perhaps the exception of those residing in Port-au-Prince and Cape Haytian, enjoy as good health as they did in their own countries.

The mountain slopes and valleys, overlooked or surrounded by lofty ridges, are comparatively cool, and are favourable to Northern constitutions. Within a few hours' ride inland farms were visited, where the temperature, cooled by the neighbouring peaks, was bracing; and in the same fields could be seen growing cabbage and bananas, potatoes and plantains, Indian-corn and sugar-cane, &c. Effective labour can be prosecuted by white men in such regions, and general good health maintained. The process of acclimation to strangers coming in was so slight as to be scarcely an inconvenience. It may be said generally that this process presents no greater obstacle to emigration than does the similar process in several of our new States.

The physical configuration of the island is such that a decided difference exists between its eastern and western ends in regard to health. In the eastern or windward portion of the island, occupied by the Dominican republic, the principal mountain chains run in lines approaching an east and west direction. The valleys between them are therefore swept during the greater portion of the year by the trade winds, which in that latitude come from directions east and north-east. These valleys are thus constantly supplied with pure air from the sea, and malarious influences are rapidly dissipated.

On the other hand, the west end of the island, occupied by Hayti, is walled in on its eastern or leeward side by chains of high mountains running in irregular curves from north to south. It would appear that these act to some extent as barriers to the trade winds; and to this fact, coupled with the influence of neighbouring marshes and mangrove swamps, it is due in a great measure that Port-au-Prince and the country about it have so bad a reputation in regard to health.

As to the large towns, there can be no doubt that the want at present of any practical application of sanitary knowledge causes them to rank far lower in regard to health than they otherwise would. Among the leading historical events connected with Hayti and St Domingo which have stamped themselves upon the public mind are the dreadful epidemics, principally yellow fever, which ravaged the English, the French, and the Spanish armies successively landed upon the coast.

The victims were Europeans, and their sad fate interested millions, so that in the public mind St Domingo and yellow fever became almost synonymous. It is a matter of history that the most fatal expedition—that of the French at the beginning of this century—conducted its operations mainly in the Haytian part of the island.

But this may be accounted for by the manner in which these troops were used. Where actively employed, they committed many indiscretions, and were devoid of many of the necessary comforts to which even the soldier is accustomed; especially was their clothing utterly unfitted for the climate in which they served.

Add to this, operations were carried on without regard to the peculiarities of a climate which seems to demand that every one shall avoid for a few hours all labour under a tropic mid-day sun.

But the greatest loss of the French was experienced while cooped up in the towns, or on shipboard, while being besieged by the negroes, and, as we have shown in the early chapters, in many cases forced to resort to dog-meat for food.

But probably their greatest losses were occasioned by the harassing nature of their conflicts with the negroes, who, laying aside all established tactical rules of organisation and manœuvre, simply became a vast body of skirmishers, retiring when attacked to their woods and hills, and then harassing, by ambushed and detached fire, old troops who had not yet learned the great art of modern warfare, of independently availing themselves of advantages offered for shelter by the nature of the ground.

The English expedition to St Domingo, which is sometimes referred to, so far as can be ascertained, was not attended by any greater loss of life from disease than might have been expected with the imperfect sanitary regulations of military forces which have existed down to a recent period.

One of the medical officers attached to the English army remarks upon the cause of the great sickness of the troops in saying, "They were overworked, dispirited, and shut up in towns where they were deprived of every comfort, and thus gave way. They pursued a diet opposite to that of the French; eating meat freely, and drinking ardent spirits; and being of plethoric habit, were quickly susceptible to the heat. The French, on the contrary, prepared themselves by gentle purges, ate little meat, and drank little wine, and that of the lightest kind, being particular to get a tepid bath each day."

Yet another writer says, "We have seen in St Domingo and Guadaloupe bodies of white troops, always active and in movement, execute on the largest scale field fortifications, and conclude their tasks with as much celerity as though they had lived all their life in Europe. And they resisted the attacks of tropical disease much better than those of the garrison who lived in idleness."

"The losses of the Spanish army from illness were largely

due to the utter lack of sanitary care; and the Commissioners are satisfied that those losses have been enormously exaggerated. The Commissioners have given special attention to the matter of health; and besides getting information from other quarters, they have charged two medical gentlemen to report specially upon it. Their conclusion is this:

"The popular idea that the Dominican territory is particularly unhealthy, and that persons visiting it are periodically liable to yellow fever, is entirely erroneous. The average general health and longevity is quite equal to, and probably greater than, that of the United States, as a whole. Immigrants are not liable to any more disturbance of general health in the process of acclimation, than are persons who pass from the old to the new States of the United States; and, saving upon the sea-coast, the process is so gentle as to escape notice. Taking the year through, as much agricultural work can be done without affecting health as can be done in our middle and western States, and with greater results. Persons in all circumstances can here enjoy, by selecting their locality, a delicious climate and abundance of fruit, with far less liability to diseases of the lungs, to scarlet fever, and other fearful epidemics, and without any liability to yellow fever."

The yellow fever in St Domingo, of which it is not a native, is different from that experienced in Philadelphia, as described by Dr Rush, and is not contagious; even in Cuba it is much overrated, for even there it is confined to localities always on the coast.

The moment one retires to the interior or the hills, there is no danger. So evident is this, that the little village of Guanabacoa, hardly two miles from Havana, has had one battalion of newly-arrived troops perfectly safe during the fever season, while another, stationed in Havana, lost half its men.

As regards St Domingo, my own experience, confirmed

by that of almost every member of the Commission, was that we could find no trace that yellow fever had ever prevailed in any of this part of the island as an epidemic.

A fellow-passenger, previously alluded to, and who, for over twenty years, had been a resident medical man at Santiago, assured me that, though he had been in every quarter of the globe, he had never met with a climate so undoubtedly salubrious as that of St Domingo; and while not denying that yellow fever was as likely to visit the coast-line as an epidemic as any of the other West Indies, said it had never yet done so, except in the case of accumulated numbers of foreign troops.

His views of sanitary measures for new-comers, being also those found in many reliable authorities, it may be said that, if attended to, they would undoubtedly be accompanied with good results. These are simply a gentle purge before landing, obviated in the case of those who have been sea-sick. A sparing use of fruit on first arrival. No matter what the nature of the outside clothing, which may be a light tweed or linen, a flannel shirt should invariably be worn next the skin. A very moderate use of wines, and especially ardent spirits; the free use of water, and ice unlimited, if to be had; a daily bath, cold in the morning, and tepid in the evening, is of great service to the health.

Tafia, a superior quality of the native rum, if made into a punch with lemon and ice, is cooling to the blood.

If to these are added exercise or labour, avoiding mid-day sun, and also great fatigue, general health would be as good here as in any part of the world to those residing on the coast, while in the interior there is nothing to apprehend on the score of health.

Two seasons are distinguished in the island—winter and summer. From the month of May to October, the rains are abundant, but diminishing in their quantity towards the latter month. From February to April, usually the season is known as the dry. In May and June the rains are not only heavy, but accompanied with thunder and lightning. The following is from M. St Mery:—

"CLIMATE AND TEMPERATURE.

"The island consisting partly in mountains and partly in plains, causes a great variety in the climate and temperature. This variety is especially produced by the situation in the region of the trade winds, as the wind coming from the east, towards which the island presents its whole length, finds in the intervals of the chains of mountains so many channels of circulation, by means of which it refreshes and tempers the mountains, an advantage that the plains, where portions of the mountains sometimes interrupt the passage of the wind and change its direction, do not partake in. Besides, a crowd of local circumstances, such as the elevation of the land, the quantity of water that runs over it, and the scarcity or abundance of wood, have a sensible influence upon the effect of the climate.

"If some powerful cause did not balance the action of the sun under the torrid zone, which darts its rays almost perpendicularly during about three months in the year at St Domingo, the temperature of this island would be insupportable to man, or at least to the man that nature had not formed on purpose for the climate. But this cause is in the wind, of which we have just spoken, the salutary effects of which soften those of the sun.

"To the benign influence of the wind may be added that of the almost equal length of the days and nights, and that of abundant rains, which continually fill the air with a fluidity always desirable, and which, falling in profusion on the surface of the island, produces, with the assistance of the evaporation caused by the heat, a sort of coolness in the air.

"The eastern wind blows at St Domingo, as in the rest of the Antilles, almost all the day long, during the greatest part of the year. It begins pretty regularly about nine or ten o'clock in the morning; rising as the sun rises towards his meridian height, and even after he begins to descend towards the west, it continues with unabated strength till two or three hours before sunset. This wind is commonly called at St Domingo the *sea breeze*, in opposition to that which I am now going to speak of.

"The name of *land breeze* is given to a wind which cools the nights, and which blows from the interior mountains. It generally begins to be felt about two or three hours after sunset, and continues till sunrise.

"The effect of these two breezes forms a curious contrast. That of the sea, coming from the circumference towards the centre, is seen advancing in that direction, agitating the leaves and other volatile bodies near the coast. The land breeze has an effect exactly opposed, and the more the situation approaches the centre of the island the sooner does it manifest itself.

"It must not, however, be imagined, that the succession of these breezes is so very regular as not to be subject to any variation. At certain times of the year, and particularly during the equinoxes and solstices, the sea breeze becomes very strong, sometimes even impetuous, and, during several days, blows without interval, or with but short pauses; during which time the land breeze is not felt at all. At such seasons the violence of the sea breeze usually augments at the rising of the sun, as if encouraged by his presence.

"At other times the land breeze predominates, which happens, for instance, in the tempestuous seasons. As almost all the tempests come from the interior part of the island, as soon as they begin to overspread the sky the sea breeze dies away, leaving the empire of the horizon to that of the land, which spreads in every direction, but with unequal rapidity, thick dark clouds, loaded with thunder and lightning, and pouring down deluges of rain. After the tempest is over, the land breeze continues predominant for the night, and even till the next day, when the sea breeze drives it back to its retreat in the mountains.

"From the combined effect of the two breezes, comes an almost continual agitation in the air, which necessarily has a great deal of influence on its constituent qualities. With the sea breeze the air acquires the quality that gives to the lungs what is necessary to resist the heat and to cool the blood, which an abundant perspiration tends to heat and impoverish. But it is for the cheering return of the land breeze that the inhabitants of St Domingo wait with impatience. This refreshing breeze gives to the whole body a calm sensation that the soul soon participates; it invites sleep, renders it restorative, and, in the high lands, it strengthens the fibres, and even prolongs life."

In the low grounds, the thermometer does not descend below 84° F., and ascends as high as 91°; but in the high lands, as has already been stated, the temperature is equable and agreeable.

Notwithstanding this, however, the inhabitants scarcely agree upon what periods of the year ought to be designated winter and summer. Those who live to the west and south and midland parts consider the time between April and

November as including the winter months or season of storms, the inhabitants of the northern districts reckon just the reverse, but neither of them speak of spring or autumn.

The best season, however, for the new-comer to land and become easily acclimated may be said to be any time after October.

In reference to the common belief that all the West India islands are the home of innumerable insects of a venomous nature, it may be said that this is quite wrong. The scorpion, so much dreaded by the Northern mind, I saw very infrequently in St Domingo, and then it was not the wicked, alarming thing I had imagined; and its sting is never dangerous, however inconvenient in its effects.

Scorpion.

The tarantula and lizard I have already alluded to, and there only remains the centipede to speak of, which is rarely met with, and then no more unpleasant in its effects than those of the Southern States. But this beautiful isle has no such pests as we possess in the galaxy of venomous reptiles and snakes, and even the primeval forests are void of any wild animals.

Centipede.

The natural productions of this island it would be impossible, in a volume like this, to describe. Suffice it to say, that, in addition to those already mentioned, the soil and climate are capable of producing almost every variety known in the world; while of the various woods, many almost unknown to commerce, the supply is unlimited. The most interesting subject for the emigrant would naturally be the land question; and of land there is abundance of every kind, which for many years is likely to be had at a reasonable rate. The tenure at present is very peculiar, the system in vogue being that known as the "Communero," a term which must not be confounded with that of land of the commune.

The first arises from the fact that landed property, at the time of the conquest of the island, and during the following centuries, was held in the manner then prevailing, as a consequence of feudalism. Society being divided between lords and vassals, masters and slaves, the land was made productive by the sweat of the unfortunates who did not reap and enjoy its harvests, and it passed undivided into the hands of the privileged heir, in conformity to the laws of primogeniture and entail, in order to preserve the lustre of family names. Religious communities considered as corporate moral persons and feudal lords, also possessed landed property: and as they had no family pride, and their only interest was that of the corporation, their property, however indivisible, became a resource for the poor colonist, who, unable to acquire an estate gratuitously, or conditioned on a burden of service, as did the nobility, found a means of living by his own work by renting monastic lands, paying a certain annual fee, or the offering of tithe, and the first-fruits of his crops.

The original owners held by a complete title, and most of them were provided with a document called royal guarantee (Amparo Real), by which the king guaranteed the validity of their acquisitions. At the death of the proprietor of an estate in the country, of whatever description, whether lots, farming, sugar, or pasture lands, his children and wife, if he had any, inherited that property, as measured and marked, that is, contained within known limits, and fixed on the plat and survey.

The proprietor having been married, under the rule of conjugal community of property, his surviving wife was entitled to one half of the land, and the children born during the marriage to the other half. The family continuing to live on their estate, contained within the same limits, though possessed by a plurality of owners, established certain rules among themselves in order to live together, each by one's own work, without actually dividing the farm; each of the brothers and sisters having a right equal to that of each of the others, and the widow her own, equal to that of them all.

When these brothers married and had children, that division of shares was further subdivided, that is, in theoretical right, but not in fact,—every one holding proportionate to his rights with reference to the extent of the entire tract inherited as shown by the titles.

The causes that originally prevented the actual division of the ground were various—

1st, The high cost for surveying, which, multiplied according to the divisions made, would not only absorb, but exceed, the small value of the lands.

2d, The nature of such property itself, which cannot in fact be conveniently and equitably divided, all being united as constituent parts of a farm, viz., the savanas, or plains, for the pasture of horned cattle, horses, and sheep; the woods, supplying timber, and whose shade is indispensable to animals during the heat of the day, and throughout the hot season; the palm groves, furnishing boards and covering for the building of huts, and food for swine, and the fibres of which supply cordage to the country people; finally, the lands fit for cultivation, and running waters or ponds for the use of both man and beast.

As it would be impossible to give pasture, wood, arable land, and water to each of the owners, or to deprive them of a single one of these elements without causing them irreparable damage, the necessity arises for harmonising their interests through community of possession under a common title. When any of the proprietors wishes to sell his share, after having offered it to his co-owners and been refused, he can sell it to a stranger, who enters not into the community of the family, but into that of the proprietorship as co-owner.

From this arises the curious custom of buying a right, by which any inhabitant of a commune can for $50 or $100 secure a right which gives him the privilege of the land just as much as though he owned it, upon which he can settle, and build, and cultivate as much as he likes, without further tax or rent; this he buys from some one of the co-owners, each of whom has a right to his proportion. By a curious custom, however, which has become a law, a man who buys a right to settle or occupy land does not necessarily buy any privileges of mahogany-cutting; this is a separate matter, and neither does the person buying the right to cut mahogany in a certain tract secure thereby any claim to the land.

Of course, such customs can only exist without trouble in a country where land is abundant and the population small; and it matters little at present, because the land is not measured. Thus a person buying for $50 the right to enter a communero tract, that may comprise several leagues, can take any part or all of it that is not occupied, no matter how much it may be, provided he does not interfere with the improved land of any one else, or the land from which is drawn their supplies of timber. To secure his title he must, however, occupy and use it. If, however, such person temporarily leaves his house for a year or more, and it burns down, and the improvements are not kept up, any other person has the right to enter upon and hold his tract.

Naturally from this condition of affairs there is sometimes considerable uncertainty about titles, and the most undoubted one is that where the owner can show undisputed possession for thirty years back, as that makes a good title.

In regard to the public lands, there is no certainty as

regards the quantity, for even in the time of the Spaniards the archives had almost entirely disappeared; and this again is subject to the curious system of the "Communes," which consist of the districts over which the "Ayuntamientos" rule, and who hold rights in all unclaimed lands for the commune. But these lands cannot be sold except by permission of the general Government, although the commune can give such a lease as is equal to a title.

There is no difficulty, however, in securing plenty of good land at a merely nominal sum; and, as an illustration, an American has bought within a short distance of St Domingo city nearly three hundred acres of land for some $1200, upon which were some improvements of the value of about $600. He has held this land about three years, and now has fourteen thousand coffee-trees growing, hundreds of bread-fruit, tamarind, orange, lemon, lime, and aguacate trees, with acres of the cocoa-tree set out.

From corn grass alone, this enterprising individual has been deriving a revenue of from $100 to $150 per month, without there being an ear of corn. In addition to these he has over four thousand banana-trees just commencing to bear.

This is no singular case, but one that can occur with any ordinarily intelligent industrious man.

The data furnished by authorities as to population are very meagre and unsatisfactory. An estimate was recently made by the ecclesiastical court, counting by parishes, which gave a total of 207,000. There are evident signs of errors in this estimate. For instance, the capital was set down at ten thousand; while it is obvious to the careful observer who counts streets and houses, that there cannot be over six thousand, if so many. Comparing these figures of the ecclesiastical court with certain known facts, and with all the evidence we could gather from intelligent witnesses and personal observation, the Commission estimate that the actual population of the republic does not exceed 150,000. This does not include the many who have voluntarily expatriated themselves on account of continual disturbances, nor the few who have been banished.

It seems probable that more than nine-tenths, perhaps nineteen-twentieths, are native Dominicans. The others are—first, coloured emigrants from the United States; secondly, European traders, who do not settle anywhere, but sojourn at commercial points. Negro blood preponderates very largely in Hayti, but the pure negro of African type is not common even there. White blood preponderates largely in Dominica, but pure whites, in the popular sense of the word, are not numerous. The majority are of a mixed race, much nearer white than black.

The great majority, especially along the coast, are neither pure black nor pure white; they are mixed in every conceivable degree. In some parts of the interior considerable numbers of the white race are to be found, and generally in the mixed race the white blood predominates. The Dominican people differ widely in this particular from the Haytians, among whom the black race is in complete ascendancy. The cultivated and educated, such as the President, members of his Cabinet, senators, judges, and local magistrates, compare well with the same classes in other countries, and the uneducated appear equal to the same class in any country with which we are acquainted. They seem to be practically destitute of prejudice of class, race, or colour. In their intercourse with each other and with strangers, they are courteous in manner, respectful, and polite. In all their relations with them the Commissioners found them kind and hospitable.

The testimony shows them to be an honest and inoffensive people, among whom, in the rural districts, a person may travel alone and unarmed all over the country with treasure without danger. All of the numerous parties attached to the Commission, which traversed various parts of the country, bear the same testimony concerning the people. The judicial officers stated that high crimes, such as murder, arson, burglary, and the like, are nearly unknown among them. No pauper class exists, and beggary is almost unknown. They are temperate people, and drunken men are rarely seen. Among popular vices is that of petty gambling, which is indulged in openly and extensively, especially by the Spanish portion of the population.

They are all Roman Catholics, except the American emigrants sent out in 1824 and succeeding years, who, with their descendants, now form a number of settlements, and amount to several thousand persons. These are mostly Methodists and Baptists. They live among the Catholics in peace and harmony. No intolerance or religious persecution can be discovered among them. The people are generally poor, living in cheap and humble dwellings, which, though well adapted to their country, might appear rude and uncomfortable to those accustomed to houses made for a more rigorous climate, but, as compared with those of the labouring class in Europe, infinitely superior. In the country, almost every family possesses all the land they desire to cultivate, which is generally one small field, for an acre or two well tilled is sufficient, in this fertile land, to furnish a family with their food. The reason they unanimously assign for not cultivating more is, that amid constantly recurring revolutions it is very uncertain who may reap the crop. Besides, there is no market here for surplus produce.

As regards the future, this question of population is a very satisfactory one, if St Domingo should become allied to any strong Government; for five years' emigration would entirely change its character, as has been the case in California.

It has been the fashion among some of our politicians to urge the purchase of Cuba, even at the price of one hundred millions of dollars, and it has a large and extensively mixed population, with all their habits, ideas, and customs fully established, with still a larger number of slaves and coolies.*

* The author takes the liberty of referring the reader interested in this subject to his previous work on Cuba, in which he will see how, even under

But here is an almost virgin island, more desirable in every way, with a free, limited, and simple people, who have no particularly fixed habits, ideas, or customs, that would not readily assimilate to those of the new-comers. One-tenth of the above-named sum, expended in improving the means of communication, in exploring and seeking information of its resources, with the change that American machinery and enterprise, accompanying emigration into the island, would bring, would in a few years give us an island equally valuable as Cuba, and aptly illustrate the fact that our institutions and civilisation are adapted to any climate and to any people.

As a great deal has been said in reference to the finances and the land concessions of the Dominican Government, I here append the result of the searching investigations of the Commissioners. First, in reference to the

"PUBLIC DEBT.

"The Commissioners made a careful and prolonged investigation into the important subject of the indebtedness of the Dominican Republic, collecting all the information that could be communicated by the officials whose special duty it was to know every detail of the finances and the liabilities of the Government, all that could be obtained from the records in the public offices, from the statements of claimants of every kind who could be heard of and found, and from the explanations of the President and his chief officers in regard to the whole and each item thereof. They also received from the Senate a list of claims and their respective amounts pending before that body, which is appended.

"The following summary statement exhibits briefly the result of those inquiries as to 'the debt of the Government and its obligations, whether funded and ascertained and admitted, or unadjusted and under discussion.' The receipts of the last three years have been mostly used for previous war debts, and for the cancelling of outstanding paper money. The latter, which originally amounted to the sum of $2,628,300, left in circulation by Cabral, has been nearly all redeemed by customs receipts, as was also the amount of $243,070 in Spanish war bonds.

---

a despotic and shortsighted Government, this island has, within only a few years comparatively, and principally owing to the introduction of American machinery, been developed. The author believes the day St Domingo becomes one of the United States, that day is the value of Cuba lost to Spain.

I. The salaries due amount to		$600,000 00
II. Bonds, treasury notes, &c., viz. :—		
1. Spanish war bonds, amount issued, .	$324,160 00	
Amount cancelled, . . .	243,070 00	
Amount outstanding, . .	81,090 00	
2. Treasury notes, nominal balance in circulation, $147,575.18, at the price fixed by senatorial decree, $400 for one dollar in silver, gives really	368 93¾	
3. Notes of credit (new paper money), nominal balance out of the Controller's office, $88,832.30; at 30 for one silver dollar, . .	2,961 07	
4. Obligations of the present Administration, issued by the Controller, .	9,761 36	
5. Obligations of the present Administration, issued by the Controller, at 6 per cent., . . .	1,153 00	
Total of bonds, treasury notes, &c. . .		95,334 36¾
III. Sundry debts and loans due towns and individuals, .		49,443 02½
DEFERRED DEBT.		
IV. Bills and obligations of Cabral's Administration, unpaid because of doubtful origin, the gross amount of which is, ...		221,845 77
Note.—This debt is now in process of consolidation, and may be reduced to less than one-third of its nominal sum.		
V. Notes of National Bank, countersigned by the General Treasurer, ...		4,130 00
VI. Sundry loans bearing interest (back interest not included),		293,511 23
VII. Loan, without interest, subject to rebate for advances, .		20,223 20
VIII. Debt of 1859 :— Amount not known, because it is not known whether any was redeemed during the Spanish Administration. It cannot exceed $50,000 or $60,000, reckoned at .		50,000 00
Total debt, ...		$1,334,487 59¼
IX. Pending claims :—		
Of Jessurun & Son, claim before Senate, for loan of $100,000 in 1857, contested since, and now under consideration by the Chamber of Accounts, .	$100,000 00	
Of Jessurun & Son, for hire of schooner *Amelia* in 1857, less than . .	10,000 00	
Of Rofman & Lowenthal, and others,	14,000 00	
Of General Baez, for spoliations, .	70,000 00	
Of W. L. Cazeneau, for spoliations in 1863,	10,000 00	
Total, ...		204,000 00
X. Of J. C. Castillanos, francs 131,719 40.		
Of A. Postel, francs 5,007.		
Total of debt and claims in dollars, about .		1,565,831 59¼

" The following statement of the receipts for 1870 is here presented, in order to give, as far as possible, a complete view of the financial condition of the Dominican Republic :—

RESULTS OF THE INCOME OF THE GOVERNMENT FOR 1870.

1. *Customs Receipts.*

Item	Amount	Total
Tonnage,	$27,206 60	
Entrance fees,	1,469 95	
Light-houses,	679 01	
Anchorage,	1,469 95	
Pilotage,	1,429 27	
Lighterage,	216 00	
Interpreter,	614 20½	
Signal-men,	594 16½	
Quarantine,	430 16½	
Wharfage,	6,793 38	
Recargo, municipal,	1,105 36½	
Recargo for steamer,	5,886 14	
Water,	241 00	
Import dues,	601,393 64¼	
Export dues,	71,419 20½	
Coast fees,	7,511 11	
Deposits,	132 43	
Additional entrance fees,	14 00	
		$728,605 58¾

2. *Direct and Indirect Taxes.*

Item	Amount	Total
Registry and mortgages,	$2,147 06½	
Licences,	12,721 86¾	
Stamped paper,	18,574 50	
Postage stamps,	1,083 69	
Postal income,	929 42¾	
		35,466 55

3. *Public Property.*

Item	Amount	Total
Sales and rents,		150 00

4. *Sundries.*

Item	Amount	Total
Sundries,		8,462 62¼
Total,		$772,684 75¼

" The Commissioners believe that the statement of the public debt given above includes all the indebtedness or obligations for which the Dominican Republic is in any degree liable, as well that which it considers valid and binding as that which it regards as unfounded or overstated by the claimants. Throughout the inquiry it was urged upon the Dominican authorities that every claim known to exist, of whatever character, should be exhibited to the Commission, whose object was not only to determine the precise amount that was justly due and binding, but to get at the bottom and find the utmost limit of these obligations, setting forth everything for which the Government could, under any circumstances, be made liable.

"The above account contains much that the Dominican Government believes to be partly or wholly groundless, and some which, upon inspection, will appear questionable. There was brought to the notice of the Commission a claim of Messrs Jessurun & Son, of Curacoa, for upwards of $500,000 for money advanced to the Dominican Government, with interest, this being the same loan of $100,000, in 1857, mentioned in the preceding list of the pending claims by the same parties. On being asked if he had any statement or explanation to make regarding it, Mr Jessurun, who submitted the claim, declined to make any. This claim has been already for a considerable time before the Dominican Government, which refuses to consider more of it than the amount named in the foregoing list, and of that it is believed but a small portion will be allowed.

"The debt was incurred for arms and provisions in time of war, when the property furnished was estimated at $100,000, on which compound interest, at 18 per cent., was to be allowed. It is claimed by the Dominican Government that, soon after the original contract was made, the Government turned over to these claimants a ship and cargo valued at $70,000 dollars, and that subsequently other payments were made, which, taken together, reduce the amount to a sum much below that named in the foregoing list. The claim is now pending before the Dominican Senate, and undetermined. Among the pending claims is one of President Baez for destruction of property.

"It is alleged by the claimant that the Spanish Government recognised this claim as valid, and ordered an examination to fix the amount, but the Commission cannot understand how this claim could be valid against the Dominican Government.

"Another claim for damages, amounting to $10,000, made by W. L. Cazeneau, seems to be of a similar nature."

Passing over all of the statements, so freely made in the United States, of grants of land having been made to prominent officials, as utterly without foundation, I shall give a glance at some concessions of lands, rights, and privileges that are still in force, many others which had been previously granted being now entirely void; and it may be said that, if the terms of these concessions are complied with and fully carried out, St Domingo will receive a fair *quid pro quo* for that she bestows.

I cannot refrain, however, from expressing a wish that our Government had seen fit to accept this island as a territory, and, taking charge of its development and interests, had retained in its own hands the control of roads, mines, and telegraph. In doing this it would more rapidly develop the resources of the island, would give confidence to the settler, and enable at once this island to take a place in the moneyed and commercial world as a spot worthy of the attention of the largest capitalists.

The United States Commission, as directed by the resolutions of Congress, made diligent inquiry to ascertain what proportion of the territory is covered by foreign claims or by grants and concessions, and generally what concessions and franchises have been granted, with the names of the respective grantees. The following list, condensed from an official statement furnished by the Dominican Secretary of State, with accompanying documents, and confirmed by the testimony, gives an answer to this inquiry:—

A grant to J. W. Fabens, or a company organised for the purpose, dated July 3, 1868, of a portion of the public lands, on condition of making a geological survey. This is a contract authorising Fabens, by himself, or any company organised for the purpose, to make a general geological examination and survey of all the provinces and districts at the expense of said company, reports to be made every three months, as the survey progresses, to the Dominican Government, to enable it to offer for sale the mineral and agricultural lands of the localities examined, also an annual report of said company: to receive one-fifth of the public lands so surveyed, excepting coal lands, to be set apart as the quarterly reports are rendered. This survey is now in progress. The parties owning the franchise and paying the expense are chiefly New York capitalists.

A grant to R. M. Funkhauser, of New Jersey, October 7, 1868, for a line of mail steamers between New York, New Orleans, and the Dominican Republic, with a provision that 5 per cent. of the import and export dues on all merchandise carried by said line be allowed to the owners of steamers. This line is now run by Spofford Brothers of New York.

A grant to Ed. H. Hartmont, to take guano from the island of Alta Vela, in consideration of the loan of May 1869. As this loan was for a large amount, and has given rise to a great many statements from those opposed to the annexation scheme, it may be as well to state here, that it was originally to be negotiated for the sum of £420,000, and was to be brought out in London; and that, as security for its payment, certain liens and concessions were made of lands and privileges which have since been voided, except that of the Alta Vela privilege, as the Dominican authorities claim, for non-fulfilment of contract.

Fifty thousand pounds were to be paid down on the conclusion of the contract, but owing to some revolutionary troubles, only some £3000 were so paid at once, but subsequently a further sum was paid, and the Dominican authorities acknowledge in their books an indebtedness to Hartmont & Co., of London, to the amount of £38,095, 4s. 9d., which they contend is the sum received, but for which there is a claim of £50,000 at 6 per cent., and which the Dominicans had under discussion; this is the principal part in the above statement of interest-bearing loans.

A grant to Fred. H. Fisher, of New York, September 9, 1869, for building a railroad from Santiago to Yuna river or Samana peninsula; to Felix Montecatini, August 3, 1867, renewed and extended April 5, 1870; to Shumacker & Augenard, for railroad from Ozama river to San Christobal; to Julian Grangerard, June 3, 1870, for building a railroad from Azua to Los Caobas; to Levi Guilamo, November 4, 1870, for constructing telegraph lines necessary in the republic; to Carlos Baez, May 8, 1870, for rent of salt works at Bani; to Telesforo Volto, for salt works at Beata Island; to Industrial and Progressive Company, November 5, 1866, to work copper-mine at El Cobre, San Cristobal; to W. L. Cazeneau, January 18, 1867, copper-mine at Monte Mateo, San Cristobal; to the same, July 12, 1869, copper-mine at Mano Matuey, and at Loma de la Boca de Diamarte, San Cristobal (the last three being consolidated under law of August 10, 1870); to Cambiaso & Co., October 24, 1867, copper-mine at Boca de Cuajo, Upper Haina, San Cristobal; to St Domingo Company (Geological Survey Company), February 25, 1870, the mining circuit, Buenaventura, Upper Haina, San Cristobal, by virtue of geological survey, to be modified to conform to geological contract; to Felix Montecatini, March 19, 1867, mining district in Cuajo San Cristobal (void), renewed to Shumacher & Augnard, July 28, 1870; to St Domingo Company, September 16, 1870; mining district of Camu.

The Dominican Government has made no grant or concession of land to any foreign Government or nation except the United States.

To the grants to foreigners by the Government above enumerated must be added some by municipalities. Of these the only ones which seem to the Commission to require notice here are those to certain parties, citizens of the United States, of lands and lots in the village of Santa Barbara, on the Bay of Samana, granted by the authorities of that town from its property as follows:—To J. P. O'Sullivan, December 1, 1868, of 930 feet fronting on the harbour and extending back several hundred feet, varying in depth in different parts, at $62 per annum rent for twenty-one years; also, 84 feet and 90 feet to the same at $4 rent for each, December 11, 1869. These leases are made perpetual, provided there be no law to prevent the same. To J. W. Fabens, December 11, 1869, of 1683 feet, fronting on the harbour, in perpetuity at $112 per annum. These grants cover a large part of the unoccupied available front of the harbour. There was also a lease by the municipal government of the city of St Domingo of a wharf front of limited extent and importance to W. L. Cazeneau.

And here my labours must come to an end; but before taking my leave of the reader, I will answer a question that has often been addressed to me since my return, "Is St Domingo such a desirable, beautiful land?"

With a free government, and such an immigration as annexation to the United States would bring, I believe in a few years St Domingo would be the jewel state of our Union, not even excepting California. It has been the lot of the writer to traverse every section of his own land, and he knows no state or section more attractive; for here the labourer will find ample occupation, while to the man of means or cultivation a field is open to amply reward his investments, or give him unlimited sources of pleasure, in establishing homes that shall rival the most beautiful of so-called sunny Italy itself.

It is only since the writer's visit to Europe that he has fully comprehended the reason of the admiration of the early Europeans for the sunny lands of the tropics; and he believes that were Santo Domingo settled and rendered habitable, that thousands of our citizens, who now spend their winters on some parts of the continent, looking for a climate they never find, would here discover a winter residence unrivalled in any part of the world.

But what stronger evidence can be quoted than the words of that venerable cosmopolite Dr Howe, who, on receiving a serenade from some Dominicans, said:—

"People too often overlook or forget the good they have, and think only of their sufferings and wants. Since I have been here, people have been talking continually to me about the disadvantages under which they labour—of the convulsions, and civil wars, and oppressions, and all that. There is another side of the picture. I find myself in danger of having my reason carried away by my senses. All my senses are, as it were, subjugated by the surroundings. I find the most beautiful island I have ever seen. The balmy atmosphere, the mild and even temperature—everything addresses itself to my sense *de bien etre*. My eyes are dazzled by the beauty of enchanting scenery. My sense of taste is gratified by the luscious and abundant fruits that are everywhere around us; and now comes your music, and so charms away my sense of hearing, that I find all my senses enlisted and carried away in your favour; and although

I may not say what I shall advise my countrymen to do on the subject of annexing the Dominican Republic, I feel strongly inclined to annex myself and my family to this beautiful island."

HINTS TO EMIGRANTS OR TRAVELLERS.

St Domingo may be easily visited by steamer from New York once a month. Any time after October it will be found a delightful trip, even if never leaving the steamer except while she is in various ports.

From St Domingo, the trip may be extended to Puerto Rico, Curacoa, St Thomas, Jamaica, and either across or around Cuba to the United States. The money of most value in use is American gold and silver.

The emigrant is advised to take all supplies with him in the shape of clothing, which need be only light woollen or linens, with woollen underclothing of a light kind.

For those who intend prospecting the island, a good M'Clellan saddle-tree, with stirrups and stirrup leathers only, of russet leather, will be found better than anything on the island; with this a felt saddle-cloth and small saddle-bags.

High boots and shoes are best of russet leather, on account of the mud. A poncho or waterproof cloak will be useful.

A small mess-chest with a stout tent-fly will make the traveller with his own supplies absolutely independent of hotels or hospitality.

Extract of beef in small cans or jars will prove worth its weight in gold in a place where fresh meat is seldom to be had, and then only of pork, the free use of which is undoubtedly the cause of so much sickness in the tropics.

A stout wood-knife is always, and a revolver sometimes useful; and a shot-gun may be of service where there is no field for a rifle.

A pocket Spanish Dictionary will sometimes get one out of a difficulty, and sometimes—into one.

DOMINICAN MANIFESTOES.

DIOS. *PATRIA.* *LIBERTAD.*

REPUBLICA DOMINICANA.

Independence or Death.

DOMINICANS !—

Your President, Cabral, seeing himself attacked by his enemies from every side, took the criminal decision of sending, on the 19th December, Senor Paul Prujol to Washington, for the purpose of proposing to the Government of the United States the sale of your country.

Hasten, then, Dominicans, ye that have shed, with so much readiness, your blood for the independence of your country. There are hardly three years since ye hastened to punish in removing the man without faith that to-day wishes to sell you to the stranger.

Dethrone from power the man Cabral, so unworthy of your confidence, and of the supreme honour that ye have bestowed on him of making him your ruler.

The Government of Hayti desires but one thing of you: it is to live in peace and good friendship, to respect your independence, and give you all the assistance that it is able to place at your service.

Lose not an hour, Dominicanos, in removing the culpable. Recognise without delay an honest Government, that respects all your rights, and feels the necessity of maintaining with your neighbours the Haytians, and your friends, that peace and tranquillity that shall foster the commerce and prosperity of both states.

B. BAEZ.

JOSE MARIA CABRAL, General of Division of the National Armies, and Superior Chief of the Revolutionary Movement, &c.

CONSIDERING that the shameful act of selling the republic to the United States of America by the Government of the traitor Baez, is apparently justified by accrediting to him the American Commission that comes with the purpose of realising this act:

Considering that all Dominicans are bound to protest in a solemn manner against an act so infamous, &c.:

It is decreed—

1. That all the authorities, as well civil as military, that exist in the Dominican nation, are bound to manifest to the American Commission its protest against the treason of the President Baez, in wishing to annex the Republic to the United States of America.

2. The authorities that shall not do this will be considered as accomplices in this infamous negotiation, and judged at the proper time by tribunals that, for this purpose, will be formed in the headquarters of provinces, when *shall be realised the triumph of the revolution.*

Given, &c., San Juan (really in Port-au-Prince), February 4, 1871.

El General, &c.,

JOSE MARIA CABRAL.

DOMINICANS !—

Buenaventura Baez sells you to the American in the same manner as Santana sold you to the Spaniard !

And this without a single condition ! Slavery with all its despotism, the loss of all your interests, death, the extermination of your race, threatens you, awaits you with all their horrors. Dishonour will cover you for ever if you lance not a cry of reprobation against the assassination of your dearest affections, &c.

Prove then, ye the descendants of the conquerors of the English in Najayo, and of the French in Palo Hincado, once more to the world that ye have the undoubted right to be free and sovereign, and sufficient courage to know how to remain so.

Dominicans, more than half a million of dollars has been given to Baez in payment of his treason, &c.

COMPATRIOTS, &c.

PATRIOTS OF ALL PARTIES, &c.

SOLDIERS OF THE COLUMN of February 27, &c.

Bury in eternal oblivion your contemptible rivalries, and make the infamous traitor Baez abandon for ever the victim he takes to the sacrifice, &c.

Endeavour to have inscribed for ever on your banner this immortal legend—

UNION, INDEPENDENCE, PROPER REPUBLICAN PROGRESS, LIBERTY OR DEATH !

GREGORIO LUPERON.

CAPOTILLO, *February*, 1871.

(Also printed in Cape Haytian, where the above bandit procures supplies.)

GENERAL STATISTICS PERTAINING TO HAYTI.

The following shows of what this island is capable, under proper administration. The Spanish portion, it has been shown, has never been sufficiently populated, or peacefully governed for a lengthened period, to give any important or reliable results; but being the virgin part of the island, nearly three times the extent of Hayti, and of much more productive climate and soil generally, some idea can be formed by comparison of what it might be capable.

General Statement of the Productions and Manufactures of the French Part of St Domingo in the year 1791.

The island was divided into fifty-one parishes, containing—

Sugar plantations,	792	Cocoa plantations,	69
Coffee do.	2810	Limekilns,	313
Cotton do.	705	Brick yards and potteries,	61
Indigo do.	3097	Number of negro hands employed,	455,000
Tanneries,	3		
Rum distilleries,	173		

The products of the above, and its accompanying business, gave rise to a commerce which comprised more than one-third of the whole of that done by France. A comparative table shows there was—

Exported from Hayti in 1789–1820.

	1789.	1820.		1789.	1820.
	lbs.	lbs.		lbs.	lbs.
Clayed sugar,	47,516,531	2,787	Indigo,	758,628	...
Moscobado,	93,573,309	2,514,502	Molasses,	25,749	...
Coffee,	76,835,219	35,137,759	Dyewoods,	6,768,634	1,919,748
Cotton,	7,001,274	346,389	Tobacco,	...	97,600
Cocoa,	...	556,424	Mahogany, ft.	...	129,500

In 1789, the money value of these exports amounted to over twenty-eight millions of dollars; and at a glance it will be seen, in comparison with the year 1820, what an immense falling off there was under the negro regime; and the following tables will show what an immense difference exists in the Hayti of to-day and the St Domingo of the past,—the sugar and molasses product being utterly extinct

The whole Island, 1835–36–40.

	1835.	1836.	1840.
	lbs.	lbs.	lbs.
Ginger, . .	8,710	16,000	8,136
Hides,* . .	24,951	14,891	39,627
Wax, . . .	10,900	16,000	19,862
Coffee, . .	48,352,371	37,662,672	46,126,272
Cotton, . .	1,649,717	1,072,555	922,575
Cocoa, . .	397,324	550,584	442,365
Dyewoods,†. .	13,293,737	6,767,902	30,283,205
Tobacco,‡ . .	2,086,600	1,222,716	1,725,389
	ft.	ft.	ft.
Mahogany, . .	513,316	4,954,944	4,072,641

In 1857–8, the coffee crop exported amounted to over 33,285,000 lbs. This is exclusive of that used in the island, and that remaining unpicked.

The importations of 1858 were equal to nearly $4,000,000; the exportations, $6,500,000. Of these—

	IMPORTATIONS.		EXPORTATIONS.
	Per cent.		Per cent.
From England, . . .	19.84	...	36.74
„ United States, . .	55.76	...	21.75
„ France, . . .	13.34	...	20.42
„ Other places, . .	11.06	...	12.09

Since that period the amounts produced have rather decreased than increased, and the Government may really be said to be bankrupt, since it cannot redeem its paper currency.

TREATY concluded between the PLENIPOTENTIARIES of their MOST CHRISTIAN and MOST CATHOLIC MAJESTIES, concerning the BOUNDARIES of the FRENCH and SPANISH POSSESSIONS in the ISLAND of ST DOMINGO, June 3, 1777.

PREAMBLE.—In order to effect the said treaty, the two sovereigns have named the following plenipotentiaries, to wit—On the part of his Most Christian Majesty, his Excellency the Marquis of Ossun, grandee of Spain of the first order, field-marshal in the army of his Most Christian Majesty, knight of his orders, and his ambassador extraordinary and plenipotentiary at the court of Spain; and, on

* Principally from St Domingo.

† Principally the product of the logwood, planted by the French for hedges, and now overgrown.

‡ Principally from St Domingo.

the part of his Most Catholic Majesty, his Excellency Don Joseph Monino de Florida Blanca, knight of the order of Charles III., counsellor of state, and first secretary of state for foreign affairs. The said plenipotentiaries, after having conferred together, and made a mutual communication of their full powers, have agreed on the following articles:—

Article I.—The boundaries between the two nations shall remain perpetually and invariably fixed at the mouth of the river D'Ajabon, or River of the Massacre, on the northern side of the said island, and at the mouth of the river Pedernales, or Des Anses à Pitre, on the southern side, in the terms specified in the second article; observing only here, that if, in future, any doubt should arise as to the identity of the rivers Pedernales and Anses à Pitre, it is already decided that it is the river commonly called by the Spaniards the river Pedernales, that the plenipotentiaries mean to point out as the boundary.

Article II.—Seeing that the last survey, taken by the Viscount of Choiseul and Don Joachim Garcia, in quality of commissioners, conjointly with the respective engineers and inhabitants born in the country, has been executed in the most exact and minute manner, with a perfect knowledge of the arrangement made between the French and Spanish commandants on the 29th February 1776; and seeing that they had before their eyes the different tracts of territory, and were fully capable of clearing up all doubts and ambiguities that could arise from the wording of the said arrangement; and further, seeing that landmarks have been planted by a common accord all along the frontier, and that more correct plans have been taken in which the said landmarks are distinctly represented; for these reasons, the undersigned plenipotentiaries stipulate, that the said instrument, made and signed by the said commissaries on the 28th August 1776, and in which all the points, rivers, valleys, and mountains, through or over which the line of demarcation passes, are clearly and distinctly pointed out, shall be inserted in, and make part of the present article, as follows:—

Description of the boundaries of the Island of St Domingo, as fixed at Attalaya the 29th of February 1776, by the definitive treaty, *sub sperati*, concluded between their Excellencies, Don Joseph Solano, knight of the order of St Jago, brigadier in the royal army of his Catholic Majesty, governor and captain-general of the Spanish part, president of the royal court, inspector of the regulars and militia, superintendent of the crusade, sub-delegate judge of the revenue of the posts, and plenipotentiary of his Catholic Majesty; and Victor Therese Charpentier, Marquis of Ennery, count of the Holy Empire, field-marshal in the army of his Most Christian Majesty, great cross of the royal military order of St Louis, inspector-general of infantry, regulars, and militia of the French Leeward Islands, and plenipotentiary of his Most Christian Majesty.

The said plenipotentiaries having signed the said original treaty by seniority of age, delivered, in consequence, their instructions of the same date to the undersigned, Don Joachim Garcia, lieutenant-colonel in the army of his Catholic Majesty, commanding the infantry of the trained militia of the Spanish colony; and Hyacinthe Louis Viscount de Choiseul, brigadier in the army of his Most Christian Majesty, named as commissaries to put in execution the articles of the said treaty, which fix invariably the boundaries of the possessions of the two crowns; to erect pyramids, plant landmarks, where necessary, to preclude for ever hereafter all disputes that might disturb the harmony and good understanding between the two nations, and to make out, with the assistance of a sufficient number of engineers, the topographical survey, to which the undersigned refer for fuller explanation; observing that it has been impossible to sign it, as mentioned in the treaty, by the chief engineer, Mr Boisforêt, employed by a superior order in the functions of his office.

In execution of the said treaty, the line of demarcation of the boundaries begins on the northern coast at the mouth of the river D'Ajabon or Massacre, and ends on the southern coast at the mouth of the river of the Anses à Pitre or Pedernales, on the banks of which rivers pyramids have been erected, as marked in the plan; the two first bearing No. 1, and the two last No. 221, with the inscriptions graved in stone, *France*, *Espana*. The plan clearly explains all the rest according to the real position; observing well that when the right or left of the line is spoken of, it is meant the right or left according to the route followed by the commissaries; and that, with respect to the rivers and streams, the right or left means the right or the left in going from the source towards the mouth.

In going up the D'Ajabon or Massacre, its waters and fishery in common form the line of frontier as far as the pyramid No. 2, of the little island divided by the pyramids, Nos. 3, 4, 5, and 6, conformably to the treaty, and as this line is not a tangent one, to the furthest elbow of the Ravine à Caïman, the marsh being impassable.

The two pyramids, No. 7, mark that the waters united into one arm between the two little islands, the river becomes in common, and forms the line as below.

The second island is divided by the pyramids from No. 8 to No. 17 inclusively, as represented on the plan, though, in conformity to the treaty, it should be divided by a right line from one extremity to the other, which forms a fork where the right arm of the river takes the name of Don Sebastian, and the other the name of Left Arm of the Massacre. But the particular plan that served as the basis of this article, representing the island as an ellipsis, and divisible only by one right line, was so incorrect, that it became necessary to take a new one, such as it now appears in the general plan; and the island has been divided by two lines which meet; in order to avoid doing prejudice, conformably to the fifth article of the treaty, to the essential interests of the vassals of his Catholic Majesty, whose land would have been bereft from them by a division of one right line.

From the pyramid No. 17, the river of the Massacre and the stream of the Capotille form the boundary of the respective possessions as far as the landmark No. 22. In this interval there are two pyramids, No. 18, placed on the banks of the Massacre, which is crossed by the high road from the town of D'Ajabon to that of Ouanaminthe; two at the mouth of the stream of the Mine, No. 20, and two landmarks, bearing the same, No. 21, at the bottom of the mouth, where are the settlements of Mr Graston, and where two little streams join, which form that of Capotille. The line ascends along the deep-banked stream on the left as far as No. 22, where ends the plantations that it surrounds in going on to No. 23, and the top of the hill which it runs along to No. 24, on the Piton des Ramiers.

From this point the line runs to the top of the mountains of La Mine and Marigallega, in following the old road of the Spanish rounds as far as the landmark No. 25, at the point formed by the little savanna of Sirop, on the plantation of the late Mr Lassalle des Carrières; it continues along some coffee grounds, surrounded with a hedge of lemon-trees, belonging to the same inhabitant, whose overseer is Mr Maingault, till it comes to the Piton des Perches, and then descends in a right line by Nos. 26, 27, and 28, in the savanna of the same name, on the right side of which, and by No. 29, the line ascends the Montagne des Racines, that of Grand Selles, Chocolate, and Coronade, where is placed No. 30. Hence, keeping the same mountain in an open road, the line comes to No. 31, placed on the slope of the Piton de Bayaba, where the line cannot be mistaken going over the summit of a mountain, with an open road which runs over the top of the Morne à Tenèbre by No. 32, over the Piton des Essentes as far as No. 33 of Filgueral, leaving to the right the sources of Grand Rivière, which run in the French part, and, on the left, the head or stream of the Eperlins, which runs in the Spanish part.

From No. 33 the line continues along a well-marked road, and crosses some deep hollows, represented on the plan, till it comes to the Montagne Traversière, on the top of which, and along by No. 34, it goes to No. 35, which cuts the stream called the Ruisseau des Sables; 36, 37, on the road, in common along a great wood, 38 on the stream of Ziguapo or Chapelets, where, by the branches of the mountain of the same name, the line comes to the top of it at No. 39, whence runs the branch or ridge called the Montagnes des Chandeliers, along which the line now goes, passing by the landmarks Nos. 40, 41, 42, till it comes to 43, placed at the confluence of the Ruisseau des Chandeliers and Grand Rivière, having to the right the valley of the river, and to the left the inaccessible hollow of the stream.

From No. 43, the bed of Grand Rivière, is the line of boundary for the two nations as far as the Guardhouse of Bahon, where is the pyramid No. 44 and the mouth of the stream of this name, mentioned in the treaty, and which the commissaries could not follow from the Montagne des Chapelets nor that of Chandeliers, in their western route, as a line of boundary, because it rises far in the south in the mountains of Barrero, Cannas, and Artimisa, without forming a junction with that of the Chapelets and Chandeliers; besides, being settled with the Spanish hattes, which are very considerable, and which come out to the river, where they have their plantations, provision-farms, and ecclesiastical revenue lands. Considering that these particular circumstances could not be known when the treaty was concluded; and to draw the line from ridge to ridge from the left bank of the river to the mouth of the stream of Bahon, would be of no manner of use to the French nation, from the small quantity and bad quality of the land which would remain between the line and the river; and considering, besides, that it would be cutting off the water from the cattle, which would prejudice the vassals of his Most Catholic Majesty, without benefiting those of his Most Christian Majesty; for these reasons the undersigned commissaries have agreed, and their generals have approved of it, that, between the two above said Nos. 43 and 44, the Grand Rivière should be the national boundary; and that, in order to facilitate the communication here, the road shall be in common, crossing the river on one side as on the other, everywhere where the badness of the road, or the nature of the land, or of the said river, may render it necessary.

From the Guardhouse of Bahon the frontier line ascends the ridge which ends at the pyramid, and from its summit it goes by Nos. 45, 46, 47, 48, and 49, in winding round the present plantations of two French inhabitants, Couzé and Laurent, these being on the right, and leaving to the left the possessions of Bernardo Familias, till it comes to the Guardhouse of the Valley, where the landmark 50 is planted.

From this point the line ascends the mountain called the Montagne Noire, along a patrole road well known, and halfway up the side of the mountain is graven No. 51 on two rock-stones, with the inscription, France, Espana. On the summit of the mountain is placed No. 52, at the beginning of the present plantations of Mr Milscent, and the line of boundary runs along his coffee plantations, which are on the ridge in going to the Nos. 53, 54, 55, 56, and 57, along the present plantations of Mr Jouanneaux, passing by the Nos. 58, 59, to the head of one of the branches of the Ravin Sec (Dry Ravine), and over the Piton or hill of the same name, to the top of the mountain, in keeping close to the plantations of Mr De la Prunarède.

The Nos. 60 and 61 are at the head of the Ravin Sec; 62, 63, and 64, on the same ravine, round the present plantations of Mr Larivière; and from 65 to 69 inclusive, the line is formed by the boundaries of the plantations of Mr Lasserre, which are on the left of the summit of this mountain. To No. 69 the line follows a road, in common, which goes, in ascending to the top of the mountain, and winds round the plantations of Messrs Potier, Laleu, Gerbier, and Béon, which lie on the left with the landmarks, from No. 70 to 79 inclusive, placed at the sources of the Ravin Mathurin, on the different straights of which it is formed.

From the Piton or eminence, where Mr Béon is settled, the line goes along an open road on the ridge as far as No. 80, which is at the head of the Gorge Noire, between the present plantations of Messrs Colombier, Mathias, and Nolasco, from the house of which last the line runs along the ridge, in descending to and ascending from certain ravines, till it comes to Nos. 81, 82, and 83, along the coffee plantations of Duhar on the height, called the height of La Porte, which is opposite the wood of the same name; and on the top of the said height, in an open road, the line descends round the plantation of Mr Dumar as far as the pyramid 84, erected at the old Guardhouse of the Bassin à Cayman, on the left bank of the river.

On the right bank, opposite No. 84, is the pyramid No. 85, where the plenipotentiaries placed the first stone at the foot of the hill beginning the mountain of Villa Rubia; the line goes now up to the top, where is placed the landmark No. 86, and, descending by one of the branches to No. 87, it takes the summit of the mountain on the plantations of the Baronness de Piis, which it follows still, leaving the slope to the right towards the valley of Dondon, and to the left in the Spanish part till it comes to the present plantations of Mrs Collière, which lie beyond the top of the mountain, as well as those of Mr Chiron, which have all been enclosed by the landmarks

Nos. 88, 89, 90, 91, and 92, at which last the line begins again, and follows the ridge of the mountain, opposite the above-mentioned valley, as far as No. 93, at the mountain called the Montagne des Chapelets, and from its top it descends to Nos. 94 and 95, in crossing the ravine which joins the plantations of Mr Soubira, to come to No. 96, on those of Mr Moreau, and from this point it descends, in a right line, to the river called the Rivière du Canot, on the left of which is the pyramid No. 97, at the point of the opposite branch which descends from the Marigallega.

The frontier line now continues ascending, in a right line, to the top of the Kercabras, No. 98, and follows the ridge along by the plantations of MM. Lécluze and Tripier, as far as Nos. 99 and 100, whence it turns round the plantations of MM. de Montalibor, Touquet, and Gerard, by the landmarks, Nos. 101, 102, 103, to 104, placed at clumps of rocks on the height of the settlement of Valero, and below the second habitation of Touquet and Rodanès.

From this point the frontier line continues, as straight as it was possible, by an open road on very rough ground, crossing Red Stream (Ruisseau Rouge), No. 105, and Ruisseau Maho as far as the landmark 106, and then ascends, obliquely, the mountain of the Cannas or Lataniers, on the summit of which is No. 107, whence it descends to the Ravine à Fourmi, and to the pyramid 108, on the left bank, between the settlements, now given up, of the Spaniard Lora, and those of the Frenchman Fauquet, possessor of the land known in the treaty under the name of Beau Fossé, then the partner of Fauquet.

Crossing the Ravine à Fourmi, the line comes to the pyramid 109, at the right side of the branch by which it ascends the mountain of Marigalante, passing by the Nos. 110, 111, as far as No. 112, when the slopes on each side go, one to the French and the other to the Spanish part, and here it begins to descend to get to the mountain, from whence the water runs into the river called Rivière du Bois d'Inde, by the landmark 113, graven on a rock; 114 placed on a branch of the mountain; 115 on the stream called the Ruisseau de Roche Plate; 116 on another stream called Ruisseau des Eperlins; 117 on a ravine; 118 on the height called Hauteur Pelée del Dorado; 119 at the hollow called Gorge du Coucher; 120 at Brulage of the Montagne Sale; 121 and 122 in the savanna of the said mountain, on the sides of the high road, and, first ascending to the top, it descends to No. 123, which is at the source of the stream called Ruisseau à Dentelles, between the said mountain Sale and the mountain called Montagne Noire des Gonaïves, on which the line ascends by No. 124 to 125, where the undersigned, finding the summit inaccessible, were obliged to wind round it, through the Spanish territory, to come at the opposite side, in the direction of the frontier line, which as in all other inaccessible places, was measured by the rules of trigonometry, from No. 125, passing 126 at the Piton, or Mount of the Savanna de Paez, and 127 at the Pont de Paez, indicated by the treaty.

Hence the frontier line continues on towards the summit of the Coupe à l'Inde, passing by the landmark 128, at the hill called the Petit Piton de Paez; 129 at a spring in the valley; 130 in the middle of the said valley, crossing the high road called the road of Coupe à l'Inde, between two mountains running along the height to where they join again, and descending to No. 131, which is in a hollow of the said mountain Coupe à l'Inde, the ridge of which is followed by the line, passing No. 132, on a rock; 133 at the foot of a clump of inaccessible rocks, called Hauteurs des Tortues, as far as No. 134, on the height and on the side of the road, called Chemin de la Découverte; inaccessible during the greatest part of its ridge, as far as the sources of the Rivière du Cabeuil; but notwithstanding, the Nos. 135 and 136, are placed in the Vallée des Cedras, and 137, in the Vallée Polanque; the mountain continues to slope on one side in the Spanish, and on the other in the French territory, the line goes by the landmark 138, placed above the Sources du Cabeuil, on the mountain called by Spaniards De los Gallarones.

The line now goes on above the Sources du Cabeuil, and along by the landmarks 139 and 140, on the summit where the Découverte joins to the Montagne des Cahos, to the landmark 141, near the plantations of Cebère and Gui; it continues along by the Nos. 143 and 144, graven on three rocks; 145, 146, by the side of the present plantations of Poirier; 147 and 148, on the land of Raulin, to 149, where it begins to descend, and comes to the first plantation of Fiëffé, going, on the Spanish side, the top of the Montagne des Cahos, and which is bounded by the landmarks 150, 151, 152, 153, 154, and 155, in returning to take up and follow the ridge as far as the second plantation, which joins that of Cazenave, and both these are surrounded by the Nos. from 156 to 160 inclusive.

The line, passing by No. 161, goes along from summit to summit on the ridge of the mountain (which cannot be mistaken) to the landmark 162, at the beginning of the plantation now belonging to Perodin, and which is enclosed by the Nos. 163, 164, and 165, whence it takes again the ridge of the mountain as far as No. 166, along the present plantation of Cottereau, lying over the ridge to the left, and enclosed by the landmarks from the said 166 to 171 inclusive; hence going along the summit of a branch of the mountain, the line comes to Nos. 172 and 173, by the side of the plantation of Ingrand, where the summit becomes inaccessible to the greatest height of Black Mountain (Montagne Noire) or Grand Cahos, the summit of which marks the national boundaries as far as the falls of the river called the Guaranas, which joins the White River (Rivière Blanche) at the place the French call Trou d'Enfer, where, on the high road, is placed the landmark 174.

From this place the frontier line runs along the ridge of the mountain of Jaïti, one slope of which is in the Spanish and the other in the French part, as far as the summit called the Piton de l'Oranger, which it goes straight over to the landmark 175, graven on a rock, and along by the Nos. 176 and 177, in the flat-land of the said mountain, called Reposoir (Resting-place), continuing along the possessions of Hubé, and pursues its way over the next mount to the No. 178 ; whence it goes, in descending along an open well-marked road, to No. 179, in the little savanna of Jaïti, and then continues on to the great savanna, where formerly was the guard-house of that name, crosses the savanna running towards south-east along by the landmarks 180, placed in the middle, and 181, at the point, going in the same direction, to the post of Honduras, crossing a very deep ravine running along the branches of the mountain on the left, till it descends to No. 182, placed in the Savanna des Bêtes (Savanna of Beasts), and to 183 on the right bank of the River Artibonite, which it crosses at this point to come to No. 184, on the left bank, 185 on the stream called the Ruisseau d'Isidore, and arrives at 186, the Guardhouse of Honduras.

To go up to the summit of the mountain called the Montagne à Tonnerre, it passes a second time the Ruisseau d'Isidore ; at No. 187 the line goes up again by Nos. 188 and 189, towards the ridge, which is a well-known boundary by the division of the slopes, as far as Nos. 190, 191, and 192, to come to the rock of Neybouc, on the side of the high road, and on each side of which are graven the relative inscriptions and the No. 193.

From the said rock at the foot of the height called Neybouc, over which the line continues on, being inaccessible, the undersigned went to it along the Spanish part, to place on the summit the landmark 194, whence the line, in an open and well-marked road, goes along the height called the Hauteur de la Mahotière, and along the ridge of the mountain to descend (across a hollow) to the Ravine Chaude, which it crosses near its junction with the Rivière des Indes or Horse-shoe River, which the undersigned crossed for the first time, and placed on the left bank the landmark 195, constrained by the badness of the passage on the right bank to traverse its straggling current and its little islands, to come to the Guardhouse of the Deep Valley (Corps de Garde de la Vallée Profonde) and to No. 196, placed on the side of the present plantations of Colombier.

From the said guardhouse the undersigned, crossing the river, placed No. 192 on a rock of the first branch, and continuing to open the line, in cutting the branches and hollows of the great mountain, along by the landmarks 198 and 199, as far as 200, to the Fond des Palmistes, on account of the impossibility of following any one of them, to take, at No. 201, the ridge which they ran along by Nos. 202 and 203, as far as 204; and, crossing the hollow by No. 205, to come at the river Gascogne, they placed the landmark No. 206 on the left bank; 207 on a branch of the mountain; 208 in a flat spot; and all the three along by the plantations of Mousset, settled between river Goscogne and the Ravine des Pierres Blanches.

From No. 208 the line crosses the ravine in a southern direction, running along by the settlements of Maucler and Guerin, over the branches of mountain which lead to No. 209, on the greatest height of the mountain of Neybe, where are to be seen the ponds; it follows the summit of this mountain as far as No. 210, where the guides pointed out the Bajada Grande or Grande Descente (Great Descent), adding that it was impossible to continue the road along the summit of the mountain, designated in the treaty as the national boundary; and descending along the Spanish part, the undersigned went to the foot of the Great Descent, and there fixed, on the side of the high road, the landmark 211, from which, crossing the lake or Etang Saumâtre, and directed *on the point of the mountain which enters the furthest into the said lake, from the southern part, near the Barguadier* (shipping place) *of the savanna of the White Ravine or Ravine River*, the line comes to No. 212, graven on a rock at the said point, whence it ascends towards the summit of the mountain, goes by the landmark 213 on the road to the mountain called Montagne du Brulage, crosses the hollow called Fond Oranger, and, after rising to the opposite height, descends to No. 214, graven on a rock in another hollow at the bottom of the settlement of Pierre Bagnol, and following the said hollow, arrives at No. 215, at the junction of another hollow at the foot of the plantation of the said inhabitant.

From this point the line, going in a southern direction, cuts the mountain on which Bagnol is settled, till it comes to No. 216, graven on a rock where the White Ravine (which has not had water since the great earthquake), joins that which takes its rise on the land of Beaulieu and Soleillet, to preserve their present plantations, which are on both sides of the ravine, and goes over the top of the mountain Majagual or the Mahots, forming the line as far as the branch which descends to Nos. 217 and 218, in two dry streams along the plantations of Soleillet.

The line now continues by the stream on the right, along a well-marked road, on the sides of which all the large trees are marked (for want of stones fit for landmarks) as far as the head of the

Pedernales or Rivière of the Anses à Pitre, the line marking the several turnings traced on the plan across the branches, and coming upon the great mountain, passing by the Piton or Brulage à Jean Louis, by the savanna of Boucan Patate—that of the Discovery and its Little Pond—to the view of the mountain of La Flor on the left, along the Dark Hollow, the Source of Miseries, the settlements of the runaway negroes of Maniel, difficult stream and deep stream; then coming to the sources of the river called by the Spaniards Pedernales, and by the French River of the Anses à Pitre, on the banks of which the undersigned placed landmarks, each bearing No. 219, with the double inscription.

The bed of this river is the boundary of the two nations; it was, followed down to its mouth, on the southern side, observing that along the first part its waters often disappear. The inscription and No. 220 were graven on a rock in the middle of the bed of the river, which does not run at this spot; and at its mouth are erected two pyramids, No. 221 on the sides, with the respective inscriptions, in sight of the two guardhouses.

The undersigned, in order to execute this important operation with the greatest precision, have always had before them the treaty of 29th of February 1776; and, except the division of the second little island and the demarcation of the line between Nos. 43 and 44, on account of the reasons above mentioned, accompanied with a sufficient number of men knowing the different places along the line, besides guided by their own honour, having a sincere desire to fulfil the desire of their sovereigns, in favour of the good and tranquillity of their respective subjects, having besides the example of harmony and sincerity given them by the plenipotentiaries, they have marked out the present plantations, and caused the inhabitants who had overshot the line on either side to draw back, according to the stipulations of the 4th and 5th articles of the treaty, and the 2d, 6th, and 7th, of the instructions, except Mr Voisins, who is mentioned as having voluntarily abandoned his position; observing that everywhere a mandate was published declaring pain of death against any one who should pull up, carry away, or remove the landmarks or pyramids of the line, and that every one who should overshot it should be punished according to the exigency of the case.

The commissaries being perfectly agreed on all contained in the present description, written in the Spanish and French languages, have hereunto set their names.

Done at the Cape, 28th August 1776.

Signed, CHOISEUL.
JOACHIM GARCIA.

[For further details see M. St Mery, "Spanish St Domingo," vol. i.]

NOTES upon the MINES of SPANISH ST DOMINGO, translated from the Report of DON JUAN Y NIETO BALCARCEL, Mineralogist to the King of Spain.

Six leagues to the east of Cotuy exists a mine of gold, which was anciently worked, and produced annually more than a million of crowns; but having fallen in, it has ever since remained in this state. I have been there to examine it, and have penetrated to the bottom, where it had fallen in. It could, at an expense of about a thousand crowns, be reworked, and the ore separated from the water, the ground being very high and dry.

I went also to examine the neighbouring hills, which are of the same quality.

At half a day's journey farther east there is a mine of blue copper very rich in metal, containing a great quantity of ore; but the proprietor, who knew not its richness, having died, as also his slaves, the mine remained more than thirty years without being worked. I went there, and made an assay of the ore; I found it gave a fifth of gold; and I do not doubt that this metal could be found as pure as from its third bed.

It is to be desired that some capitalists would undertake the working of this mine, which, as I have said, has lain unworked for many years; and though Cotuy has received the patent of your Majesty, dated February 3, 1790, it has not sought to realise its value. This is why I do it to-day, with its consent; and, with the aid of God, I hope that in less than a year the royal fifths will produce much. I hope also that, in consequence, laborious and enterprising men will present themselves, who will bring into value the numerous mines of silver and other ores of which I possess a knowledge.

From this mine I have been to examine that which is in the district of Jarabacoa, at one day's journey from the town of La Vega. It was previously worked, and contained a great quantity of silver; but being fallen in, it has remained in this state. Beyond this are some ancient establishments made by the French, where can be found some very rich mines of silver, called Sami, which, according to ancient tradition, are of a greater richness than those of Potosi. When the French came to establish themselves in the vicinity, these mines were worked by Don Diego de Cacerees, who abandoned them. In the Black Mountain, "Sierra Prieta," which is very high, there are some mines of iron which I have discovered.

In the village of Banica, at seventy leagues from St Domingo, there exists a very abundant sulphur mine. I have extracted a small quantity from it, which I discovered to be of the best quality.

In the valley of Bani, part of the south, there are many quarries of alabaster, and there exists a great number also in the town of Monte de Plata and the valley of Neyba.

Not far from the mines of blue copper, which I have mentioned, there are two mines of silver.

In the jurisdiction of Santiago, near to the Yaqui river, there exists a mine of silver, and a great quantity of copperas.

In the valley of Neyba is a mine of rock-salt, of great renown, and which supplies Santiago and several other places.

At twelve leagues from the same town, in the canton of Zazica, there has been discovered in a hill upon the river a mine of silver, that I have recognised but imperfectly, on account of the weather.

In several other places besides those I have indicated, I have had information of many other mines of various metals, and particularly of gold, silver, lead, and tin.

In the river Bao, beyond Santiago, in the south, in crossing an arm of this river, can be seen a mountain, of which the ascent is almost impossible by reason of its precipitous height. This mountain is the asylum of many runaway negroes, who have taken refuge there, and who live in a state of absolute liberty. I learned from some of these negroes that this mountain contained much gold, of which they showed me some grains.

In the confines of the jurisdiction of the town, or the valley of San Juan and of Guaba, they showed me some diamonds found in the cavities of the hills.

Upon the banks of the river Bao, of which we have just spoken, not far from the habitation of Don Diego de Andujar, there is a mine of very rich gold, from which has also been taken some emeralds. I went to examine this mine, and it appeared that the aborigines obtained gold in nuggets from the banks of the river up to the top of the hill, upon which were the walls of a convent of Franciscans.

I went to the mines of Guaraguano, situated at ten leagues from Santiago, which had originally been of great renown, but being fallen in, they had ceased to be worked; they are, however, very rich.

I returned afterwards to Santiago, from whence I went to Cienaga, that is called very rich. In the possession of Don Diego de Andujar is a place named Las Mazelas, where a number of persons were lately occupied in getting out gold.

At Jaina, near Buenaventura, at the habitation Gamboa, which belongs to Don Nicholas Guridi, and which was depopulated by Don Diego de Herredia, in a place named Guayabal, upon the route from

La Vega, at half-way between that place and Santiago, is a mine of silver, very rich, which has been sunk and opened, and eight or ten slaves are now at work there.

In crossing La Croix, in the same canton of Arriva, not far from San Miguel, there exists another mine of silver, also very rich, and which needs but some labourers to produce much.

In crossing the river Jaina, by the road which conducts to San Cristobal, and to the habitation of Don Juan de Abedanos, to the right of the road, there exists a hill upon which grows not a single plant, but which contains a mine of quicksilver. I have hastily examined it.

In going from St Domingo to the village of Higuey, near to the town of Seybo, twenty leagues to the east, there is found in a hill a mine of tin, containing some portions which had been founded and worked by a goldsmith of St Domingo. Still farther on, within the limits of Higuey, at thirty leagues from St Domingo, there is another mine of silver that the Indians worked formerly, but which has since been neglected. According to what many persons who have entered this mine and extracted ore have told me, it is very rich, and has been but very little worked. Your Majesty, with few advances, would be able to draw from it great profit.

In the mountains of Maniel, distant twelve long leagues from St Domingo, there is found much grain-gold. These mountains, which are called horrible, and which many persons have attempted to penetrate, but have been unable to do so, are not inaccessible however.

[He also refers to many other places as containing various minerals, and closes his report in saying]—

Finally, I can compare this isle to that of Tarshish, from whence Solomon drew the gold that he employed in the ornamentation of his temple.

THE END.

VALUABLE STANDARD WORKS

FOR PUBLIC AND PRIVATE LIBRARIES,

PUBLISHED BY HARPER & BROTHERS, NEW YORK.

☞ *For a full List of Books suitable for Libraries, see* HARPER & BROTHERS' TRADE-LIST *and* CATALOGUE, *which may be had gratuitously on application to the Publishers personally, or by letter enclosing Five Cents.*

☞ HARPER & BROTHERS *will send any of the following works by mail, postage prepaid, to any part of the United States, on receipt of the price.*

MOTLEY'S DUTCH REPUBLIC. The Rise of the Dutch Republic. By JOHN LOTHROP MOTLEY, LL.D., D.C.L. With a Portrait of William of Orange. 3 vols., 8vo, Cloth, $10 50.

MOTLEY'S UNITED NETHERLANDS. History of the United Netherlands: from the Death of William the Silent to the Twelve Years' Truce—1609. With a full View of the English-Dutch Struggle against Spain, and of the Origin and Destruction of the Spanish Armada. By JOHN LOTHROP MOTLEY, LL.D., D.C.L. Portraits. 4 vols., 8vo, Cloth, $14 00.

NAPOLEON'S LIFE OF CÆSAR. The History of Julius Cæsar. By His Imperial Majesty NAPOLEON III. Two Volumes ready. Library Edition, 8vo, Cloth, $3 50 per vol.

Maps to Vols. I. and II. sold separately. Price $1 50 *each*, NET.

HAYDN'S DICTIONARY OF DATES, relating to all Ages and Nations. For Universal Reference. Edited by BENJAMIN VINCENT, Assistant Secretary and Keeper of the Library of the Royal Institution of Great Britain; and Revised for the Use of American Readers. 8vo, Cloth, $5 00; Sheep, $6 00.

MACGREGOR'S ROB ROY ON THE JORDAN. The Rob Roy on the Jordan, Nile, Red Sea, and Gennesareth, &c. A Canoe Cruise in Palestine and Egypt, and the Waters of Damascus. By J. MACGREGOR, M.A. With Maps and Illustrations. Crown 8vo, Cloth, $2 50.

WALLACE'S MALAY ARCHIPELAGO. The Malay Archipelago: the Land of the Orang-Utan and the Bird of Paradise. A Narrative of Travel, 1854–1862. With Studies of Man and Nature. By ALFRED RUSSEL WALLACE. With Ten Maps and Fifty-one Elegant Illustrations. Crown 8vo, Cloth, $3 50.

WHYMPER'S ALASKA. Travel and Adventure in the Territory of Alaska, formerly Russian America—now Ceded to the United States—and in various other parts of the North Pacific. By FREDERICK WHYMPER. With Map and Illustrations. Crown 8vo, Cloth, $2 50.

ORTON'S ANDES AND THE AMAZON. The Andes and the Amazon; or, Across the Continent of South America. By JAMES ORTON, M.A., Professor of Natural History in Vassar College, Poughkeepsie, N. Y., and Corresponding Member of the Academy of Natural Sciences, Philadelphia. With a New Map of Equatorial America and numerous Illustrations. Crown 8vo, Cloth, $2 00.

WINCHELL'S SKETCHES OF CREATION. Sketches of Creation: a Popular View of some of the Grand Conclusions of the Sciences in reference to the History of Matter and of Life. Together with a Statement of the Intimations of Science respecting the Primordial Condition and the Ultimate Destiny of the Earth and the Solar System. By ALEXANDER WINCHELL, LL.D., Professor of Geology, Zoology, and Botany in the University of Michigan, and Director of the State Geological Survey. With Illustrations. 12mo, Cloth, $2 00.

WHITE'S MASSACRE OF ST. BARTHOLOMEW. The Massacre of St. Bartholomew: Preceded by a History of the Religious Wars in the Reign of Charles IX. By HENRY WHITE, M.A. With Illustrations. 8vo, Cloth, $1 75.

LOSSING'S FIELD-BOOK OF THE REVOLUTION. Pictorial Field-Book of the Revolution; or, Illustrations, by Pen and Pencil, of the History, Biography, Scenery, Relics, and Traditions of the War for Independence. By BENSON J. LOSSING. 2 vols., 8vo, Cloth, $14 00; Sheep, $15 00; Half Calf, $18 00; Full Turkey Morocco, $22 00.

LOSSING'S FIELD-BOOK OF THE WAR OF 1812. Pictorial Field-Book of the War of 1812; or, Illustrations, by Pen and Pencil, of the History, Biography, Scenery, Relics, and Traditions of the Last War for American Independence. By BENSON J. LOSSING. With several hundred Engravings on Wood, by Lossing and Barritt, chiefly from Original Sketches by the Author. 1088 pages, 8vo, Cloth, $7 00; Sheep, $8 50; Half Calf, $10 00.

ALFORD'S GREEK TESTAMENT. The Greek Testament: with a critically revised Text; a Digest of Various Readings; Marginal References to Verbal and Idiomatic Usage; Prolegomena; and a Critical and Exegetical Commentary. For the Use of Theological Students and Ministers. By HENRY ALFORD, D.D., Dean of Canterbury. Vol. I., containing the Four Gospels. 944 pages, 8vo, Cloth, $6 00; Sheep, $6 50.

ABBOTT'S FREDERICK THE GREAT. The History of Frederick the Second, called Frederick the Great. By JOHN S. C. ABBOTT. Elegantly Illustrated. 8vo, Cloth, $5 00.

ABBOTT'S HISTORY OF THE FRENCH REVOLUTION. The French Revolution of 1789, as viewed in the Light of Republican Institutions. By JOHN S. C. ABBOTT. With 100 Engravings. 8vo, Cloth, $5 00.

ABBOTT'S NAPOLEON BONAPARTE. The History of Napoleon Bonaparte. By JOHN S. C. ABBOTT. With Maps, Woodcuts, and Portraits on Steel. 2 vols., 8vo, Cloth, $10 00.

ABBOTT'S NAPOLEON AT ST. HELENA; or, Interesting Anecdotes and Remarkable Conversations of the Emperor during the Five and a Half Years of his Captivity. Collected from the Memorials of Las Casas, O'Meara, Montholon, Antommarchi, and others. By JOHN S. C. ABBOTT. With Illustrations. 8vo, Cloth, $5 00.

ADDISON'S COMPLETE WORKS. The Works of Joseph Addison, embracing the whole of the "Spectator." Complete in 3 vols., 8vo, Cloth, $6 00.

ALCOCK'S JAPAN. The Capital of the Tycoon: a Narrative of a Three Years' Residence in Japan. By Sir RUTHERFORD ALCOCK, K.C.B., Her Majesty's Envoy Extraordinary and Minister Plenipotentiary in Japan. With Maps and Engravings. 2 vols., 12mo, Cloth, $3 50.

ALISON'S HISTORY OF EUROPE. FIRST SERIES: From the Commencement of the French Revolution, in 1789, to the Restoration of the Bourbons, in 1815. [In addition to the Notes on Chapter LXXVI., which correct the errors of the original work concerning the United States, a copious Analytical Index has been appended to this American edition.] SECOND SERIES: From the Fall of Napoleon, in 1815, to the Accession of Louis Napoleon, in 1852. 8 vols., 8vo, Cloth, $16 00.

BALDWIN'S PRE-HISTORIC NATIONS. Pre-Historic Nations; or, Inquiries concerning some of the Great Peoples and Civilizations of Antiquity, and their Probable Relation to a still Older Civilization of the Ethiopians or Cushites of Arabia. By JOHN D. BALDWIN, Member of the American Oriental Society. 12mo, Cloth, $1 75.

BARTH'S NORTH AND CENTRAL AFRICA. Travels and Discoveries in North and Central Africa: being a Journal of an Expedition undertaken under the Auspices of H. B. M.'s Government, in the Years 1849–1855. By HENRY BARTH, Ph.D., D.C.L. Illustrated. 3 vols., 8vo, Cloth, $12 00.

HENRY WARD BEECHER'S SERMONS. Sermons by HENRY WARD BEECHER, Plymouth Church, Brooklyn. Selected from Published and Unpublished Discourses, and Revised by their Author. With Steel Portrait. Complete in 2 vols., 8vo, Cloth, $5 00.

LYMAN BEECHER'S AUTOBIOGRAPHY, &c. Autobiography, Correspondence, &c., of Lyman Beecher, D.D. Edited by his Son, CHARLES BEECHER. With Three Steel Portraits, and Engravings on Wood. In 2 vols., 12mo, Cloth, $5 00.

BOSWELL'S JOHNSON. The Life of Samuel Johnson, LL.D. Including a Journey to the Hebrides. By JAMES BOSWELL, Esq. A New Edition, with numerous Additions and Notes. By JOHN WILSON CROKER, LL.D., F.R.S. Portrait of Boswell. 2 vols., 8vo, Cloth, $4 00.

www.ingramcontent.com/pod-product-compliance
Lightning Source LLC
LaVergne TN
LVHW021224110826
845150LV00002B/238

9781425563912